D1611014

Boston BRUINS

Greatest Moments
& Players

by Stan Fischler

Sports Publishing Inc.
www.SportsPublishingInc.com

Layout and design: Erin J. Sands
Dust jacket design: Terry N. Hayden
Editor: Joanna L. Wright
Copy editor: David Hamburg

Photos courtesy of AP/Wide World Photos, Steve Babineau, Boston Public Library, Bruce Bennett Studios, Stan Fischler and Tom Sarro.

ISBN:1-58261-063-0
Library of Congress Number: 99-65969

Printed in the United States.

Sports Publishing, Inc.
www.SportsPublishingInc.com

To all the Boston hockey people who over the years made my coverage of The Game more pleasurable—Herb Ralby, Walter Brown, Nate Greenberg, Harry Sinden, Don Cherry, Bobby Orr, Joe Fitzgerald, John Carlson, Eddie Andelman, Dale Arnold, Mike Milbury, Karen Buregian, Derek Sanderson, Bob Woolf, Mark Witkin, Pat Burns, Lynn Patrick, Brad Park, Jean Ratelle, Gerry Cheevers, Phil Esposito, Bob Beers, John Cunniff, Peter McNab, Terry O'Reilly, Wayne Cashman, John Bucyk, Cam Neely, Adam Oates, Raymond Bourque, Steve Freyer and Fluto Shinzawa.

Table of CONTENTS

Boston BRUINS *Acknowledgments*

Since the Bruins were the original American team in the National Hockey League, it goes without saying that there have been a lot of Beantown heroes over the past 75 years.

Unearthing information about them was not difficult because so many in the print business have chronicled their exploits from the very beginning, in 1924, to the present. Without the assistance of these valuable sources of research, this book could not have been written.

I also delved into my own books about the Bruins, written independently or co-authored with the likes of Derek Sanderson, Brad Park and John Ferguson. In some cases original material from my books was used here. Those books used for research material follow:

I've Got to Be Me by Derek Sanderson with Stan Fischler

Those Were the Days

Grapes by Don Cherry with Stan Fischler

Fischler Hockey Encyclopedia

Fischler Ice Hockey Encyclopedia

Coaches

Stan & Shirley Fischler's All-Time Book of Hockey Lists

More Hockey Lists

Hockey Stars of 1969

Hockey Stars of 1970

Hockey Stars of 1971

Where Have They Gone?

Hockey's Great Rivalries

Hockey Stars of 1972

Hockey Stars of 1973

Hockey Stars of 1974

Hockey Stars of 1975

Hockey Stars of 1976

Bobby Orr and the Big, Bad Bruins

Thunder and Lightning by John Ferguson with Stan and Shirley Fischler

Hockey Action

Bad Boys 2

More Bad Boys

Ultimate Bad Boys

Heroes of Pro Hockey

The Flakes of Winter

Hot Goalies

Play the Man by Brad Park with Stan Fischler

Heroes and History: Voices from the NHL's Past! by Stan and Shirley Fischler

Thanks to all of the following authors, as well as the Boston media, including the current beat writers for their 1998-99 work, which helped in the research of this manuscript: Bud Barth, Doug Chapman, Mike Colageo, Kevin Paul Dupont, Michael Felger, Carmine Frongillo, Joe Gordon, Steve Harris, Bill Keefem, Mike Loftus, Nancy Marrapese, Michele McKenzie, Gene O'Donnell and Phil Stacey.

In addition, the following books provided worthwhile background for various chapters:

In the Crease by Dick Irvin

High Stick by Ted Green with Al Hirschberg

Red's Story by Red Storey with Brodie Snyder

Goaltender by Gerry Cheevers with Trent Frayne

Life after Hockey by Michael A. Smith

Hockey In My Blood by John Bucyk

Total Hockey: The Official Encyclopedia of the National Hockey League

Trail of the Stanley Cup, Volume I, by Charles L. Coleman

The Brothers Esposito by Phil and Tony Esposito with Tim Moriarty

More Hockey Stars from the Canadian Sports Album by Ron McAllister

Hockey Heroes by Ron McAllister

The Mad Men of Hockey by Trent Frayne

When the Rangers Were Young by Frank Boucher with Trent Frayne

The Hockey Book by Bill Roche

Dick Beddoes' Greatest Hockey Stories by Dick Beddoes

God Save the Players by Neil Offen

Hockey Is My Life by Phil Esposito and Gerald Eskenazi

Sports Tales and Anecdotes by Frank G. Menke

The Patricks: Hockey's Royal Family by Eric Whitehead

Also, special thanks to those worthies at Fischler Hockey Service who painstakingly sifted through the mounds of research material so that a coherent manuscript could be completed: Christina Attardo, Candice Blizzard, Andrew Buzin, Shawn Field, Louis Garuccio, Adam Raider, Jonathan Scherzer, Amy Spencer, Jason Wagner and Beth Zirogiannis.

And to Joanna Wright and her sidekicks at Sagamore/Sports Publishing, a Standing O for the totality and enormity of their assistance.

Last, but certainly not least, a tip of the fedora to John Halligan for steering us toward Mike Pearson, who was behind the project from the beginning.

Boston BRUINS

Foreword

Difficult as it is to imagine as the millennium approaches, my links to Boston hockey extend beyond half a century.

In fact, one of my first favorite teams was the Boston Olympics, who played in the old Eastern Amateur Hockey League. I'd catch them on Sunday afternoons at the old Madison Square Garden, playing the New York Rovers, a Rangers farm team.

The Olympics—a Bruins farm team—had some wonderful personalities who became instant favorites of mine. Maurice Courteau was the goaltender and, as far as I was concerned, the best in the world until Harvey Bennett came along. Up front the Olympics had Al "Fishy" Dumond, a swift little forward, and Russ Kopak, who was even swifter. Ty Anderson, an EHAL legend, was on defense, always wearing a helmet when nobody else did.

Olympics-Rovers games were classics, not unlike those between their parent clubs, the Bruins and Rangers. It's worth noting that many of those stars on the O's—Pentti Lund, Eddie Barry, Allan Stanley and Fernie Flaman, among others—eventually graduated to the Bruins.

As a native new Yorker, and a hockey nut, my ambition was to see a game at Boston Garden.

This goal was fulfilled in 1952. In those days the Rangers and Bruins traditionally played home-and-home games starting on Thanksgiving eve in New York, followed by the second half on Thanksgiving night at the Garden.

I caught the game in Manhattan and then grabbed the midnight bus at the Greyhound terminal diagonally across from Madison Square Garden. It was a long ride but well worth it. From the moment I stepped off the bus, I fell in love with Beantown and have felt that way ever since.

In 1954-55, after getting my first full-time hockey writing job, I got to know Bruin personalities on a more professional basis. Lynn Patrick, Jim Henry and Eddie Sanford were among my top Bruins through the 1950s. Then there was Jack McIntyre, who beat Terry Sawchuk in sudden death to help the Bruins to an amazing upset of the Red Wings in the 1953 playoffs.

By the time the 1960s were ending, I began to look at the Bruins from a different perspective. My first book was *Bobby Orr and the Big, Bad Bruins,* followed by the ghosting of Derek Sanderson's autobiography, *I've Got to Be Me.*

It would not be an understatement to tell you that collaborating with Turk was one of the most enjoyable episodes of my professional career.

In addition to print work, I've remained close to the Bruins as a television journalist through the 1970s, the 1980s and the present.

I had the pleasure of interviewing the likes of Mike Milbury, Ray Bourque et al. Not to mention the thoroughly irrepressible Don Cherry, with whom I co-authored the book *Grapes.*

I never thought I'd get to like another coach as much as Cherry, but then Pat Burns came along, and in his own way has been as likable and entertaining as vintage Grapes.

As far as the player rating is concerned, I considered several factors to determine who was or wasn't to be included. Ability and longevity were the obvious criteria, but I also considered personality—as in Derek Sanderson—and uniqueness, as in Myles Lane, the only Bruin ever to become a State Supreme Court Justice.

Obviously, it was a subjective selection, but then again, subjective has always been my middle name, along with Irwin.

Whatever the case, enjoy.

Stan Fischler
New York, June 1999

Boston BRUINS

Greatest Moments & Players

Bobby Orr—The One and Only

Bobby Orr is Boston hockey. Period.

He is the bottom line. The franchise. The logo. The everything.

One could argue until the cows come home that Eddie Shore may have been better in his time and that Ray Bourque certainly has been more durable.

Some critics—this author included—have noted that the Blond Whirlwind conquered the National Hockey League in an era when talent had been diluted through expansion.

Really, when all is said and done, the points are irrelevant.

A century from now, when historians review the evolution of the ice game, they will put Robert Gordon Orr's name in italics because he was not only special, he was the ultimate performer, combining defense with offense in a manner that never was matched before or since.

While it has been fashionable to label Wayne Gretzky "The Greatest Hockey Player of All Time," it remains a fact of life that Gretzky never on the best nights he ever had could match the totality of Orr's game.

The magic of Gretzky always has been the numbers, which artfully concealed his lifetime deficiencies as a checking forward. The beauty of Orr was that the Bruins defenseman simply had no weaknesses. None. Nada!

He could do anything the best forwards could do—and then some—and the numbers underline the point. On defense, he was nonpareil.

The Hockey News rated him the greatest defenseman of all time. Bypassing Gretzky, the immortal Gordie Howe named Orr, "the number one player of all time."

In his prime, Orr was evaluated as the "Perfect Hockey Player." He played defense well enough to have won the Norris Trophy in 1968, 1969, 1970, 1971, 1972, 1973, 1974 and 1975. Offensively, Orr was no less awesome, and although he was technically listed as a backliner, he won the Art Ross Trophy for the league scoring championship in 1970 and 1975.

Orr's legion of admirers would cite chapter and verse to underline his position among hockey's definitive leaders. Harry Sinden, who coached Orr when the Bruins won the Stanley Cup in 1970, perceived aspects of Orr's play that were superior to those of Gordie Howe.

"Howe could do everything but not at top speed," said Sinden. "Hull went at top speed but couldn't do everything. Orr would do everything, and do it at top speed."

That was true only during those precious few years when Orr was not under the knife or recuperating from knee surgery. After two NHL seasons, he underwent two operations.

By the time Orr retired in 1979, he had amassed an impressive collection of silverware. Apart from the Norris and Ross trophies, he had won the Calder Trophy as rookie of the year in 1967; the Hart Trophy as the NHL's most valuable player in 1970, 1971 and 1972; and the Conn Smythe Trophy as the most valuable player in the Stanley Cup playoffs of 1970 and 1972.

"I thought that the Ranger team I played on in 1972 was good enough to win the Stanley Cup," said Hall of Famer Rod Gilbert. "We played Boston in the Finals that year and the series went six games before the Bruins eliminated us. The difference, in the end, was Bobby Orr."

In that classic final-rounder between two outstanding teams, Orr orchestrated the winning goal in a manner that only could be described as inimitable. But first, a flashback: trailing the series, three-games-to-one, the Rangers rallied to win Game Five in Boston, setting the stage for Game Six at Madison Square Garden. Suddenly, momentum had shifted to the Broadway Blueshirts, who now had the advantage of home ice. There was a feeling among the press corps that, yes, the Rangers were capable of winning Game Six and then heading back to Beantown for the decisive seventh match.

But Orr blew away such fantasies with one sterling maneuver just past the 11-minute mark of the first period.

Seemingly trapped at the right point by Rangers defensive forward Bruce MacGregor, Orr somehow pirouetted around his checking foe and delivered a blistering drive that eluded goaltender Gilles Villemure. In the third period, Orr set up teammate Wayne Cashman to give the visitors a 2-0 lead which enabled them to cruise through the rest of the game and win their second Stanley Cup in three years.

Ironically, the star on the other side of the handshake line was a mini-Orr named Brad Park, who, like many others who admired Boston's Number Four, could not quite match the many outstanding elements of Orr's game.

Apart from the sheer quality that Bobby delivered night in and night out, other elements should be considered. Primary, of course, is the ability he had to fill arenas throughout the NHL during its first critical expansion period from 1967-68 through the early 1970s.

In 1967, the league daringly doubled its size from six to twelve teams and continued adding clubs thereafter. Conservatives among the NHL hierarchy—including president Clarence Campbell—questioned whether expansion would work in such cities as Philadelphia, Pittsburgh, St. Louis and Los Angeles. That expansion succeeded could be directly attributed to The Orr Effect.

Orr not only was the ultimate artist, he also was exceptionally good-looking. During an era when helmets were not mandatory, Bobby's golden locks, flying in the breeze created by his exceptional speed, proved as attractive as his other stickhandling assets. Wherever he skated, he drew capacity crowds, and those crowds enabled expansion to work.

Equally important was his impact on the playing of the game.

Through the post-World War II years, big-league hockey's style was basic. The maskless goaltender remained in the crease and was dedicated to only stopping pucks.

Forwards skated up and down their lanes in attempts to arrange scoring situations. Defensemen essentially were dedicated to patrolling their blue line and keeping the enemy from threatening their goal. Rare was the backliner —that's precisely why they were named BACK-liners—who took off on an offensive foray.

When Orr arrived in the NHL at the start of the 1966-67 season, it was as if he had never heard of the traditional method of playing defense. He attacked as often as he defended and carried through to an extreme the shibboleth that "the best defense is a good offense."

But it worked. In spades.

"All Bobby did," said teammate Phil Esposito, "was change the face of hockey all by himself."

This was possible for two reasons: a. Orr did it so expertly that there was no reason to dissuade him from revolutionizing The Game, and, b. The once-hapless Bruins began getting better and better as Bobby's point totals soared. And the more Orr scored, the more other young defensemen began reconsidering their own conservatism behind the blue line.

Soon, the Rangers' Park became a reasonable facsimile—or The Poor Man's Orr—and after Park there was Denis Potvin of the New York Islanders as well as Paul Coffey of the Edmonton Oilers.

While speed was a major element in his repertoire, Orr could also call upon his immense stickhandling, passing and shooting skills, not to mention his innate playmaking radar. "When someone once asked me about Bobby's best move," chuckled Gordie Howe, "I told the fellow that it was putting on his skates!"

It is amusing in retrospect but the one thing the youthful Orr could not do as an aspiring stickhandler in Parry Sound, Ontario, was write his name clearly enough to satisfy his amateur hockey coach. One day, before the entire kids team, the coach showed the youngsters a piece of paper with Orr's signature. Bobby was eight years old at the time and had not mastered the Palmer method of proper penmanship.

"Look at this scrawl," the coach barked. "I want you to look at the way Bobby Orr signs his name. Why, he can't even write properly. So, how can a kid who can't even sign his name play hockey? He can't, that's what, he can't."

The coach was in error. At each level of youth hockey, Bobby was so far ahead of his peers that he began to attract attention outside his hometown. In those days of the six-team NHL, it was possible for big-league clubs to permanently latch onto the services of amateurs by the time they reached their early teens. And so it was with Orr.

A Boston Bruins scout noticed him while scouting a game in Gananoque, Ontario, when Orr was 12 years old. The bird-dog recommended that the big club put a lock on Orr and the Bruins did just that by merely putting his name on what then was called a "Protected List."

That done, the Bruins patiently waited for Orr to mature. His ripening as a hockey star was faster than anyone can imagine. By the time he was 16, he had become the talk of Canada, and the Bruins, then a last-place club, began the usual ritual of touting a teenager who had never played a professional game as the eventual Messiah who would save the franchise.

The NHL establishment then became shaken by the kid from Parry Sound because of what neither Gordie Howe nor Rocket Richard had done when he was invited to

the bigs: Bobby brought an agent with him. His representative, Toronto attorney R. Alan Eagleson, stunned the Bruins' manager Hap Emms with the declaration that Orr would not come to Boston unless he was rewarded with a contract commensurate with his ability. At this time, it was an outrageous demand, particularly in view of the fact that Orr had yet to play a single game as a professional. Emms objected to Eagleson's presence but Orr replied, in effect, no Eagleson, no Orr.

The result was a two-year, $150,000 contract that caused reverberations throughout the league. Although nobody knew it at the time, Orr was helping to organize and perpetuate an NHL Players' Association with Eagleson at the helm.

As it happened, nobody ever could have imagined that Eagleson and Orr not only would ultimately sever their business and personal relationships but also would engage in one of the bitterest battles between agent and athlete in the history of sports.

That, however, would come later. In the late 1960s the Orr-Eagleson tandem became noticed in hockey circles in direct proportion to the rise of the Bruins. Although the club missed the playoffs during Bobby's rookie season, the Beantowners described a steady ascent toward the NHL pinnacle. What's more, the growth spurt was accelerated by a monumental trade with the Chicago Blackhawks that brought—among others—Phil Esposito to the Bruins.

The chemistry between the tall, somewhat awkward-skating center and the fluid defenseman was distilled in Hockey Heaven. Orr and Esposito intuitively knew where the other would be and as a result, Bobby was able to integrate himself into any attacking formation that involved the Esposito-Ken Hodge-Wayne Cashman line. They were like perfectly meshed gears as the machine descended on enemy goaltenders. But always, the ice dance was choreographed by Orr.

"In many ways," said Philadelphia Flyers general manager Bob Clarke, "Bobby was actually too good for the rest of us in the NHL when I played against him."

As far as the Boston Garden faithful were concerned, Orr's primary purpose was to help deliver a Stanley Cup to the city which had not owned the silverware since 1941, when the Bruins defeated the Red Wings in four straight games.

By the 1969-70 season the Orr-Esposito tandem had turned the Hub sextet into a powerhouse. They were known as Bobby Orr and the Big, Bad Bruins for good reason.

Orr not only led the league in scoring (120 points) but also had the most assists (87), while Esposito had a league-leading 43 goals.

To reach the Stanley Cup, the Bruins initially had to conquer a competitive New York Rangers club which managed to tie the series at two games apiece after Boston had soared to a two-games-to-none lead. Orr & Co. disposed of New York in the next two games and followed that with respective four-game sweeps of the Chicago Blackhawks and St. Louis Blues.

The final-round triumph hardly was surprising, but the fourth game, at Boston Garden, was a thriller since the expansion Blues had pushed the game to the limit, forcing overtime after holding the Bruins to a 3-3 tie after regulation time.

But no sooner had the sudden-death period begun than Boston forced the issue.

Center Derek Sanderson outfought his checkers behind the St. Louis net and slid a pass to the onrushing Orr. At precisely the 40-second mark, Bobby tipped the puck past goalie Glenn Hall for the Cup-winner.

A split-second later, Blues defenseman Noel Picard instinctively hoisted Orr with the blade of his stick, sending our hero hurtling through the air with his wand lifted in

In another stroke of irony there was the matter of Orr's excellence in relation to the rest of his team. What better example than the 1970-71 season, during which the Bruins were defending their Stanley Cup.

Over the regular season Boston dominated as few clubs ever have in the NHL. The Bruins finished with a record of 57-14-7 for 121 points. Orr played in 78 games and totaled 37 goals and a league-leading 102 assists. It seemed as if nothing could stop the Hub juggernaut.

But there are times when one player is so good that his teammates become overconfident and tend to depend on him too much. Such was the case with Orr and the Bruins during the infamous first playoff round in April 1971.

Facing a veteran Montreal Canadiens club, the Orr-led Bruins underestimated their foe. After defeating the Habs, 3-1, in the opener, Boston found itself drawn into a prolonged seven-game series culminating with an unexpected 4-2 Canadiens triumph on April 18, 1971, at Boston Garden.

In his prime, Orr was evaluated as the "Perfect Hockey Player." He played defense well enough to have won the Norris Trophy in 1968, 1969, 1970, 1971, 1972, 1973, 1974 and 1975. Offensively, Orr was no less awesome, and although he was technically listed as a backliner, he won the Art Ross Trophy for the league scoring championship in 1970 and 1975.

---

the traditional goal-scoring signal. The thunderous cheer that almost rocked Boston Garden off its foundations matched any ovation for any Beantown championship dating back to Babe Ruth's days with the Red Sox.

Photos of the winning goal immediately published thereafter suggested that Orr had actually delivered the winner while in mid-air, which hardly was the case. But the pulsating panorama was enough to capture the hearts of New Englanders from Cape Cod to Gloucester and, to this day, the photo of Orr's goal remains the most spectacular piece of photography to stamp a Bruins championship.

Actually, the photo was more symbolic than anything else because it epitomized the thousands of other Orr maneuvers that never were actually captured as vividly in photographs. There were so many that, as one *Boston Globe* reporter, Fran Rosa, once said, "We just stopped counting."

Which is not to suggest that Orr was perfect. Certainly, his physique was vulnerable and had been as early as his junior hockey days. Knee problems hampered him almost from the very moment when he entered the NHL and would curtail a career that certainly would have added another decade had he been healthy.

Orr & Co. were stunned to the very core by the upset, which was due in large part to a cockiness rooted in the thinking that the Big, Bad Bruins were invincible because of Bobby. The lesson was hammered home and by 1971-72 the embarrassed club went about its mission to regain the silverware.

This time there were no mistakes. After a 54-13-11 finish, the Bruins were not going to allow overconfidence to be their downfall, although there was good reason to be cocky. Orr had played 76 games and tallied 37 goals and 80 assists for 117 points while Esposito led the league with 133 points.

The Bruins picked apart the Toronto Maple Leafs in a five-game opening round and routed St. Louis in a four-game semi final sweep. Even the powerful Rangers—paced by Brad Park, Ed Giacomin and Rod Gilbert—could only take two games from Boston in the finals. Orr capped his remarkable playoff by leading all players in assists (19) while tying for the points lead (24) with Esposito.

Orr's excellence transcended the hockey rink. To a man, his teammates regarded him not only as a superstar, but as a super individual as well. Considering his stature,

Orr was remarkably self-effacing and down-to-earth. Nobody summed up Bobby better than his teammate, John Bucyk, who authored the following words in his autobiography, *Hockey in My Blood:*

"Bobby is very shy away from the hockey rink. You can hardly hear him talk and he's always been this way except on a few occasions when he's got mad on the ice or yelled at the referee. He hates interviews because he has to talk and he doesn't like cameras, either. He's almost got an inferiority complex. He always seems embarrassed to talk about things he does on the ice, an important goal he may have scored for example, and you can detect this image in most of his interviews.

"Once in a while I'll hear how Orr wasn't back in time to cover up for some goal but what these second-guessers don't realize is that he's also a forward. Having Bobby Orr on defense is having four forwards on the ice. He skates up ice, takes a shot, and is back down covering our zone before you know it. I've seen opposing players time and again get the puck near the blue line when Bobby's down in their end and by the time the other player reaches our blue line Bobby is on his back.

"When it comes to the youngsters and charities, Bobby Orr is even greater than he is on the ice. He does a lot for charities and handicapped children. I've seen him in a rush to go somewhere, even to a game, but he'll always stop and say hello to a youngster in a wheelchair, or to a little kid who wants an autograph."

In the end, however, it was the ice exploits that made Bobby so special.

"Orr is able to execute certain maneuvers that another guy wouldn't dare try," said Harry Sinden, former Bruin coach. "For instance, there's an old rule in hockey that if you're the last man between the opposition and your own goal and you have the puck, you shoot it out or pass it—you never try to stickhandle past an incoming man. Bobby stickhandles."

And Orr had tricks he hadn't even used—yet. Sinden revealed that during each practice, Bobby experimented with techniques that had never been seen on hockey rinks before. No doubt they would be unveiled in a game when least expected and most needed.

After watching Orr single-handedly wreck the Rangers in the 1970 playoff, columnist Larry Merchant of the *New York Post* observed, "Orr is one of those rare athletes who revolutionizes his game, as Babe Ruth did, as Bill Russell did. Bobby Jones [golfing great of the 1920's] once said of Jack Nicklaus, 'He plays a game with which I am not

A young Bobby Orr before he donned his now-famous No. 4. Orr won the Calder Trophy as best rookie in 1966-67.

familiar.' Orr plays hockey in a way that makes old-timers feel like dinosaurs, too."

Orr single-handedly revised all concepts of modern hockey defensive play. "It seems obvious," said Merchant, "that Orr will have a far-reaching impact on the game; that by glamorizing defense he will influence youngsters who can skate well to play it, and coaches who want an extra offensive force to encourage good skaters to play it. Power-

Bobby Orr checks the curve of his blade while former Bruins trainer John "Frosty" Forristall looks on.

What made Orr so impossible to stop was his uncanny combination of speed, strength and savvy. "He has 16 versions of fast," said teammate Derek Sanderson. Orr's bowed legs made him more difficult to knock over, and his powerful arms and 5-foot-11, 190-pound physique allowed him to brush past bruising defensemen as if they were nothing but annoying mosquitoes. On top of that, he was an intelligent athlete.

Nobody admired Orr more than Don Cherry when Grapes coached the Bruins. Like others before and after, Cherry understood that there was little he could tell Bobby about playing the game.

"Nobody coached Bobby Orr," said Cherry. "He was the greatest hockey player I have ever seen, Gordie Howe and Wayne Gretzky included. I felt that there was little I could do to improve on Orr's perfection. From time to time, though, I would drop little hints here and there.

"Actually, it was not easy to deal with Bobby on any level—player or friend—because he was such an unusual person and I don't mean that in a negative way. It was simply that with all the pressures on him, socially, physically, and otherwise, he became a significantly detached individual, one who was conspicuously wary of others.

"A case in point: I was brand new at the job in Boston and really hadn't had a chance to sit down with Bobby. One day I noticed him sitting alone in a hotel coffee shop in Chicago. I walked over, sat next to him and tried to make conversation. At first, he seemed friendly so I began thinking about what subjects might interest him. I knew he was from Parry Sound, Ontario, a town on Georgian Bay, so I figured it would be a good idea to talk fishing. 'Whaddya catch?' I asked him and immediately we swung into a chat about hooks, lines, and sinkers.

"At first he seemed very enthused about the chat but then, like a smart defensemen divining an attacking play, he quite obviously sensed that the only reason I was talking about fishing was to make conversation with him—and he clammed up. I didn't lose him forever with that incident, but it did take me a while to get to know him.

"Unfortunately, Orr didn't have a press agent who could trumpet the good works he did very quietly. Bobby would visit a Boston-area hospital three times a week just to cheer up the sick kids. He didn't tell anybody, not even his close friends on the team and certainly not me. But one day I had to take my son, Timothy, to the children's division of Massachusetts General Hospital and I began chatting with some of the nurses. They told me that my All-Star defenseman was a regular visitor.

ful skaters like Bobby Hull and Gordie Howe would get more ice time and be able to help more on defense."

The standard Orr play appeared so simple that onlookers wondered why it was so difficult to defend against. Bobby would skate out of the Boston zone with the puck, then pass it off to a teammate. At that point he would race toward the enemy goal, taking a return pass in full stride. Then he was ready to shoot the puck, drive toward the goal or set up a play for a teammate with a pass.

> "Orr is one of those rare athletes who revolutionizes his game, as Babe Ruth did, as Bill Russell did. Bobby Jones (golfing great of the 1920's) once said of Jack Nicklaus, 'He plays a game with which I am not familiar.' Orr plays hockey in a way that makes old-timers feel like dinosaurs, too."
>
> — New York Post Columnist Larry Merchant

"Orr wouldn't tell anyone because, despite his widespread appeal, he loathed the limelight. Game after game, win or lose, whether he was the hero or insignificant, the reporters would chase after him. If we won a game, 3-0, the newspaper guys wouldn't seek out the goalie who got the shutout or the guy who scored the hat trick, they'd want to see Bobby. This bothered him to the extent that he began to hide in the trainer's room just so that some of his teammates could get some of the limelight."

Orr's rainbow evaporated almost as quickly as it appeared on the hockey horizon. After Boston's 1972 Stanley Cup win, Bobby was never the same, literally, figuratively and physically. He betrayed his weaknesses during the 1973 playoffs when, without his teammate Esposito, who had been injured, he could not lift the Bruins past the opening round, and they were upset by the Rangers. Again, in 1974, he was stymied by Fred Shero and the Flyers. He never again played on a Cup-winner and soon became embroiled in an intense and prolonged contract dispute with the Bruins' owners.

If the NHL became too dependent upon Orr, so, too, did Bobby become too dependent upon Eagleson. Had Orr been left to his own devices, it is likely that he would have remained a Bruin until he was compelled to hang up his skates. But Eagleson was calling the shots, and Bobby did what nobody familiar with the NHL scene had ever believed possible: he left the Bruins and wound up signing with the Chicago Blackhawks in 1976.

In some ways, the declining days of Orr were reminiscent of those of Babe Ruth, who will always be associated with the New York Yankees. Ruth's final season was spent playing for the Boston Braves. Orr did his thing in the Windy City. For both, it was terribly anticlimactic.

On the few occasions when his left knee was not causing him excruciating pain, Orr displayed signs of the glorious past. But the flashes of finesse were insufficient for the Blackhawks, the fans and, most of all, Bobby himself.

He announced his retirement in 1979 and, like Ruth, seemed out of place on the sidelines. His long-term friendship with Eagleson ended abruptly and bitterly for both sides.

In 1979, amid much pomp and circumstance, Orr was named a special assistant to NHL president John Ziegler but, again, the marriage was not binding. Less than two years later Orr, complaining that he was not more than a figurehead, said he would no longer work with the league.

Returning to his beloved Boston, Orr maintained his income by doing endorsements, and, in 1981, he became the unofficial advisor (agent) to Bobby Carpenter, the teen-aged wonder from Massachusetts who was selected first in the NHL draft by the Washington Capitals.

More recently, Orr became a partner in the Boston-based sports agency Woolf Associates.

As a player agent, Orr frequently was seen in various parts of the country. While his status as a player grew majestically with time, his status as an observer of hockey showed a similar growth. Bobby was always ready to offer suggestions on developing young talent.

In the spring of 1999 he made this observation about taking steps to make players better in junior hockey:

"They're trying to restrain the kids too much," Orr said after he was named to the career Canadian Hockey League all-star team at the Memorial Cup. "Let the kids go. Let them be creative.

"Those four years I spent playing in Oshawa (for the Generals) were four of the best years of my life. And one thing I am thankful for is I was never asked to change the way I played. I liked to skate and take the puck and go, and that wasn't the way a defenseman was supposed to play. The Bruins (the Generals' parent club when Orr played there) never tried to change me."

And a good thing too, because after the arrival of Orr on the hockey scene, they threw away the mold.

Raymond Bourque, the Ultimate Bruin

Raymond Jean Bourque

Born: Montreal, Quebec; December 28, 1960

Position: Defense

NHL Teams: Boston, 1979-present

Awards/Honors: Calder Trophy, 1980; King Clancy Trophy, 1992; Norris Trophy, 1987, 88, 90, 91, 94

Ray BOURQUE

There is something extraordinarily deceptive about Raymond Bourque that tends to ever-so-slightly cloud the glitter that is his due.

Part of it has to do with his subdued personality; another is rooted in the historic fact that two decades of stardom have failed to produce a Stanley Cup for Boston. Finally, there is a style that is well honed in all aspects, but conspicuously less than sensational.

Nevertheless, the Montrealer's name will be inscribed in the books as a nonpareil who could best be called a defense version of Gordie Howe—artistic, indestructible and menacing when challenged.

"He's Ray Bourque and he's unbelievable," said Pat Burns, who had the good fortune to coach the Bruins captain in the last years of the 1990s in Boston. "There isn't anyone else out there like him."

What has made Bourque unique—among many factors—is his durability. The French-Canadian has played one of the most trying positions in sports at the highest level for two decades. During the 1998-99 season he was nominated for the Norris Trophy as the NHL's best defenseman for the fourteenth time.

"Being nominated for the Norris is like being nominated for an Oscar," said *Buffalo News* columnist Jim Kelley, president of the Professional Hockey Writers' Association. "You win even when you lose."

Bourque has won the Norris five times, was runner-up five times and was third three times. Those credentials are testimony to the man's ability to take the ice night after night and deliver a vigorous, inspiring performance with little fuss or fanfare.

"I don't know when it will end," Bourque declared during the 1998-99 playoffs.

"I'm still looking at it like a little kid. I still feel like I've got something to prove. Every day I have to prove myself and that's how I've played this game my whole career."

Because he has been a Bruin for his entire career, Bourque inevitably is compared to Boston's all-time favorite hockey player, Bobby Orr. The comparison is legitimate in one sense—both were defensemen. But while Orr's style featured flamboyant end-to-end rushes for a team sprinkled with superstars, Bourque's game has been more subtle but no less productive over the long haul.

"Ray was often the focal point for my days when I was playing," said Sabres coach Lindy Ruff, a forward-defenseman who more recently became Buffalo coach. "I broke in in 1979—the same year as Bourque. When I played against him our coaches wanted us getting on him and finishing checks.

"I was one of those guys who, as a forward, had to go in there and try and seek him out (and hit him) when I was forechecking even to the extent that it was three or four seconds after he passed the puck.

"Twenty years later he was still the focal point, playing 30 minutes a game and still the guy the opposition had to wear down."

That was true not only during the regular season but also into the playoffs, and even as Bourque climbed in years. At the age of 38, during the 1999 playoffs, the defenseman was unsparing of his body. Facing the rugged Sabres in the second round, Bourque played more minutes than stars who were 15 years younger. In one match he logged 35 minutes and 19 seconds.

The captain, as always, was an inspiration. Before the start of the fifth game of the series he rose in front of his teammates and delivered a short yet poignant message.

"Don't take this moment for granted," Bourque said, his voice tinged with emotion.

Bourque's speech not only inspired his teammates and the Boston press but Buffalo writers as well. One of them was Jerry Sullivan of the *Buffalo News*.

"He told them he'd been in the NHL for 20 years. He'd been in a lot of Stanley Cup playoffs. One thing he learned was that you never know when you're going to get this far again. Don't cheat yourself by failing to give your best.

"Then the Bruins went out and made their captain proud. Facing elimination, they played their best game of the series, driving Dominik Hasek from the net in a three-goal second period and holding on for a 5-3 victory that sent the series back to Buffalo for the sixth game."

The Bruins, whether it's alumni like Mike Milbury or contemporaries such as defenseman Kyle McLaren, inevitably are impressed by Bourque.

"When a guy of Ray's stature speaks, you listen," said McLaren. "He didn't want to lose. His emotions were running very high. Everyone was feeling it after he said a few words. It really got us going.

"He's the best teacher for everyone in this dressing room, and I think everyone in this room took what he said to heart."

In one sequence, Bourque was blasted on a questionable check by Alexei Zhitnik, shook off the aftereffects, climbed back onto his skates and quarterbacked the ensuing power play. "What's more," noted Jim Kelley, "he did it brilliantly."

Consistency has been the hallmark of Bourque's game no matter who the coach might have been in any particular season. In 1989-90, when Mike Milbury ran the Bruins, he unequivocally called Bourque "the best player in hockey. Better than Wayne Gretzky and better than Mario Lemieux."

At the time of Milbury's words, both Gretzky and Lemieux were at the very tops of their games. As forwards, they inevitably would score more goals and total more points, but those who favored a more comprehensive game understood Milbury's point. So did Bourque.

"My first priority has always been defense," said Bourque. "Goals and assists, they're important. But I've always taken a lot of pride in keeping the other team from scoring. That's why I'm out there."

Coaches from Milbury to Burns also had Bourque out there because he has been a steadying influence on those around him: He rarely loses his temper and always has been an understated personality in the dressing room, even as captain.

This trait also has been evident in "down" times for Bourque, particularly when he was edged out of the Hart Trophy race in 1989-90 by Mark Messier who then was with the Edmonton Oilers. The difference was two points, a small matter that caused a big deal among some

Bostonians but, significantly, not Bourque.

"You lose, you lose," said Ray. "Two votes? You might think about that a little. When it's that close, it can go one way or the other. Obviously, I was a little disappointed because that chance doesn't come by too often for me. But the guy who won it, deserved it."

Perhaps, perhaps not. What matters is that Bourque did not require the Hart nor any other Trophy to underline his magnificence as an iceman. Those who have played with him, both past and present, confirm that Raymond exudes an aura that automatically lifts the game of those around him.

One such player was Dave Ellett, a defenseman whose NHL career appeared to be over when he arrived in Boston at the start of the 1997-98 season. Playing under Pat Burns and alongside Bourque proved a tonic for Ellett, whose game was revived for at least two seasons.

"What I learned watching Ray is that he loves The Game," said Ellett. "Every day—even at practice—he can't wait to get on the ice. He couldn't possibly have lasted so long in this game if he didn't have that passion.

Bourque eyes the action from his bench.

"Another key element is that he never puts himself before the team. Ray has always been a team player and I've told younger players that if they're smart, they'll sit and watch this man and listen to what he has to say."

Even the best players sooner or later have to lose steps to Father Time. That Bourque has been able to keep pace over two decades has been an unending source of amazement to teammates and foes alike.

"He never seems to allow his age to affect him in a negative way," said Bruins forward Rob DiMaio. "I don't believe that he thinks he's that old because he doesn't play old."

Bruins broadcaster Andy Brickley, who was a Bruins teammate of Bourque for four seasons, called the defenseman "a freak of nature."

Brickley theorized that Bourque's durability is partly a

function of learning the game inside out to a point where he minimized his mistakes. "He also became very disciplined in his lifestyle and off-season conditioning. For years, Ray trained very, very hard in the summer but it was something that rarely was discussed when others evaluated his stamina. This was particularly true when it came to his lower-body strength."

Among those tutored by Bourque were Glen Wesley, Gord Kluzak, Don Sweeney, Garry Galley and, most recently, Hal Gill. "Ray has had a positive effect on every one of them," said Brickley. "He can take a guy who had bounced around for six or seven years and turn him into an asset."

Reporters have often found Bourque to be reticent about discussing his game. "He remained anything but a self-promoter," said Kevin Paul Dupont of *The Boston Globe.*

A counterattack is launched by Bourque.

NHL backline bunch.

"Bourque was the stalwart of the NHL team's rear guard in the two-game 'Rendez-vous 87' series against the national team of the then-Soviet Union and the kingpin for Team Canada in the six-nation Canada Cup international tournament," recalled Frank Orr of the *Toronto Star*.

Ray not only annexed the 1987 and 1988 Norris Trophies but also demonstrated that many of Bobby Orr's qualities—which captured the imagination of Boston Garden fans in the early 1970s—are evident in him.

"He reminds me so much of Bobby Orr," said Bruins general manager Harry Sinden. "Ray is so shy and innocent like Orr was when he came up. He has so much poise it's incredible; so much hockey sense. I get goose bumps from watching him."

On "Phil Esposito Night" at Boston Garden on December 3, 1987, Bourque stole the show with a display of class and dignity. He surprised the Garden crowd by giving up his number seven jersey in favor of 77. It was the same move that Esposito himself made when he moved from the Bruins to the New York Rangers in 1975. "I gave Phil back his number. He worked so hard here and he deserved it," said Bourque. "This is something that I was involved in and that feels great. It's his night, but it was a great thrill for me."

"On most nights he would rather take a Brett Hull slapper to the nose than talk about his own play."

Bourque: "People still think of me as being shy. I prefer to think of it as down-to-earth. Besides, if people want shy they should have seen me when I first showed up in Boston at eighteen. If they think I'm shy and withdrawn now, I was the definition of these words back then."

In much the same manner that Denis Potvin was overshadowed for years by another gifted defenseman, Bobby Orr, so too was Bourque burned by Paul Coffey's press clippings. It wasn't until the 1986-87 season that the French-Canadian blueliner became the top banana of the

Bourque has enjoyed dozens of special nights since becoming a Bruin in 1979. And the comparisons to Orr do have a certain validity. Certainly, Bourque's biggest asset on the ice is his skating ability. He has speed and agility that are almost unmatched in the NHL. "I use my speed when the club is on a two-on-two or three-on-three rush," Bourque explained. "If I can get up into the play, then it's an odd-rush in our favor." His puckhandling ability is on par with his skating skill. Ray is just as liable to skate the puck out of the zone as he is to pass it.

Nor does his shot suffer any lack of potency because of his other talents. "Bourque is dangerous anywhere he has the puck and he can put the puck anywhere he wants," said an NHL scouting report. "He can shoot pucks from his goal line, through the air, and hit the opposition net dead center. His shot is hard, even from that distance, and lands in the net as if it were fired from a gun."

He demonstrated that during Game One of the 1988 Wales Conference championship against the New Jersey Devils. With the score tied 3-3 in the third period, Bourque snared a loose puck inside the Jersey blue line and blasted a shot past goalie Bob Sauve for the game-winner.

Bourque can also play the physical game with the best of the NHL backliners. He is not afraid to use the body, and his play in the corners is often fearsome. Bourque's upper-body strength is what allows him to fire a rocket from the point, as well as pin a man along the boards.

Raymond Jean Bourque was born on December 28, 1960, in Montreal, Quebec. His sparkling career began with Verdun of the Quebec Major Junior Hockey League. "Ray is the best defenseman to come out of the QMJHL," said Rodrique Lemoine, owner of Bourque's junior team, the Verdun Blackhawks. "He is...a second Bobby Orr. He is even bigger and stronger than Orr."

Drafted first overall in the 1979 Entry Draft by Boston, Bourque was touted as the turn around player of the Bruins' defense corps. "The future of the Boston Bruins on defense has been turned around pretty good in the last couple of hours," chortled Sinden at the time of the draft. "Bourque has all the talents. He's a good skater, an exceptional shot, a fine playmaker, a team leader." The praise was well deserved. He won the Calder Trophy as the NHL's top rookie in 1980, as well as making the NHL First All-Star Team. He's been a member of the team eleven times since then and has also earned six spots on the Second All-Star Team.

Until the mid-1980s, Bourque betrayed a woeful lack of leadership and often seemed quite willing to sacrifice offense for defense. But maturity changed his attitude and his style.

In 1987, he won the James Norris Trophy for best defenseman in the league. He captured 52 of 54 possible first-place votes and was one of the most impressive winners

of the trophy since Bobby Orr won unanimously in 1970. He led all defensemen in scoring that season, posting a career-high 72 assists and 95 points in 78 games.

"I would have been very disappointed if I had not won it [the Norris Trophy] that season because I felt I had a really good year," said Bourque. "Over the years I haven't said anything when I didn't get it. But I said to myself that once and for all I had to get my hands on the trophy."

He has also logged his share of international ice time. Bourque has played on three Canada Cup teams (1981, 1984 and 1987) and in Rendez-vous '87, which stepped up the level of his play.

"For me, the most important part of it is, when you reach a certain level in your play, you need some place to check it out," expressed Bourque. "Playing with so many great players on an NHL All-Star Team or Team Canada and against a team as good as the [then] Soviets is the best place to do it. I'm certain every player in the NHL feels that way, no matter what you hear."

Bourque's value to the Bruins was underlined during that 1987-88 season. He paced Boston to a strong second-place finish in the Adams Division and playoff triumphs over the Buffalo Sabres, Montreal Canadiens and New Jersey Devils. Because of his skill and durability, Bourque was frequently asked by then-coach Terry O'Reilly to log extra ice time. Thus it was hardly surprising for Ray to play 25-30 minutes per game. Eventually, fatigue set in, and Bourque seemed tired and less than effective in the Bruins' 1988 Stanley Cup final loss to Edmonton.

But the fatigue factor always was temporary. Bourque's reboundability astonished just about everyone who studied his style. Opponents such as Joe Juneau, who saw Ray in his prime, still remained awed by the supposedly over-the-hill defenseman in 1998-99.

"I really admire what he's done," said Juneau. "When I broke into the league, I can remember wanting to be a player just like Ray."

It is reasonable to believe that this will be the case well into the 21st century.

> "I'm still looking at it like a little kid. I still feel like I've got something to prove. Every day I have to prove myself and that's how I've played this game my whole career."
>
> —Ray Bourque

The 1929 Bruins finished the season 26-13-5 and captured their first Stanley Cup with the help of Eddie Shore, pictured at the far left, back row.

Edward William Shore

Born: Fort Qu'Appelle, Saskatchewan;
November 25, 1902; died March 16, 1985

Position: Defense

NHL Teams: Boston, 1926-40; New York Americans, 1940

Awards/Honors: Hart Trophy 1933, 35, 36, 38;
Lester Patrick Trophy, 1970; Hall Of Fame, 1947

Eddie SHORE

*I*t would be impossible for even Hollywood to script the life of Eddie Shore, simply because too many of the episodes would be considered preposterous to the average viewer.

But those who played with—and unfortunately against—the "Edmonton Express" knew that even the most far-fetched tales about Shore were likely true.

Absurdly fearless, totally talented and dedicated to his profession like nobody before or since, Shore was a defenseman who was so extraordinary a skater that he instinctively became an intrepid puck-carrier and thus added a new dimension to his game—defender-on-the-attack—decades before another Boston skater, Bobby Orr, would subconsciously copy his style.

During an era when hockey featured more wood-chopping than the Canadian northwoods, Shore was virtually indestructible. Opponents understood that if they could neutralize the Boston Bruins' defenseman, the game would be theirs. A game involving the Montreal Maroons exemplified the brand of assaults inflicted upon Shore.

One of the Maroons tore open Eddie's cheek with his stick blade, and another sliced his chin. One after another, the Maroons belabored Shore. Late in the game, he was clobbered in the mouth. He fell to the ice minus several teeth and remained inert for fourteen minutes while doctors worked him over. When Shore was finally removed to the dressing room, medics discovered he had suffered a broken nose, three broken teeth, two black eyes, a gashed cheekbone, and a two-inch cut over the left eye. The assortment of wounds would have been sufficient to sideline lesser athletes for more than a month. Shore donned a Bruins uniform for the very next game.

During the early 1920s, Shore's reputation carried across western Canada. He starred in the Pacific Coast League, alternately playing for Regina, Edmonton and Victoria. Soon his reputation for consummate defensive play carried to the East, where the NHL was undertaking its most ambitious period of expansion.

Boston, already a center of amateur hockey, was selected as the first American NHL franchise. The Bruins' owner, millionaire grocery magnate Charles F. Adams, spent liberally to develop a winner. The Bruins, however, were militantly inadequate until the Pacific Coast League folded in 1926 and a number of superior players became available on the open market.

Adams opened his wallet and obtained a seven-man package including Shore, Frank Boucher and Duke Keats —all future Hall of Famers. The tab was $50,000 for all seven, which made it one of the best bargains in sports. (By today's fiscal standards, the seven would have been worth $5,000,000.)

Shore arrived in Boston with suitable fuss and fanfare, and on November 16, 1926, made his debut in a Bruins uniform. The Boston *Transcript* commented: "Eddie Shore caught the fancy of the fans. The new defenseman is tall, yet sturdily built. His speed is exceptional and he handles his body and stick well."

Within two years, Shore had guided the Bruins to their first Stanley Cup championship and had firmly established professional hockey as a major sport in Beantown. Fans who had never before seen a game were captivated by the iron-muscled defenseman who, at once, seemed to be blunting an enemy attack, wheeling with the puck, and then launching a counterattack against the opponent's goal.

"Shore's abnormally long stride built up a momentum that carried him down the ice with frightening speed," said

writer-editor Ed Fitzgerald. "His chilling disregard for personal safety enabled him to maintain peak speed to a point well beyond the limit dared by lesser men. The result was that he came up consistently with plays that other stars were lucky to duplicate once in a lifetime."

There was a dark side to Shore that struck fear in the hearts of opponents from the day he broke into the NHL until his retirement. It was more than his penchant for rough play that made him an intimidating force.

One episode explained why Eddie was such a scary figure. The incident in question developed during a Leafs-Bruins game in the 1933-34 season. It was December 12, 1933, at the Boston Garden.

Exactly what inflamed Shore to detonate one of the most widely discussed episodes in hockey history remains debatable to this day. However, most observers agree that the incident started when the Leafs were killing a pair of overlapping penalties and simultaneously nursing a lead. Toronto coach Dick Irvin dispatched defensemen Red Horner and King Clancy on defense, and inserted Ace Bailey up front as his lone penalty-killing forward. George Hainsworth was in the nets.

Bailey was a splendid stickhandler and tantalized the Bruins on this occasion with some uncanny bobs and weaves until the referee whistled a stoppage in play. At that point Ross summoned Shore to the bench and whispered some advice to him. When Shore returned to the face-off circle, Bailey won the draw and continued to dazzle the Bruins with his footwork. Exhausted at last, Bailey skimmed the puck down the ice into the Bruin end of the rink. Shore retrieved it and began picking up speed in his inimitable locomotive fashion.

Confusion regarding subsequent events arises at this point in the play. Frank Selke, Sr., who was—at the time of the incident—assistant general manager of the Leafs, contended that Shore tried to round Clancy, was tripped by the minuscule Toronto defenseman and lost the puck to the Leafs. Selke assumed Shore was intent on retribution and charged at a player who he thought was Clancy. Actually it was Bailey, who had dropped back to Clancy's vacated defensive position and whose back was turned to Shore.

Sport magazine editor Al Silverman, in an extensive article about Shore, asserted that Eddie was bodychecked by Horner and went after the Toronto ruffian after he recovered from the fall.

"Raging," said Silverman, "Shore went after Horner, mistaking Ace Bailey for Horner."

"Whether he mistook Bailey for Clancy," wrote Selke in his book *Behind the Cheering,* "or whether he was annoyed by his own futility and everything in general, nobody will ever know."

But this much is known. Shore gained momentum as he moved back toward the play in Boston territory and soon was skating at full speed as he approached Bailey from behind. According to Selke, he struck Bailey across the kidneys with his right shoulder. The impact of the blow was so severe that Bailey did a backward somersault resembling a gymnast's trick; but he landed on his head with such force that onlookers could hear the crack all over the vast arena.

Selke, who was sitting in the front row of the press box, had one of the best vantage points in the building. He described the incident this way: "Shore kept right on going to his place at the Boston blue line . . . Bailey was lying on the blue line, with his head turned sideways, as though his neck were broken. His knees were raised, legs twitching ominously. Suddenly an awesome hush fell over the arena. Everyone realized Bailey was badly hurt. Horner tried to straighten Bailey's head, but his neck appeared to be locked. Red skated over to Shore, saying, 'Why the hell did you do that, Eddie?'

"Shore, little realizing how badly Bailey had been hurt, merely smiled. His seeming callousness infuriated Horner, who then hit Shore with a punch on the jaw. It was a right uppercut which stiffened the big defensive star like an axed steer. As he fell, with his body rigid and straight as a board, Shore's head struck the ice, splitting open. In an instant, he was circled by a pool of blood about three feet in diameter."

At that moment the Bruins, as one, vaulted the boards and charged Horner, but teammate Charlie Conacher rushed to Horner's side and the two held their sticks in bayonet position. "Which one of you guys is going to be the first to get it?" Conacher demanded. The Bruins suddenly conducted an orderly retreat to assist Shore and see if Bailey was still alive.

For nineteen minutes Bailey lay unconscious while doctors worked frantically over him. An ambulance was summoned to rush him to the hospital, where he teetered precariously on the brink of death. He had suffered a cerebral concussion with convulsions, and appeared incapable of recovery. Before he was removed to the hospital, Bailey looked up at Selke from the dressing-room table and pleaded, "Put me back in the game; they need me."

As Selke and others suspected, Bailey was in danger of dying at the time, and only immediate surgery would save him. A day after the injury, two brain surgeons familiar with the type of damage were found in Boston. They operated on Bailey, thinking he had suffered only one concussion. After the initial surgery, however, they discovered he had suffered two, and a week later, a second operation was performed.

Few held out hope for the player, and the Toronto management made plans to have Bailey's body shipped back to Canada. Two weeks after the injury, Ace appeared to be slipping into an irretrievable condition, but he was attended by two unflaggingly spirited nurses who kept urging him to "keep fighting."

Eddie Shore in his prime

Suddenly, Ace took a turn for the better, and he was released from the hospital two weeks later. Shore, meanwhile, had taken a turn for the worse in the eyes of hockey fans and officials. He was suspended by the NHL, and cries for his permanent suspension were heard from New York to Chicago.

When he was sufficiently recovered, Bailey graciously minimized Shore's dilemma by saying, "We didn't see each other coming."

When Eddie heard that, he replied, "I wish we had, I'd have slugged him—and nobody ever got hurt that way but Shore."

The Bruins sent Shore on a recuperative vacation, and a month later the NHL concluded that since Eddie had never before suffered a match penalty for injuring an opponent, he would be reinstated. He returned to the Bruins lineup in January 1934, neither penitent nor restricted in his play because of the furor.

From time to time, other enterprising NHL owners cast covetous eyes at Shore and hoped to lure him away from the Bruins, but, of course, neither Adams nor manager Art Ross would part with their meal ticket. By far, the most absurd offer for Shore was generated by the New York Rangers.

Colonel John Hammond, president of Madison Square Garden, suggested to Lester Patrick, the Rangers' manager, that it would be to the Rangers' advantage if they obtained Shore. Patrick realized that Hammond was naive about hockey but had no choice except to listen to his boss. Colonel Hammond demanded Patrick offer Myles Lane, a young, modestly talented defenseman to the Bruins for Shore.

Patrick obliged and, reluctantly, telegraphed the bid to Ross: Myles Lane for Eddie Shore. A day later Ross cabled back what has become a legendary squelch. The Bruins' cable read: LESTER: YOU ARE SO MANY MYLES FROM SHORE YOU NEED A LIFE PRESERVER.

Teamed with such stalwarts as Lionel Hitchman, Dit Clapper and Cooney Weiland, Shore was named the NHL's most valuable player in 1933, 1935, 1936 and 1938. Not surprisingly, Eddie was voted to the First All-Star Team in 1931, 1932, 1933, 1935, 1936, 1938 and 1939.

Shore was no less galvanic nor capable at age thirty-seven, when the 1938-39 edition of the Bruins finished first with thirty-six wins, ten losses—sixteen points ahead of the runner-up Rangers. The Broadway Blueshirts tested the Bruins to the limit in a best-of-seven series that ranks among the classics. During one interlude, Shore rammed the Rangers' pesky center Phil Watson into the boards with such vigor that Watson's teammate Muzz Patrick felt obliged to come to the rescue. The robust Patrick, who once had been the amateur heavyweight champion of Canada, walloped Shore so hard that Eddie absorbed a broken nose and a black eye.

Significantly, though Patrick had won the battle, Shore helped win the war. Eddie had his wounds patched and then replied by steering his mates to a four-games-to-three win over the Rangers.

The Bruins next were challenged by the Toronto Maple Leafs, who were powered by Harvey "Busher" Jackson, a future Hall of Famer. In the pivotal third game of the series, Shore defused Jackson with a crunching bodycheck that dislocated the Toronto player's shoulder. The Bruins won the series four games to one and annexed the Stanley Cup.

Edward William Shore was born November 25, 1902, in Fort Qu'Appelle, Saskatchewan, and spent his early years working on the family farm. His youthful passion was breaking wild horses, and his interest in farming inspired him to enter the Manitoba Agricultural College in Winnipeg.

Shore's interest in hockey was tangential, at best, and might never have been cultivated had it not been for his brother, Aubrey, who challenged Eddie to try out for the school team. Eddie accepted the challenge, and he mastered every aspect of the sport. When the Shore family suffered from financial hardship, he quit college and began his professional hockey career. He had been steeled by the harsh Saskatchewan winter and imbued with the work ethic by his parents.

Armed with these assets, Eddie was to continually startle the world with his extraordinary exploits. Nothing said it better about Shore than an incident which took place on the night of January 2, 1929.

> "His chilling disregard for personal safety enabled him to maintain peak speed to a point well beyond the limit dared by lesser men. The result was that he came up consistently with plays that other stars were lucky to duplicate once in a lifetime."
>
> — Writer-Editor Ed Fitzgerald

En route to meet his teammates, who were boarding a train that would take them to Montreal for a game with the Maroons, Shore got stuck in a traffic jam and missed the express train by a few moments. In those days, there was no airline service to Montreal and no further trains that night.

But Shore knew the Bruins already had a defenseman on the injured list and his presence was needed. He was determined to reach Montreal. Unfortunately, a mid-winter blizzard was reaching its peak, and only the most hardy would even venture out into the streets of Boston.

Eddie contacted a wealthy friend, explained his predicament and persuaded his pal to supply him with an automobile and a chauffeur. But after five miles of plowing through the storm, the driver told Eddie he would not continue at the wheel. Shore took over and headed for the Green Mountains and the perilous route to Canada. When snow gathered on the windshield, Eddie opened the top half of the glass and bore the brunt of the icy wind and storm. By the time they had reached the halfway point to Montreal, the car had slid off the road four times.

The auto reached the Quebec border at three in the afternoon, but soon fell into a deep ditch. Shore hiked a mile to a farmhouse and persuaded the farmer to hitch a team of horses to his car and put it back on the road. That done, Eddie resumed driving, arriving at the team's quarters, the Windsor Hotel, at 6:00 p.m. Manager Art Ross was there when Shore arrived and recalled the sight of him:

"His eyes were bloodshot, his face was frostbitten, his fingers bent and set like claws after relentlessly gripping the steering wheel so long, and his unsteady gait showed that his leg was almost paralyzed from tramping on the foot brake."

Ross was reluctant to allow Shore to play that night, but Eddie would not be stopped. Except for a two-minute penalty he was assessed early in the game, *Shore played the entire sixty minutes*. He played one of the greatest games of anyone's career.

"On defense," Ross recalled, "he smacked the hard-driving Maroons left and center and the Bruins finally won the grueling game by a score of 1-0. I might add that Shore also found the energy to score that one goal!"

It is quite possible that had Shore entered the NHL at an earlier age—he was twenty-four when he joined the Bruins—he would have won even greater acclaim.

As it was, Shore played fourteen seasons in the NHL, thirteen and a half with the Bruins. He finished his NHL career with the New York Americans. Four times he won the Hart Trophy as the league's most valuable player and was named to the All-Star Team seven times. The best estimates place Shore's total number of stitches in excess of 970. His nose was broken fourteen times, his jaw shattered five times, and all his teeth had been knocked out before his career had ended. He barely missed being blinded in both eyes and nearly lost an ear.

Prior to the post-World War II era and the eventual arrival of Bobby Orr, Shore remained the most dominant Boston hockey personality. And even in comparison with the inimitable Orr, Shore was—because of his violent side—in a class by himself.

Eddie lived hockey to the very end. After concluding his playing career with the Americans, he bought the Springfield Indians of the AHL and operated that franchise through the late 1960s, when it was taken over by the L.A. Kings.

He passed away on March 16, 1985.

Milt Schmidt is best known as the center for the Bruins' famed "Kraut Line"
with wingers Woody Dumart and Bobby Bauer.

Milton Conrad Schmidt

Born: Kitchener, Ontario; March 5, 1918

Position: Center

NHL Teams: Boston 1936-42, 1945-55

Awards/Honors: Hart Trophy, 1951; NHL Scoring Leader, 1940; Lester Patrick Trophy, 1996; Hall of Fame, 1961

Coaching: Boston, 1954-61, 1962-66; Washington, 1974-76

Milt SCHMIDT

The saddest part of Milt Schmidt's career—if one can call it sad—was that the majestic center excelled in the National Hockey League in the pre-television era.

It is unfortunate only in the sense that so many of his multiple talents escaped the realm of videotape, leaving us with very little tangible evidence of what was a most remarkable career.

If one were to compare the Schmidt style to another Hall of Famer, it would have to be a forward such as Gordie Howe. In addition to his skill, Milt possessed a fearlessness that often was translated into hand-to-hand combat with his foe. As leaders go, he was a captain's captain.

Not that Schmidt was a slouch when it came to production. He led the NHL in scoring in 1940, was picked to the First All-Star Team three times and was voted the Hart Trophy as the league's most valuable player in 1951, all as a member of the Bruins.

Schmidt's career, unfortunately, was shortened by World War II. Milt, along with his "Kraut Line" buddies, Bobby Bauer and Woody Dumart, enlisted in the Royal Canadian Air Force at the very height of his career and thus "lost" the best three years of playing time. Nevertheless, he played for four first-place teams and two Stanley Cup winners.

Apart from his own personal achievements, Schmidt was the pivot on a remarkable forward line whose roots could be traced to the city of Kitchener, Ontario. Milt and his boyhood pals, Bauer and Dumart, originally gained recognition on a local team known as The Greenshirts.

Bauer and Dumart, the oldest of the trio, were signed by the Bruins and assigned to their farm team, the Boston Cubs. When the two arrived at Boston Garden, they immediately made an appointment with Bruins' general manager Art Ross. They insisted that their center, Schmidt, was as good if not better than they were as professional prospects.

Ross did not want a seventeen-year-old in Boston and rebuffed the lads, but they persisted and Ross finally mailed a letter to Kitchener inviting Schmidt to the Bruins' training camp in the autumn of 1936.

A week later, Ross received a letter from Schmidt, accepting the invitation and promising that he "would work all summer to save the money needed to report in Boston and would pay his train fare and board."

Schmidt made his NHL debut late in the 1936-37 season, and even though he scored two goals, he nurtured doubts about his future. He mailed his first paycheck home to his mother with a note saying, "Better bank this for me, mom; it may be the last I'll get."

Once the trio got the feel of big-league hockey, they became a dominant factor for the Bruins and a hit with the fans. They were alternately known as "The Kraut Line," "The Sauerkraut Line" and "The Kitchener Kids."

The Krauts not only played together, traveled together and relaxed together, but they also presented a united front when it came to contract-signing time. "We felt if we went in together, asked for exactly the same salary for each, and took a stand in our dealings we'd be better off," Schmidt said.

So close were The Krauts that when Schmidt married Marie Peterson in 1946, Dumart and Bauer had to toss a coin to decide which one would be best man. When Bauer married, Schmidt and Dumart had also tossed. When, in 1948, Schmidt became the father of a daughter, Nancy, he announced that Dumart and Bauer were *both* godfathers!

This closeness was often reflected in the scoring statistics. During the 1939-40 season, when the Bruins finished first, Schmidt led the league in scoring with fifty-two points, while his linemates were tied for second with forty-three points apiece.

Not surprisingly, "The Kraut Line" enlisted as a unit in the Royal Canadian Air Force and played from time to time against other service teams. While stationed in England, where Schmidt played as often as possible when not performing his duties as flying officer, he was as popular as ever.

Milton Conrad Schmidt was born March 5, 1918, in Kitchener, Ontario—a German-Canadian community, originally named Berlin—until the outbreak of World War I. The youngest in a family of six, Milt attended King Edward Public School and began playing hockey almost as soon as he was able to walk.

It was young Schmidt's good fortune to meet Montreal Canadiens' goalie George Hainsworth, who had grown up in Kitchener, at a trophy presentation in King Edward School. Hainsworth gave the dark-haired Schmidt words of encouragement that remained with him through his lengthy career.

The hallmark of Milt's play, both as a youth and later as an NHL star, was a muted ruggedness. "Schmidt," said one longtime admirer, "was a gentleman's hockey player—until someone started pushing his teammates around."

It had been feared that Schmidt, like so many other NHL stars returned from the war, would have lost his touch, but Milt regained his form and in 1946-47 enjoyed the best productivity—twenty-seven goals, thirty-five assists, sixty-two points—of his entire career. Author Ron McAllister remembered that year for a different reason: "Towards the end of the 1946-47 season, the Bruins' defense was riddled with injuries, and Schmidt, who was always a team player, made one of his few suggestions. He asked Coach Dit Clapper to try him on defense until some of the players returned to duty. Once there, he demonstrated his amazing versatility by playing a terrific game; in fact, he did so well that the management and fans were all for leaving him there.

"But good sense prevailed. It was decided to make full use of Schmidt's leadership qualities. He belonged up with the forward lines, leading the team, so when the 1947-48 season got under way, he was back in his old position between wingmen Dumart and Bauer."

Even the retirement of Bobby Bauer failed to put the brakes on Schmidt, and in 1950-51, still teaming with Dumart, he produced twenty-two goals and thirty-nine assists for sixty-one points. It was enough to win him the Hart Trophy.

Schmidt's ability to withstand pain was legendary. During the 1948-49 season, he was injured during a

Bruins-Maple Leafs playoff following a collision with Toronto's Cal Gardner.

McAllister: "Schmidt tumbled over backwards in a hard fall on the Garden's ice. It was clear to everyone that Schmidt was badly hurt. His left arm hung helplessly by his side, and dangled like a dead branch when he was assisted to his feet. Milt refused to return to the bench, however, and went right back into the game. Driving himself relentlessly, he continued to lead his team in its effort to crack the four-four tie. He had to hold his stick with one hand, but he clung to it grimly, and kept boring in on the Leaf defense. Even the Toronto crowd yelling for a Leaf win found itself cheering for Milt Schmidt too, who was trying to skate the home team into defeat, literally single-handed."

On March 18, 1952, the Bruins held a "Schmidt-Dumart Night" and talked Bobby Bauer out of retirement for that one game. After elaborate pre-game ceremonies, The Krauts got down to the business of winning a hockey game against the Chicago Blackhawks. Boston won the game 4-0, clinching a playoff berth in the process, and Bauer went back into retirement.

Schmidt remained an active player until 1955 when he was given the coaching reins of a struggling Boston hockey club. He stayed on until 1962-63 when Phil Watson was called in to take charge. But Watson could not rejuvenate the Bruins and Schmidt took over again in the middle of the 1962-63 season. He remained at the helm of the Bruins as general manager from 1966 until 1973 and enjoyed two Stanley Cup triumphs, in 1970 and 1972, with the help of trades he had engineered.

Easily, the greatest accomplishment of Schmidt, the manager, was a deal he made with the Chicago Blackhawks. He sent goalie Jack Norris, defenseman Gilles Marotte, and center Pit Martin to Chicago in return for forwards Phil Esposito, Fred Stanfield, and Ken Hodge.

In the view of some experts, it was the most one-sided deal in NHL annals and was directly responsible for the Cup victories in 1970 and 1972.

Long-ago retired, Schmidt holds his beloved jersey.

Milt left Boston in 1974 to become the first general manager of the new Washington Capitals franchise, but it was a move that generated nothing but woe. The Caps, under his administration, never became competitive and Schmidt eventually left the disaster scene, returning to Boston where he went to work for the Bruins in the ticket-selling department and then ran the Boston Garden Club.

Schmidt remained a fixture around Boston Garden through the 1990s, always upright, always reflecting the greatness of his past.

John Bucyk awaiting a centering pass.

John Paul Bucyk

Born: Edmonton, Alberta; May 12, 1935

Position: Left Wing

NHL Teams: Detroit, 1955-57; Boston, 1957-78

Awards/Honors: Lady Byng, 1971, 74; Lester Patrick Award, 1977; Hall of Fame 1981

John BUCYK

Durability and score-ability were the trademarks that enabled John Bucyk to gain a slot in the Hockey Hall of Fame. Either way, he was a winner.

His big-league career spanned the seasons 1955-56 through 1977-78, all but the first two of which were spent with the Bruins.

Over that twenty-three year period, Bucyk tallied 556 goals, 813 assists and 1,369 points in 1,540 games. "Whatever we paid John," Bruins president Weston Adams once said, "he was worth."

Bucyk's value was manifold. He was big enough and strong enough to intimidate merely with his size; his shot was accurate enough for him to reach the 51-goal mark in 1970-71; and he had the playmaking ability to achieve 65 assists that same season.

"When I was coaching Boston in the mid-1970s," said Don Cherry, "Johnny was the best in the league in the corners and on the power play. There was no one else like him."

That's what the Detroit Red Wings originally thought when they nurtured the young left wing through their amateur system in the early 1950s. Born in Edmonton of Ukrainian parents, Bucyk lived a hard, tough life as a youth in the poorest section of the Alberta city.

"My father died when I was eleven," Bucyk recalled, "which meant that my mother had to work at more than one job to keep us going. She would work as a potato-picker on the side. My brother and I both worked in the same drug store, but fortunately the owner let us off early when we had hockey practice."

"Since I was older, Johnny naturally looked up to me," said his brother Bill, "and, of course, I would always be in a

yell at him to keep it up because sometimes he'd get nailed. His skating improved some, but he was still down on his ankles a lot when he left me. But he had a great big heart and would do anything you told him."

Bucyk often credited former NHL goalie and Edmonton icon Ken McAuley with having a substantial influence on his hockey development.

McAuley helped make Bucyk the complete hockey player by doing something drastic to improve his skating. He enrolled him in a figure skating school.

"He was so damn awkward. He'd step on the ice and fall, go a few steps and fall. The faster he'd try to go, the more he'd stumble. But he had great determination, great desire and could he hit! Uhmpf! I felt if the kid had that kind of desire, he should be given a chance to make it. So I had him play with the North Edmonton Outlaws all next season, a sort of pick-up team, just to give him more

---

"Johnny had so much desire. That's the thing I remembered most. But his skating wasn't too good, so I would make him go out between periods and skate, skate, skate. I remember telling him keep his head up too—I'd yell at him to keep it up because sometimes he'd get nailed. His skating improved some, but he was still down on his ankles a lot when he left me. But he had a great big heart and would do anything you told him."

—John Bucyk's pee-wee hockey coach Bob McGee

---

little higher calibre of hockey than him. So he would always have a target.

"We didn't have hockey sticks so we'd use old broom-sticks, and for pucks we'd use old tennis balls or stones or frozen balls of manure from the milkwagon horses.

"We didn't have any pads so we'd use old magazines stuck under our socks, old Eaton's catalogues. We used to put Johnny in goal a lot because he was the smallest. He was good too. I remember later, when some of us did get hockey sticks, they'd sometimes break. So we'd get old tin cans, flatten them, and wrap them around the broken part of the stick to hold it together and then tie string around that."

When John was 10, his pee-wee coach was Bob Magee, who remembered Bucyk very well.

"Johnny had so much desire. That's the thing I remembered most. But his skating wasn't too good, so I would make him go out between periods and skate, skate, skate. I remember telling him keep his head up, too—I'd

skating. When he wasn't playing for the Oil Kings, he was playing for the Outlaws.

"Well, he improved but not enough. So the next summer I told him I was going to enroll him in this figure skating school. He didn't like it, thought it would be sissy, but I told him he *had* to learn to skate if he wanted to play pro hockey someday. He couldn't turn right, see. He'd coast. Turn left but not right. He'd fall down. At this point even Clarence Moher had given up on him, saying, 'Goddam Ken, cut that kid, he won't help you.' But I said no. He had guts. He had a great shot, a fine head and he wanted to excel so badly. It was finally arranged that Johnny would take private lessons one whole summer. Just him and the instructor so nobody would laugh at him."

Bucyk's outstanding junior play enabled him to catch on with the Red Wings-sponsored Edmonton Flyers of the Western Hockey League. It was the same organization which had sent the likes of future Hall of Famer Glenn Hall and hard-nosed defenseman Larry Zeidel to the NHL.

As a rookie, Bucyk pumped in 30 goals and had 58 assists. Still only nineteen years old, he won the WHL rookie of the year award and played tough enough to arouse attention from Detroit's general manager, Jack Adams.

"I was nicknamed 'The Beast' in the WHL," Bucyk recalled. "I guess there were 'Hate Bucyk' clubs all around the league."

Adams certainly didn't hate him. The Motor City hockey boss signed Bucyk for the 1955-56 season in which he played 38 NHL games. "Unfortunately," said Red Wings coach Jimmy Skinner, "John was playing out of position most of the time. Back then, he was a stubborn kid and he had to learn some things the hard way."

Bucyk's sophomore year in Detroit hardly was impressive, although he managed 10 goals and 11 assists in 66 games. He might have continued with the Red Wings except for a major upheaval in Boston and Detroit. Following a playoff upset that saw the Red Wings ousted in the first round, Adams decided to unload Glenn Hall. Coincidentally, the Bruins had become disenchanted with Terry Sawchuk and, thus, two monster deals were consummated.

When the dust had cleared, Sawchuk was back in Detroit, Hall in Chicago and Bucyk—dealt even-up for Sawchuk on July 24, 1957—found himself a Bruin.

The timing couldn't have been better. Boston already had a big winger named Vic Stasiuk and acquired a clever center, Bronco Horvath, who couldn't get along with New York Rangers coach Phil Watson. Coincidentally, the same three players had skated together on a line with Edmonton. Horvath played in the middle with Bucyk on the left and Stasiuk on the right.

As well-known NHL offensive trios go, "The Uke Line" was different in that it lacked a true superstar. Stasiuk was a lumbering skater whose tenacity outdid his skills. Remarkably slow for a big-leaguer, Horvath nevertheless was a creative playmaker armed with an accurate wrist shot.

Although Stasiuk and Bucyk legitimately called the Ukraine their ancestral home, Horvath was of Hungarian descent but obliged the media by allowing them to dub the unit The Uke Line.

"When the line was in its heyday," author Al Rosenberg noted, "Bucyk spent most of the time in the shadows. Horvath was the crowd's favorite and Stasiuk had a following of his own."

Bucyk, now enjoying life after hockey.

In the first two years of the line's existence (1957-58, 1958-59), Bucyk scored 21 and 24 goals, respectively, at a time when anyone who passed the 20-goal level was considered a .300 hitter in hockey.

"The three of us worked well together," Bucyk explained. "Each of us knew where the other two fellows would be. Bronco and Vic turned out to be the big scorers, whereas my job was to get the puck out of the corners."

It was while he was playing on The Uke Line that Bucyk received his infamous nickname, "The Chief." In his autobiography, *Hockey in My Blood*, John explains the origins of his alias:

"Bronco Horvath gave me the nickname 'Chief' when

The chief at the peak of his career.

the Ukes coincided with the decline and fall of big-league hockey in Boston.

Following the 1958-59 season, the Bruins missed the playoffs for eight consecutive years. But this was no fault of John Bucyk. Actually, his game improved through the whole ugly mess, as he skated with whomever management chose to align him.

For a time he skated with Murray Oliver at center and Tommy Williams on the right. The unit was called the BOW Line but enjoyed considerably less success than the Ukes.

It wasn't until Bobby Orr turned pro in 1966 and Phil Esposito was obtained from Chicago in 1967, along with Ken Hodge and Fred Stanfield, that the Bruins' fortunes turned.

While Orr and Esposito received the most credit for the Boston hockey renaissance, Bucyk also was a positive factor in providing overall balance for the Bruins' attack.

Esposito centered the first line with Ken Hodge and Wayne Cashman, but when they were checked to a standstill, a second line, composed of Bucyk and John "Pie" McKenzie on the wings and centered by Stanfield proved wonderfully effective and productive.

Underrated by the Blackhawks, Stanfield emerged as a crackerjack two-way center, whereas Pie McKenzie worked the ice like a tireless hornet, constantly disrupting the foe while melding neatly with his linemates.

That Stanfield and McKenzie were a boon to Bucyk is evident by John's stats. He reached his personal-high 51 goals while playing with them and also made it to the Stanley Cup Finals in 1970 for the first time since 1958, the year he arrived in Boston.

"I had waited a dozen years for that moment," said Bucyk, who played on Cup-winners in 1970 (vs. St. Louis) and 1972 (vs. the Rangers).

Bucyk wasn't kidding about the long wait. He had previously played in the 1956 finals for Detroit, who lost to Montreal, and in the 1958 finals when the Habs beat the Bruins. In his first game of the 1970 finals, Johnny came up with a hat trick in the 6-1 romp over St. Louis. Boston would go on to sweep the Blues en route to the Cup.

"Everything I had ever hoped for in a hockey game came true with 40 seconds gone in overtime," Bucyk said of

we were playing together in Edmonton because I used to dig the puck out of the corners so well and feed it back to him at center. We used to call Bronco 'The Colonel' because he'd park himself in front of the net and holler at me to go in the corner and dig the puck out. So one day somebody mentioned to Bronco that he acted like a chief bossing the two Indians around on his line. Bronco told the fellow Johnny Bucyk was the chief because I was the guy who used to sneak into the corners and lead the attack to get the puck. Bronco said I used my stick like a tommyhawk to steal the puck."

By 1961, both Stasiuk and Horvath had outlived their usefulness in Beantown and had left the Bruins. Although nobody could have foretold it at the time, the dissolving of

"John was the kind of player I didn't appreciate until I played on the same line with him. When I played in New York, I knew that he was good, but I didn't appreciate how much he did for the team on the ice with his knowledge and how much he did for the team off the ice."

—Bruins player Jean Ratelle

the final game of the 1970 playoffs. "I was sitting on the bench right next to McKenzie and actually I didn't see [the goal] go in. It all happened so fast. Orr broke down the side and in. Noel Picard tripped him, Bobby went flying and the next thing I knew the red light was on. I couldn't believe it at first!

"What were my first thoughts?

"To get hold of that Stanley Cup!

"Clarence Campbell made the Stanley Cup presentation and it felt great, something that can't be put into words, to receive the Cup from him. Skating around the Boston Garden with the Stanley Cup was one of the greatest moments of my life. The fans gave us a standing ovation. A tremendous roar literally rocked the Boston Garden. My hair stood on end. It just didn't stop."

During both Cup runs, Bucyk was the productive centerpiece. Over a fourteen-game span in 1970, he scored eleven goals and eight assists. In 1972, over a fifteen-game span, his numbers were 9-11-20.

The 1972 triumph over the Rangers would be the last Cup victory for Bucyk but certainly not the last of his meaningful moments. While teammates such as McKenzie and Derek Sanderson departed for the newly formed World Hockey Association, Bucyk remained a loyal Bruin.

Even as age braked his speed, he excelled in the mid-1970s and was given a new life when center Jean Ratelle was obtained from the Rangers and worked as Bucyk's pivot.

"John was the kind of player I didn't appreciate until I played on the same line with him," said Ratelle. "When I played in New York, I knew that he was good, but I didn't appreciate how much he did for the team on the ice with his knowledge and how much he did for the team off the ice."

Considering that he had been notorious for his tough play in Edmonton, it was rather shocking that Bucyk twice (1970-71, 1973-74) won the Lady Byng Trophy. Teammate Bobby Orr, however, was surprised John did not claim the award sooner.

"It's a trophy that's given to the player who shows sportsmanship play, without earning penalty minutes, and combines it with great ability," Orr said. "He deserved it. In fact, I thought Chief should have won it long before he did."

Bucyk also was recognized for his humanitarian work off the ice when in 1976 he was named winner of the Charlie Conacher Memorial Trophy. At the time, Bucyk was vice-chairman of the Heart Fund for Massachusetts.

"The more involved I became in it, the more satisfaction I received from it," said Bucyk. "Then, I got to know some kids who never would have made it without the very complicated heart surgery which was made possible by the research the fund supports. I realized that if I could help with that, then I was doing something worthwhile."

In truth, "worthwhile" is an accurate description of Bucyk as a member of the Bruins family. He retired as an active player after the 1977-78 season but has remained a member of the organization ever since.

With little fuss or fanfare, John Bucyk has earned the title of Mister Bruin as much as anyone who ever donned a Boston hockey uniform.

Phil Esposito, moving into scoring position.

Philip Anthony "Phil" Esposito

Born: Sault Ste. Marie, Ontario; February 20, 1942

Position: Center

NHL Teams: Chicago, 1963-67; Boston, 1967-75; New York (R), 1975-81

Awards/Honors: Hart Trophy, 1969, 74; Art Ross Trophy, 1969, 71, 72, 73, 74; Lester B. Pearson Award, 1971, 74; Hall of Fame, 1984

Phil
ESPOSITO

*I*f ever there was a hockey career that could be dubbed schizophrenic, it belonged to Phil Esposito.

Actually, Esposito's 18-year big-league stint could be divided three ways—his early years with Chicago, his final years with the Rangers, and the glory seasons in Boston.

Esposito's impact as a Bruin was so powerful in contrast to his efforts in the Windy City and the Big Apple that it is virtually forgotten that Phil played for any team but Boston.

Nor did it matter to his image that Phil was variously known as a "garbage collector" and complainer of the first order.

All that really mattered was that Espo swept 717 pucks behind the men in the cages during his career. He turned goaltender's garbage into his "G-O-A-L-D," and the Midas touch of his quick wrists earned him one MVP award, five scoring titles, two Stanley Cup championships and a sea of ink in the NHL record books.

Throughout his career, Esposito was overshadowed by his teammates—the golden namesakes of hockey. In Chicago it was *The Golden Jet*, Bobby Hull, and in Boston, *The Golden Boy*, Bobby Orr. As a result, people were skeptical about Espo's true ability. He was accused of being a selfish glory seeker who scored goals by hanging out in front of the net and depositing rebounds. But Esposito countered his critics by saying, "Then why don't others do the same?"

Phil admitted he would have loved to score classic goals with the finesse of Orr or the power of Hull, "But I haven't got that hard shot," he said. "I could shoot from 60 feet out all season and not get a goal. A player must do what he does best." Thus, Phil did it his way.

Which way is that? Chip Magnus, a reporter for the *Chicago Sun-Times*, captured it best when he wrote, "We see Phil move into the slot, waiting, just off the right corner of the net. Keith Magnuson belts him back into the net post and Phil recovers. Jerry Korab traps Esposito's stick with his own, digs with an elbow, spins Phil around.

"Stan Mikita moves in and rocks Phil with a hip check as he swings past. Magnuson returns, sending a shoulder into Esposito's spine . . . Phil is once more bounced by Magnuson, but he regains his balance, gets the puck and scores."

Esposito began his NHL career in 1963 with the Chicago Blackhawks. Following a quiet rookie season, he returned to the Hawks as the center for Chico Maki and Bobby Hull. Phil averaged 23 goals per season over the next three years, but more important, Espo helped Bobby Hull lead the league in goals scored over his duration.

Esposito, however, was not to remain a permanent fixture in Chicago. Coach Billy Reay and manager Tommy Ivan were disenchanted with Espo's playoff performance and decided to trade him. In May 1967, the Blackhawks and Bruins concluded a six-player deal. Esposito, center Fred Stanfield and winger Ken Hodge were sent to Beantown in return for defenseman Gilles Marotte, crafty center Pit Martin and goalie Jack Norris. Hockey columnists regarded this deal as "the most one-sided trade in modern hockey history." Time would prove them prophetic.

Bobby Orr (left) and Phil Esposito helped establish the Big, Bad Bruins as one of hockey's most feared teams of the early 1970s.

The trade didn't surprise Esposito, but the thought of joining a team full of guys that he'd grown to hate bothered him. Espo said, "To me, guys like Ted Green and Bobby Orr have been the villains. I don't know how I'll adjust to playing alongside of them." But the Bruins were understanding. They gave Espo the confidence he needed by immediately naming him the team's alternate captain.

Phil led the NHL with 43 assists in his first season with Boston and, by adding 35 goals to his totals, emerged as a substantial offensive threat.

Bobby Hull commented on the progress of his former linemate by saying, "The difference is that when Phil was with the Blackhawks he had to give me the puck all the time. Now, he can keep it for himself. He's gone from being the little toad in the big pond to being the big toad in the little pond that turned out to be a big pond. Boston thought that Bobby Orr would lead them out of the wilderness. But Bobby couldn't do it alone. Orr and Esposito; they complemented each other."

The following season, coach Harry Sinden placed Espo and Ken Hodge on the same line and finished off the trio by adding Ron Murphy. The threesome decimated opposing defenses and established a line-scoring record of 263 points. Phil was TNT offensively, feeding his teammates for 77 assists and 126 points, also an record. Never before had a player topped the 100-point plateau; Espo accomplished it with plenty of points to spare.

Judging by Esposito's accomplishments, a case could be made for him as one of the finest centers of all time. He was a First Team All-Star in 1969, 1970, 1971, 1972, 1973, 1974 and 1975. Both in 1969 and 1974, he was voted the Hart Trophy as the NHL most valuable player. He led the league in scoring in 1969, 1971, 1972, 1973 and 1974. He wears a pair of Bruins' Stanley Cup rings—from 1970 and 1972. In addition, Esposito was considered the pivotal factor for Team Canada in its four-games-to-three (one tie) victory over the Soviet national team in September 1972.

Yet, there were those who found a flaw in Esposito's armament. His critics charged that he was a selfish hockey player who lacked the ability to combine defensive aspects with his offensive game.

Clearly, one of the most traumatic moments in Bruins history—not to mention Esposito's—occurred when he was dealt by Harry Sinden along with Carol Vadnais to the New York Rangers for Brad Park, Jean Ratelle and Joe Zanussi.

The date was November 7, 1975. The deal not only shook up New Englanders, it had a terrible effect on his coach at the time, Don Cherry.

Derek Sanderson (left) talks to former teammate Phil Esposito at the Boston Garden in January 1973.

In his autobiography *Grapes: A Vintage View of Hockey*, Cherry remembered the moment when he visited Esposito's hotel room to tell him about the deal.

"I knocked on his door. Phil opened it and I walked over to a chair near the window and sat down. Phil sat on the bed.

"Me: 'Phil, I might as well give it to you straight; there's no use beating around the bush. Phil, you've been traded.'

"His body contorted. He was in physical and mental agony. He got up, sat down; got up again, sat down again. At least five minutes went by before he even said a word; then the words came blurting out.

"Phil: 'Grapes, please tell me, they traded me to *any team but the New York Rangers*.' (Funny how things work out. Much later Phil told me that the Rangers were the best team he could have gone to. He was made for New York.)

"I looked out the window and watched the raindrops

> "Phil was superstitious, but not nearly as much as some people thought. The one thing he insisted upon was that his sticks and gloves be laid out in front of him in the dressing room before each game. Heaven help the trainer or player who would accidentally kick those sticks or move those gloves.

—Don Cherry

course down to the window sill. Then, I looked at Phil and saw the tears filtering down his face. I couldn't hold it back any longer.

"Me: 'Yes, it is the Rangers.'

"Phil: 'But, Grapes, when I signed my contract with Harry I said I wouldn't ask for a no-trade contract. All I asked was that Harry give me his word that I would go to any team *except* the New York Rangers. And we shook on that.'

"Me: [To myself] 'You should have known that old Yogi Berra saying that verbal agreements aren't worth the paper they're written on.'

"Life had to go on and I had a team to coach. At least I *thought* I had a team to coach. When the guys finally convened on the bus heading for the Vancouver Coliseum there was a deathly silence that carried over to the practice. As the guys glided around the ice, Bobby Orr, who had been sidelined with one of his injuries, sidled up to me and asked whether I had played a part in the deal. I admitted that I had. 'Look,' he said, 'I don't want to sound as if I'm bragging or anything but why couldn't you guys have waited till I came back to see how the team would have played me back in the lineup. Maybe we would have been all right.' I told him that Harry and I felt that there was not time to waste, otherwise the Rangers might have nixed the deal.

"I left Orr and got ready to launch into the accelerated part of the skate. I blew the whistle, which meant the guys were supposed to move into high gear, but nothing happened. There was no reaction, as if I hadn't even blown the whistle. I blew it a second time and, again, it was as if my whistle were mute.

"I knew I was on the spot. They were a sullen bunch and I knew there would be trouble for a while because Phil and Vad had meant a lot to them. But we went on with the practice until there was a *real* downer: Phil and Vad came by the rink to pick up their sticks and skates and to make their good-byes.

"Needless to say, there wasn't a dry eye in the place as the two veterans moved around the dressing room, shaking hands with everyone. My heart was with them, but my mind said the deal had to be made if the team was to be straightened out."

Nobody understood Esposito better than Cherry, which is why the deal was so difficult for Grapes to accept. In a sense, Phil and Don were kindred spirits.

Cherry: "Esposito, to me, was one of the most colorful persons ever in the NHL. I have to laugh when people would say he scored 'garbage goals.' Phil would laugh, too, and say, 'Who cares what they call them—they all look like slap shots in next morning's papers. Who cares how they go in, as long as they count?'

"The thing I will always remember most about Phil was the 1972 Canada Cup. He had the courage to go on TV between periods and say that the team and players didn't deserve the abuse Vancouver fans and fans across Canada were heaping on them. He said that the players were truly doing their best and that, instead of booing and ridiculing, they should all get behind the team. It's the first time a hockey player rallied a country. Phil Esposito turned around the fans, the media—and most of all, he turned around the players. I think Phil Esposito won the Canada Cup that hot night in Vancouver.

"There were some who charged that Phil was more interested in his own point total than the welfare of the team. I never felt this way. I honestly think that Phil figured he was doing the best for the club by playing three- and four-minute shifts instead of coming off the ice sooner. Maybe he was right. He won a lot of scoring championships and he also played on two Stanley Cup-winners.

"Unfortunately, Phil's demand for ice time did have an adverse effect on others, particularly Andre Savard, a young French-Canadian center for whom the Bruins had high hopes. Andy's line would generally follow Phil's onto the ice, except that Phil always stayed on extra long. I can still see poor Andy's face as Phil would go through two or three extra shifts. Andy would sit astride the boards waiting and waiting and waiting for Phil to get off. We all said that Andy sat astride the boards so long waiting to get ice that by the time he got married he'd be sterile!

"Among Phil's high priority sensitivities, his hair ranked right at the top. He loved his hair and would treat it accordingly. After a game, he would sit in his brown-and-white kimono, apply a white solution to his hair and then sit with the conditioner settling in to make it even more beautiful. I remember one night, we were playing a crucial game at Boston Garden and as I patrolled the area behind the bench I noticed the back of Phil's neck. A dark substance was running down his neck. 'Phil,' I said, 'you look like you're oozing dark blood.' He felt the back of his neck, looked at his palm and said: 'Grapes, I'm gonna kill that hairdresser!'

"Phil was superstitious, but not nearly as much as some people thought. The one thing he insisted upon was that his sticks and gloves be laid out in front of him in the dressing room before each game. Heaven help the trainer or player who would accidentally kick those sticks or move those gloves.

"Esposito's natural talent for scoring once prompted me to ask him how he had learned to become such an efficient goal machine. 'Grapes,' he said, 'when I'm goin' good I just get the puck and fire it at the net and I just figure the net hasn't moved in fifty years so I'm bound to be on target. The rest will take care of itself. It's like being a baseball pitcher; he should never aim the ball, just rear back and throw it. I never aim the puck because I know that when I aim it I'm not goin' good.'

"Phil could score from any angle. I once saw him split the enemy defense, fall to his knees and, while still on his knees sliding toward the net, put the puck in the top corner of the cage."

Esposito never was the same after his trade to the Rangers. The adjustment was extremely difficult for Phil, who at first complained about conditions in Manhattan. But he gradually came around and, although he never regained his Stanley Cup form of the early 1970s, he won the hearts of New York fans.

In the midst of the 1980-81 season, Phil startled the hockey world by announcing his retirement—then and there—and moving behind the bench as an assistant coach and later a broadcaster.

Philip Anthony Esposito was born February 20, 1942, in Sault Ste. Marie, Ontario. He was not very highly regarded as a youthful skater, but the Chicago Blackhawks thought enough of him to place him with their St. Louis farm team in the early 1960s. It was there that he learned to employ his size and quick shot to his advantage.

The season following his retirement, Esposito was named color commentator for the New York Rangers, although many believed his future in hockey was in the executive suite as the general manager of a major league club. Sure enough, Phil soon found himself running the Rangers from the GM's suite. He remained in New York as vice-president and GM from 1986 to 1988. On December

Espo: A goal scorer's goal scorer

3, 1987, his jersey number 7 was retired in an emotional ceremony at the Boston Garden.

In 1990, Esposito would continue his hand in hockey, helping to orchestrate the expansion of NHL into Tampa Bay. He served as GM and alternate governor of the Lightning until 1998, before joining up with Fox Sports Net as a hockey analyst. He returned to Boston for the 1999-2000 season as a broadcaster.

Mr. Zero—Frank Brimsek.

Francis Charles (Frankie "Mr. Zero") Brimsek

Born: Eveleth, Minnesota; September 26, 1915

Position: Goaltender

NHL Teams: Boston, 1938-43, 1945-49; Chicago, 1949-50

Awards/Honors: Vezina Trophy, 1939, 42; Calder Trophy, 1939; Hall of Fame, 1966

Frank **BRIMSEK**

It has been the Bruins good fortune over the decades to be blessed with top-flight goaltenders, from Tiny Thompson to Byron Dafoe. But if one had to single out one puck-stopper who etched the most distinguished career between the pipes for the Hub sextet, it would be Frank Brimsek—alias "Mister Zero."

One would be hard-pressed to find an American-born player who made a more emphatic impact on "The Game" than Frank Brimsek. Were it not for a World War II stint in the United States Coast Guard—which significantly disturbed his future—Brimsek might well have emerged as the greatest exponent of goaltending ever known.

As it was, his career featured a number of truly sensational chapters from the moment it was announced he would depose the remarkable Tiny Thompson in the Boston Bruins' net.

In Frankie's rookie season of 1939, he won both the Calder Trophy as the best newcomer in the league and the Vezina Trophy for his outstanding play in the nets—the only American player ever to accomplish that achievement. That year, Frankie also was voted to the First All-Star Team. He repeated as the Vezina winner in 1942 and was the First All-Star Team goalie as well. Brimsek was named to the Second All-Star Team six times during his Boston career. With Frankie in the nets, the Bruins won the Stanley Cup twice and three times finished first.

He was an American legend in hockey. In 1966, Brimsek became the first United States player of professional hockey to be elected to the Hockey Hall of Fame.

Brimsek had quite a sensational break in the majors. In 1937, he had been assigned to Boston's American League farm club, the Providence Reds. Boston's goaltender was none other than Thompson, known to the hockey world as "the goalie without a weakness." Thompson was the best in the business, a four-time Vezina Trophy winner. Prospects didn't look good for the American kid buried in the minors.

It was quite by accident that Brimsek got his first chance to play in a big-league game. Thompson developed an eye infection, and Art Ross, the general manager and coach of Boston, sent for Brimsek. Frank was nervous. It was tough enough to fill for any goalie, but the pressure was colossal, considering the kid was being asked to fill the nets for the great Tiny Thompson.

His jitters vanished once the game started. Frankie, then only 23 years old, won his NHL debut by the score of 3-2. Three nights later, with Brimsek in the nets, the Bruins beat the Detroit Red Wings.

Thompson recovered, and Frankie was sent back to Providence. But Ross had liked what he had seen. He now had a dilemma on his hands. Popular with the fans, Thompson was great and had been Boston's solid rock for ten years. At 33, he would have several more outstanding seasons.

Trading Thompson would not go over well with the multitude of Bruin supporters, especially if Tiny's replacement failed. Ross journeyed to Providence to take another look at Frankie, who turned in a couple of shutouts while Ross scouted him. On November 28, 1938, Tiny Thompson was dealt to the Red Wings for $15,000.

On December 1, 1938, in a game against the Montreal Canadiens, Frankie Brimsek went into the nets not as a replacement for an injured Thompson, but as the regular goalie for the Bruins. Although the game was played at the Montreal Forum, Brimsek was aware there were critical eyes watching his every move.

The evening turned into a disaster. Montreal, which had only won once in its eight previous contests, beat Boston 2-0. In Detroit, the exiled Thompson beat Chicago 4-1. It left little doubt that Ross had made a mistake.

Brimsek was down but not out. It took only the next seven games for him to become a hockey legend. Playing the next match against the Chicago Blackhawks, Brimsek recorded his first NHL shutout as Boston beat Chicago by a score of 5-0.

However, the fans were not yet warming to him, and Frankie did little to improve his image. He had an idiosyncrasy of wearing red hockey pants instead of the team's then gold, brown and white colors, and his footwork left much to be desired. But his glove was quick and his confidence was enormous. The Boston fans would be in for a surprise.

Two nights later, the same teams met in Boston. It was Frankie's first appearance before the hostile Bruin fans. Brimsek claimed he could feel the coolness from the crowd.

Brimsek's next game was against the New York Rangers. Although the Rangers belted him with 33 shots on goal, Frankie stopped them all and earned his third straight shutout by a score of 3-0. He had 192 minutes and 40 seconds of scoreless goaltending. Thompson's modern record of 224 minutes and 47 seconds was in reach.

By now, even the Boston fans were wildly supporting Brimsek. The Bruins were so confident of Frankie's ability that they often sent five men into enemy territory, leaving Brimsek to fend for himself. The next game was against Montreal at the Boston Garden. Boston jumped to a 2-0 lead in the first period, while Frank held Montreal scoreless. The amazing string of scoreless goaltending ran into 212 minutes and 40 seconds. At the 12:00 minute mark of the second period, the tension in the Garden grew. At 12:08 the arena went wild! Brimsek, in only his fifth game as the Bruins' regular goalie, had erased Tiny Thompson's scoreless record. However, with less than a minute to go in the second period, four Bruins were caught down ice, and Herb Cain took a pass from George Brown and dumped the puck in the Boston goal. Brimsek's marvelous streak had ended at 231 minutes and 54 seconds. Boston went on to win the game, 3-2.

Thanks largely to the talents of the young American goalie, Boston was now in first place. Brimsek next shut out Montreal 1-0. Next up were the Detroit Red Wings and the first face-to-face meeting with Thompson. Both goalies played well, but Boston won 2-0. Frankie cut down the New York Americans next, by a score of 3-0. It was his third straight shutout, and his sixth in seven games.

Brimsek went after his own record in the next game against the Rangers. He held New York scoreless during the first period. During the second period, Phil Watson put the puck in the net for the first goal on Brimsek in 220 minutes and 24 seconds of hockey. When Frankie reached down to

Brimsek (1) front and center on the 1938-39 champs.

retrieve the puck, the fans gave him a standing ovation. Frankie Brimsek had done the impossible—he had won over the Boston fans and made them forget Tiny Thompson.

Francis Charles Brimsek was born on September 26, 1915, in Eveleth, Minnesota. His interest in hockey, oddly enough, was accidental. His older brother John was the second-string goaltender on the Eveleth High School team, but what he really wanted to be was a defenseman. John moved up to the blue line, and brother Frank took over in the nets.

After playing at Eveleth High, he goaltended for a short time at St. Cloud Teachers College. He decided to give the pros a shot and, in 1935, Frankie traveled to Baltimore for a tryout with the Eastern Amateur Hockey League. He failed.

Hitchhiking back home to Minnesota, depressed and disappointed, Frank was about to land in hockey by accident once more. Running out of cash while in Pittsburgh, Frankie stopped off at the old Duquesne Arena to see if he could borrow money for food. Lady Luck shone again on the Minnesota native, as the Pittsburgh team in the Eastern League, the Yellow Jackets, needed a goaltender. Frankie got the job. For two years, Brimsek was that club's goalie.

In the fall of 1937, Ross signed Brimsek to a pro contract. He had never even seen the young man play. Assigned to the Providence Reds, Boston's American League farm club, Frankie waited in the minors. In 1938, Brimsek, barely one year out of the amateurs, was Boston's goalie.

Looking back on that rookie season, Frankie said, "Tiny was such a great goaltender. I had to be good or they would have chased me right out of Boston."

During that spectacular rookie season, Brimsek finished with a brilliant 1.59 average and had 10 shutouts. He had given up only 70 goals in 44 games. Rightfully, he was awarded both the Calder Trophy and the Vezina Trophy.

Frankie played for Boston for five sparkling seasons, winning the Vezina Trophy again in 1942. At the end of the 1942-43 season, he enlisted in the United States Coast Guard. He played for the Coast Guard sextet in the Eastern League and then served aboard a patrol craft in the Pacific.

After the war, Frankie gave the National Hockey League another try. He returned to Boston for four seasons, but his comeback was a great disappointment. He had lost his edge. The Bruins kept waiting and hoping for the magic to come back. It never did. Boston traded Frankie to the dismal Chicago Blackhawks in 1949. There, Brimsek bombed terribly, and he retired after one season.

Frank had retired at the relatively young age of 34. He had been the best and he had been unique, an American-born, American-developed goaltender, excelling at his craft. He had played on Stanley Cup winners. He had stood alone on the mountaintop, the finest in his profession. The war had caused him to lose his skill, and Brimsek had little choice but to hang up his skates.

After he retired, Frankie settled in Virginia, Minnesota, a small town only five miles from Eveleth. He became an engineer for the Canadian National Railroad, guiding freight trains between the various cities in Canada.

His goaltending for the pre-war Boston Bruins will forever be cited by hockey's *cognoscenti* as the definitive work of its time. Frankie Brimsek proved beyond a doubt that an American could make it in the Canadian-dominated National Hockey League.

Along with Milt Schmidt and Woody Dumart, Bobby Bauer was one of the original Kitchener Kids.

Robert Theodore "Bobby" Bauer

Born: Waterloo, Ontario; February 16, 1915; died September 16, 1964

Position: Right Wing

NHL Teams: Boston, 1935-42, 1945-47, 1951-52

Awards/Honors: Lady Byng Trophy, 1940, 41, 47; Hall of Fame, 1996

It was hard not to like Bobby Bauer, even if you had the misfortune of playing against the Kitchener Kid.

Bauer played the game according to Hoyle or whoever it was who wrote the rules that said THIS is the proper way to work in the National Hockey League.

He was an exemplary performer whose skill only was overshadowed by the fact that he played on the same line as his childhood chums, Milt Schmidt and Woody Dumart.

As a unit, The Kraut Line ranked with the top forward combinations the NHL has ever known, and because the trio remained together so long, the skill of the others often concealed the third man.

> "He had a knack for getting between the boards and the opposing winger and making a play. He had a good shot, was a good skater and stick handler and he had a way of finding holes. He and Milt would pass the puck back and forth. I got the garbage goals."
>
> —Woody Dumart

This was a forever thing with Bauer since he and his two mates originally were combined as a forward unit when they still were in the minors at Providence of the American Hockey League.

In 1936-37, the Reds coach, Albert "Battleship" Leduc, combined Bauer with Schmidt and Dumart and thereby created what became known as The Kitchener Kids Line.

Like the others, Bauer was born in Kitchener-Waterloo, Ontario—originally known as Berlin, Ontario, before World War I—and knew Schmidt and Dumart from the old neighborhood.

Bauer originally gained national attention in 1933-34 playing for Toronto's St. Michael's College, which won the Memorial Cup, symbolic of Canada's junior championship. He then transferred to his hometown team, the Kitchener Greenshirts, who won the 1935 Memorial Cup. Although Schmidt and Dumart also were members of the Greenshirts, they did not play on the same line with Bauer.

Originally, the Toronto Maple Leafs—through their affiliation with St. Michael's College—had hoped to sign Bauer but the Bruins got to him first. In 1935 Boston signed him after Bruins boss Art Ross personally scouted him, as well as Dumart, who also was signed.

Ross overlooked Schmidt for the moment but Bauer and Dumart implored Ross to keep an eye on their younger buddy, which he did. Eventually, Schmidt would become part of the Boston hockey cast.

The three were reunited as Bruins in 1937-38 and spent the next four years together, making some of the most beautiful music ever seen at Boston Garden.

"They had the ring of 'The Rover Boys in Andorra,' or 'The Golden Boys on Center Court at Wimbledon,'" commented Herbert Warren Wind of *Sports Illustrated*. "They were the stuff of devoted boyhood chums scaling the heights together, all for one and one for all."

Bauer emerged as the cleanest player of the group and had the silverware to prove it. He won the Lady Byng Trophy for good sportsmanship in 1940, 1941 and again in 1947.

Anyone who followed the Bruins closely in the pre-World War II days knew that there was nothing phony about the brotherly feeling among the Kitchener Kids—also known as the Sauerkraut, or Kraut, Line.

In 1939 Great Britain and Canada entered the war and gradually, one by one, Canadian-born NHL players enlisted in the armed forces. Bauer, Dumart and Schmidt decided that they would join the Royal Canadian Air Force as a threesome and in 1942 they went off to fight the real wars.

In their last game before leaving for service, the Kitchener Kids totaled eight scoring points in an 8-1 rout of the Montreal Canadiens. At the finish, players of both teams plucked them up and carried them off while the Boston Garden organist played "Auld Lang Syne."

Long after the incident, Bauer remembered it as one of the most touching moments of his life. "The ovation," Bobby said, "at the height of my youth, sort of grabbed me."

Bauer was one of the precious few servicemen who managed to play hockey while serving in the armed forces. As was the case with many army, navy and air force units, hockey players combined to form service teams. Playing for the RCAF Flyers, Bauer helped the sextet to an Allan Cup, emblematic of Canada's senior championship. At the time, it was the second-most revered trophy in hockey behind the Stanley Cup.

Along with his airmen buddies, Bauer returned to the Bruins in 1945. While other NHL players-turned-servicemen lost their edge during the war, Bauer appeared to be in mint condition.

It is noteworthy that his most productive season came after the war, when he tallied 30 goals and 24 assists in 1946-47.

That was the good news.

The bad news for Bostonians was Bauer's declaration

that he was hanging up his skates to join the Bauer family hockey equipment business. At the time, Bauer set a record of sorts, becoming the only NHL player to quit after a season in which he scored 30 goals, the equivalent at the time of hitting .350.

There was, however, an asterisk after Bauer's retirement decision because he actually returned to the NHL for one more game.

On March 18, 1952, the Bruins staged a Schmidt-Dumart Night at Boston Garden.

Bauer came out of retirement for that game to play alongside his buddies one more time against the Chicago Blackhawks. Schmidt had 199 goals at the time and incredibly was set up by Bauer and Dumart for his 200th goal. At that point the public-address announcer intoned for the last time, "Boston goal by Schmidt, assists from Dumart and Bauer."

Granted that Bauer retired too soon, but the accolades then and now prove that he will never be forgotten.

Woody Dumart: "He had a knack for getting between the boards and the opposing winger and making a play. He had a good shot, was a good skater and stickhandler and he had a way of finding holes. He and Milt would pass the puck back and forth. I got the garbage goals."

Milt Schmidt: "I always maintained Bobby was the brains of our line. It's like winning the Stanley Cup all over again to have all three of us in there."

A member of the Hall of Fame, Bauer suffered a fatal heart attack at the age of 49 in 1964.

Bobby Bauer—he retired too soon.

Dit Clapper in his early years as a forward.

Aubrey Victor "Dit" Clapper

Born: Newmarket, Ontario; February 9, 1907;

died January 20, 1978

Position: Right Wing

NHL Teams: Boston, 1927-47

Awards/Honors: Hall of Fame, 1947

Coaching: Boston, 1945-49

I n a way, it's amazing that Aubrey Clapper became almost a forgotten man among Boston's most marvelous athletes.

Dit, as he was known to the Boston Garden faithful, not only was a major league star of elegance and versatility, he later became a Bruins coach and one of the rare iron men of the franchise.

Tall, handsome—with his hair always parted neatly down the middle—Clapper left his imprint in many ways.

He was the first National Hockey League player to last in the majors for twenty full seasons—all of them with the same team. He starred as a right wing for the first nine years of his career and then reverted to defense, where he proved no less adept.

Aubrey "Dit" Clapper played first in the NHL as a star forward and the last ten years as a topflight defenseman, all with the Bruins.

As a forward, he was a Second-Team All-Star in 1931 and 1935. As a defenseman, he was a First-Team All-Star in 1939, 1940 and 1941, and a Second-Team All-Star in 1944. His championship dossier includes three Stanley Cups and six first-place teams.

Although Clapper preferred the role of pacifist, his temper occasionally boiled out of proportion to his character. His most notorious eruption took place during a game with the Montreal Maroons. An opponent named Dave Trottier jammed the butt end of his stick into Clapper's face. Normally, this would have resulted in a penalty, but referee Clarence Campbell (who eventually became president of the National Hockey League) failed to detect foul play.

Clapper took the law into his own hands and jumped Trottier, whereupon Campbell skated to the scene of the crime. "Clapper," said the referee, "you're a dirty sonofabitch!"

The accusation was doubly surprising to Clapper because everyone in the NHL realized that the distinguished Campbell was a Rhodes Scholar and not given to profanity.

"What did you say?" demanded Clapper.

"I said you're a dirty sonofabitch," he repeated. Instead of leaving bad enough alone, Clapper followed up his tirade with a right cross to Campbell's head, sending the referee staggering back into the arms of the pleased players.

The act of punching out a referee was considered severe enough to warrant a long-term suspension. Instead, NHL president Frank Calder slapped a $100 fine on Clapper and a mild tongue-lashing.

Pressed as to why the punishment was so light, Calder revealed that he had received a report from referee Campbell that tended to shift the blame away from Clapper.

"I was talking loud," Campbell admitted, "when I

should have been throwing them into the penalty box."

Clapper is best remembered for his gallant efforts as a forward and a defenseman, not to mention his Beau Brummel appearance. Dit dressed meticulously and exuded class. He was the same way on the ice. *The Canadian Press,* in describing Clapper, noted that he was "the Jean Beliveau of his day," a reference to the classic Montreal Canadiens center of the 1950s, 1960s and early 1970s. Today, Clapper would be compared to a Wayne Gretzky.

Aubrey Victor Clapper was born February 9, 1907, in Newmarket, Ontario. After playing amateur hockey in the communities surrounding his home, he showed enough

powerful in history. That Boston club won the Stanley Cup with Frankie "Mister Zero" Brimsek in goal and "The Kraut Line" of Milt Schmidt, Woody Dumart and Bobby Bauer spearheading the attack.

During Clapper's final seasons with the Bruins, he assisted Ross with the coaching chores and then took over as the full-time coach after retiring in 1947. He gave up coaching after two seasons and retired to Peterborough, Ontario, where he made an unsuccessful run as a Liberal candidate in a federal election.

Although he was away from the NHL scene in retirement, Clapper continued to follow the professional

> ## "Dit Clapper was 'the Jean Beliveau of his day,' a reference to the classic Montreal Canadiens center of the 1950s, 1960s, and early 1970s. Today, Clapper would be compared to a Wayne Gretzky."
>
> ## —The Canadian Press

promise to earn a contract with the Bruins in 1927 when Art "Uncle Arthur" Ross was constructing one of the strongest teams to grace NHL ice.

Within two years of his debut, Clapper had outshone virtually every forward in the league. During the 1929-30 campaign—his most productive—Clapper totaled forty-one goals and twenty assists for sixty-one points in a forty-four-game schedule. (That was the one season in which the league allowed forward passing from zone to zone.)

Dit, of course, did not work alone. He was fortunate to be aligned with the gifted center Cooney Weiland and left wing Norman "Dutch" Gainor to form what was to become "The Dynamite Trio," a gallant and effective scoring unit.

Clapper once recalled that his first goal—scored but ten seconds into his first shift—and his 200th goal, which was the winner in a game against Toronto at Maple Leaf Gardens in 1942, were his most memorable.

Many hockey critics regard the 1941 Bruins team, on which Clapper was a defenseman, as one of the most

game. When Bobby Orr began starring for the Bruins in the late 1960s, comparisons were made by the experts who rated the stars of different eras. When Orr surpassed Clapper's lifetime mark of 228 goals and 248 assists, Dit never pouted but, rather, toasted the lad from Parry Sound, Ontario.

Dit was so enthralled with Orr's Bruins that, in April 1970, he returned to Boston at his own expense to see if the Bruins could win their first Stanley Cup in twenty-nine years.

"I'm looking forward to drinking champagne out of that Cup," Clapper enthused. "It's been such a long time."

The Bruins obliged by winning the Cup, and Dit returned to his home a happy man. The Boston club retired his number 5 jersey along with his shoulder pads.

After being inducted into the Hockey Hall of Fame, Clapper died on January 20, 1978. *The Canadian Press*, in a long and glowing obituary, stated that Dit was "one of the NHL's all-time greats." And that he was, on the attack as well as on defense.

Terry O'Reilly was the consummate power forward.

Terry O'Reilly

Born: Niagara Falls, Ontario; June 7, 1951

Position: Right Wing

NHL Teams: Boston, 1971-85

Awards/Honors: All-Star, 1975, 78

Terry O'REILLY

O f all the players Harry Sinden brought to the National Hockey League, none was more Sinden's type of player than Terry O'Reilly.

Sinden once summed up what it takes to be a Bruin, and his explanation tells everything one needs to know about O'Reilly's meaning to his team.

"The most important thing to any player," said Sinden, "is his teammates. It's not important how he feels about the coach, the fans or the press. What matters is how he feels about his teammates and how they feel about him."

No Bruin ever felt more keenly about his teammates than the right-winger from Niagara Falls, Ontario. O'Reilly, all 6-1, 199 pounds of him, was the quintessential Bruin. *Boston Herald* columnist Joe Fitzgerald, who closely followed the Bruins during the early 1980s, summed up the prevailing opinion of O'Reilly as well as anyone.

"When Wayne Cashman hung up his skates, Harry Sinden had to find another captain," noted Fitzgerald. "My suspicion is that it took Harry a split-second to conclude his search. O'Reilly was his kind of guy.

"Long after Terry is gone, his name will stand for the way they play hockey in Boston. It's violent, passionate, emotional hockey, played with the heart, and what it comes down to is giving a damn, and no one gives more than O'Reilly."

After playing his Junior hockey for the Oshawa [Ontario] Generals, O'Reilly was drafted by Boston in the second round of the 1971 Entry Draft—14th overall—and the Bruins wondered about their move. So did Terry.

"They figured that someday I would learn how to skate," he said. "I was kind of excited going to Boston. I got a map of New England, and Boston looked interesting—it was right there on the ocean. But then I thought, 'Holy mackerel! These guys just won The Stanley Cup!' That's when they were just booming. I thought I would be buried in the minors three or four layers deep."

O'Reilly was elevated for one NHL game in 1971-72, spending the other 60 games with the Bruins' American League farm club, the Boston Braves. It was at the time of the World Hockey Association's birth, and a few Bruins had defected to the WHA. Terry knew that his time was not far away. "There was room at the end of the bench for me, and once you get your foot in the door . . ."

He played in 60 games (9-8-17-134) but did get an opportunity to watch the big club very carefully. It was an enriching experience and one he never forgot.

"I would sit on the bench," said Terry, "and watch the way Bobby Schmautz and Ken Hodge shot the puck. I would watch Bobby Orr skate and the way Wayne Cashman went into the corner and the way Johnny Bucyk played the wing. I would pick out their strong points and then try to imitate them in practice."

O'Reilly's exuberance was both contagious and worrisome. He was the type of individual who had diffi-culty braking his emotions and sometimes it worried teammates such as defenseman Don Awrey.

"We'd have to skate laps when practice was done," Awrey recalled. "So Cashman or myself would have to grab Terry's jersey and hold him back, because if we allowed him to set the pace, the rest of us would drop from exhaustion."

The early O'Reilly was more prominent for his fists than his shots.

He was not the NHL's best fighter, but he certainly was one of the most energetic jabbers the game has ever known. As a result, Boston Garden's Gallery Gods eagerly awaited his next bout—whenever it would occur.

"One night I scored a goal against Toronto," O'Reilly remembered, "and when I got back to Boston the next day everyone was congratulating me on the fight I had had. It was as if no one noticed the other things."

That's not quite accurate. The "other things" certainly were noticed by those who know hockey best, particularly teammates such as Bobby Orr.

"I always felt," said Orr, "that if everyone played like Terry played, we'd never lose a game. He just won't quit."

It showed in his stats; the harder O'Reilly tried, the bigger his numbers grew. By 1975-76 he had cleared the 20-goal plateau (23-27-50) for the first time and by 1977-78 had reached 90 points (29-61). He was not the very soul of smoothness but nobody seemed to care.

"On skates," chuckled Orr, "Terry was about as smooth as a stucco bathtub."

He was soon named "Taz," as in Tasmanian Devil, which was about as appropriate a hockey nickname that ever was coined. O'Reilly's employer, who was always careful about doling out praise, never held back when it came to Terry.

"In Boston, Montreal, Toronto—in cities all over the league—thousands of people will pay money to watch Terry O'Reilly play hockey," said Sinden. "Why? He's fun to watch and he works so hard."

In 1977-78 O'Reilly became only the second player in NHL history to lead his team in both scoring and penalty minutes (211) and nobody but opponents complained about the latter.

Like many Bruins of that era, O'Reilly considered the

O'Reilly swerves into attack formation.

1978-79 club one of the best.

"In the years since 1972 we had some good teams at Boston, and I don't think any was better than the '78-79 team," said O'Reilly. "We were a hardworking club with a lot of balance and I always thought Don Cherry did an excellent job of coaching to get the most out of the talent we had. He had us working—some writers called us the 'Lunch Pail Brigade,' meaning we were a team of good, hardworking, honest hockey players."

The only problem was that Scott Bowman's Montreal Canadiens were in the middle of a dynastic four-straight Stanley Cup run. But the Bruins nearly ended that run on

May 10, 1979. It was the seventh game of the Stanley Cup semifinals at the Forum in Montreal. Like other Bruins, O'Reilly felt that if they won that game, they'd go on to win the Cup, no matter who they played in the finals.

In an April 1980 interview with *Hockey Digest*'s George Vass, O' Reilly described that game in these words:

"I don't think we've ever been more steamed up for a game than we were for that one. We knew what we were up against in the Forum, but we also remembered the first two games, each of which we could have won, if we hadn't made a few mistakes.

"We got the first goal in the seventh game. It came in

the middle of the first period, and though the Canadiens tied it quickly, we came out of the period tied 1-1 feeling pretty good about our chances.

"The second period was all ours. We scored a couple of goals, both by Wayne Cashman, to take a 3-1 lead. We didn't get many shots, but we made the most of our opportunities. The Canadiens, at the same time, were getting a lot of chances, but Gilles Gilbert was playing outstanding for us in goal.

"We couldn't hang on to that two-goal lead in the third period, Montreal tying the game early. But with less than four minutes left, Rick Middleton put a shot past Ken Dryden, the Canadien goalie, and we had a 4-3 lead.

"All we had to do was hang on for less than four minutes and we'd beat the Canadiens. They were pressing, but if we played it smart, we'd come out all right and then go on to the finals.

"Somehow, though, whenever you've got the Canadiens in trouble, they seem to get out of it. There was only a couple of minutes left when we got a stupid penalty for too many men on the ice. As usual, the Canadiens made the most of it. Guy Lafleur scored a power-play goal with just over a minute to go to tie the game 4-4 and it went into sudden-death overtime.

"We should've won it in the overtime. We had plenty of chances to score. I got the puck and took a shot, but it went wide of the net. If I'd been more accurate, the game would've been over and we'd have gone to the finals.

"But I shot wide, and after about nine minutes of overtime Yvon Lambert scored the goal that won it for the Canadiens."

If there was any complaint about O'Reilly, the player, it was because of his awkward skating, which suggested a lumberjack snowshoeing through the Canadian tundra.

"My problem," O'Reilly explained, "was that I couldn't skate very well because, as a kid, I played goalie for four years. I didn't skate as much as the other players. After my first year in Boston, I skated for three hours each day all summer."

Terry compensated well. He mastered the art of manipulating the puck with his skates and often would put on a show for his teammates during off-day scrimmages.

"You should have seen him," enthused Cherry. "No stick. Just O'Reilly and the puck and the boards. All three of them take a beating, mind you, but O'Reilly could make the puck talk."

He never fully controlled his temper and once was suspended three games for bumping a referee. Anyone who saw the Bruins in the next three matches would admit that Terry was conspicuous by his absence.

"When Terry was out," said Cherry, "we were a mediocre club because when he's in the lineup, he adds life, spirit and hard work."

Not surprisingly, he became a frequent winner of the "Most Popular Bruin" award from Boston Garden's Gallery Gods and played his entire career for the same franchise.

While O'Reilly was adored by players, coaches and fans alike, nobody appreciated him more than Don Cherry. In his autobiography, Grapes provided the following insights into the coach-player relationship:

"If any enemy seriously fouled a player like Bobby Schmautz, that player, more likely than not, would be carved up without warning. But if that very opponent fouled Terry in the same way, O'Reilly would go after the guy, tap him on the shoulder, allow him to turn around, invite him to fight and then permit the enemy to strike the first blow. The Marquis of Queensbury would have been terribly proud of him. The problem was that O'Reilly's ritual hurt the team. Invariably, he would wind up with an additional two-minute penalty for going after the guy and a five-minute major for fighting. The other fellow would get away with just a five-minunte penalty.

"Try as I might, I couldn't convince O'Reilly that he was being too nice, but one of the best fighters in the league cured Terry of his etiquette. We were playing the Los Angeles Kings, when Dan Maloney was the Kings' number one gunfighter. I had been cautioning O'Reilly that he had to stop permitting the enemy to take the first punch at him. I didn't want him to go around sucker-punching the opposition but, on the other hand, I didn't want to see him getting hurt by being too nice. Well, on this night Maloney not only hit him first but he did a pretty good number on Terry. It was a painful experience but Maloney had done me a favor because, now, Taz made sure he got the first punch in before the other got started jabbing.

"I found Terry to be a very paradoxical character. As tough as he was on the ice, that's how lamb-like he was when he wasn't in uniform. He was an avid antique collector. If he had one flaw, it was a vicious temper.

"Sometimes Terry pushed his courageousness too far. He and his wife, Lourdes, were vacationing one spring in Acapulco when Terry decided to go for a swim. As it happened, he misjudged the waves and the undertow and, before he knew it, he had drifted out far beyond the acceptable limit. Strong as he was, he still had a difficult time making headway with all the waves and the undertow. In time it became apparent that he was in trouble—big trouble. Just when it appeared that he might fade out of sight, a couple of lifeguards spotted him, swam like the devil through the waves, and reached him just in time. It took them half an hour to haul him in, but they did and, thoroughly exhausted by the ordeal, they laid him out on the beach.

"Apart from the fact that he had nearly drowned, O'Reilly also had pulled his ankle so badly in the rescue operation that he could hardly walk, but he finally pulled himself together and headed back to his cabana, limping all the way. As he walked along the beach, he passed a bunch of guys who had hang gliders, surfboards and other gismos. One of the fellows noticed Terry and began goading him. 'Hey, big fella, let's see ya do some surf gliding.'

"Terry politely shook his head, but the guy persisted. 'No, thank you sir,' Terry repeated, but the hustler wasn't satisfied. 'How come,' he snapped. 'Are ya yellow, or too cheap?'

"The man who had just come this close to drowning and was hobbled by a bum ankle looked over at his adversary and replied: 'I'll show you who's yellow,' and proceeded to grab the guy and bury his head in the sand. You just don't say things like that to Terry O'Reilly.

"Of course, I've said a few things to O'Reilly, but sometimes my words went flying past him like a slapshot aimed wide of the net. The classic example took place one day when Terry, Dwight Foster, Mike Milbury, Peter McNab and I were helping Terry move to his mansion in Georgetown. The address, by the way, is One Cherry Lane. (Terry says he's changing it to One Cheevers Lane.)

"When it came time to load the fridge, I said, 'Terry, we better take all the food out of the fridge before we pick it up.' 'No, Grapes,' he laughed. 'Remember, you're not my coach in the summer. I don't have to listen to you now. The stuff won't come out.' There was not much I could say to that, so I watched as Terry, Mike, Peter and Dwight lifted it.

"A split-second later, the door flew open and everything poured out of the refrigerator. It looked like Fibber McGee's closet. After the last bottle of milk hit the ground, I patted Terry on the shoulder. 'Taz, old boy,' I said, 'you should always listen to your coach.'

"Terry really demonstrated the kind of friend he is during a family crisis. In 1979, our son Timothy had to have a kidney transplant. As you can imagine, we were all

absolutely devastated. He was on a dialysis machine, and the whole ordeal was extremely hard to take. Rose and I were tested to see whether or not our kidneys were compatible for a transplant, but as it turned out, our daughter Cindy's kidney was almost identical to Tim's. Cindy was a miracle throughout the whole thing. She just said, 'Take mine,' without hesitation.

"The whole experience was getting to be a little hard for me, so much so that I began to look forward to road trips so I could get out of Boston. I left the whole burden on Rose's shoulders.

"Some people might wonder how I could leave my family at a time like this; how could I even function. Well, when you're a professional, you have to work all the time. You separate one aspect of life from another. I didn't realize the seriousness, the importance of the operation, until I saw both Cindy and Tim being wheeled into the operating room. Then, I finally realized the sacrifice Cindy was making.

"Throughout all of this, the Bruins won twenty of our first twenty-two games. Someone asked Terry why we had gotten off to such a good start and he said, 'Well, we had a meeting and decided that Grapes was having enough trouble, so let's give him one less thing to worry about.' That's the kind of guy Terry is and that's the kind of guys they all are. They all went to donate blood so that Tim would have enough blood for the operation. Now you see why I loved them."

"The name Bruins has always commanded respect," O'Reilly explained.

"Whenever someone asked what I did for a living, I'd say I played for the Bruins. Just saying it would send a chill down my spine."

That is exactly how most Boston fans reacted when they watched Terry O'Reilly in action.

The Stitched-Mask Man, Gerry Cheevers.

Gerald Michael (Gerry "Cheesy") Cheevers

Born: St. Catharines, Ontario; December 7, 1940

Position: Goaltender

NHL Teams: Toronto, 1961-62; Boston, 1965-72, 1976-80

Awards/Honors: Hall of Fame, 1985

Coaching: Boston, 1980, 84; 1984-85 (shared with Harry Sinden)

He was Billy Smith before the notorious Islanders' wild man came along. Among the long list of feisty professional goalies, Gerry Cheevers ranks right up there with such fist-flailing stoppers as Harry Lumley, Legs Fraser and Ron Hextall.

Not that it was a problem for Cheevers, but he did play for a team whose theme was go-go-go into the opposition end and let defense take the hind post.

Bobby Orr's Big Bad Bruins were the perfect match for Cheevers' Big Bad Behavior.

But it should never be forgotten that behind the netminder's bombast was a superbly competitive athlete. More than anything, he was a winner. Cheevers shared the goaltending with Eddie Johnston on the Boston Bruins' last two Stanley Cup championship teams in 1970 and 1972.

In 1973, he was voted the best goaltender in the World Hockey Association. He was the number one goalie for Team Canada in 1974 during the series against the Soviet All-Stars and was durable enough to span two decades as a professional.

Few could match Cheevers' competitive zeal. His policy was strict and honest: when you lose, it's like being shot on the battlefield, and don't go shaking the hand of the enemy for that! Such was the case in 1971, when goalie Ken Dryden and the Montreal Canadiens upset Cheevers' Bruins. At game's end, the teams lined up for the traditional handshaking ceremonies, but Cheevers had already made a quick exit to his dressing room.

"I wanted to tell Dryden when it was all over that he'd done a big, big job, but I didn't," said Cheevers. "When the teams met in a straggly line at center and shook hands, I wasn't among those present. I've never congratulated a guy for beating me. I sure as hell didn't feel like gripping Mahovlich's paw, and Harper's and Lemaire's. They put lumps on me and took my money; why should I applaud them?"

Later, Cheevers called over Jacques Beauchamp, a journalist who was heading to the plane that would carry the victorious Canadiens—and Dryden—back to Montreal. "Jacques," he said, "when you get on the plane, tell that giraffe [Dryden] he had one hell of a series. Tell him congratulations for me, Jacques."

Congratulations enveloped Cheevers many times during a career that included 418 regular-season National Hockey League games and 88 playoff matches. His goals-against average was 2.89 for the regular-season campaigns and 2.69 for the playoffs.

In a sense, the figures were deceptive because Gerry goaled for a Bruins club that invariably accented offense—Phil Esposito, Bobby Orr and Ken Hodge were the big guns—and ignored defense. Which meant that Cheevers was pretty much on his own.

Nicknamed "Cheesy," Cheevers set an NHL record during the 1971-72 season, when he played goal through 32 unbeaten games "He was one of the all-time greats when it came to money games," said Esposito, a longtime team-mate.

Former coach Don Cherry cites one example of Cheevers as "the best money goaltender" for Dick Irvin's book *In the Crease*: "We're playing Pittsburgh in the playoffs and Cheevers beats them the first two games in Boston. We were gonna beat them for sure, but at home they were pretty tough so I decide to rest Cheevers and start Gillie Gilbert in the third game. So when we get to the rink Cheevers goes out and gets a Pepsi and has a couple of hot dogs because I told him he wasn't starting. After the warm-up, he's sitting in the dressing room relaxing and Gilbert suddenly breaks out in hives five minutes before the game is

gonna start. So I go to Gerry and he's full of hot dogs and everything, which he shouldn't have done, but that's Gerry. I told him, 'You're playin' tonight.' So what happens? He digs down, goes out, and plays the best game of his career. As far as I was concerned, his game that night was better than any of the overtime games we won, or any other game.

"That's the kind of a guy he was. If you got up 6-1 you knew he might let in two or three easy ones late in the game. He was tough on coaches that way. But if it got to 6-4, he wouldn't let a pea get by him."

Gerald Michael Cheevers was born on December 7, 1940, in St. Catharines, Ontario, and seemed destined for a career with the Toronto Maple Leafs, who owned his rights during the early 1960s. He was obtained by the Bruins in 1965 and, after a few trips to the minors, made it to stay in the NHL in 1967, at a time when Boston's fortunes were on the rise.

The rise of Cheevers to stardom surprised many who remembered him as a second stringer in Toronto.

"Toronto had Johnny Bower," said Cheevers, "who was playing very well for them and then in 1964, they picked up Terry Sawchuk in the draft. I knew there was no way I was going to win a job from a pair of greats like that. Actually, when they drafted Sawchuk, they dropped my name from the protected list. But nobody claimed me. The next year they left me unprotected again, and Boston grabbed me for the $30,000 draft price. I was glad of it."

A knee injury was, perhaps, the best accident that befell Cheevers and the Bruins in his rookie season with Boston. The Bruins demoted him to Oklahoma City, where he met coach Harry Sinden. The young mentor was sensitive to the new goaltender's problems and helped put him back in the groove.

"He was a bit down on himself for not having stuck with the Bruins," Sinden recalled. "But I figured we could straighten him out in Oklahoma, and we did. The team seemed to rally in front of him, and we went on to win our first championship that year."

Sinden was promoted to the Bruins the following year, but he didn't forget Cheevers. In November 1966, Johnston suffered an eye injury. Normally, the substitute goaltender, Parent, would replace the starter, but Sinden wasn't follow-ing the book. He elevated Cheevers from Oklahoma City and immediately started him in the Bruins goal. He tied New York, 3-3, shut out Toronto, 4-0 and beat Montreal, 2-1, in his first three games. He was returned to Oklahoma City in January 1967, finished the season there and won the Harry Holmes Memorial Trophy as the Central League's outstanding goaltender.

During the summer of 1967, the Bruins were com-pelled to make a serious decision about which goaltenders they would protect in the draft. It wasn't a simple matter because they owned Johnston, Cheevers and Parent—as well as the very promising young Doug Favell. Only two could be retained. Parent appeared to be the first choice, followed by Cheevers, Johnston and Favell, but Schmidt and Sinden protected Johnston and Cheevers and lost the other pair to the Philadelphia Flyers.

"That put pressure on Eddie Johnston and myself," said Cheevers, "but as far as I was concerned, I was anxious to prove that I belonged in this league as a matter of general principle, anyway."

Superficially at least, it appeared that Cheevers had not only won himself an NHL job, but managed to bump Johnston in the process. The kid played 44 games while the veteran played 20. Cheever's average was 2.83 and the veteran's record was 2.87, but management's feeling about the pair was tacitly expressed during the playoffs with Montreal. Sinden stubbornly stuck with Cheevers as the Canadiens won four straight games. It was a bit of strategy that invited—and received—criticism.

"I probably cost our team one game in that series," Cheevers told Montreal author Gil Smith. "But we lost two of those games by the margin of a single goal, and a break or two might've made the difference."

Management was not persuaded that it had committed an error by not using Johnston in at least one game, claiming many of the Bruins had never played in playoff competition before. They came right back with Cheevers and Johnston in 1968-69. In many ways, the pair had come along neatly, if not splendidly, as a goaltending tandem.

Inevitably, fans were hanging banners over the Boston Garden balcony: "WE'RE BELIEVERS IN GERRY CHEEVERS."

After the Bruins won the Stanley Cup in 1972, Cheevers jumped to the Cleveland Crusaders of the World Hockey Association and remained in the WHA until 1976, when he returned to the Hub sextet. It was no coincidence that Cheevers' return marked another upturn in the Bruins' fortunes. His habit of pursuing and stickhandling the puck delighted Boston Garden fans, and his goaltending still had a snap of sharpness.

Gerry remained a Bruins goalie until his retirement after the 1979-80 campaign, when he was named Boston's coach. The transition from the nets to the bench was not an easy one. "It was," said Cheevers, "a tremendous learning experience."

Coaching did not agree with Cheevers. In time, he was released by the Bruins and became a TV hockey analyst for the Hartford Whalers (now the Carolina Hurricanes). Still, he is remembered as a championship goalie.

Cheevers played for two Stanley Cup winners, which is more than most goaltenders can claim. Talking to Dick

Cheesy: Never at a loss for words.

Irvin, Cheevers summed up his feelings: "I think the only high you can have in hockey is winning the Stanley Cup. When you decide to become a pro and make hockey your living, you have to try to be the best. If you decide to become a lawyer, you want to be the best. In sports, you want to win championships. Once in a while I sit back and feel mad or disappointed that the teams I was with as a player and a coach could never beat Montreal when we played them in big ones. But we won a couple of Stanley Cups, so I know somewhere along the line I succeeded."

He succeeded in spades. Cheevers was inducted into the Hall of Fame after 13 seasons in the NHL. Perhaps Harry Sinden said it best when he observed, "Certainly we had Bobby Orr and Phil Esposito, but I'm sure we couldn't have won the Cups without Gerry Cheevers."

Ed Johnston eyeballs the puck on its way into his body for another save.

Edward Joseph Johnston

Born: Montreal, Quebec; November 24, 1935

Position: Goaltender

NHL Teams: Boston, 1962-73; Toronto, 1973-74;
St. Louis, 1974-78; Chicago, 1978

Coaching: Chicago, 1979-80; Pittsburgh, 1980-83
and 1993-97

Ed
JOHNSTON

*U*nquestionably the last of the outstanding old-time goalies was Ed Johnston, who nearly died as a result of an injury suffered between the pipes.

Johnston was the last big-league goaltender to play an entire season (1963-64) without being replaced.

It was remarkable in many ways, particularly since he was being paid only $8,500. Johnston revealed to author-broadcaster Dick Irvin what happened after he finished that year with a 3.01 goals-against average, third best in the league, with six shutouts.

"After the season I went in to see the manager, Lynn Patrick, and told him I thought I had a thousand dollars coming to me because they would give me a bonus if I had an average of 3.00. He said, 'Did you read the fine print? You had 3.01.' But he gave it to me!"

There are many ways to define Johnston's excellence, but one way to begin is to explain how well he played when the Bruins were at their absolute worst at the start of the 1960s.

Those were the days when goaltenders were beginning to wear masks, but Johnston was not one of them. It was 1962-63 and Ed had just replaced Bobby Perreault as the Bruins' goalie.

Johnston was a husky Montreal-born youngster who had previously belonged to the goalie-rich Montreal Canadiens. Johnston stepped between the goal pipes at the start of the third period on November 14, 1962, and again on December 15. He played a total of forty-nine games and finished the season with a poorer goals-against record than his humorous predecessor. However, for reasons known only to management, Perreault was dismissed to the minors and Johnston was given the Bruins goaltending job. It was a dubious triumph.

With exclusive rights to the Bruins nets in the 1963-64 season, Johnston gave up 211 goals for a 3.01 average. Boston won only eighteen games that year and finished dead last. It was difficult to determine just how good—or bad—Johnston's goaltending was because Boston's defense seemed to be competing with its offense for some sort of ineptitude award. He did manage six shutouts and was sturdy enough to play all seventy games, but the feeling persisted that he would be, at best, an adequate goalie and that was that.

The following year the Bruins alternated Johnston with Jack Norris, a relative unknown who was useful only in that he provided a comparison with Johnston. If Johnston was inept with a 3.47 goals-against average, Norris was worse at 3.70, and the Bruins again finished in sixth place. But the new order was coming, and in 1965-66 there was evidence that Boston's goaltending deficiencies would soon be remedied, even though they still had Johnston, whose record was getting worse rather than better.

The source of hope was Bernard Parent, another Montrealer, who had an admirable record as a junior goaltender in Niagara Falls. For a while it appeared that Parent might be more than an average player, but a couple of severe beatings altered his reputation. He finished his rookie season with a 3.69 average to Johnston's 3.72 and a reputation as a potential star.

In time the Bruins' high command would conclude that their goaltending future could best be handled by Johnston and Gerry Cheevers. Parent was grabbed by the Philadelphia Flyers in the 1967 Expansion Draft. As it happened, it was a positive move for the Flyers, but the Bruins hardly suffered, although the near-fatal injury to Johnston could have crippled Boston's goaltending machine, if not Eddie himself.

The grim episode took place on the night of October 31, 1968. Coach Harry Sinden had advised Eddie that he would be starting that night in Detroit's Olympia Stadium. Johnston was handling some routine warm-up shots when he was suddenly struck down by a flying puck that came from the corner. He was hit on the side of his head above the left ear and was carried to the dressing room.

At first Johnston's injury seemed to be a routine pre-game accident that would soon heal. He was dispatched to Detroit's Osteopathic Hospital, where doctors kept him under observation for four days. When he was released, ostensibly recovered, he took an early-evening flight back to Boston.

"They got me on the plane," said Johnston, "but anything I know about arriving home is what I've learned from Ted Green and Sammy Videtta, who met me at Logan Airport."

Johnston didn't remember being sick on the flight, but all indications were that he was terribly ill. When Green greeted him at the airport, he was appalled at Johnston's appearance.

"Teddy has told me," Johnston added, "that I looked so bad there was only one thing to do."

Stan Fischler Collection

Goalie Ed Johnston and Bobby Orr defend against the Minnesota North Stars.

Green rushed the goaltender to Massachusetts General Hospital, where doctors pondered whether or not to perform an operation to relieve a blood clot. They eventually rejected the idea but kept Johnston in the hospital until December of that year.

Time proved a great healer for Johnston, and by January 4, 1969, he told Sinden he was ready to play. He held the Minnesota North Stars to a pair of goals in a 2-2 tie at Bloomington, Minnesota, and found his old groove with a two-goal tie with Detroit at Olympia on January 23.

Other goalies may have suffered more injuries than the man they called "EJ," but not many. It is a matter of record that Johnston suffered three of his seven broken noses in a stretch of ten days. "I broke it in New York and took eighteen stitches. There used to be this little doc at the Garden there, Yanagisawa, who we all called Kamikaze, and he'd just reach up and give the nose a quick twist to bang it back into place. The next night in Boston I broke it again for twelve more and then we went into Montreal and I broke it again. But did I have sense enough to put on a mask? No way."

Johnston remained a Bruin until 1972-73, when he was traded to Toronto. A year later he was sent to the St. Louis Blues and, in 1977-78, was traded to Chicago. He played four games for the Blackhawks that year before calling it a career.

In Dick Irvin's book, *In the Crease—Goaltenders Look at Life in the NHL*, Johnston summed up how he felt about his career:

"I was playing at the same time as some of the greatest goalkeepers that ever played. You had Bower, Plante, Sawchuk, Hall, Gump, and myself. Playing with people like that was just great.

"With the kind of equipment we had we were black-and-blue right from training camp through the whole year. All we wore on our arms was just a little padding and our underwear. I had no protection at all on my skates. My toes were always hurt. I'd walk around the whole year with swollen toes. That year I played every game. I broke my nose three times and had the lobe of my ear sliced off. But with only one goalkeeper you were afraid to come out of the net. Somebody would step in and you might be gone.

Goaltender Ed Johnston (1) enjoyed a great rapport with fellow Bruins netminder Gerry Cheevers. He was a member of Team Canada during the 1972 Summit Series versus the Soviets.

That's the way it worked for everybody.

"Today, I don't think a guy could play 84 games, for a lot of reasons. Travel is probably the biggest. Sometimes in the course of a week you play in two or three different time zones. But the equipment is much better now. It's great with the helmets, the arm pads, the way they're protected everywhere. They've got the thing underneath their chin. The biggest advantage they have today is the equipment. It really is."

Johnston should know. He hasremained close to the game ever since packing in his pads, serving as head coach of the Pittsburgh Penguins from 1980-1983 and again from 1993 to 1997, posting an overall record of 232-224-60 and leading the team to two division titles. He was general manager from 1983-1988 and had the distinction of drafting Mario Lemieux with the first pick of the 1984 NHL draft.

Originally, Johnston stepped into the coaching ranks as head coach of the Chicago Blackhawks' AHL affiliate in New Brunswick. After one season in the minors, he was named head coach of the Blackhawks in 1979 and led his team to a division title. He was hired by the Penguins the following season.

Johnston also served as GM of the Hartford Whalers from 1989-1992, then returned to coach the Pens again, from 1993 through 1996-97.

Eddie Westfall receives the Bill Masterton Trophy from Carole Masterton in 1977.

Vernon Edwin (Eddie "No. 18") Westfall

Born: Belleville, Ontario; September 19, 1940

Position: Right Wing

NHL Teams: Boston, 1961-72; New York (I),

1972-79

Awards/Honors: Masterton Trophy, 1977

Ed **WESTFALL**

*I*f ever there was a player who made sweet use of adversity, it was Ed Westfall.

He had the ill fortune to have played for some of the worst teams in Bruins history

early in his career. And then Easy Ed enjoyed the good fortune to be a member of

Boston's Stanley Cup-winners in 1970 and 1972.

Somewhere in between, Westfall learned the art of penalty-killing so well that he

ranks among the best shorthanded experts ever to grace the ice.

His partner with whom he generally worked against enemy power plays was Derek

Sanderson, who learned the craft well from The Master.

Together, Westfall and Sanderson were without peer for their time and were favor-

ably compared with the Toronto Maple Leafs tandem of Nick Metz and Joe Klukay,

who, in the late 1940s, developed penalty-killing to its highest form.

As a checking forward, Westfall invariably was dispatched to guard such sharpshooters as Bobby Hull and handled that portion of his work so well that he was recommended for the Hockey Hall of Fame, although he lacked enough political support to gain induction. Those who had seen Eddie in his prime insist he was every bit the defensive forward that Bob Gainey was, and the latter is in the Hall of Fame.

"Eddie was one of the all-time greats," said Sanderson. "When I came up, he was the established veteran and I was the rookie. He was supposed to take care of me, be my roomie and keep me under his wing. And he did. He taught me the ropes, and he was a gentleman—one of the classiest guys in the game."

What made Westfall such an effective player?

Al Arbour, who played against Eddie and then coached him on Long Island, said it succinctly. "Westfall was a guy with a lot of intelligence and that's what made him such a good player."

That intelligence was apparent during a Bruins career that began in 1961-62 and concluded exactly a decade later, following the Cup victory. At that point Westfall was claimed by the New York Islanders on June 6, 1972, in the Expansion Draft.

Many observers believed the Bruins had erred in allowing Westfall to remain unprotected. After all, since he had been their savior so many times in the past, there was every reason to believe he would be their savior again.

It was, in fact, Westfall, as much as Bobby Orr, Phil Esposito and Ted Green, who was a mainstay of the team that had grown admirably during the late 1960s. One example comes to mind.

As hockey catastrophes go, the present Bruins had regarded the loss of Bobby Orr through injury as the most telling disaster that could traumatize the team. That was a reasonable estimation until the night of February 2, 1969.

Disabled with an injured knee, Orr was forced out of the Boston lineup at a time when the Bruins were gliding along on a sixteen-game unbeaten streak; more important, they were making their first serious overtures for first place in more than two decades. On February 2, the Detroit Red Wings visited Boston Garden, motivated by the lure of a playoff berth.

The visitors smelled victory at midpoint in the game. Boston was playing two men short, while the Red Wings had one player in the penalty box. Detroit's power play was nullified by the Bruins defense, and the puck fell onto defenseman Don Awrey's stick. He wound up and moved the puck ahead to Westfall, who was both the most ubiquitous and the least-recognized Boston skater.

Awrey's pass was too slow for Westfall, so Eddie had to decelerate, and still the puck lagged behind them. There was only one thing to do—a difficult maneuver—but

Westfall executed the play as if it were second nature to him. "He caught the puck with his skate," said coach Harry Sinden, "and moved it up to his stick blade, and away he went."

True, Westfall was in motion, but he was being pursued by Frank Mahovlich on the left and Gary Bergman on the right. In that situation, a less composed player would have looked frantically for a teammate or rushed a pass to nowhere in particular, as long as it freed him from danger. Instead, Westfall moved closer to the net, which was guarded by Roy Edwards.

"First I had to think whether Edwards would commit himself," Westfall diagnosed after the game, "then I was hoping Mahovlich wouldn't catch up. When Edwards didn't move I had to think fast. The few times previous to that when I had breakaways I didn't score because I went high."

This 6-1, 189-pound forward gave the banal expression "utility player" great dignity. Unlike a number of his colleagues, whose cerebration is conspicuous by its nonexistence, Westfall in that split second thought out his possibilities. Knowing that high shots were foiled by Edwards and others, he felt it was time for a change.

"This time," Westfall recalled, "I decided to go low."

The shot blurred past Edwards and nestled into the left corner of the net. It gave Westfall what he described as "a great feeling," and for good reason. The goal was his 15th of a season in which he would finish with 18 goals, 24 assists, and 42 points, the most he'd ever collected since becoming a Bruin in 1962-63. More than that, the goal represented something more than a personal record. It told the world that the utility player in his way was as relevant to the team's success as were the players with fat five-and-six-figure contracts.

"The Bruins discovered," wrote John Ahern in the *Boston Globe*, "if they hadn't already realized it, that they have another super player and without him that wonderful win streak would not have reached No. 17."

The "discovery" of Westfall was not made by a single hockey expert; rather it seemed to be a happening involving many individuals, including coach and teammates.

"It wasn't only that goal," said Sinden. "He does everything and this time he was playing every position except goal. I look around on the ice and I see a lot of our guys playing well . . . Then I look again and Westfall would be doing it all. It was a tremendous job.

"But I want to ask a question and I'll bet there's no one in hockey who can give me the answer. I just want to know when he played a poor game. If he ever did it had to be before he was in organized hockey."

Sinden's memory was limited then by his relatively short tenure as NHL coach. Westfall *had* played a poor game, in fact, many poor games; but that was long ago, when many of the Bruins played abysmally, as if by reflex, as soon as they put on the colors of the Boston club.

He became a Bruin during the 1961-62 season when Phil Watson was the Boston coach and last place was the team's regular stopping-off place. He became a Bruin because he wanted to make it just a little bit more than the next fellow. He made a point of finding ice to practice on during the summer of 1961 so that when he arrived at training camp in Niagara Falls, Ontario, he was a step quicker than his rivals. It was that step the Bruins brass found so appealing.

"Eddie was skating in midseason form when the rest of the squad took the ice for the first time," said Lynn Patrick, then manager of the Bruins. "He caught Watson's eye and from that time on he took a regular turn."

Not having been a member of that team, Sinden, of course couldn't recount the numerous *faux pas* that Westfall had committed in those fumbling years. But Bruins publicist Herb Ralby remembered them, and as he once noted in a magazine article, "his inexperience stood out like a beacon light."

Westfall's mistakes multiplied until the Boston management found the goals-against figure too high for the club to

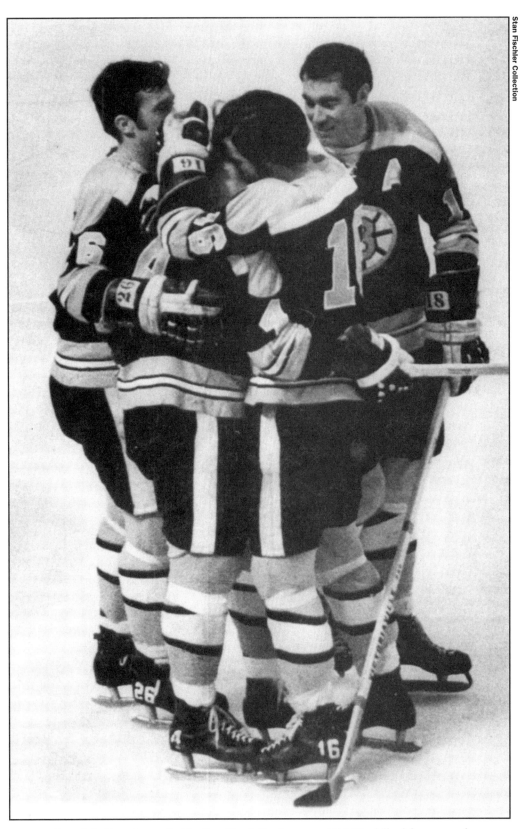

From left, Don Awrey, Bobby Orr, Derek Sanderson and Ed Westfall celebrate a goal.

tolerate. He was shipped to Kingston of the defunct Eastern Pro League for the 1962-63 season—or at least for the start of that campaign. The demotion didn't wear well with the pleasant-smiling young man.

"At first," he revealed, "I didn't think I needed to be

sent down. But it turned out the other way. I not only learned all over again how to play defense, but I regained my confidence. I found I could experiment a lot. I found out what I could do best and what I was weakest at."

It was no coincidence that the man who infused

Westfall with a surplus of hockey knowledge was Kingston's coach, Harry Sinden. When Kingston's right wing was injured, Sinden tried Westfall at the forward position and discovered his adaptability quotient was high.

"If I hadn't been sent to Kingston," Westfall admitted, "and hadn't had the chance to play, I never would have been aware of certain aspects of passing the puck up from the defense to the forward. I had never given it much thought before then. But when I had trouble digging the passes out of my skates instead of getting them right on my stick, I decided in the future to put my passes right on the forward's stick."

Westfall actually became a utility player in junior hockey, playing both forward and defense for the Niagara Falls Flyers of the Ontario Junior A League. He usually played more than half a game for coach Hap Emms and

Bruins had a full complement of defensemen at the start of the schedule but ran into a painful series of injuries. At first, coach Milt Schmidt used Westfall as a penalty killer and then as a defenseman. When the forwards began beating a trail to the hospital, Schmidt transferred Westfall to the front line.

"Say, Eddie," a railbird mentioned one day, "you're getting as much ice time as Bobby Hull and Gordie Howe."

"Listen," Westfall shot back, "I'll take all the ice time I can get!"

In time Schmidt began employing Westfall as Hull's "shadow." It was an onerous task, but one that Eddie performed so well that the role became permanent. By the 1966-67 season, rookie coach Sinden began experimenting with Westfall at center, his fifth position in four and a half years with the team.

"Eddie was one of the all-time greats. When I came up, he was the established veteran and I was the rookie. He was supposed to take care of me, be my roomie and keep me under his wing. And he did. He taught me the ropes, and he was a gentleman—one of the classiest guys in the game."

——Derek Sanderson

---

often would be required to spend up to fifty minutes on the ice.

"As a result," said Westfall, "I never really learned to bodycheck properly until I came up with the Bruins. Leo Boivin taught me how to hipcheck when Leo was with the Bruins."

An awkward skater, whose strides reminded one of a sailor walking the deck during a hurricane, Westfall required one final demotion to the minors in 1963-64 before he acquired the poise to remain in the NHL. Even when he returned, life was not without its small tortures. There were nights when he wished there was a tunnel running straight from the dressing room to his home. Yet he nurtured the hope during those depressing seasons that some day the Bruins would see the light.

"I never wanted to be traded," he insisted. "I thought about it and then I'd think of the years ahead. I knew things couldn't stay bad forever. It had to get better and if the organization had faith in me, I felt I had to have faith in it. It certainly paid off. Soon I began to I feel like a prosperous businessman. My life was good."

The pivotal season for Westfall was 1964-65. The

"The next move," quipped Westfall, "is to get myself some goalie equipment. I've never been in the nets before but that opportunity may arise any day and I should be ready."

His unique position as swing man complicated the possibilities of a bonus for goal scoring. "My contract is a difficult one to negotiate," he revealed late in the 1968-69 season. "There is no set price on many of the things I do, as there is with goals and assists. Perhaps in fairness to myself, I should devise some method of bookkeeping on such things as how my record stacks up against that of the man playing opposite me."

Westfall remained content with compliments, rather than statistics. "He's the big spoke out there," said defenseman Ted Green, who suffered through the Bruins' years in the NHL trough. "All he does is make the big play every time we need the big play. It's great to see him scoring. But he does so many things to stop the other team from scoring you can't name them if you spend all night trying."

Students of the Bruins of the seventies contended that Westfall's most memorable game was the fourth match between the Canadiens and the Bruins in the 1969 East Division final. The teams were locked in a 0-0 tie early in the game when Garnet Bailey was penalized for interference. Sinden, who described Westfall as "one of the league's best penalty killers," sent his man out to stall the Montrealers.

"We were back in our end," said Westfall, reconstructing the play, "when Dallas Smith set me up with a good pass."

Instead of wheeling back toward his own defensive zone, Westfall thought he might just fool the enemy with a surprise attack. His shot was blocked by tiny goalie Rogatien Vachon but it rebounded to the charging Westfall. "It came right back to me and I took a swipe at it with my stick."

By this time, Montreal defenseman Jacques Laperriere enveloped Westfall, with his left arm over the Bruin's neck and his right around his waist. Eddie was plunging headfirst towards the ice like a kamikaze, but the damage had been done. Fully horizontal, Vachon, stared longingly at the puck as it rolled into the right corner of the net.

"So long as it went in," said Westfall, "I'm satisfied. I'm not going to be fussy about how it got past him."

The Canadiens rebounded to tie the score and then Westfall went out to kill still another penalty with teammate Derek Sanderson. The 14,659 fans in the Garden had difficulty discerning which team had the penalty and which one the power play. Boston, with Westfall in command, hustled the Canadiens into the visitors' own end of the rink. The puck squirted loose behind the net. J.C. Tremblay, the Montreal defenseman, lost it to Sanderson, who sliced out in front of the net and tucked the disk behind Vachon.

Montreal wouldn't die easily, and on this night the Habs punctured the Bruins' defenses in the third period as they searched for the tying goal. But, with less than two minutes remaining, Westfall sent Bobby Orr into the clear for what developed into the game's winning score.

What was most remarkable about Westfall's extravaganza was not so much his lucrative evening but rather the collection of headlines he gathered in the local journals. "BRUINS' WESTFALL ALWAYS A WINNER" was the banner in the *Record-American*. "WESTFALL FINALLY 'DISCOVERED,'" the *Globe* disclosed.

John Ahern, who covered the game for the *Globe*, took due notice that the reporters rarely pushed to the far corner of the Bruin dressing room. "It has been pretty lonesome in that corner for many seasons," said Ahern, "with only an occasional scribbler stopping by to ask for a quote. On Sunday it looked like a football huddle. Silent men, bend-

ing over slightly, were taking in every word, and Eddie was talking like a quarterback."

"Sometimes," said Sinden in another part of the room, "we have to wonder why there isn't more talk about him. Probably we're to blame for it. We just expect him to do everything and he does it. What a hockey player!"

Sinden wasn't expressing a local opinion. On the other side of the ice, Montreal's coach, Claude Ruel, was glumly enthused about the Bruins winner. "Very good man," was the terse comment of the French-Canadian mentor. "Very good man!"

"When they use that word 'steady,' they're leaving a great deal unsaid. There is a tendency to think of the individual things which Eddie does well without adding them all together," said Coach Sinden. "He's one of the league's best penalty killers. In an emergency we can drop him back to defense, although fortunately that has not been necessary this season. He's a remarkably good defensive forward and a two-way right winger who is contributing to the scoring of this team."

Eddie's deeds reinforced these claims. When other, more loudly trumpeted Boston players failed, Westfall saved the team. As John Ahern so aptly noted on February 3, 1969, after Eddie had almost single-handedly beaten the Red Wings, "Now it is known definitely: the Bruins can play without Bobby Orr."

Westfall should have remained a valuable Bruin well past the 1971-72 season, but the Bruins had to sacrifice someone to the expansion draft and chose Easy Ed, although they no doubt regretted the move, in retrospect.

As soon as he joined the Islanders, Westfall was named captain and helped turn the baby franchise into a playoff contender by the 1974-75 season.

Westfall remained an integral part of the budding dynasty until the 1978-79 season. Prior to the Islanders-Bruins game at Nassau on March 13, 1979, Westfall revealed that he was going to retire. The 38-year-old veteran of two Stanley Cup triumphs had played in 50 games in 1978-79 and scored five goals and 11 assists. He still was an effective penalty-killer and the club's top face-off man. After making his announcement at a pre-game press conference, No. 18 enjoyed a 7-2 triumph over his old team, Boston. "I always wanted to see a game like this played on the day I announced my retirement," said Westfall after it was over. "It was the way I dreamed it would be."

Following his retirement, Westfall became a television analyst for Sports Channel New York and continued as a Fox Sports Net New York TV analyst through the 1990s.

Always he remained a credit to the game, whether he was on or off the ice or behind a microphone.

Ted Green watches as teammate Jerry Toppazzini clears the puck from in front.

Edward Joseph (Ted "Terrible Teddy") Green

Born: Eriksdale, Manitoba; March 23, 1940

Position: Defense

NHL Teams: Boston, 1960-69, 1970-72

Coaching: Edmonton, 1991-94

Ted **GREEN**

Pound for pound, Ted Green was the toughest of the post-World War II Bruins and—with the exception of Eddie Shore—the meanest player ever to don the black, gold and white.

Like the immortal Shore, Green would do anything to win a hockey game. Anything. And he learned very early in his hockey career that shortcomings in the realm of skill could be compensated for by brute force.

A castoff from the powerful Montreal Canadiens farm system, Green arrived in Boston as an unpolished defenseman determined to fight his way onto the Bruins' varsity.

"I had one philosophy," Green recalled, "and that was this—the corners were mine. Any man who tried to take a corner away from me was stealing from me. I get mad when a man tries to steal from me."

At first it was difficult for the Eriksdale, Manitoba, native. He was surrounded by a mediocre team that remained out of playoff contention through the early 1960s, although Green found a tutor in a boxy-looking defenseman with snake hips named Leo Boivin.

A future Hall of Famer, Boivin taught Green the art of bodychecking and intimidation. Teddy learned well and, by the late 1960s, had become one of the best punchers in the National Hockey League. He also earned notoriety for his forays to the left of the rule book.

One night in a game against the Rangers at Madison Square Garden, Green "speared" New York center Phil Goyette in a corner of the rink. Goyette doubled over in pain and appeared to be seriously hurt.

The episode so infuriated Rangers president William Jennings that he exploded in a post game news conference, calling Green "an animal," adding that "a bounty should be put on his head." Right or wrong, Green had become regarded by the enemy as a terror and was smart enough to use his notoriety as an asset.

"One thing in my favor—when you played the way I did then—was reputation," Green recalled. "Players on the other teams knew that I was going to get them. They had to be thinking about it. I got a lesson from [Leo] Boivin. He'd crack an arm when they tried to get around him. That was my style."

Green's game changed somewhat in the late 1960s, once the Bruins acquired superior players such as Bobby Orr and Phil Esposito. The combination of their high-quality game, as well as the addition of tough stickhandlers such as Derek Sanderson, John McKenzie and Wayne Cashman, took the burden of intimidation off Green's shoulders and spread it around the rest of the tough club.

Still, when the term "Bobby Orr and the Big, Bad Bruins' was heard, Green still was regarded as the baddest of the "Bad." Yet the respect with which he was held by teammates had reached such a high level that Teddy wore the captain's "C" on his jersey and was considered the team leader both on and off the ice.

Because of his toughness and his powerful supporting cast, Green exuded invincibility. He seemed indestructible until the autumn of 1969, when a catastrophic episode would change Ted Green's life.

"Green lived by the sword through eight violent NHL seasons," wrote Canadian author Trent Frayne, "and finally was felled by it."

The episode, known throughout the hockey world as the notorious Green-Maki incident, conjures up the same dreadful memories the Titanic disaster might for seafaring folk or the Apollo 1 tragedy does for astronauts. It happened on September 21, 1969, in Canada's capital city, Ottawa. Green's good friend and teammate, Derek Sanderson, was his companion during the hours preceding the tragedy and remembered them well.

"We were going to play the St. Louis Blues that night," said Sanderson. "It was a nothing exhibition game and Teddy and I decided to spend the afternoon with a walk around Ottawa. We strolled to the Parliament Buildings to relax a bit and talk about how management likes to take advantage of players."

Curiously, Green and his attorney, Bob Woolf of Boston, had just hammered out a new, long-term contract with the Bruins that was the best Teddy ever had. Except that Green had not gotten around to signing it. "I shouldn't be playing tonight," Green told Sanderson as they walked past the capitol. "I'm not going to hit St. Louis. I'm not going to get into any trouble. I don't want anything to do with this game—this exhibition—until I'm signed. When I'm signed, I'll start hitting. Then I'll play my usual game, but, until then, forget it."

Considerably younger than Green and quite impressionable, Sanderson listened carefully to everything the old pro had to say and absorbed every word of it. That night, sidelined because of a knee injury, Sanderson sat in the stands and watched Green carefully, remembering what he had told him. As the impending clash neared, Derek Sanderson studied the movements of players on both teams.

"Wayne Maki tried to go around Green," said Sanderson, "but Greenie had him pretty well lined up. All of a sudden Maki slashed Teddy. Now Greenie wasn't going to take that, so he punched Maki. It was a short jab and Maki went down. When Maki got up he speared Greenie, stuck his stick right in his gut. Teddy retaliated by slashing Maki across the arm and then he turned to go to the penalty box. That was it. There was no sense making a big thing out of it because it was only an exhibition game."

Unfortunately, it was merely the prelude to the disaster. Up until that time, Green had never clashed with Maki. In fact, he hardly knew who he was. "I wasn't particularly concerned about him," wrote Green in his autobiography, *High Stick*.

"As I trapped the puck behind the net the kid hit me from behind, and I got a little ticked off, as I always do when that happens. But my first obligation was to clear the puck. I kicked it with my skate up to my stick and shot it out around the boards to our right wing. Then I turned to take care of the guy who hit me.

"By that time, we had both moved in front and a little to the left of our net. I reached out with my gloved left hand and shot Maki in the face. He went down by the side of the net. Figuring that was the end of that, I turned away, but then Maki speared me.

"Where at first I had just been annoyed, now I was sore as hell, and I hit Maki with my stick just below the shoulder at the biceps, knocking him off balance and, I think, down on one knee."

Boston's Ted Green (6) scraps with the Rangers' Larry Cahan at center ice.

Ted Green does not remember precisely what happened after that; and for good reason. Maki's retaliatory blow nearly killed him.

"As Greenie turned," Sanderson recalled, "Maki hit him right smack over the head. Teddy went down on his side. He just stretched out on the ice, stunned, although he wasn't bleeding very much."

To a man, the Bruins realized their pal was in real trouble, and they couldn't decide whether to rush to Green or beat up on Maki. Bobby Orr was one of the first off the bench and he immediately knocked Maki down. The St. Louis player grabbed a stick for protection but he might as well have picked up a piece of cotton candy.

"Ace Bailey went after Maki," Sanderson remembered, "and hit him on the side of the face real hard."

Meanwhile, others were tending to Green who, by now, had been taken to the dressing room. Although his condition was worsening rapidly, he still knew he had been victimized. "I'll kill that little bum!" he said. Those who were with Green realized that his words were slurred. His injury, they sensed, was more than a superficial wound.

Then it became obvious. The left side of his body was paralyzed; the right side of his head above the temple was crushed. Green could not move his left hand, nor could he lift his left leg. The worst, short of death, had happened. His brain had been damaged.

"Looking at him on the stretcher," said Sanderson, "was the most depressing sight in the world. It looked as if his eyes were in the back of his head. He was absolutely motionless."

Long afterwards, Green still remembered little about his movements from the ice to the dressing room. He said he recalled goalie Ed Johnston and the trainer, Frosty Forristall. Somebody mentioned an ambulance, and Green tried to say something but the words were not available. Soon he was taken to a hospital. The throbbing pain in his head became more and more intense.

Then he passed out.

It is not unusual for a hockey player to be hospitalized, but Green was in grave condition that September night. He had lost his speech, and he had become desperate. He realized that something very serious had happened to him;

so serious that he needed the last rites of the church.

Fr. Jean-Paul Hupé, head chaplain at the hospital, was at Green's bedside. He said he was surprised when Ted signaled for the last rites. As he delivered a prayer for the sick, one of the toughest men ever to lace on skates cried.

"I cried," Green later wrote, "because my head hurt, and I cried because I didn't know if I was going to die when I wanted so badly to live, and I cried when I thought of my wife, Pat, and my kids and my parents and my brothers."

A young neurosurgeon, Dr. Michael Richard, operated on Green. Several bone fragments had been driven right into the brain. For two and a half hours, Dr. Richard worked over the fallen player until he was satisfied that all that could be done to save Ted Green had been done. Then, everybody prayed.

The believers say their prayers were answered. Others say that Dr. Richard did one hell of a good job. In any event, Teddy Green still was alive the next day, although he was far from well. Close Bruins friends sneaked through hospital barricades to see him. Sanderson was one of them.

"He told me he had lost a lot of pride," said Sanderson, "and he was embarrassed by the incident. He said he never should have lowered his stick—'I should have clobbered him with it'—but Greenie wasn't speaking too clearly and it really hurt to see him like that."

Now that it was apparent Green would live, the next question was whether he'd be able to speak again, and then the long shot—could he ever play? A total of three head operations were necessary before the results were in. For the most part, they were surprisingly affirmative. His speech still was not perfect and there was considerable question about his ability to play big-league hockey again, but the doctors said he could try.

In September 1970, the night before the Bruins opened training camp, Green sneaked out and pulled on his skates for the first time since he had almost died in them.

He wanted to be sure the rink was empty before he took those critical strides that would determine whether he could earn his living as a hockey player once again. He said he didn't want to "look foolish in front of the guys, falling on my rear end."

It was a different Ted Green. The clash with Maki left him with a protective plate in his head and a strange, constricting helmet which doctors insisted he wear at all times when playing. He put his blades on the ice and gingerly took one stride and then another until he realized that nothing much had changed. Now he was ready to skate with his teammates.

"At our first practice," said Bruins center Phil Esposito, "everybody was standing around, waiting for Teddy to come out. This would be a big moment for him. When Teddy finally joined us on the ice he started skating slowly at first, then gradually picked up steam. He really

surprised me."

The Bruins needled him. They told the prideful defenseman he looked better now than before his injury. He smiled. Reporters pestered him with questions about the new season.

"I haven't really been hit yet," he said. "Nobody's taken a run at me. But I know that will come. There are a couple of areas where I don't have my confidence yet."

The new season began and he donned the black-gold-white Boston jersey. Opening night at the Garden that year was on against the Montreal Canadiens. Green recalled his return to hockey in *High Stick*:

"The Boston fans gave me a night at the Garden that my wife and I will never forget. And the warmth and understanding of the fans, who bore with me through some bad games and overlooked some bad play, will stay with us forever.

"On my night in Boston, I was showered with gifts. When I stepped before the microphone to try to express my thanks, all the emotions of the past year rushed together to form a lump in my throat. So I couldn't speak for a moment.

"Just then, a voice called out from the balcony. 'That's okay, Teddy, we love you anyway!' It was a fan. A friend.

"I was back home again."

One, two, three games played and all was well. Then a dozen, and Ted Green still was there. "There were certain games when the injury bothered me—mentally, not physically," he said, "but I got over most of that. By mid-season—by Christmas—I was my old self again."

And he was, too. Playing against his arch foes, the Rangers, Green was slugging away again. The only difference was that the "new" Green wore a helmet. "I certainly don't want to look foolish by getting injured again because I was asinine enough not to wear a helmet," he said.

Green had always known pressure. As the Bruins' "policeman" before their championship days, he was expected to bear the brunt of the fighting and protect the smaller skaters. When he was claimed from Montreal on June 7, 1960, Stanley Cups were the furthest thing from the mind of anyone in Massachusetts.

Green: "The Bruins were in deep trouble, a fifth-place team needing help almost everywhere, when they bought me from the Canadiens. They were last in 1960-61, for the first of five straight years, and they went eight seasons without making the playoffs. Lynn Patrick, one of the nicest guys I know, later told me my aggressiveness had caught his eye, and he felt that even if I didn't score much (I never do) I could make waves with the Bruins. I guess he was right. I played for them through those bad years, and though we weren't going anywhere, I kept fighting.

"Actually, the 'Terrible Teddy' reputation was built up over those four years, from the 1961-62 season through the

1964-65 season. As a Boston regular, I amassed over 100 penalty minutes each year, and even increased that number as I went along. The first season I spent 116 minutes in 66 games in the penalty box. The next three years, playing 70 games each year, I had, in order, 117 minutes, 145 minutes, and 156 minutes.

"I was proud of that record then, but I can't say I'm particularly proud of it now. It's pretty stupid to get banished by the referee for breaking rules, although sometimes you can't help it. In any contact game, you'll break some rule, intentionally or otherwise, but hockey is so fast you'll often get away with it. I think I picked up a good deal of penalty time because of my reputation. Since the officials watched me closely, they naturally caught me more often.

"My wife didn't like my reputation any more than I did. I remember once early in our marriage she asked me why I played so hard.

"'Look,' I told her, 'they expect this of me right now. This is the only way I'm going to stay up. If I don't knock people down, which is what fans expect me to do, I don't keep my job. I'm learning. The more I learn, the more they'll depend on my ability instead of my roughness. Right now I'm the team policeman. If somebody gets hit, it's up to me to go after the guy. This helps attract attention to the Bruins, because we're not winning.'

"Terrible Teddy Green. The tough guy of the National Hockey League. That was the reputation I had before Maki bashed in my skull with his stick. I didn't like the name or the reputation. I played hockey hard, and sure I hit, because it was my job to it. In my younger days maybe I went out of my way to find a fight, but not later. Two, three years before Maki hit me, I had stopped being Terrible Teddy Green. I held my ground, I battled for puck control, I hit back when I got hit. But that was to protect my part of the ice, my goalie, my partner, and myself."

Ted Green was now a good, tough hockey player who refused to look for trouble, although he never backed down from it. His comeback reached its peak when the Bruins won the Stanley Cup in 1971-72. Green was a key contributor.

With the formation of the World Hockey Association in 1972, Green accepted the offer of the New England Whalers and jumped to the new circuit. The members of

Ted Green shows one of the St. Louis Blues some of his most indelicate stick work.

the Whalers had so much faith in the rejuvenated Green that he was made captain of the team. His role with the new club was to serve as the veteran and leader of the team; he responded very well to the challenge, and showed that there was plenty of quality hockey play left in him.

Ted captained New England to the playoff championship in 1972-73 and remained with the Whalers until 1975-76, when he was traded to Winnipeg. As a member of the Jets, he skated for Avco Cup-winning teams in 1975-76 and again in 1978-79. Green finished his playing days that season, culminating an 18-year professional career that was as turbulent as any.

Though his playing days were over, Green remained an active part of professional hockey. He joined the Edmonton Oilers in 1981 as an assistant coach and was a part of each of the Oilers' five Stanley Cup championships. He succeeded John Muckler as head coach on June 27, 1991, before assuming the position of assistant to the president for the next three seasons. In 1997-98 he returned behind the bench as an assistant to then-coach Ron Low.

Obviously, hockey will always be a part of Ted Green's blood, and nobody ever shed more blood for the Boston Bruins than the always-dependable number six.

Bill Cowley, stickhandler extraordinaire.

William Miles "Bill" Cowley

Born: Bristol, Quebec; June 12, 1912

Position: Center

NHL Teams: St. Louis, 1934-35; Boston, 1935-47

Awards/Honors: Hart Trophy, 1941, 43; NHL scoring leader, 1941; Hall of Fame, 1968

Bill **COWLEY**

The art of stickhandling has undergone many changes over the years, and some of those alterations were directly affected by the speed of the game. But few players were as clearly superior at the art of puckhandling at any time than Bill Cowley, who starred for the Bruins both before and after World War II.

During the pre-1943 era, Cowley commanded the most attention. It was before the introduction of the center red line in 1943, at a time when hockey's tempo was slower than it would later be.

Not that it would have mattered to Bill, whose stick skills would have enabled him to excel at any tempo. Oddly enough, those very attributes would be discovered in Paris, France, of all places. The year was 1934, and Cowley was a 21-year-old center accompanying the Ottawa Shamrocks on an extended European tour.

Cowley's magic helped the Shamrocks to thirty-three wins, no losses and two ties. The virtuoso performance caught the critics' eye and led to a professional contract. Within a decade of that junket, Cowley had accomplished everything a major-leaguer could hope for, and then some. He won the Hart Trophy as the National Hockey League's most valuable player in 1941 and 1943. He led the NHL in scoring in 1941 and was chosen to the First All-Star Team in 1938, 1941, 1943 and 1944. He made the Second All-Star Team in 1945 and was a member of the 1939 and 1941 Stanley Cup-championship Bruins.

Cowley's problem—if it can be called a problem—was that he played on the same team with the formidable and infinitely more colorful "Kraut Line" of Milt Schmidt, Bobby Bauer and Woody Dumart. The trio's exploits frequently overshadowed the effortless grace and subtlety of Cowley, who was every bit as good as his more illustrious mates.

During the 1938-39 season, Cowley teamed with Charlie Sands, a smooth-skating wing, and Ray Getliffe, a hard worker who knew how to get the job done. The unit jelled neatly and soon was rated over the Krauts.

The Bruins finished first that year, and by playoff time, coach Art Ross had made some changes to thwart the New York Rangers, their first-round opponents. Cowley was switched to center for Roy Conacher and Mel Hill.

At the conclusion of regulation time in the opening game, the teams were tied 1-1. Ross divined the Rangers' strategy—stifle Cowley with blanket checking and do the same to Conacher—and summoned Cowley to his side. "We've got to fool them," he said. "They're watching Conacher so carefully it would be better to feed Hill."

Cowley could have been forgiven if he had raised an eyebrow. At that time, Hill was regarded as a Grade B shooter, at best, who scored only ten goals all season. Cowley listened to his boss and then decided that Hill would get that puck if he had to present it to him on a Lazy Susan.

The sudden death had begun and the teams conducted a series of thrusts and counter-thrusts with no result. That they were evenly matched was obvious, and it was equally clear that only a very special play would decide the contest. The first twenty minutes of sudden death ended without result, as did the second overtime period. It appeared that the third sudden death would conclude without result, when Cowley took control of the puck with less than a minute remaining.

Cowley crossed into Rangers territory and lured the big New York defenseman, Murray Patrick, toward him. Patrick couldn't quite get to Cowley in time, and the Bruin eluded him, skated into the corner and fed a perfect pass to Hill, who was camped in front of goalie Dave Kerr. Hill deposited the puck behind Kerr at 19:25 of the third

overtime. When the red light flashed, it was 1:10 a.m.

The second game was virtually a carbon copy of the first. It was 2-2 at the end of regulation time and, once again, Ross employed the same strategy with Cowley—feed Hill. With eight minutes and twenty seconds gone in the first sudden-death period, Cowley charged the Rangers' defense. As the New Yorker braced for his shot, Bill deftly dropped the puck back to Hill, who fired a forty-footer into the twine. The time was 8:24 of the first overtime, and the Cowley-Hill combine was the talk of the hockey world.

The Bruins took Game 3 in more traditional form by a score of 4-1, but then it was the Rangers' turn. They won the next three in a row and seemed destined for a major upset as the teams lined up for the seventh and deciding game at Boston Garden.

Again they were deadlocked, this time 1-1 at the end of three periods. Wearied from the heat of an April evening, the teams slogged through one, then a second sudden-death period without producing a score. With more than seven minutes elapsed in the third sudden death, the Bruins moved to the attack. Roy Conacher fired the puck at goalie Bert Gardiner, who earlier in the series had replaced Kerr. Gardiner nabbed the rubber in the webbing of his glove and flipped the puck into the corner of the rink, expecting one of his defensemen to retrieve it. But Cowley got there first.

The crafty Boston center continued behind the goal, using the cage as a blocker, viewing the goal area for a possible opportunity. There was Hill, somehow unguarded. Again, Cowley distributed the perfect pass and, before Gardiner could move, Hill sped it home at exactly eight minutes of the third overtime. The Bruins had won the series four games to three.

William Miles Cowley was born June 12, 1912, in Bristol, Quebec. The youngest member of the Cowley clan of four boys and a girl, Bill received his first pair of skates at Christmas, 1924, when he was twelve years old.

But early disappointments prompted Bill to consider abandoning the sport entirely. He launched his youthful playing career as a goalie, and gave up a dozen goals in the first period. His teammates convened before the second period began and decided that Cowley was to be moved out to his favorite position—left wing.

Author Ron McAllister, writing in his book *More Hockey Stories,* recalled: "Cowley put on his best skating effort, and although his team lost the game by the close margin of two goals, he had the time of his life. All was well until he overheard two teammates grumbling after the game:

"'We could'a won that game if Bill Cowley had been able to skate!'"

"Hurt to the core when in his own opinion he had helped to almost win the game, Bill hurried home determined to forget hockey. Early the next morning, however, he had apparently changed his mind. When the family arose on that bitterly cold December day, its youngest member had already made twelve trips down to the creek carrying buckets of water to make a frozen pond in the backyard." And the young man who almost gave up the game set out to begin his own "private practice" to improve his skating skills.

Cowley broke into the NHL with the St. Louis Eagles in 1934. When the Eagles folded at the close of the 1934-35 season, he signed with the Bruins. Before reporting to Beantown, his career was nearly ruined. Playing softball in Ottawa, he badly injured his knee.

Wrote McAllister: "The knee was still causing trouble when he reported to the Bruin training camp for the season of 1935-36. During the rugged practice sessions, with dozens of farm team prospects showing their very best, Bill Cowley struggled to look as good as he had when Boston picked him for the club. The one thing he noticed more than anything else was that the Bruins were loaded with prospective center men. Cowley's injured knee became a dismal handicap.

"As the first scheduled game of the season rolled around, Bill Cowley, to his surprise, remained at the training camp although many others had been sent away. Confused, he couldn't understand why the Bruins kept him when they had so many centers who seemed more promising. When the team was announced for the opening game against Montreal, the players gathered round to hear who was to face Hooley Smith, Baldy Northcott, Jimmy Ward, Bob Gracie and the rest of the famous Marauding Maroons.

"Tiny Thompson of course was slated for goal, and Eddie Shore and Babe Siebert were taking the ice on defense; Cooney Weiland, Dit Clapper, Red Beattie and the other regular players were assigned to the select group. Bill, alone by the boards, had almost decided he was on his way home, when he heard his name called out.

"' . . . and, Cowley—you'll start at left wing!' He felt his face burn as everyone looked around, and he tried to appear nonchalant as though he had known all along that he'd be on the team."

Cowley played three games on the wing before the veteran defenseman Babe Siebert took the coach aside. "That kid can fly," Siebert said. "Put him at center and he'll rattle in the goals."

In his fourth game with the Bruins—against the Canadiens at Montreal—Cowley was at center. The game was tied in the third period when Bill moved into high gear and sped off on a breakaway with Siebert right behind. As he passed Montreal's blue line, goalie Wilf Cude crouched into position.

Bill "Cowboy" Cowley captured the Hart Trophy as Most valuable player in 1941 and 1943. The slightly built center was one of hockey's most consistent scorers and best playmakers throughout the 1940s.

"Beat him—it's your play, kid," came Siebert's yell.

Cowley moved right in on goal, wheeled across the goal mouth, and seemed ready to swerve behind the net. Cude was duped by the maneuver and Cowley backhanded the puck into the net.

It was the start of a career that spanned eleven years in Boston. Cowley retired after the 1946-47 season, having suffered a broken left hand, a jaw broken in five places, torn knee ligaments, a shoulder separation and assorted cuts and bruises.

Following his retirement, Cowley coached teams in Renfrew, Ontario and Vancouver, before settling in his native Ottawa. He was elected to the Hockey Hall of Fame in 1968.

Ralph "Cooney" Weiland—one of Boston's best at breakaways.

Ralph "Cooney" Weiland

Born: Seaforth, Ontario; November 5, 1904;

died July 13, 1985

Position: Center

NHL Teams: Boston, 1928-32; Ottawa, 1932-34;

Detroit, 1934-35; Boston, 1935-40

Awards/Honors: NHL scoring leader, 1930;

Lester Patrick Trophy, 1972; Hall of Fame, 1971

Coaching: Boston, 1939-41

Ralph Weiland—otherwise known as Cooney—became as well known in Boston as Bunker Hill and North Station.

If ever there was a cornerstone Bruin of the pre-World War II era, Weiland was it. He launched his career in Beantown in 1928 and played for the Bruins until 1932, returning again in 1935. He concluded his National Hockey League career as a Bruin in 1939.

By any standard of comparison, Weiland was a superlative center. He was the balance wheel on Boston's Dynamite Trio, playing between Dit Clapper and Dutch Gainor when the Bruins won their first Stanley Cup in 1929. He scored forty-three goals in forty-four games that year.

Cooney led the National Hockey League in scoring in 1930 with the Bruins, but two years later he was dealt to the Ottawa Senators and then the Detroit Red Wings.

"Weiland," said former goalie and author S. Kip Farrington, Jr., "was a great face-off man, one of the best I've ever seen. He also was—like Hooley Smith and Frank Nighbor—an excellent three-way stick checker. He was a master of the poke, sweep and hook checks."

He played well for Detroit, but the feeling was that Weiland would be at his best back in Boston. One night, in 1935, Bruins' manager Frank Patrick met with his Detroit counterpart, Jack Adams.

"If I had Cooney Weiland," Patrick said, "Boston would be able to make the finals."

"If I had Marty Barry," Adams retorted in reference to Boston's big, dour center, "Detroit would win the Stanley Cup."

That did it, and a trade was made that, literally, helped both teams. Cooney moved between Gainor and Clapper, while Barry was inserted between Larry Aurie and Herbie Lewis to form the set of forwards chiefly responsible for Detroit's first Stanley Cup triumph in 1935-36. Weiland guided the Bruins to a pair of first-place finishes and another Stanley Cup in 1939.

Ralph Weiland was born November 5, 1904, in Seaforth, Ontario. He turned pro with the Minneapolis Millers and then graduated to the Bruins. In his book, *Skates, Sticks and Men*, Farrington noted that Weiland had a vast repertoire of ice skills.

"Cooney was outstanding at breaking up power plays and getting the puck in breakaways out of the end zone when the Bruins were playing shorthanded," wrote Farrington. "I believe his greatest night was January 1, 1931, in Madison Square Garden in a game against the Rangers. The Bruins and the Rangers were tied 3-3 in the third period, with about ten minutes to play, when Cooney was tripped from behind while he was going in alone to shoot against John Roach.

"Cooney slid headfirst into the boards and was knocked cold. By the time he was revived, the game was eight minutes into overtime and the Bruins were playing

not one but two men short. Cooney returned to the ice and a minute later broke away and started in toward goal in a duplication of his play in the third period. Only this time he scored the winning goal *before* he fell and slid into the boards again. Momentarily, Cooney was out again, but he had won the game, 4-3."

Weiland produced a 100 percent effort, whether he was a winner or a loser. During his one full season with the Ottawa Senators, he was the leading scorer for the last-place club. Yet, it was his precision handling of the subtle skills of the game that caught the attention of experts.

"The finest individual face-off that I can recall, and the most important in a terrible spot, occurred in the Stanley Cup semifinals between Boston and Toronto in April 1939," said Farrington.

"There was a rule that year that if anyone other than the goalie fell on the puck in his defensive zone, there was a face-off. Weiland faced off with Bingo Kampman, the tough defenseman and the Maple Leafs' best face-off man. The puck was square in front of the net, the Bruins were leading by one goal, and there were about five minutes to play. The referee blew his whistle, the puck dropped—away it went, and wound up across the Toronto blue line into their zone. Nobody was able to touch it on the way back. I will never forget it."

Following the Bruins' 1939 Stanley Cup victory, Weiland retired to become coach of the Boston sextet. They finished first in 1939-40 and 1940-41 and also won the Stanley Cup in the latter season.

Surprisingly, Weiland achieved even more acclaim as a collegiate coach than he did in the majors. He was recommended for the Harvard coaching job in 1950 by Farrington and turned the Crimson team into an Ivy League power. Between 1950 and his retirement in 1971, Weiland was named New England Coach of the Year in 1955, 1957, 1961 and 1962—and the American Hockey Coaches Association Coach of the Year in 1957 and 1971. He retired as Harvard hockey coach in 1971 and that same year was voted into the Hockey Hall of Fame. A year later, he received the Lester Patrick Trophy for his outstanding service to amateur hockey in the United States.

Ralph "Cooney" Weiland

Wayne Cashman: tough, skilled, determined.

Wayne John Cashman

Born: Kingston, Ontario; June 24, 1945

Position: Left Wing

NHL Teams: Boston, 1964-83

Coaching: Philadelphia, 1997-98

O ne simply could not find a more team-oriented player than Wayne Cashman, whether the sport were hockey, football or croquet, whether the city were Boston or Bangkok.

Cash, as he was known to friend and foe alike, lived for Bruins victories, starting with his rookie season, 1964-65, until he concluded his career in Beantown following the 1982-83 campaign.

To say that Wayne would do anything to win a hockey game would not be an overstatement, considering some of his real-life antics for the Hub sextet.

One episode in particular says it all, simply because of the bizarre nature of the encounter.

Facing the Los Angeles Kings during the 1977 playoffs, the Bruins had established a 3-2 lead as the series moved back to The Forum at Inglewood.

With elimination staring them in the face, the home club resorted to what they hyped as "the greatest pregame show in hockey history."

Trailing, three games to two, the Kings needed all the help they could get. And when they skated onto the ice, they thought they had gotten it. More than 16,000 fans got to their feet and cheered for five minutes.

Finally, the noise subsided and singer Frank Mahoney moved into the spotlight on ice, where he was to sing "God Bless America," which had been designated as the good-luck song of the Kings.

This would be the turning point, the Angelenos hoped, as the houselights dimmed. Mahoney took the mike, but none of the 16,005 in attendance could hear a word of the tune. "Mahoney's microphone was dead," reported *Sports Illustrated's* Peter Gammons. "Forum officials tried to locate the source of the electrical malfunction, but in time they gave up."

While the Kings frantically wondered what was happening to their good-luck charm, Cashman smiled sardonically in the shadows. He *knew* what was happening because he had made it happen.

Tipped off about the gala Kings' production, Cashman—with a little help from Bruins' trainer Frosty Forristall—had sabotaged the ceremony. Armed with a well-sharpened pair of scissors, the Bruins captain had sliced the vocalist's microphone cord.

The guerrilla action worked. Boston scored three goals in the first eight minutes and outshot the Kings, 30-7, over two periods. In the end Boston won, 4-3, but only after the backchecking Cashman had broken up a two-on-one in a spectacular display of defensive hockey.

Coach Don "Grapes" Cherry was so enthused about the series-clinching effort that he chirped, "God Bless Wayne Cashman" in the victorious dressing room.

Normally, Wayne would earn his living in more traditional ways, such as scoring goals, crafting offensive maneuvers and, most of all, playing a physical game that delighted Cherry most of all.

"I knew at an early age that I'd never be a fifty-goal scorer," Cashman explained, "so I spent my career doing what had to be done."

Sometimes it meant fighting the meanest men in the league, such as Dave "Hammer" Schultz, originally of the Philadelphia Flyers (Broad Street Bullies) and later the Kings. During one encounter, Schultz insisted that Cashman warned that he would "cut my eyes out."

Whether it was with Schultz, Orland Kurtenbach or Dennis Hextall, Cashman never walked away from a fight, but his pugilism tended to obscure his hockey talents. It was those very skills that enabled Cash to blend so snugly on Boston's top line with Phil Esposito and Ken Hodge.

Gammons: "It was Cashman who always did the dirty work in the corners to get the puck out in front of the net to his high-scoring and highly publicized linemates."

Cashman hit his stride on Causeway Street during the Bruins' 1969-70 Cup run, tallying five goals and four assists in fourteen playoff games. He followed that spring with a 79-point season (21-58) and sparkled again in the 1971-72 playoff with four goals and seven assists in fifteen post-season games.

Although headline-grabbing was never Cashman's forte, he always was a player's player, appreciated most by his peers both in and out of the dressing room. "He's one of the best wings ever to play the game," said goalie Gerry Cheevers, who teamed with Cashman on two Stanley Cup-winners. "If I was picking an all-time NHL team, he would be one of my five left wings.

"Granted, he didn't have the flair of a Bobby Hull, but championships aren't won only by the flashy guys. They're won in the corners and along the boards, and Cashman was the best of our era when it came to playing in the corners and along the boards."

Rather than jump to the World Hockey Association, as some of his 1971-72 Stanley Cup teammates did, Cashman remained a loyal Bruin for the remainder of his career although he never played on another championship team.

More important, he developed a leadership mode that eventually led to his succeeding legendary John Bucyk as team captain. The turnabout from workhorse youngster to inspirational leader was a curious one to those who observed Wayne's maturation.

"When he was younger," said Cheevers, "Cash never used to say a thing. Then, he became captain and began talking with the young players—sometimes cheerleading, sometimes being brutally blunt. Cash becoming captain was the most important thing that had happened to the team at the time."

The beauty of Cashman was not merely his down-to-earth quality but a sense of humor that ranged from subtle to zany, depending on the occasion. One such episode involved an encounter with police following a team party. Cashman was taken to the station house, where he was informed that he could make one telephone call—presumably to a lawyer.

"Twenty minutes later," wrote Gammons, "a small Oriental knocked on the station house door and announced, 'Chinese food for Mister Cashman.'"

Cashman's loyalty to his teammates was legendary. He was particularly fond of Phil Esposito as a linemate and friend. When Espo was traded to the Rangers, Cashman took the departure of his comrade harder than most. The Bruins were in Vancouver at the time of the announcement, and coach Don Cherry was one who chronicled the reaction of his stickhandlers.

Although Cherry never mentioned Cashman by name in his autobiography, *Grapes*, many Bruins-watchers believed that it was Wayne to whom Don referred in a tale about the players being in a hotel room together after the deal was announced:

"He began ranting and raving about what a lousy deal we had made. I listened and listened and, after about an hour, I could take no more, so I got up and left. But I told some of the other guys to keep an eye on him, because I could tell he was going to get himself into trouble. They didn't heed my warning and a short time later he proceeded to demolish the room—literally. Had you seen the place, you would have guessed that a large bomb had been planted there, because there wasn't a single piece of furniture that wasn't in splinters.

"It wasn't difficult for the hotel detectives to get wind of the ruckus but, the funny thing was, they wouldn't allow anything to be put back into place until photos were taken of the damage. The next morning, when we were about to leave, I phoned the player involved. He thought I was calling to bawl him out, or even to fine or suspend him for what he had done to the place. Instead, I said, 'I left a red tie at your place last night. Can you check to see if it's still there?'

"He asked me to wait a minute. I could hear furniture being moved, glasses falling. Then he returned to the phone and said, yes, he had found the tie. I said, 'Good, bring it to the bus.' Was he ever happy that I had only called about the tie!

"Some people have criticized me for not disciplining him severely for his outburst, but I wouldn't think of it. For one thing, he wrote a cheque for a couple of thousand dollars in damages as he left the hotel. For another, over the years he had given his heart and soul to the Bruins. When the going got rough, he was there. You couldn't ask for a better ally to be in the trenches with you in time of war."

Cashman worked those trenches through the 1982-83 season and was one of the club's most distinguished captains. His teammates finger the Esposito trade as the event that had a most profound effect on the Cashman psyche, if not the team as a whole.

"The guys who got the headlines—like Esposito—were either gone or injured as in the case of Bobby Orr," said Cheevers. "Everybody on the team had to learn to become a worker like Cashman."

The Cherry teams of the late 1970s always will be revered for their "Lunchpail Athletic Club" philosophy which enthralled Boston hockey fans in the years immedi-

ately following the post-Orr era.

"Now we had to do what Grapes kept telling us we had to do," said Cashman. "We had to work. We didn't have anyone who thought of himself as a star, not even guys like Jean Ratelle. Everyone was equal, from Ratelle to the last guy on the bench. The three key words for that team were toughness, work, control."

Occasionally, Wayne would ignite a sparkling game with his scoring touch, although the grinding game remained his forte. But on April 2, 1978, the spark led to an explosion: four Cashman goals in an 8-3 rout of the hated New York Rangers.

Until that contest, Cashman had five career hat tricks, but it had taken him ten years in the NHL to score four goals in a game. In the end though, Wayne will never be remembered for any specific goal as much for his spirit.

For a decade, he was the very soul of the Bruins and once summed up his basic belief with these words: "Talent above the shoulders and below the belt is as important as individual scoring totals."

It was a tenet that Cashman took with him once he concluded his career and turned in the direction of coaching. He did basic training as an assistant with the Rangers, as a scout and later assistant coach for five seasons.

From 1992-93 through 1995-96, he served as an assistant coach with the Tampa Bay Lightning. He became an assistant coach for Team Canada in the 1997 World Championships after working in a similar role with the San Jose Sharks during the 1996-97 season.

He finally reached the head-coaching level on July 7, 1997, taking over the Philadelphia Flyers bench. Although he compiled a 32-20-9 record, Cashman was not allowed to finish the full campaign and was demoted back to assistant coach on March 9, 1998, in a sudden reshuffling.

More importantly, Wayne retained his dignity and composure, accepting the altered status, and continued to work diligently for the Flyers organization, where he remained through the 1998-99 season.

Nevertheless, Cashman always will be remembered as a Bruin first and foremost and one of the toughest of them all.

"He was the meanest and toughest on that Bruin team of the late 1960s and early 1970s," wrote Gammons.

And the ultimate leader from the mid-1970s through his retirement.

"I knew at an early age that I'd never be a fifty-goal scorer, so I spent my career doing what had to be done."

—Wayne Cashman

Jean Ratelle, Boston's answer to Jean Beliveau.

Joeseph Gilbert Yvon Jean Ratelle

Born: Lac Ste. Jean, Quebec; October 3, 1940

Position: Center

NHL Teams: New York (R), 1960-75; Boston, 1975-81

Awards/Honors: Lady Byng Trophy, 1972, 76; Masterton Trophy, 1971; Lester B. Pearson Award, 1972

Jean RATELLE

To some Boston hockey fans, it borders on sacrilege to list Jean Ratelle among the all-time Bruins because he played more hockey for the Rangers than he did for the Beantowners.

That said, one cannot discount his contributions to the black, gold and white after his arrival on Causeway Street on November 7, 1975.

The lithe French-Canadian had one of the toughest acts to follow, having to skate in the footsteps of Phil Esposito, for whom Ratelle had been dealt.

Diametrically opposite the effusive Espo in personality and style, Ratelle nonetheless skated his way into the hearts of knowledgeable local rooters with a combination of skill and dedication. Without much fuss and fanfare, he did the job that had to be done, along with former Ranger Brad Park, who also moved from New York to Boston in the same trade.

Among the many reasons Ratelle was beloved, none more succinctly summed it up than a headline in the *Boston Globe*: EVEN AT 38, RATELLE ACTS LIKE A ROOKIE.

What Ratelle brought to Boston—and what he lacked for a number of earlier years as a Ranger—was a consistency about his game that would complement his innate gifts of skating, stickhandling and overall creativity.

It wasn't until he played for Don Cherry that Ratelle achieved all the expectations that had materialized early in his career. Even those reporters who covered hockey on a casual basis were instantly appreciative of Ratelle. One was the *Boston Globe*'s Bob Ryan.

"Others skate," observed Ryan, "but Ratelle glides. Others arrive on the scene as if escorted by seventeen motorcycle cops, but Ratelle is already there."

Ironically, Ratelle as a Ranger never particularly impressed Cherry. Before the monster deal, Grapes had his eyes on Park. "I never really saw that much of Ratelle," said Cherry. "Every time we played New York we won 11-1 or something, and I never noticed him. But once he became a Bruin, Jean became absolutely the most perfect man to play my system."

Cerebral almost to a fault, Ratelle became the thinking man's Bruin. He saw the ice much the way Wayne Gretzky would in later years.

"Some people noticed Ratelle's effectiveness with the puck," former teammate Gregg Sheppard explained, "but they didn't see what a great positional player he was. I very rarely saw an opposing center score a goal from the slot with Jean on the ice."

Cherry: "Jean was terrific at picking passes off in front of our net."

The Cherry system did not encourage high scoring in the manner to which Ratelle had been accustomed when he played alongside Rod Gilbert and Vic Hadfield for the Rangers' GAG Line.

In his best season on Broadway, 1971-72, Ratelle passed the 100-point plateau with 46 goals and 63 assists. As a Bruin, Jean peaked in 1976-77 on the strength of 33 goals, 61 assists and 94 points.

Curiously, the Lunchpail Athletic Club under Cherry often was billed as "A Team without a Star," a gratuitous kick in the derriere to Ratelle.

Ryan: "Maybe Ratelle's public relations problem was that people spent so much time writing about the Bruins being a team without a star that they came to believe it. What is a star, if not somebody who does every damn thing you need him to do?"

Credit for Ratelle's success late in his hockey life belongs to Bruins boss Harry Sinden for having the wisdom to perceive Jean's potential. "I knew he was a good player," reflected Sinden, "but I had no idea how good he was until he joined our team. I always recognized his offensive ability but I hadn't realized that he was such an excellent defensive

player, too."

In a sense, Ratelle was an anomaly on a boisterous team that took its cue from the flamboyant Cherry. Characters abounded in the dressing room, but it was Jean's calm that impressed even a hard-nosed character such as captain Wayne Cashman.

"Jean was the man everyone wanted to be," said Cashman, "because he was able to maintain such peace in his life. He wasted no time being a jerk, going off on tangents like many of us did. He was totally devoted to his family and that's all he needed to be happy."

Sinden couldn't have been happier because out of six seasons, Ratelle outpointed Esposito over the same campaigns. For example, in 1975-76, the newly acquired Bruin outscored his Ranger counterpart by 23 points. Again in 1976-77, Ratelle came out 14 points ahead. Ratelle's dominance waned considerably in the following season when he bested Esposito by three points. The men switched positions in 1978-79, when Esposito tallied 78 points, six more than Ratelle. In 1979-80, Esposito won the race by five points, despite playing 23 more games. The next season, the last for both players, saw Ratelle reclaim his lead, doubling Esposito's assists and besting him by 17 points. Over the course of their final six seasons, Ratelle had the advantage over Esposito by a total of 46 points.

"Jean turned into our version of [Hall of Famer] Jean Beliveau," added Sinden. "He was a classy player and a classy guy, just like Big Jean."

Unfortunately, Ratelle—unlike Beliveau—never played for a Stanley Cup-winner, a fact that always gnawed at him. "There was nothing that I would have liked more than win a Cup," Ratelle acknowledged.

That said, his dossier overflowed with kudos. His highlight games were many, but few could match Game 4 of the 1979 Boston-Montreal series.

In that tournament, the Bruins trailed in the semi-finals, two games to one, as Game 4 went into overtime, thanks to two goals by Ratelle. Early in the sudden death, Boston caught the Canadiens in a line shift. Bruins defenseman Rick Smith sent a pass to Rick Middleton, who already had beaten Canadiens defenseman Serge Savard. As Middleton skated down the left side, Ratelle glided along the right boards. Rick sent a perfect cross-ice pass to Jean. As Ratelle broke in on goalie Ken Dryden, Jean switched from backhand to forehand with apparent ease and slid the puck past Dryden.

The Boston crowd exploded in a celebration that lasted long after the game was over. While Jean was in the locker room answering questions, the sellout crowd of Beantown faithful remained outside the Garden for over an hour, chanting, "Ratelle, Ratelle."

Even as he approached age 39, Ratelle played as if he was in mint condition. "He had the body of a 25-year-old when he was 39," said Harry Sinden. "Even then he had that strong, lean body and the legs were still there. He was fortunate, not having suffered any serious injuries."

What surprised some was that the Rangers had not fully exploited Ratelle's talents and that his best years were in a Boston uniform. "They damned near ruined Jean in New York and it was pretty stupid," said Don Cherry. "They wore him out for the playoffs in New York. They never gave him a day off from practice. They had him on the ice every day and made him burn himself out before the playoffs. That's why he never did much in the playoffs with the Rangers. Look at how he changed in Boston; averaging more than a point a game in the playoffs.

"I told Jean once that if I saw him in practice the day after a game, I'd fine him. I knew that he wasn't the strongest guy in the world and he was up there in years and still killing penalties and working the power play and taking all the important face-offs. You've got to be crazy not to give a guy like that a day off, especially when you know he busts his tail and always keeps himself in shape."

By 1981 Ratelle's body was telling him that it was time to pack it in—and he did, while receiving well-deserved accolades.

"I was always impressed with Jean as both a player and a human being," said Sinden. "He was very proficient in both areas."

Ratelle pivots in front of Buffalo defenseman Jim Schoenfeld.

Al Arbour, who both played and coached against Ratelle, put it another way. "Jean always made things look easy. Playing against him was like playing a chess game. He waited for you to make the first move and at the slightest mistake he'd pass the puck or go around you.

"He never looked that fast until he was right on top of you and then he would be by you with that great natural stride. When I coached the Islanders, I would tell my players, 'Don't give him any extra room and play him tight,' because he was so deceptive."

Former teammate Rod Gilbert claimed that Ratelle's longevity not only was a product of his skating and stickhandling skill but because of the respect he inspired in the opposition, as well as in his teammates.

"If anyone tried messing around with Jean," said Gilbert, "he was immediately protected by his teammates. He had the respect of the league because he was a classy player who used legal tactics. He was dedicated to the game and he inspired other players."

This special character was recognized after his retirement. In 1985 Ratelle was elected to the Hockey Hall of Fame. More recently, he became the Bruins' New England scout and, in 1999, completed his 22nd season as a member of the Boston organization.

And to think that at one point, he was Mister Ranger! Sorry, Jean Ratelle will best be remembered as a Bruin.

Brad Park was one of the league's premier offensive defensemen.

Douglas Bradford "Brad" Park

Born: Toronto, Ontario; July 6, 1948

Position: Defense

NHL Teams: New York (R), 1968-75; Boston, 1975-83; Detroit, 1983-85

Awards/Honors: Masterton Trophy, 1984; Hall of Fame, 1988

Coaching: Detroit, 1985-86

To both Boston and New York hockey fans alike, the Brad Park saga simply reeks of Jekyll and Hyde.

Which part is Dr. Jekyll and which Mr. Hyde is for the individual fan to decide, but this much is certain: there never was a hockey player so beloved in one city (New York) who was so hated in the other (Boston), only to have the roles reversed after eight years.

That Park's career was launched on Broadway and concluded near Bunker Hill gives a superficial idea of the man's story line. That Brad skated in the shadow of Bobby Orr for eight seasons is a meaningful sidebar to the defenseman's career.

What really matters is that Park was appreciated at home and away throughout the National Hockey League because of his all-round excellence.

He was a total performer at the highest level, a fact that firmly was acknowledged by his induction into hockey's Hall of Fame.

Precisely how Park's career would have evolved had he not been traded by the Rangers to Boston—with Jean Ratelle and Joe Zanussi on November 7, 1975—is anybody's guess.

Perhaps a career that seemed to be fading on The Great White Way would have been rekindled under the stewardship of John Ferguson and Fred Shero. Then again, it may have continued in a precipitous decline that would have negated any hope of Hall of Fame membership.

"As time wore on," said Jerry Kirshenbaum of *Sports Illustrated,* "the New York press and public had soured on him, concluding he was overweight, overpaid and—though only 27—maybe even over the hill."

What we know, of course, is that from the moment he donned the Hub colors, Park became as much a part of the local sports fabric as Phil Esposito before him.

Even Boston's Italian-American community, which had worshipped Espo, quickly took Brad to their hearts. Joe Palladino, who owned the Three B's restaurant, where he had a boccie court installed in a back room expressly for Phil, called the defenseman "Parko."

Why Parko?

"Brad played so well for the Bruins," Palladino explained, "that I gave him an Italian name!"

Brad Park

Once he arrived in Boston, Park set up his family compound in suburban Lynnfield. He long ago admitted that his impression of New England's Hub suddenly changed for the better. "Before I was traded," he revealed, "all I had really ever seen of Boston was the airport and the rink. I just didn't realize there were so many pretty areas.

"When I was with the Rangers, I lived out on Long Island. It took over an hour to drive to Madison Square Garden for games and there were sixty-five traffic lights and two tolls. In Boston it took me just twenty minutes to get to the rink and only one light. And no tolls!"

Playing 43 games for the Bruins in 1975-76, Park totaled 53 points (16-37) and 95 penalty minutes. Pretty soon, a banner was hung in Madison Square Garden—

BRAD PARK WE MISS YOU. PLEASE COME HOME.

There was no going home again, if "home" was to be New York. Playing under coach Don Cherry, Park performed like the First-Team All-Star he had been in three seasons as a Ranger, if not better.

For a glorious—but all too brief—period, Park teamed with Orr to give Boston the greatest power-play quarterback tandem the league has ever seen. However, a knee operation forced Orr to the sidelines after only ten games, and Park faced similar surgery that would keep him off ice for the last 21 regular-season games.

The trauma caused up and down Causeway Street when Orr bolted to the Chicago Blackhawks the following season was eased by Park's return, not to mention other changes produced by Sinden and Cherry.

Gregg Sheppard, a 5-8 center, replaced Esposito and tickled the Garden crowd with his scrappiness. Gerry Cheevers and Gilles Gilbert gave Boston the best one-two goaltending combination and Ratelle was outscoring Esposito.

Mostly though, it was Park's ability to step into a commanding role once Orr moved from Massachusetts to Illinois. And it was Cherry's ability to realize that an alteration in Park's style would make Brad a better, all-around performer.

As a Ranger, Park was used in a do-it-all role, which meant that he not only had to defend and score but also was called upon to play policeman and lug the puck from one end of the rink to the other. Cherry said nix to that. He wanted his top blue liner to concentrate on defense first and let the rest of the hockey business fall into place.

"Brad was not as flashy as he had been when he came to Boston from the Rangers but he became a better player," said Cherry. "If you could forget about Orr for a moment, there was no defenseman I would rather have had than Brad Park."

Admittedly, Park's offensive instincts remained, but he was more than willing to adapt to the Cherry style. Brad never claimed that he was the second-coming-of-Orr, although the New York writers harped on that theme so often, it made it seem the other way around.

"Bobby Orr was the greatest hockey player I had ever

Boston's Bobby Orr (4) tussles with Rangers' rear guard Brad Park (2) in the first and only fight between the superstar defensemen.

seen," Park allowed. "I never said I was as good as he was although others did. But people kept saying, 'Hey, Park, who are you kidding? You're no Bobby Orr.'

"I always had a lot of confidence and I always enjoyed a challenge. I was influenced by Orr and sometimes I'd find myself trying to rush end-to-end like he did and I've had to remind myself to stop it."

Another difference between Park and Orr was in their media dialogue. Bobby was more cautious and diplomatic with the press, while Brad was given to more outspoken comments that, while honest, hardly could be considered diplomatic.

As a Ranger, Park raised the red flag before the Bruins to its highest level when he co-authored (with your's truly) his autobiography, *Play the Man*, which hit the stands in the Spring of 1972 prior to the start of the Boston-New York Stanley Cup Finals.

Written while he still was a loyal, Boston-hating member of the Blueshirts, Park lashed out at his Bruins rivals as "a bunch of bloodthirsty animals" and further accused them of everything from padding statistics to

taking sneak punches.

The result was just as anticipated; New Englanders became enraged and, more particularly, so did Orr & Company. *Play the Man* inspired the Bruins more than the Rangers and, wherever possible, the high command used it as a propaganda weapon.

"We got a lot of mileage out of that book," remembered Tom Johnson, who coached the Bruins at the time. "At least Derek Sanderson had the good sense to write about broads."

Play the Man sold well but, in the end, the Rangers lost the 1972 finals to Boston and, of course, the book was said to be a factor—albeit small—in the final result.

However, it did suggest that if Park ever was traded by New York, it would be to somewhere like Los Angeles, St.Louis or Minnesota. "Boston," Brad admitted, "was the last place I expected to go."

Park's pals, including Ratelle, believe that he was terribly hurt by the deal. "It was tougher on him than me," Ratelle allowed. "Brad was in his prime at the time whereas I was mentally prepared to leave New York. It was a shock

Park became the heir apparent to Bobby Orr.

Steve Babineau

accurate shooter who could develop an attack and then retreat in time to intercept an enemy counterthrust.

His game was embellished by a fluid skating style that often underplayed his speed, as well as a storehouse of power that proved deceptive because of his relatively modest size.

It was Park's misfortune never to have skated for a genuine powerhouse. He was the ice general and captain of a modestly successful New York Rangers team in the late 1960s and early 1970s, but never tasted the Stanley Cup champagne. After his trade to the Boston Bruins, he played for a team already in a decline, but the team remained competitive because of Park's combative play.

Because he played in the shadow of some of the all-time great backliners, Park may not have received the media attention he merited, but the experts took due note of his excellence. Brad was voted to the First All-Star Team in 1970, 1972, 1974, 1976 and 1978. He made the Second Team in 1971 and 1973.

More than anything, Park was a refreshing player to watch and, in some ways, a throwback to an earlier, more robust, era of defensive play.

"One of the glorious aspects of sports," said author Roger Kahn, "is having your spirits renewed by Brad Park."

for him."

Once the shock had abated, Park gave Sinden the best hockey any general manager could expect—and did so through the 1982-83 season, after which he was signed as a free agent by the Detroit Red Wings. He played two more seasons in the Motor City before finally retiring.

When one considers a career that spanned the years 1968-1985, a number of conclusions can be made. One is quite clear, and that is that there was only one missing item in Park's collection, and that would be a Stanley Cup ring.

The consummate contemporary defenseman, Park was the master of the hip check, as well as an exceptionally

Park's own spirits occasionally were deflated by Bobby Orr's presence in the same league. A defenseman like Park, Orr has long been regarded by many as the most-holy-blessed-be-he in hockey since the invention of the puck. Playing second fiddle to a superstar like Orr couldn't be the easiest thing in the world, but Park made the adjustment.

"If I have to be number two," Brad explained, "I might as well be number two to a super player like Orr."

Park had been super, or close to it, ever since he became a Ranger in 1968-69. An instant regular, he learned the ropes, took punches in the chops and scored goals almost immediately. His early career almost came to an end with similar suddenness.

The Rangers were playing the Red Wings, and dangerous Gordie Howe was still playing for the Detroit sextet. Park was guarding Howe, notorious for his great strength, durability and viciousness. "Watch Howe!" Brad was warned. "He likes to club you with his elbows."

Park remained vigilant and when Howe confronted him, the young Ranger bodychecked the veteran cleanly, depositing him on the ice. But then Brad became less vigilant and a few minutes later Howe's stick flashed, cracking into Park's Adam's apple.

For an instant, it appeared as if the blow might have ended Park's career. Brad fell, unable to swallow, gasping for breath. Ranger trainer Frank Paice dashed across the ice and calmed the kid until he was fully revived and able to skate off the ice under his own steam.

As Brad passed Howe, he turned to his assailant and rasped, "You sonofagun. It could have been my eye. From now on, when you're skating around me, you damn well better keep your head up."

The flak was never heavier than in the spring of 1974

But it was just as exhausting for Park, mostly because his Ranger teammates failed to generate as much zest as he did. As a result, the Flyers edged New York, four games to three, and advanced to the Stanley Cup Finals.

Injuries severely braked the careers of both Park and Orr, but it was the latter who was ultimately forced to retire prematurely, while Park, plagued with knee problems, continued to play, although at a more modest pace.

"In some ways," said Don Cherry, "Brad was a better player after all the injuries because he began to pace himself. He wouldn't take as many chances on offense and that meant he was in better position on defense so he was caught out of position much less."

The pain had so troubled Brad that it was freely predicted that he would retire by 1980, but he kept coming back, and when the 1981-82 campaign began, he was back on the Bruins' blue line, playing as smart a game as he ever had in his life.

Unfortunately for him, a number of younger, flashier defensemen such as Denis Potvin of the New York Islanders and Randy Carlyle of the Pittsburgh Penguins were scoring

---

> ## "I always had a lot of confidence and I always enjoyed a challenge. I was influenced by Orr and sometimes I'd find myself trying to rush end-to-end like he did and I've had to remind myself to stop it."
>
> —Brad Park

---

when the Rangers met Philadelphia's ferocious Flyers in the semifinal round of the playoffs. Dave Schultz, number one hitter on the Flyers, made a point of zeroing in on Park early in the third game of the Cup round. First he bodied Brad heavily in the corner, and then, as play swung up-ice, Schultz charged into Park a second time and knocked him down, straddling the semi-defenseless Ranger and pouring punches at his face.

The Flyers' theory was simplicity itself—beat up on the best Ranger [Park] and Philadelphia would grind out a series victory. "You can't be a hitting team sixty minutes a game," countered Park. "It's exhausting."

more than Park, although not necessarily playing better defense. The high-scoring defensemen got the accolades and Brad, as he had been during the Orr era, was relegated to the shadows.

But the purists remained appreciative of his skills, particularly his "submarine body-check," in which he'd thrust his hip into the path of onrushing attackers, catapulting them upside down to the ice. In 1977 and 1978, Park was one of the primary reasons the Bruins reached the Stanley Cup finals.

It was a case of close, but no cigar; the story of Park's hockey-playing life despite a remarkably efficient career.

Adam Oates, the thinking man's center.

Adam Oates

Born: Weston, Ontario; August 27, 1962

Position: Center

NHL Teams: Detroit, 1985-89; St. Louis, 1989-92; Boston, 1992-97; Washington, 1997-2000

O nce upon a time there was a radio program called "Mister Keene, Tracer of Lost Persons." Each week, the hero would find people who—for whatever reason—had disappeared.

Had Mister Keene been around for the past fifteen years, he certainly would have "discovered" Adam Oates several times.

Not that it was Oates' fault that he constantly was overlooked by smart hockey people who should have known better. Yet it happened over and over and over again.

The oversights began during the early 1980s, when Adam left his native Weston, Ontario, for the prestigious Rensselaer Polytechnic Institute in Troy, New York. As the kingpin of RPI's offense in 1984-85, Oates tallied 31 goals and 60 assists for 91 points, but it was as if it all happened somewhere in the South Sea Islands.

Oates seemed to be overlooked by everyone until the Detroit Red Wings signed him as a free agent on June 28, 1985. As it happened, this proved to be one of the best free agent signings in NHL history.

Over four seasons, culminating with 1988-89, Oates got progressively better and seemed destined for a long career in the Motor City. But in one of the most bizarre misjudgments, the Wings dispatched up-and-coming Oates—along with Paul MacLean—to St. Louis for Bernie Federko and Tony McKegney, both of whom were on the last legs of their careers.

Oates was even better with the Blues. Centering for Brett Hull, he surpassed the 100-point mark for two straight seasons (1989-90 and 1990-91) and appeared to be a fixture in the Mound City for years, but the St. Louis management seemed enthralled with a pair of disappointing Bruins, Craig Janney and Stephane Quintal.

Harry Sinden was delighted to make the exchange that brought Oates to Boston on February 7, 1992. It didn't take very long for Sinden to look like a genius again.

"Adam became the playmaking, go-to-the-net Number One center the Bruins had needed ever since Barry Pederson had left town in 1986," commented Kevin Paul Dupont of the Boston Globe.

"Someday, maybe, someone will discover the obvious —that Adam Oates will put up the points wherever he goes, whatever the job. The discovery is no discovery at all."

Previously, Janney had been the center, doling sweet passes to Cam Neely, but Oates was even better. The Oates-Neely duet made beautiful music together, and Adam's passes soon put him right behind Mario Lemieux (1.36) and Wayne Gretzky (1.33) in terms of assists-per-game average. Adam checked in at 1.08 and was, by 1993-94, being rated one of the NHL's ultimate playmakers.

"The best part of it for me," said Oates, "was finding a guy in the open so all he had to do was tap the puck into the net. That's such a picturesque play."

Certainly, the beauty part of Oates' five-and-a-half year Boston stint was his ability to make Neely a better player— and just about any other wing who was lucky enough to play on his line.

"What I liked about Adam," said Brian Sutter, who coached him in Boston, "was that he got his points no matter who he played with and that he wasn't concerned when changes had to be made."

His ability to adjust was superb. When rookie Joey Juneau came to Beantown, Oates steered him to a 102-point season. After Juneau was traded to Washington, Adam made yet another adjustment.

"I had to go to the net more and try to get more shots," he remembered.

During his early NHL years, Oates was labeled weak defensively, but he shored up that aspect of his game and became a gifted two-way center and one of the league's best at winning face-offs. Without question, he has made the most of his skills, and his teammates—as well as foes— would be the first to admit same.

"Adam uses everything," asserted veteran Dave Reid, who teamed with him as a Bruin. "You can tell that he played lacrosse [Oates was a junior ace at the sport] by the way he protects the puck with his body. What he used to do with the lacrosse stick and a ball he now does with a stick and a puck. He's just really smart."

A voracious reader and intellect, Oates had to make an adjustment to the smaller Boston Garden ice surface after playing on traditional rinks in Detroit and St. Louis.

"It worked well for me," said Adam. "Skating is the weakest part of my game and in Boston Garden, I got to touch the puck more."

He also got to register more points as a Bruin than ever before. In 1992-93 he scored a career-high 45 goals and similarly, a career-high 97 assists for 142 points while only being hit with 32 penalty minutes. Oates always plays hard but clean.

"A lot of goals he scored as a Bruin," added Reid, "were the result of hits he had made deep in the other team's zone."

Sinden: "There were other point-getters who got three or four points a game and got them for other reasons than Adam did. He fought his way to every point he got."

Oates' second century-plus point season in Boston was 1993-94, when he rang up 32 goals and 80 assists for 112 points, not to mention three goals and nine assists in thirteen playoff games.

Despite his marvelous run on Causeway Street, Oates tended to be overshadowed by the crack scorers. Fortunately, it never was a sore point with the even-tempered pivot.

"In the NHL," he explained, "the goal-scorers get the attention, not the guys who make the passes. And that's just fine by me. When I played in Detroit, Steve Yzerman got all the attention and when I was in St. Louis, I skated in the shadow of Brett Hull.

"Once I came to Boston, I was behind Ray Bourque and Cam Neely. Nevertheless, the fans in Boston appreciated what I did and that was all that ever mattered to me."

By the mid-1990s, Oates had etched his name alongside the NHL's créme de la créme. As good as his passes were, so, too, he became a scoring threat, especially on the Bruins' power play.

"Before I came to Boston," he said, "I generally played the point on the power play and I was usually on the off side so I didn't take many shots. As a Bruin, I became as much a trigger man on the power play as the set up man.

"Once you start scoring, you get to like the feel of it and start looking for more opportunities."

Oates continued to be a productive Bruin through the 1996-97 season and was a regular contender for the Lady Byng Trophy for ability combined with good sportsmanship. Hockey-savvy Boston fans took him to their hearts and he responded in kind with remarkable playmaking.

His favorite assist?

"In Philadelphia I stepped in over their blue line and pulled up," Oates said. "Steve Leach went wide right and cut to the net. I floated a pass about 10 feet in the air, past two defenders, and it landed perfectly so all Steve had to do was one-time it in. I remember thinking 'Yes!' when I saw the puck go in."

After 63 games of the 1996-97 campaign, Adam had a commendable total of eighteen goals and fifty-two assists for seventy points. But Sinden was unhappy with the club's direction and on March 1, 1997, the general manager completed one of the most extraordinary trades of his long career.

Sinden dealt Oates, as well as goalie Bill Ranford and forward Rick Tocchet, to Washington for Jason Allison, Jim

Oates: One of Harry Sinden's best acquisitions.

Carey, Anson Carter and Washington's third-round pick in the 1997 Entry Draft.

It was a trade that benefited both teams. Oates continued to thrive in Washington, pacing the Capitals to the Stanley Cup finals in 1998. Allison and Carter—considerably younger than Oates—led the Bruins' youth movement and were particularly effective in Boston's 1998-99 playoff drive.

A decade and a half in the NHL was enough for Oates to be discovered—and certainly remembered by all Boston fans who had the pleasure of watching him play.

Cam Neely prepares to throw a bodycheck.

Cam Neely

Born: Comox, British Columbia; June 6, 1965

Position: Right Wing

NHL Teams: Vancouver, 1983-86; Boston, 1986-96

Awards/Honors: Masterton Trophy, 1994

*W*hat were the Canucks thinking?

It is a question that has been asked thousands of times since D-Day, June 6, 1986, when Vancouver traded Cam Neely to Boston—along with the Canucks' first-round pick (Glen Wesley)—for Barry Pederson.

Unquestionably, Neely emerged as the quintessential National Hockey League power forward of the late 1980s and early 1990s.

Had Neely not suffered a crippling knee injury because of a dubious check delivered by defenseman Ulf Samuelsson, one can only wonder what other heights he might have reached as Boston hockey hero. It wasn't simply a matter of scoring or bodychecking or playmaking; it was a matter of guts.

Guts. Neely had it in spades.

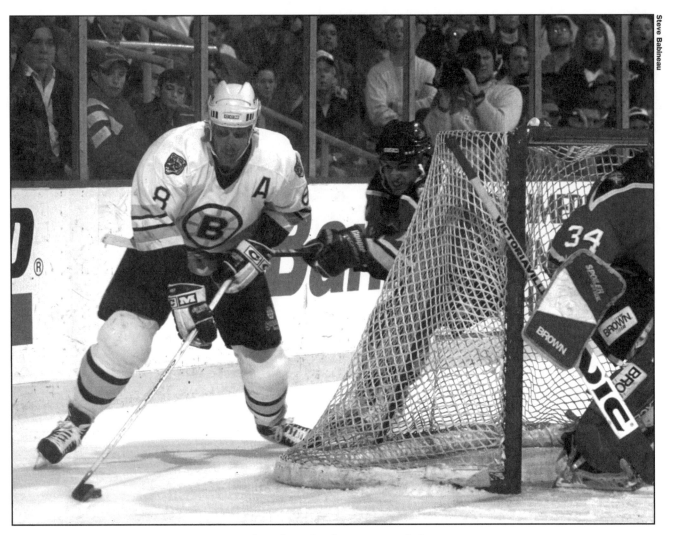

Neely in the midst of a wraparound play.

Once, in a vicious Bruins-Canadiens match, Cam was clocked on the forehead by teammate Alan Pederson's slapshot. Blood spurted through a wound that eventually would require sixteen stitches.

After having the wound temporarily sealed, Neely returned for the next period and wound up fighting Shayne Corson, who promptly punched Neely in the face and re-opened the wound, although Cam won the fight.

"Perhaps more than any goal he would score, or check he would deliver in his first few months of Bruinhood, this blood-and-guts display made the largest impact on local fans," commented Karen Guregian of the *Boston Herald*.

The aggressive action also impacted on Neely's new teammates at the Garden.

"It epitomized what Cam is all about," said ex-Bruin Lyndon Byers. "A lot of players, just after getting a slapshot in the head alone, might decide to take the night off. But he came back out on the ice. Then he fought Corson.

"I know personally that if I had gotten so many stitches in the head, I'm not sure if I'd go around looking for a fight."

Typically, Neely tried to minimize his courageous behavior. It never was his style to engage in braggadocio but he was asked to explain why he did what he did.

"It was a reaction thing," Neely said. "I was upset at the time, so I ended up dropping my gloves. After it was over and I was back on the table, I was thinking that it had been a stupid thing to do.

"But when I was out there, I wasn't thinking about being careful. I was going to play my same game that I played every night."

That game was reflected in the Bruins legacy dating back to the likes of Eddie Shore, Milt Schmidt, Wayne Cashman and others who gave the term Big, Bad Bruins a good name in the land of baked beans and cod.

"I didn't have to talk to him about what being a Bruin meant," said Harry Sinden. "I think he knew."

Not that Neely had been a student of Boston hockey history. He had been a kid who had spent his childhood shuffling back and forth between Saskatchewan and British Columbia, spending ten years in Moose Jaw, from where the likes of power forward Clark Gillies learned the ice game.

"In those days," Neely admitted, "I didn't follow Boston too much. I followed the Leafs first, then the Vancouver Canucks. But I knew that the Bruins had been one of the Original Six and that there was a lot of tradition at Boston Garden."

He became a Bruin essentially because the hockey brains in Vancouver had given up on him after he had played three seasons in British Columbia. To this day, ice savants are wondering what they missed at Pacific Coliseum. Chalk it up to hasty judgment or poor coaching or whatever, the point is that a performer who had never scored as many as forty points in any of his first three NHL seasons in British Columbia suddenly blossomed in New England.

The moment Cam put on a Boston uniform, everything began coming up roses for him and the Bruins. In his first year he was the club's leading goal scorer (36) and was second only to Raymond Bourque in points (72).

"The physical rehabilitation wasn't the hardest part," Neely remembered. "It was the mental rehabilitation. After you've gone through so much to get back—and then you have another setback—you wonder if you want to go through it all again; if it's worth it."

For a time it was worth it. After playing in only 26 games the previous two years, Neely managed 49 games in 1993-94.

Even by Wayne Gretzky-like standards, it was a remarkable run. In his 44th game of the season, on March 7, 1994, Neely scored twice and lifted his goal total for the season to 50. Thus, the bruising right-winger had completed the third-fastest 50-goal season in NHL history.

"At the beginning of that year," Neely recalled, "I wasn't even sure I'd be able to get in 50 shifts, let alone 50 goals. It was a lot more than I had expected. Frankly, I would have been happy with 30 goals because I knew that I couldn't play in every game."

"The injury was a great wakeup call. It made me appreciate what I had even more. That's the way it is for anyone who had been doing something for a while and attained a certain comfort level. But I'll always look back on that 1993-94 season and it will bring a smile to my face."

—Cam Neely

By the 1989-90 campaign, Neely had established himself as a genuine power forward. His 55 goals and 37 assists spoke volumes about his value, and longtime Bruins-watchers claimed that Cam was the second coming of Terry O'Reilly. Not surprisingly, O'Reilly was one of the first to agree.

"What I saw in Cam was the essence of the Boston Bruins," said O'Reilly. "When you think of the image of the Bruins, Cam fit that mold. He was very committed, very intense and willing to pay the price."

Neely paid the price early and often.

A questionable hit by then-Pittsburgh defenseman Ulf Samuelsson during the 1991-92 season had career-ending overtones and ignited a rivalry between the two warriors that lasted throughout Neely's career.

Cam's return from the knee injury was slow and painful. Rehabilitation exercises seemed endless but he battled through them and finally was able to return to the varsity.

Unfortunately, the injury jinx continued to plague him. During a March 13, 1994, loss to New Jersey, Neely left the game after a first-period slash tore a piece off the top of his right pinky.

Several stitches made the finger whole again and Neely returned to the game. That, however, was a minor mishap compared to the damage that would befall him less than a week later against the same foe.

On March 19, 1994, a Ken Daneyko check caused a tear to the medial collateral ligament in his right knee.

The injury was beyond traumatic for several reasons, not the least of which was that Neely had been the only player in the NHL to average more than a goal a game. He had fourteen multiple-goal games and three hat tricks. Despite missing more than a third of the season, Neely led the NHL in game-winning goals with thirteen. He also led the Bruins in power play goals with twenty.

Unfortunately, the very style that produced the goals also helped invite the injuries.

Cam Neely was a throwback to the six-team era of the NHL. But the prolific goal scorer's career was cut short by injury, and he retired following the 1995-96 season.

"Many of his goals came from his willingness to pay a price," said former Bruins coach Steve Kasper. "Cam knew where he had to be to score goals and nothing got in the way. His greatest asset was his mental toughness; his determination and persistence."

Those qualities were rewarded at the league's annual awards ceremonies in the spring of 1994 when Neely received the Masterton Trophy.

Kevin Paul Dupont of the *Boston Globe* captured the essence of Neely's game after the Masterton award with these words:

"He persevered. He scored. He lived to play a game he sometimes thought was over for him and regained his status as the game's most potent and feared power forward."

Neely recovered from the Daneyko disaster sufficiently to play again in the lockout-shortened 1994-95 season, although the numbers were not nearly as impressive as in earlier years.

"The injury was a great wakeup call," said Cam. "It made me appreciate what I had even more. That's the way it is for anyone who had been doing something for a while and attained a certain comfort level. But I'll always look back on that 1993-94 season and it will bring a smile to my face."

Once the lockout had ended, Neely played 42 games in the aborted 1994-95 season, scoring 27 goals and adding 14 assists. In the opening playoff round against New Jersey, Cam was closely shadowed by Devils checkers and produced two goals as Boston was eliminated in no time at all.

Questions were raised in the summer of 1995 about Neely's ability to carry on at his formerly-high standard. His answer was honest: "If it ever gets to the point where I can't perform the way I want, at a level that makes me happy, then I'll hang 'em up. I couldn't be a role player. It's not the way I want to be remembered."

In the interim, Neely—occasionally seen in the company of actress Glenn Close—made his film debut in the movie "Dumb and Dumber."

> "If it ever gets to the point where I can't perform the way I want, at a level that makes me happy, then I'll hang 'em up. I couldn't be a role player. It's not the way I want to be remembered."
>
> —Cam Neely

Cam's appearance didn't inspire anyone to suggest he join Actor's Studio.

"It was difficult watching myself on that large a screen," he chuckled. "Because it's you and you're always your own worst critic, you can't help but say, 'Oh, man, that doesn't look so good.'

"I was nervous watching it but at least the people who make the movies thought it was good enough to be in there."

Whether Neely was good enough to continue as the NHL's premier power forward was a matter that bore watching in 1995-96. The cumulative effect of his leg injuries had taken a toll and in 49 games he managed 26 goals and 20 assists before the final damage had been done and Cam no longer could answer the bell.

"I had always maintained that confidence had been a big part of my game," Neely concluded. "When you don't have it, you find yourself thinking too much, instead of reacting."

In the end, however, for Cam Neely it wasn't a question of mind over matter. The legs were gone and there was really nothing he could do about it.

The career that almost never happened—and then turned into a whiz-bang decade in Boston—abruptly ended in 1996.

It was much too soon when one considers Cam's age, but the knees simply wouldn't cooperate anymore, although the fire kept burning within him.

Once during the 1998-99 season, that fire caught the attention of Boston media types who reported that Neely was considering a comeback. He was working out and he was hoping but the curtain had come down on the Cam Neely Era in Boston two years earlier.

Hope as he and his followers might, the last comeback was aborted before it ever got to the ice because Cam Neely's body wouldn't allow it.

All things considered, it was one of the few battles the doughty right-winger ever lost.

Frank Frederickson

Frank Frederickson

Born: Winnipeg, Manitoba, June 11, 1895; died April 28, 1979

Position: Center

NHL Teams: Detroit, 1926-27; Boston, 1927-29; Pittsburgh, 1929-30; Detroit, 1930-31

Awards/Honors: Hall of Fame, 1958

Frank
FREDERICKSON

O ne could not logically list Frank Frederickson as one of the greatest Bruins simply because his tenure in Beantown was relatively short.

Nevertheless, the native of Winnipeg deserves mention here because, among all of Boston's professional hockey players, he ranks among the most unusual—and excellent as well. When you hear his story, you'll know the reason why.

Frank Frederickson's glorious hockey career nearly ended in the Mediterranean Sea.

Frederickson was being transferred from Egypt to Italy during World War I when the transport on which he was a passenger was hit by a German torpedo. Frederickson, who was a member of the Royal Flying Corps (later the Royal Air Force), searched for an empty lifeboat but found none.

"Suddenly, I realized that I had left my violin in my bunk," Frederickson remembered. "My violin was very important to me. So, I ran back, got hold of it and gave it to one of the captains of another lifeboat and told him to take good care of it."

Before the ship went down, Frederickson found a space on another lifeboat and, ultimately, was carried to safety. In time, he returned to Canada and resumed his hockey career.

Frank captained the Winnipeg Falcons team that won the gold medal in the 1920 Winter Olympics at Antwerp and later enjoyed a short but illustrious career as a professional.

He was a stylish center who scored forty-one goals in thirty games for Victoria during the 1922-23 season and helped that club win the Stanley Cup two years later. There have been better centers, to be sure, but not many with Frederickson's grace both on and off the ice.

Frank Frederickson was born in Winnipeg, Manitoba, in 1895. His parents came from Iceland and spoke only Icelandic in the house. Frank couldn't speak a word of English until he was six years old. Yet, when I interviewed him in 1968, his English was perfect.

At the time of Frederickson's youth, the Icelanders in Winnipeg were treated as a second-class minority group, and Frank found himself the target of insults when he would return home from school. During our interview, he recalled how he was able to find a safety valve in sports.

"My best outlet was hockey. I got my first pair of skates when I was five and had a great time learning to play. School came easy for me. After finishing grade eight, I decided I ought to earn a living and got a job as an office boy in a law firm. This turned out to be an excellent move, since the firms all sponsored hockey teams then, so naturally we had one too. It was a seven-man team, because in those days, a rover was the seventh player, in addition to three forwards, two defensemen and a goalkeeper.

"I played well and captured the attention of two of our attorneys. They took a great deal of personal interest in me, not just as a hockey player, and urged me to go back to school. So in 1914 I enrolled at the University of Manitoba, took liberal arts courses and a year later was named captain of the hockey team."

Not long after the outbreak of World War I, Frank enlisted in the 223rd Scandinavian Battalion, but when he got to England, he switched to the Royal Flying Corps and remained an airman—miraculously surviving several close calls—until the end of the conflict.

Once, during an interview in his Vancouver living room, he told me this tale: "It took a year from the time the war ended before I could get back to Winnipeg. When I

returned in 1919, a bunch of us, led by Mike Goodman, the speed-skating champion of North America, and Slim Halter, a great big, gangling six-footer who was a beautiful stickhandler, organized the Falcon hockey team and applied for admission to the senior league.

"The leaders of that league wouldn't let us in because they claimed we weren't good enough to compete with teams like the Monarchs and Winnipegs. So we did the next best thing and organized our own league composed of such teams as Selkirk, which had 'Bullet' Joe Simpson as captain. We later found out the reason we couldn't get in the senior league was because the players were from well-to-do families and wanted no part of us. But they couldn't quite get away from us that easily. We finished in first place, then played the winners of the big league in a two-game series. In a terrific upset, we beat them in two games straight, 14-2. We then defeated Lake-of-the-Woods, Head-of-the-Lakes and Fort William and went on to Toronto, where we won the Allan Cup for the senior championship of Canada, beating the famed University of Toronto.

"That was quite a triumph because it qualified us to represent Canada in the 1920 Winter Olympics at Antwerp, Belgium—the first time ice hockey was ever included on the Olympics program.

"Winning the Olympic championship was quite a feather in our cap and gave us all a lot of publicity. I had the world at my feet, but instead of returning immediately to Canada, I was asked by the Icelandic government to go there to do some experimental flying. As it turned out, I became the first pilot of Icelandic extraction to fly in Iceland.

"I flew from May to September and had to give it up at that time because they couldn't get petrol supplies. Then I went to England to try and get some of the English concerns interested in flying to Iceland but I failed in that and returned to Canada, making a stop in Toronto.

"When I got there, Mayor Church entertained me and asked, 'Now that you're back, Frank, what do you want to do?' I told him I wanted to join the Canadian air force but didn't think I could get in because there were many senior officers ahead of me. Church was a wonderful guy and a very influential man; when I got home to Winnipeg there was a telegram advising me to report to camp for duty. So, in 1920 I joined the Canadian air force.

"For all intents and purposes it appeared that my career was set for years to come. Life is funny though and out of the blue I received a letter from Lester Patrick, the Old Silver Fox of hockey, who was in Victoria, British Columbia, where he had a team in the old Pacific Coast League. It was top-notch hockey and Lester offered me what was a substantial contract in those days—$2,500 for

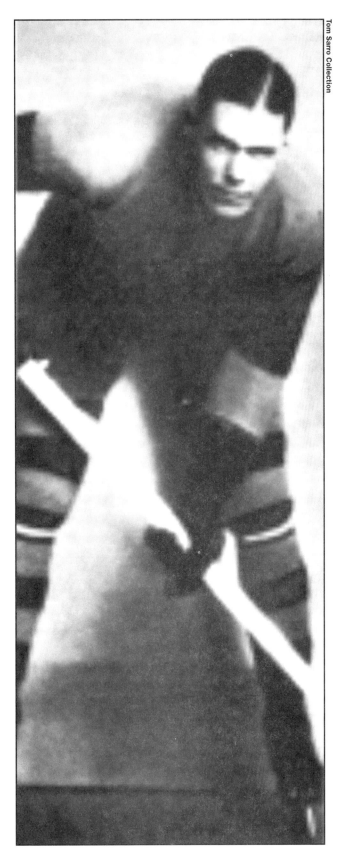

Frederickson initially signed with Detroit for $6,000.00.

twenty-four games. I call it substantial because the rest of the boys were playing for $800 or $900. I couldn't resist the offer and so found myself right back in the middle of hockey again."

In an interview in August 1970 at his home in Vancouver, Frederickson explained how he made his way to Boston via Detroit.

"Patrick had made arrangements for his players to go to Detroit, and the Detroit club signed up everyone but me. Meanwhile, Boston's Art Ross, who was a great friend of Patrick's, arranged to have me play with the Bruins, along with Eddie Shore and Harry Oliver. But I wouldn't sign up with Boston, and Ross sent me a wire threatening me with expulsion for the rest of my life. So I signed with Detroit and got $6,000, which was a lot of money then.

"When I got off the train from the West and picked up a paper in Detroit, I saw a lead story entitled,

working together in a collective effort. I learned one thing: by cooperation and joint effort you can do an awful lot more than when you're just by yourself.

"My first game as a Bruin was against the New York Rangers, who were now managed by my old boss, Lester Patrick. We beat New York 3-2 and I got three goals. Those days with Boston were outstanding from the viewpoint of competition because there were great players all over the place. New York had Frank Boucher and the Cook Brothers, Bill and Bun. Frank was as sweet a hockey player as you could find; and that line, well, there was nothing like it. But on our club we had Eddie Shore, and he was really something.

"Shore was a very colorful hockey player who put everything he had into the game but also used every subterfuge he could to win the sympathy of the crowd. He'd fake getting hurt and would lay down and roll around in

"My best outlet was hockey. I got my first pair of skates when I was five and had a great time learning to play. School came easy for me. After finishing grade eight, I decided I ought to earn a living and got a job as an office boy in a law firm. This turned out to be an excellent move, since the firms all sponsored hockey teams then, so naturally we had one too."

—Frank Frederickson

'FREDERICKSON GETS $10,000.' You can imagine how my teammates must have felt—they were getting only $2,000 and $2,500. But that newspaper story was just the same old bunk, they always have to add a little.

"As things turned out, I didn't do well in Detroit. Previously, I had been first, second or third in scoring, but now was 24th and getting nowhere at all. The problem was dissension on the team but I didn't last too long and was traded to Boston for two good hockey players.

"As soon as I arrived with my new team, Art Ross scheduled a meeting with me. At first I thought he'd give me the business, but instead, he said, 'I'm taking Dick Ferguson off the first line and I want you to take it with Harry Oliver and Perk Galbraith and work with them.' At that time Boston was the second tail-end team in the American Division, but after I got there we took the lead.

"Now, I don't say that this good fortune was due to their acquiring Frank Frederickson; it resulted from fellows

agony. Then he'd get up and be twice as good as ever. To me, Shore was a country boy who had made good; he was a good skater and puck-carrier but wasn't an exceptional defenseman like his teammate Lionel Hitchman, who was better because he could get them coming and going. But there wasn't another character like Shore. I remember once when he decided to take saxophone lessons. Art Ross, Harry Oliver, Sprague Cleghorn and myself were playing bridge, and there was Shore, alone in the hotel drawing room, playing his saxophone with the damnedest noise in the world coming out.

"Finally, Ross said to Harry Oliver: 'Jesus Christ, Harry, go and tell that silly bastard to blow on the goddamned thing and not suck on it.'

"One night we had a game and Shore came skating out on the ice—wearing a bathrobe. It was crazy and I think Art Ross encouraged him; of course, Art himself was quite a character. One night we were playing a Stanley Cup game in Ottawa and Ross objected to some bad calls the referee had made. We lost the game—and the Cup—but after it was over, Ross got us together in the dressing room and said, 'Okay, the first man who gets that referee gets a $500 bonus.' Well, we had a big French boy on our team named Billy Coutu who was straight out of the woods; the minute he saw the referee, he let him have it unmercifully and absolutely knocked him out. And, sure enough, Ross gave him a $500 bonus.

"But in the final analysis, it was a tragic episode. The matter was brought up before the NHL Board of Directors, and Coutu was suspended for life; yet it was Ross who had inspired it. I've never forgiven Art Ross for that, and it was the beginning of the end for us. Not long after that incident, a story appeared in the *Boston Herald* saying that Frank Frederickson would be handling the Boston club. It was ridiculous and I had no idea why it was written; naturally, Ross didn't like it, and when we got to New York, he didn't put me on my regular line.

"With each game he would use me less and less and finally relegated me to killing penalties. Then he went to Charles Adams, owner of the Bruins, and suggested I be traded to Pittsburgh.

"The deal was for me to go to the Pittsburgh club in exhange for Mickey McKay and $10,000. When the trade was approved, I was heartbroken, not only for myself but also for McKay, because his pride was very much hurt when he heard about the terms. Besides, I loved Boston and my family was very much settled there.

"Well, I sent the family home, and then Adams called me into his office to say, 'Frank, I'm awfully sorry, but I more or less have to take the advice of my manager and that's that.' He then handed me a check for $1,000, which was wonderful. I still have letters from fans and teammates, saying how badly they felt that I had left Boston, but I had to make do and so moved on to Pittsburgh.

"I went directly to my new team, run by Odie Cleghorn. He was a coloful chap, always dressed with top hat, spats, cane and gloves—the works, like a Beau Brummel. But I wound up getting double-crossed in Pittsburgh. I had a three-year contract with them at $8,000 a year, but my first season was a poor one and I ended up tearing the cartilage in my knee. By hockey standards I was old—37 years—and they decided to cut my contract. They gave the club to Cooper Smeaton and moved to Philadelphia in 1930.

"If they had dropped me like that today, I'd have sued. I even met with Lester Patrick, told him what had happened and said I wanted to sue. He replied, 'It would cost you more to sue in the courts than to get your contract.'

"And that was it for the NHL and me."

Following the conclusion of his playing career, Frederickson coached and managed Pittsburgh in 1930-31 and later returned to his home in Vancouver.

Frank remained a vigorous citizen, even in retirement, and followed the modern game of hockey with great interest. He died on April 28, 1979.

Bill Quackenbush (left) and Milt Schmidt

Hubert George "Bill" Quackenbush

Born: Toronto, Ontario; March 2, 1922; died
September 12, 1999

Position: Defense

NHL Teams: Detroit, 1942-49; Boston,
1949-56

Awards/Honors: Lady Byng Trophy, 1949;
Hall of Fame, 1976

Bill
QUACKENBUSH

*I*n what otherwise was a long and distinguished career, Bill Quackenbush will most be remembered as a Bruin for a play in which he was beaten, although he seemed to have done everything right.

Quackenbush had become a stalwart Boston blue liner at the time the Bruins were playing Les Canadiens in one of the most bitter series between the longtime rivals. The season was 1952 and the teams had ground down to the seventh and final game of the playoff semifinals at Montreal's Forum.

To the eyes of experts, Quackenbush was in his prime on the night of April 8, 1952. His defense work was as technically correct as any backliner of the post-World War II era, and his combative thirst was camouflaged by a seemingly mild disposition.

On this memorable night, the Bruins tough winger Leo Labine had crushed Montreal ace Rocket Richard with a devastating check in the first period. Richard did not return to the ice until the third with the score tied.

More than sixteen minutes had elapsed in the third, when Bruin veteran Woody Dumart carried the puck toward the Canadiens' zone. Butch Bouchard thrust out his stick with rapier-like speed, jabbing the puck away from Dumart. The Montreal defenseman looked up for a moment and spotted Richard near the blue line. The Rocket captured the pass as Dumart futilely tried to bat down the puck. Richard wheeled around Dumart like a speeding car skirting a disabled auto on the highway. First he reeled to center and then cut sharply to the right, jabbing the puck ahead of him with short pokes from his black-taped blade.

Quackenbush skated backward on the Bruin defense, prepared to meet the ominous challenge, for Richard was now in full flight, his eyes blazing madly, his destination known to all. Quackenbush was traveling at about ten miles per hour in reverse as Richard bore down on him with more than twice that speed. Quackenbush hurled his black-shirted body at the Canadien ace, but it was as if he were checking a phantom.

Nevertheless, Quackenbush had done his job quite well, for he had forced Richard to take so circuitous a route along the right side that the Rocket appeared to have taken himself right out of the play. "He looked to be too deep for a shot," said Baz O'Meara of the *Montreal Star,* "but then he suddenly did a deft cut to the left."

A right-handed shot playing right wing would have been cradling the puck too far to his right to release a threatening drive, but Richard, the anomaly, was a left-handed shot. Thus, the puck was on his left side, closer to the net, as he barreled past the flailing Quackenbush. "Sugar" Jim Henry, both eyes blackened from previous injuries and barely recovered from a broken nose, guarded the right corner of the net, allowing Richard nothing but the "impossible" angle shot to the far-left corner.

Almost atop Henry's bulky goal pads, Richard finally released his drive. It was low and hard and Henry never managed to touch, let alone see, the puck. "One minute I was facing him," said the Boston goalie, "waiting for the shot, the next he had whizzed by and the puck was in the net."

Montreal won the series but it was no fault of Bill Quackenbush. In fact, over a career that spanned 14 years in the majors, Quackenbush rarely drew anything but praise. He was clean enough and competent enough to win the Lady Byng Trophy in 1949 while playing for a Detroit club notorious for such sluggers as Terrible Ted Lindsay and Black Jack Stewart.

Although the temptation to join the brawlers always was quite apparent, Quackenbush resisted the lure and played a pure defense. In so doing, he made a greater impact on the game than some of his more violent teammates.

> "More than anything, Quackenbush was an extraordinary practitioner of his art. He was named to the National Hockey League's First All-Star Team in 1948, 1949, and 1951, during an era when the NHL was oozing with top-notch backliners. Bill made the Second Team in 1947 and 1953."

More than anything, Quackenbush was an extraordinary practitioner of his art. He was named to the National Hockey League's First All-Star Team in 1948, 1949 and 1951, during an era when the NHL was oozing with top-notch backliners. Bill made the Second Team in 1947 and 1953.

It is a measure of the influence of Quackenbush that some hockey writers have suggested that the NHL name a trophy in his honor to be given to the league's best defensive defenseman.

Along with winning the Lady Byng Trophy in 1949, quite an accomplishment for a defenseman, he once went a span of 137 games (over three different seasons) without taking a penalty.

Bill Quackenbush played with some of the all-time greats of the sport and was a regular when a kid by the name of Gordie Howe came to Detroit.

"He came in when he was seventeen and anyone looking at him could tell he had talent. It was just a matter of time before he became the kind of hockey player he was," said Quackenbush. "He was one of the best all-around hockey players I've ever played with."

Hubert George Quackenbush was born March 2, 1922, in Toronto, Ontario. He played his hockey on the city's innumerable outdoor rinks during the Great Depression and was ready for the big time shortly after the outbreak of World War II.

Quackenbush played on the Red Wings' 1943 Stanley Cup-winning team and played on two first-place teams. When the Red Wings finished first at the conclusion of the 1948-49 season, there was no hint that Bill would be traded, but Jack Adams stunned the hockey world by dealing Bill to the Boston Bruins.

For Quackenbush, it was a comedown in more ways than one. Not that life in Detroit was all glamor. Adams ran a spartan ship at Olympia Stadium, but conditions in Boston Garden were even worse.

The first year in Boston was not an easy one for Quackenbush or any of the other players.

"They were supposedly in financial trouble," he said. "They had traded away Nobby Warwick. They sold a couple of players straight out. They let Frankie Brimsek go to Chicago for nothing. We started the year with a rookie in goal, Jack Gelineau. Turned out he won the rookie-of-the-year award that year."

In the early fifties with the weak Boston Bruins, it was necessary to find humor where you could, and Quackenbush certainly found it in Boston.

"Our whirlpool consisted of a hose and a bucket to put your foot in. When I went to Boston I was looking forward to a new set of long john underwear, which I liked to wear. Instead I got a set of underwear with ten different numbers scratched off 'em."

Things started looking up in the spring of 1952, when Quackenbush found himself skating in the Stanley Cup semifinals against the Canadiens, and ultimately, Rocket Richard.

"The Rocket just made a super play," recalled Quackenbush. "He was one of the greatest, if not the greatest goal-scorers ever to play the game."

The play remains one of the all-time greats in hockey lore, and though Quackenbush boasts, "It's the only time in fourteen years the Rocket beat me," Richard made this type of play a common element in his arsenal against rival teams and shell-shocked goalies.

At the conclusion of the 1955-56 season, Quackenbush hung up his skates for good, opting to return to school. For seven years, he attended Northwestern University in Massachusetts at night while working as a manufacturer's agent during the day. He also raised three sons after retiring from the NHL, while at the same time earning an associate's degree in engineering.

"After about twelve years out of hockey I decided I'd like to get back into it, so I talked to Herb Gallagher at Northeastern, and went to work there as assistant coach."

In the mid-sixties, Princeton was looking for a quality coach for its men's ice hockey team. Quackenbush applied and was accepted. For six years, he coached the team, lending his vast knowledge and great understanding of the game to the young men of the university's hockey team. When, after his sixth year, the team began losing, Quackenbush stepped down as coach, but was soon back coaching a different kind of ice hockey.

In the late 1940s and early 1950s, Bill Quackenbush was one of the best defensemen in the NHL, first with the Detroit Red Wings (1942-49) and the Boston Bruins (1948-56).

"Eventually they got a girl's team there and they needed a coach. They asked me to volunteer. I felt that anything I could do to help them learn the game would be a pleasure for me. The girls were very receptive, they really wanted to learn. When I told them things, they would thank me. It was a lot of fun."

Aside from coaching the women's hockey team, Quackenbush also coached the varsity golf team. Always, he remained the same gentleman and scholar he was when he originally signed a contract with crusty Jack Adams in 1942.

There have been better defensemen than Bill Quackenbush, but none who was classier, on or off the ice. His career proves that there is credibility to the line that nice guys can survive in the war games on ice.

Fern Flaman

Ferdinand Charles "Fernie" Flaman

Born: Dysart, Saskatchewan; January 25, 1927

Position: Defense

NHL Teams: Boston, 1944-50; Toronto, 1950-54;

Boston, 1954-61

Awards/Honors: Hall of Fame, 1990

Fern FLAMAN

When Boston was represented in the Eastern Amateur Hockey League by the Olympics in the late 1930s and 1940s, the Os—as they were known—became one of the most productive farms teams ever developed.

Players such as Pentti Lund, Paul Ronty, Eddie Barry and Harvey Bennett all cut their puck teeth on the Olympics before being promoted to the big club at Boston Garden.

Among the Olympics graduates, none was more successful than Fernie Flaman, who spent sixteen years as a major leaguer.

A mere teenager when he made his NHL debut during the World War II years, Flaman was groomed for the big leagues on the Olympics, which dominated the EAHL. His teammates then included a number of aces such as Lund and Allan Stanley, who eventually would accompany Flaman to the NHL.

Fernie achieved permanent NHL status in 1946-47 with the Bruins and became an instant favorite in Beantown, where his lusty bodychecks and potent fists endeared him to the Boston Garden faithful. However, in a surprise move, the Bruins dispatched Flaman to the Toronto Maple Leafs in the 1950-51 season. Although he played on his first and only Stanley Cup-winning team (1951) in Toronto, Flaman was less boisterous and, somehow, did not seem the same when he was wearing the royal blue and white of the Maple Leafs.

Thus, it seemed eminently appropriate that the Bruins reclaimed Flaman in a trade at the start of the 1954-55 campaign. Having matured while losing none of his mustard, Flaman added spice to the Boston backline that made it one of the most feared in hockey. "Fernie was a solid bodychecker," said Hall of Famer Milt Schmidt, who was Flaman's coach in Boston. "He was at his best when the going got rough."

Some of Flaman's confrontations became legends, especially those with Henri "Pocket Rocket" Richard of the Montreal Canadiens. On one occasion, Richard attempted to elude a Flaman hip check by vaulting over the Bruin. But the Pocket Rocket only made it halfway over, at which point Flaman grabbed the Canadien and hurled him bodily into the side boards. Teamed with the equally robust Leo Boivin, Flaman was named to the NHL Second All-Star Team in 1955, 1957 and 1958.

Not surprisingly, Flaman's name frequently appears in Ira Gitler's definitive book on rugged hockey, *Blood on the Ice*. According to a poll taken of six NHL general managers in 1958 to determine the toughest hockey players they had ever seen, Flaman appeared on every list. Fernie was a disturber in every possible way—sometimes he used his body, other times his fist and, occasionally, his stick. "That Flaman," Henri Richard once said, "he bothers me more than anybody else in our league. I can't think of anyone else who gives me such a bad time. He's always got his stick between my legs or hooks my stick or something."

Early in the 1957-58 season Flaman and Henri Richard went toe-to-toe when other Bruins intervened. "First," wrote Gitler, "it was hulking Jack Bionda and Richard dispatched him."

The Bruins desperately wanted a piece of Richard. Leo Labine went after him and he, too, was belted by Richard. It marked one of the few times that Flaman failed to gain an edge—and required help from his friends.

Another who remembered Flaman was Rangers' skinny sharpshooter Camille Henry, who said his biggest mistake was angering Flaman before the season even started. "We were playing a preseason game against Boston," said Henry, "and Flaman came around the Bruin net with his head down. I was pretty cocky then, so I hit him and he fell down. He was mad after that. That turned out to be one of

the biggest mistakes I ever made, because every time we played Boston he used to nail me two or three times during the game. Flaman was the toughest player I ever came up against. He wasn't too dirty against me, but he hit me every chance he got."

Clearly, there was nothing very dainty about Flaman's deportment. He gave out punishment and he took it as well. "One night," wrote Gitler, "Flaman was intimidating some of the smaller Montreal Canadien players. Doug Harvey of the Canadiens stationed himself near Flaman at one point in the action and swung hard at the puck. He missed, but his follow-through caught Fernie flush on the jaw, shattering it in several places."

For reasons such as these, Flaman endeared himself to the boisterous crowd in Boston Garden. As Canadian author Peter Gzowski noted: "Boston fans seem to want to win all right, but winning just doesn't seem as important as some good, rough body checks . . . Win or lose, Boston fans seem to get more fun out of hockey than fans in any other city. But they like their hockey simple, and as tough as possible." From 1944, when he was a rookie in from Dysart, Saskatchewan, Flaman provided that brand of hockey.

"My first hockey was played on outdoor rinks," Flaman recalled. "I'd spend as much time as possible and listen to any person who could give me advice about the game. There was one fellow in town, who worked for the fire department and was a hockey bird-dog on the side, who recommended me. I wound up in the Bruins' chain—they had a farm team in the Eastern League called the Boston Olympics—but they had too many players, so they loaned me out to another team in the Eastern League called the Brooklyn Crescents. Next thing I know I'm skating against a club called the Curtis Bay, Maryland, Coast Guard Cutters, a wartime club that had NHL stars such as Frankie Brimsek of the Bruins, Johnny Mariucci of the Blackhawks, and Art Coulter of the Rangers. What a thrill that was; the first time I had ever been exposed to NHL players and I'm skating against them. I was in awe."

When an opening developed on the Boston Olympics, Flaman took the train to Beantown and wore the white jersey with the winged crest and soon became a fixture at Boston Garden. "They paid me $75 a week," he recalled. "I played for the Olympics for three years in one heck of a league. We'd go in to Madison Square Garden and play the New York Rovers and there would be crowds as big as those that the Rangers got."

Flaman improved to the point where the Bruins' organization moved him to its highest minor league club, the Hershey Bears of the American Hockey League. He realized that it would only be a matter of time before he replaced one of the older Bruins' defensemen. "There's a real touch of irony here," Flaman explained. "When I was a

> ## "I was pretty cocky then, so I hit him and he fell down. He was mad after that. That turned out to be one of the biggest mistakes I ever made, because every time we played Boston he used to nail me two or three times during the game. Flaman was the toughest player I ever came up against. He wasn't too dirty against me, but he hit me every chance he got."
>
> —Rangers' Camille Henry

kid, playing peewee hockey in Saskatchewan, we had numbers on our jerseys and we also had the name of an NHL player we hoped to play like. Well, the name on my jersey was Babe Pratt, who had been a terrific defenseman with the Rangers, then the Maple Leafs, and, finally, the Bruins. When I was in Hershey, Babe was in Boston. The ironic aspect of the story is that when Babe was sent down to Hershey in 1946-47, I was the guy who replaced him. That sure made me feel strange."

If Fernie wasn't the most popular Bruin, he certainly was always among the top three favorites at Boston Garden. Considering his youth, Fernie had good reason to expect that he would be wearing the black and gold for several seasons. That's why the trade to Toronto stunned him to the core.

"The trade was the lowest point in my life," Flaman said. "I had felt a part of Boston. I had played three years with the Olympics and nearly three more years with the Bruins. On top of that, it had been in the papers that I would not be traded, that I was an 'untouchable.' Next thing I know, I'm with the Maple Leafs."

Flaman spent four seasons in Toronto before GM Conn Smythe invited him into his office one day for a conference. "He asked me if I'd like to go back and play for the Bruins. That was awfully nice of him, being that my wife was from Boston and my home was there. Yes, I told him, I would like to be a Bruin again. I respected Smythe for letting me know in advance where things stood. You don't find many

people in sports as decent as he was to me."

Flaman became a Bruin again in time for the 1954-55 season and, for Fernie, it was a golden period. "The homecoming was great. I was named assistant captain and played under Milt Schmidt, who had been my teammate in the previous run with the Bruins. Working for Milt was good and the fans treated me just great. In 1959, while I still was playing, the fans tossed me a Fernie Flaman Night and presented me with a car and many other gifts. Getting the respect of the Boston fans and the Night was a highlight of my career."

Like so many other hockey "cops," Flaman experienced little pleasure in relating his battles of yesteryear. "They [the fights] were never a highlight of my career. Of the guys I played against, Gordie Howe was the toughest. We didn't fight because we had a mutual respect for one another. But we both played it hard and I'm sure I received a few nicks from him and I gave him a few, too."

Although Flaman never played on a Stanley Cup-winner after he left Toronto, several of his Boston clubs were extremely competitive and reached the Cup Finals.

His playing career concluded after the 1960-61 season and Fern went on to manage in both the American and Western Hockey leagues. In 1970, he returned to the Boston area as coach of the Northeastern University hockey team and later joined the New Jersey Devils, where he remains as a member of the scouting staff.

Woody Dumart

Woodrow Wilson Clarence

(Woody, "Porky") Dumart

Born: Kitchener, Ontario; December 23, 1916

Position: Left Wing

NHL Teams:

Awards/Honors: Hall of Fame, 1992

For starters, the man had one of the best long names of any Bruin. Woodrow Wilson Clarence (Woody or Porky) Dumart.

Others alluded to him as The Kitchener Kid, although two other linemates, his cronies Milt Schmidt and Bobby Bauer, also hailed from Kitchener, Ontario.

Like Milt and Bobby, Woody started playing hockey on the frozen, outdoor rinks in a city which then had a large German population. Before the outbreak of World War I, Kitchener had been called Berlin, Ontario, but once the war fervor took over the country, it was renamed Kitchener, after a British commanding general, Lord Kitchener.

Dumart was born in the midst of the war—December 23, 1916—and was named after the American president at the time, Woodrow Wilson.

But politics was hardly on Woody's mind once he had become adept at stickhandling.

Playing for the Kitchener-Waterloo Greenshirts in the Ontario Hockey Association's Junior A League, Dumart began as a defenseman.

Bauer was the better of the three when they were in their teens. Bobby had been drafted by the Bruins from the Toronto Maple Leafs farm club in Syracuse. He had tried unsuccesfully to have Toronto tie up both Dumart and Schmidt. When Boston claimed Bauer, Bobby turned his persuasion on Bruins manager Art Ross.

The Boston boss did put Dumart's name on his list. Then, under renewed coaxing by Dumart and Bauer, he agreed he would take Schmidt to training camp the following season.

Meanwhile, Dumart showed the brass that he might be better suited to play forward rather than defense. During the 1934-35 season, Dumart tallied seventeen goals in seventeen games, as well as eleven assists. He was ready to become a professional, so the Bruins signed Woody and sent him to their farm club, the Boston Cubs, in the Canadian-American Hockey League.

By now the Bruins' high command decided that Dumart would be more useful as a forward and switched him to left wing. It took a while for him to make the adjustment. In fact, Woody played part of the 1936-37 season with Providence of the American Hockey League where he teamed with Schmidt and Bauer.

Former NHL defenseman Albert "Battleship" Leduc was coaching Providence at the time and is credited with uniting Dumart with Schmidt and Bauer. "Leduc named them his 'Sauerkraut Line,'" noted *Toronto Star* columnist Milt Dunnell, "in recognition of a delicacy that casts its enticing aroma over Kitchener."

Woody became a Bruin to stay in 1937-38. Wearing uniform number 14, Dumart perfectly complemented Schmidt at center and Bauer on the right side.

According to Dumart, the following campaign, 1938-39, was among the most memorable in his career. The Kitchener Kids had powered the Bruins to first place, and in the first playoff round they beat the New York Rangers in a seven-game series.

"That was the year that Mel Hill was playing for us and scored all those sudden-death goals against New York. In Game Seven it was tied one-one and went into a third overtime before Mel scored for us," said Dumart.

"That was a great series and Eddie Shore's last with the Bruins. After we had all gone to the dressing room to celebrate, the crowd yelled so loud and so long for Shore that he had to skate back on to the ice."

Boston defeated Toronto, four games to one, in the finals for Dumart's first Stanley Cup.

He was on another Cup-winner in 1941, a four-game sweep of Detroit.

Following the 1941-42 season—and in the prime of his hockey life—Woody enlisted in the Royal Canadian Air Force with his pals and spent three years serving his country.

The Krauts were reunited for the 1945-46 season and remained together until Bauer retired to a business career in Kitchener after the 1946-47 season.

Schmidt and Dumart carried on, and though Woody never put up big numbers again, he remained a valued member of the Bruins. During the 1952-53 playoffs, he was a catalyst for one of the NHL's most amazing upsets.

In the opening playoff round, the third-place Bruins faced the first-place Red Wings, who had finished 21 points ahead of them. The defending champion Detroiters were overflowing with such future Hall of Famers as Gordie Howe, Ted Lindsay, Terry Sawchuk and Red Kelly. Had Detroit swept them in four straight, it would not have surprised anyone.

The key for Boston's survival was containing Howe, who was the NHL's most awesome scorer at the time, having led the league in points that year. Coach Lynn Patrick decided to gamble on 36-year-old Dumart and assigned him to check Big Gordie.

"Many people thought that Woody would run out of gas," said Patrick, "but I knew that he wouldn't."

And he didn't.

Howe was limited to a pair of goals in the six-game series, which the Bruins won four games to two. Most critics contended that Dumart's work was pivotal in the upset and that never did Howe outskate him.

"Woody was in better shape at that time than he was years earlier," said former teammate Jack Crawford. "He was skating as fast as he ever did and never got tired."

Patrick, who began coaching Dumart in 1950-51 when Lynn moved from New York to Boston, learned quickly about Woody's durability.

"When I came to Boston," said Patrick, "the first thing I heard was that 1950-51 would be Woody's last year. I knew better because he was a model for all athletes. He kept regular hours, got his rest and ate what he should. He was always ready to go, on the first day of practice or the last game of the year."

But Patrick began employing Dumart as a utility forward in the waning years and his production dipped to an all-time low of four goals and three assists over sixty-nine games in 1953-54. "Even as a utility forward he was still invaluable," said Roger Barry, who covered the Bruins for the *Quincy Patriot-Ledger*.

Nevertheless, in the summer of 1954, management decided that it had to make room for young talent, and Dumart was given his release

The Kitchener Kids (left to right), Bauer, Schmidt, Dumart.

The old, established firm of Dumart and Schmidt—as Milt Dunnell would call them—had finally been dissolved. Only Schmidt remained of the prewar Bruins, who had once dominated the league.

Woody contended that the goal he best remembered was scored in the 1949 playoffs against the Maple Leafs.

Dumart told this story to *Montreal Gazette* columnist Red Fisher in 1957:

"I might mention at this point that my old buddy Bobby Bauer, who played on the Kraut Line with Milt [Schmidt] and me, had left the Boston team by that time, and most of the experts figured that it wouldn't be too long before I'd be on my way to a pipe and slippers, too. They didn't say it out loud, but they probably had a sound basis for their thoughts, since I had scored only 11 goals during the regular season. Things turned out well, though, because I managed to stay around Boston another five seasons.

"We went into that semifinal playoff round a pretty tired team, as I remember, and we showed it too, when we lost the first two games of the best-of-seven series. The third game was played in Toronto before a Saturday night crowd, and it was a hummer.

"We started off pretty fast, jumped into a two-goal lead at one point, and figured to take that one without too much trouble. But you've got to hand it to those Leafs. They're fighters, and before we knew it, the game was all square. We finished regulation time tied 4-4.

"Well, into overtime we went, and it was rough going for the first 16 minutes or so. I was feeling pretty good because I had scored one of our four goals during the game —my second of the series by the way—but above all, I was itching for the winner.

"Shortly after the 17-minute mark, there was a faceoff to the right of the Toronto nets. Eddie Sandford went in against Ted Kennedy, a tough guy to beat at any time, but Eddie jumped on the puck and batted it back to me. I let go at Turk Broda, and in it went.

"They told me later that the puck deflected off the late Bill Barilko's hip, but we scored, and that's all that mattered."

Dumart retired to his home in Needham, Massachussets, where he had lived since 1940. He maintained hockey contacts, especially with his buddy Schmidt, who continued working at Boston Garden long after his retirement as player and then coach.

Although he never was a First All-Star (he was on the Second All-Star team in 1940, 1941 and 1947 or winner of any major awards, Dumart will best be remembered—apart from his superlative work with the Kraut Line—as a class act on a class team. Sometimes that's even better than making the Hall of Fame, although Woody did that, too.

Dit Clapper and Flash Hollett

Frank William "Flash" Hollett

Born: North Sydney, Nova Scotia, April 13, 1912; died in 1999

Position: Defense

NHL Teams: Toronto, Ottawa, 1933-34; Toronto, 1934-36; Boston, 1936-44; Detroit, 1944-46

Rare is the hockey player—Hall of Famer or otherwise—who can lay claim to have scored the goal that won a Stanley Cup for his team.

William "Flash" Hollett was one who could make that statement.

In April 1939, he applied the coup de grace to the Maple Leafs, scoring the goal that crushed Toronto and won the Stanley Cup for Boston.

It was delicious irony for Hollett, since the Maple Leafs gave him his big-league start and then unceremoniously dumped him on the Bruins for a mere $16,000.

The move eventually became a blessing, because the high-scoring defenseman would be a balance wheel for one of the best hockey clubs Bostonians have ever had the pleasure of witnessing.

Whatever possessed Maple Leafs boss Conn Smythe to dispose of Hollett is a moot question. During the 1934-35 campaign with Toronto, Flash was every bit his nickname, scoring ten goals and adding sixteen assists over forty-eight games; a handsome feat for a defenseman.

But on January 15, 1936, Hollett was sent packing to New England, where his improvement was even more noticeable.

Writing in *The Trail of the Stanley Cup*, the NHL's unofficial history, Charles L. Coleman lauded Hollett thusly: "At Boston he developed rapidly into a superb rushing defenseman under the tutelage of Eddie Shore and Dit Clapper. He was an excellent stickhandler and before long his goal production began to mount. He became very adept at setting up scoring plays as his assists total indicates."

One would have expected Art Ross to be tickled with his acquisition, but the relationship between manager and defenseman was abrasive, to say the least.

"At times," noted Toronto hockey historian Margaret Scott, "Ross berated Smythe for unloading Flash upon the Bruins. Smythe promptly offered to buy him back at the same price. Ross declined the offer.

"Once, Ross was reportedly on the brink of demoting Hollett to the minors, but instead of obeying the boss, Flash contacted the owner, Weston Adams, who scuttled the move. Hollett was a brilliant Bruin stalwart for nine seasons."

While he did feud with Hollett, Ross understood Flash's value, not to mention his versatility.

"If anyone was hurt," said Hollett, "I would move from defense up to forward. Other times, Art would use me up front as a penalty-killer."

During the 1938-39 season, Hollett became a full-fledged star. He scored ten goals—remarkable for a defenseman during those low-scoring years—and seventeen assists. On the Bruins' excursion to the Stanley Cup, he added a goal and three assists in a dozen playoff games.

It was a delightful state of affairs for Flash—also nicknamed "Busher," "Headline" and "Laughing Bill"—except for one thing. He mostly wanted to play defense with a capital D.

"I finally insisted that Ross keep me exclusively on the blue line," Hollett remembered. "Moving around so much

certainly wasn't getting me anywhere and wasn't paying off for the team as much as it could if I stuck to defense."

Hollett finally put his foot down during the 1940-41 season when Boston went twenty-three games without a defeat, an NHL record at the time. Two seasons later he topped all rear guards in points by collecting nineteen goals and twenty-five assists to erase the record (forty-one points) held by Tommy "Cowboy" Anderson.

Asked to recall his top thrill as a Bruin, Hollett remembered the Boston-Toronto best-of-seven semifinal of 1938-39. Boston led the series, three games to one, with Game Five at Boston Garden.

"We needed the one victory to eliminate Toronto, and we were grimly hanging on to our 2-1 lead with three minutes to go in the game," said Hollett. "Just then, Eddie Shore got a penalty and we were worried because we felt that we had to win this game. We didn't want to return to Maple Leaf Gardens for any more games.

"Many of the Bruins had remembered in a previous season when Boston had a 4-0 lead in the first period before Charlie Conacher led them to a comeback when the same Eddie Shore had been penalized. Because of that, nobody wanted to take any chances this time."

Ross dispatched Hollett and Milt Schmidt to the ice for penalty-killing purposes. They captured the puck and sent it back to their own end of the rink.

Hollett: "We then began moving forward and finally got the puck into Toronto's area. Milt passed to me and I faked a long shot. All the Leaf players, with the exception of Gordie Drillon, went behind the net to retrieve the puck. Except that I still had it. Drillon dropped to his knees to block my shot.

"But I faked their goalie, Turk Broda, and drew him about ten feet out of the net. Then, I got so excited I could hardly put the puck in the goal. But I did and that gave us the win, 3-1, and the Stanley Cup. I kept the photos that showed how I managed my two fakes."

One of the best Hollett stories of all time was told by his former teammate Dit Clapper, who played alongside Flash throughout his Beantown career. Clapper, who originally relayed the tale to *Toronto Globe and Mail* hockey writer Bill Roche, considered it one of his funniest NHL moments. Roche later included it in his oral history, *The*

> "I finally insisted that Ross keep me exclusively on the blue line. Moving around so much certainly wasn't getting me anywhere and wasn't paying off for the team as much as it could if I stuck to defense."
>
> —Flash Hollett

Hockey Book.

The story dates back to the 1940-41 season and, according to Clapper, was "Hockey's Mildest Brawl." Here's how Dit detailed it:

"Hollett accidentally knocked a tooth out of Syl Apps' mouth in a checking tangle at the Bruins' blue line. The incident caused what undoubtedly was (and probably still is) the tamest-language and biggest-letdown rhubarb in professional hockey history.

"I've heard plenty of chewing-matches in games and I have heatedly spoken my piece in print, too, where the hot, bad words almost melted the ice. But this spat between Apps and Hollet, both clean-playing, clean-living and non-swearing hockey stars, was absolutely tops—in reverse.

"It had been a typical Bruin-Leaf game of those days, including full-out, hard-hitting action, a tied score, and tempers getting shorter every minute. The players were primed for the right spark to start a real donnybrook as the fast, rough game stormed along.

"I was Hollett's defense partner that night when Apps, coming full tilt, evidently thought we were spread a little too wide. He faked a pass; then tried to knife between us.

"Hollett and I closed up, and it was the younger and more nimble Flash who got the big piece of Apps. The Leaf star went down, and so did Hollett. But Syl didn't get up. He knelt on the ice, shook off his right glove and covered his mouth with his hand.

"Let's get this straight: in the heat of a game on Maple Leaf Gardens ice, a visiting player might do a pretty good job of walloping Bob Davidson, Nick Metz or several other Toronto favorites of that time, but you couldn't slough Syl Apps and get away with it (not with the Toronto fans, anyway). And in retrospect, I don't blame them.

"Nearly all the players on the ice quickly formed a ring around Apps. Nobody in the Gardens, including us Boston players, wished to have him injured. However, when Syl got to his feet, blood was flowing down his chin.

"Hollett had not moved away, and I knew by the look on his face that he was the most worried person in the rink.

"But when Syl saw Flash standing near, he waved his hands excitedly and whirled over to face him—a very menacing move for the mild-mannered Apps to make.

"Brother, that was the indicator! If Apps was going to take an unprecedented poke at Hollett, a free-for-all fight of both teams would be on.

"Both benches emptied in a split second. Every Leaf and Bruin raced to the scene of the impending combat. Each was toting his stick high and ready. I could sense, too,

Flash Hollett in his prime as a Bruin.

that every fan in the Gardens was up and waiting.

"The stage was all set for the big scene. Testy-tempered Leafs were jostling testy-tempered Bruins for front-row positions. Just one punch to be swung by either Apps or Hollett—and to quote old Tim Daly, it would be 'ev'yman fur hisself.'

"However, this is what the audience of irate players heard:

"'By hum, Flash, you knocked my tooth out!'

"The traffic jam of players had crowded Apps and Hollett until they were virtually chin-to-chin. And I had been squeezed right up against them.

"Flash answered Syl's accusation, not with a punch, but with, 'For gosh sakes, Syl, I'm sorry. I didn't mean to do it!'

"Right then I began to see a magical change in the belligerent Leafs and Bruins around me. But Apps continued his seemingly threatening gestures while exploding:

"'By criminy, Flash, that was a bad thing to do to a fellow!'

"Hollett then did some glove-waving and came back with:

"'Aw gee, Syl. My stick just bounced up off your stick

and hit your face. You know how these things happen, doggone it!'

"The hostile looks on the players around me were being replaced so rapidly by wide grins, even between Leaf and Bruin, that I realized what was bound to happen.

"Somebody was going to infectiously and disdainfully laugh out loud, and I didn't want to see Apps and Hollett embarrassed. Anyway, that was all of the 'brawl' I could take while still able, under great stress, to keep a straight face.

"Also, I had been around the hockey wars, including the old, strong-language variety, long enough to realize that the popular Syl was now at a disadvantage. He had used up his entire and well-known-around-the-league supply of cuss words. Apps had gone full out with both 'By hum' and 'By criminy,' whereas Hollett hadn't even used his 'By golly,' and so on.

"Obviously, the 'fight' buildup and expectation was an all-time NHL flop. So, I managed somehow to freeze a stern look on my face; then pushed between Apps and Hollett, and declared loudly:

"'See here, fellows. Cut out that bad language! It's terrible for the fans to hear. Shame on both of you. I MEAN IT!'

"Of course, the crowd hadn't heard a word. But darned if Syl and Flash—two grand competitors in anybody's hockey game—just looked at me, startled and sheepish, then exchanged the same looks, and quietly skated away to their benches.

"Only then could I let down and really laugh. I skated rubber-legged back to our goal-cage; draped myself over it and howled. To this day I don't think the Toronto fans understood why that big lug Clapper held up the game just to laugh and laugh."

Hollett starred for the Bruins through the World War II years, and in the 1942-43 season, helped orchestrate another Stanley Cup Finals symphony, although there was one discordant note; Boston lost in four consecutive games to Detroit.

Surely, it wasn't Flash's fault. He was the playoff assist leader (9) and had a career-high 44 points (19-25) during the regular campaign.

In 1943-44 the Bruins began slipping and on January 5, 1944, Ross dealt Hollett to Detroit for defenseman Pat Egan. It was one of Ross' worst moves. The Bruins missed the playoffs while Detroit finished second.

Hollett was crushed by the deal. "Boston was like home to me," he declared.

Nevertheless, he reported to the Red Wings, and in 1944-45, Flash showed why Ross had erred. Hollett tallied twenty goals and twenty-one assists, followed by three goals and four assists in fourteen playoff games.

A year later Flash suffered pleurisy, plus groin and knee injuries.

The medical problems hurt his game and caused Red Wings general manager Jack Adams to trade Hollett to the New York Rangers. Flash refused to report.

"When I got traded," said Hollett, "I was pretty mad. When I didn't go to the Rangers, they suspended me. There were a lot of factors involved. I had a young family and the prospect of apartment living in Manhattan didn't appeal to me or my wife.

"But from a hockey standpoint, I should have gone. Frank Boucher was running the Rangers and he was a great fellow; plus the Rangers played my kind of game. I could have fit in with them because I was a playmaker and they were a passing team."

Sadly, Flash Hollett never played big-league hockey again. He eventually drifted to senior-level hockey in Ontario, playing for the Kitchener Dutchmen and the Toronto Marlboros. He ended his playing career in 1950 and retired to the Toronto area. Hollett died in 1999.

> "When I got traded, I was pretty mad. When I didn't go to the Rangers, they suspended me. There were a lot of factors involved. I had a young family and the prospect of apartment living in Manhattan didn't appeal to me or my wife.
>
> —Flash Hollett

Bill "Flash" Hollett, one of the NHL's finest rushing defensemen.

*Cecil "Tiny" Thompson was one of the NHL's most accomplished goaltenders,
having won the Vezina Trophy four times in 12 seasons.*

Cecil "Tiny" Thompson

Born: Sandon, British Columbia; May 31, 1905;

died February 9, 1981

Position: Goaltender

NHL Teams: Boston, 1928-38; Detroit, 1938-40

Awards/Honors: Vezina Trophy, 1930, 33, 36,

38; Hall of Fame 1959

Cecil
THOMPSON
"Tiny"

Were it not for the sensational exploits of Frankie "Mister Zero" Brimsek, Cecil "Tiny" Thompson certainly would be remembered as the best Boston goaltender in the history of the franchise.

In the opinion of some, Thompson actually was better than Brimsek, but the two were so close in their abilities that the issue is a moot point. Unfortunately, Thompson played in an era so distant that few are around today who can claim to have seen his excellent work, night in and night out, year in and year out.

But it was there, and the statistics support his membership in the Hall of Fame.

The native of Sandon, British Columbia, won the Vezina Trophy for the best goals-against average in 1930 (2.19), 1933 (1.76), 1936 (1.70) and 1938 (1.80).

Ironically, Thompson never meant to be a goaltender in the first place. "I wasn't crazy about it as a kid," he once admitted, "but I had to agree to go between the pipes or the other kids wouldn't let me play."

And play he did, mostly with older youngsters with whom he became a star. "Just about everyone I played against in those days was bigger than me so they nicknamed me 'Tiny,' although I wasn't crazy about it. I guess alongside them, I looked tiny."

His feats, however, were prodigious as he played amateur hockey for the Calgary Monarch Juniors, the Pacific Grain Seniors and the Bellevue Bulldogs. At 5-10, 180 pounds, Tiny wasn't tiny anymore, but the nickname stuck after he moved to Minnesota to play high-class amateur hockey for Duluth and eventually Minneapolis.

During the late 1920s, the American Hockey Association was a top minor league and Minneapolis was one of its major franchises. Thompson was discovered there in 1927-28 after posting a handsome 1.23 goals-against average. It was his third season in Minnesota, and each successive campaign was better than the previous one.

Hal Winkler had been the Bruins goaltender in 1927-28, but he was no match for Thompson. Tiny stepped in and enthralled the Boston crowd, coming up with twelve shutouts and a 1.18 goals-against average as a rookie.

Thompson's goaltending was a major factor in the Bruins winning the Stanley Cup for the first time in the club's history. He permitted a mere three goals in five playoff games and posted three shutouts!

This was a critical time for the Bruins. The franchise was young and needed heroes to gain the fans' attention. Thompson thus became the first puck-stopping icon on Causeway Street and was as much a cornerstone as Eddie Shore and Dit Clapper.

Thompson's excellence was reflected in the team's standing. With Tiny in the nets, Boston finished first, winning the Prince of Wales Trophy in 1929, 1930, 1931, 1933, 1935 and 1938.

Ironically, Tiny's most memorable game was one he lost. Playing against the Toronto Maple Leafs in the opening round of the 1933 playoffs, the Bruins were primed for their hated rivals from across the border.

The two best teams in all hockey were meeting in a best-of-five series that was tied at two games apiece after four pulsating games. The deciding contest would be played on April 3, 1933, at Maple Leaf Gardens.

Facing Thompson in the Toronto goal was veteran Lorne Chabot, who already had won a Stanley Cup with

the New York Rangers. Thompson and Chabot battled evenly over sixty minutes of regulation time.

Neither gave an inch as sudden death began. More than 100 minutes of exhaustive play still produced no result. At that point, the respective managers, Conn Smythe of Toronto and Art Ross of Boston asked NHL president Frank Calder for permission to stop the game and resume it the following night. Permission was refused and the Thompson-Chabot battle continued into the early morning.

Early in the sixth overtime, Bruins defenseman Eddie Shore attempted a clearing pass which was intercepted by Andy Blair of Toronto. Blair skimmed a pass to teammate Ken Doraty, who was in the clear. Skating in on the breakaway, Doraty cleanly beat Thompson at 4:46 of the sixth overtime—164:46 of the game.

The game was the longest overtime played to that point and even though he was defeated, Thompson received a standing ovation from the Toronto crowd.

From 1932-33 through 1937-38—six full seasons in all—Thompson never missed a game for the Bruins, although in the 1937 playoffs he suffered a severe hand wound when it was sliced by a skate. He rebounded from the injury to post an impressive 1.80 goals-against average the following season.

The 1938 playoffs were another story. Toronto swept the Bruins in three straight games, a result that infuriated Ross, who hated losing to the Leafs under any circumstances.

While Ross cast about for a replacement, Thompson played capably for Boston at the start of the 1938-39 campaign. He appeared in five games and produced a nifty 1.55 goals-against mark, which ordinarily would have insured his job.

By now, Ross was convinced that farmhand Frank Brimsek was ready for the NHL. Thompson was traded to the Detroit Red Wings. Tiny played two seasons in the Motor City and then retired.

He later became chief scout of Western Canada for the Chicago Blackhawks. A two-time First All-Star, Thompson died on February 9, 1981.

"You had to admire the guy," said Hall of Famer Sid Abel, who played alongside Thompson in Detroit. "He always made the big play."

Tiny was a big player for Boston when the Bruins needed him most.

> "Just about everyone I played against in those days was bigger than me so they nicknamed me 'Tiny,' although I wasn't crazy about it. I guess alongside them, I looked tiny."
>
> —Cecil "Tiny" Thompson

Goalie Cecil "Tiny" Thompson sprawls on the ice during a game against the Rangers.

Versatile Doug Mohns was equally adept at defense and forward positions.

Douglas Allen (Doug "Diesel") Mohns

Born: Capreol, Ontario; December 13, 1933

Position: Defense

NHL Teams: Boston, 1953-64; Chicago, 1964-71; Minnesota, 1971-73; Atlanta, 1973-74; Washington, 1974-75

Doug MOHNS

A headline running across the pages of *Hockey Illustrated* magazine once said a lot about one of the least celebrated and most underrated Bruins—DOUG MOHNS, ALWAYS ONE STEP FROM STARDOM.

It said a lot, but not in a completely accurate manner. After all, there were many nights at Boston Garden when the forward-turned-defenseman-turned-forward actually reached the marquee level that only belongs to the very best.

How could anyone forget the 1957-58 season, when the native of Capreol, Ontario, tallied thirteen points in a dozen playoff games—as a defenseman, no less!

Or, how about the 1959-60 campaign, when he rang up twenty goals and twenty-five assists for a whopping forty-five points in sixty-five games!

Doug Mohns braking to a stop.

Not to mention the fact that he was named to the NHL's Second All-Star Team as a defenseman for the opening half of the 1956-57 season. The following year he captured two awards—the Dufresne Trophy as the outstanding player in Bruins' home games and the Eddie Shore award as the best Boston player of the year.

When Mohns scored twenty goals, he believed that he would gain a spot in the NHL record book. Until then, onetime Bruin Bill "Flash" Hollett held the record for goals scored by a defenseman (20) and it seemed that Doug had done the trick as well.

"I had eighteen goals going into our final game," Mohns remembered. "I scored two in that last game and thought I had tied Hollett's record for defensemen.

"Actually, I had, but the league told me that my numbers wouldn't be recognized because I had played seven games at left wing. But all of my goals were scored as a defenseman and none at left wing. I thought I should have been listed as having tied the record."

The similarity between Hollett and Mohns transcended mere numbers. Each was a gifted skater with good size (5-11) during an era when players were considerably smaller than in contemporary hockey. Lynn Patrick, who had played against Hollett as a member of the Rangers and then coached Mohns in Boston, suggested that Mohns was a Hollett clone.

"Flash could give you a great game at wing, was a good center and also a good defenseman with a fine shot," said Patrick. "Like Flash, Mohns was a fine skater with an exceptional burst of speed. You didn't find many players who could move up and back and still retain their effectiveness."

A star junior player with the Barrie Flyers of the Ontario Hockey Association's A Division, Mohns originally was a forward in youth hockey leagues and as a top flight amateur. In 1953 he leaped directly from the OHA to the NHL, a move that few players could negotiate without at least a hiccup, but Mohns had no trouble at all.

As a rookie forward in Boston, he played in all 70 games, tallying thirteen goals and fourteen assists. It was a year when the Bruins engaged in a neck-and-neck battle for a playoff berth against the Rangers and finally made it in the final week of the season. That spring, Doug scored his first playoff goal.

"The big thing Doug had going for him," said former Bruins coach Milt Schmidt, "was that he came to play, just like Hollett. There was nothing Flash liked better than being on skates and playing, no matter where. Doug was the same way.

"He was quiet but all hockey player when he stepped on the ice, regardless of where he was asked to play. Doug could switch at a moment's notice and still give you a solid effort."

In addition to his powerful skating stride—appropriately, he was nicknamed Diesel—Mohns' arsenal included a shot that goaltenders distressingly referred to as "heavy." According to netminders, that meant that the drive was usually felt right through the goalie's padding and could jar the stick from his hands.

"I could never think of any reason how I developed it," Mohns said, "except that many years earlier, I had started the habit of leaning on my stick. Often when it slipped while I was shooting, I took an unexpected tumble. But it did have the effect of putting a lot more muscle and beef behind the shot.

"The way I saw it, too many players were too erect when they shot. They would just put arms and wrists into it. I always believed that there should be some weight behind the shot."

Boston's braintrust decided at the start of the 1956-57 season that Mohns would best serve the team as a defenseman. "I never thought I'd like playing defense," he admitted, "but after I tried it, I changed my mind."

Mohns was instructed by former Bruins' defenseman Hal Laycoe, as well as teammates Bob Armstrong and Fernie Flaman.

For the most part, the Bruins employed Mohns as a defenseman and he constantly put up excellent numbers, including a pair of forty-five-point seasons. But every so often he would get the call to move up to a forward line and never missed a step.

Mohns: "It was easier to play up front. If you're a forward and you miss your check you still have a defenseman behind you. But when you're a defenseman and a guy gets past you, there's nobody left but the goalie.

"Even when I was a forward, I would think like a defenseman. I'd always try to get back and cover the opposing forward and sometimes I would do that too soon instead of following up on a shot.

"Nevertheless, I always felt that one of the greatest thrills in hockey was stopping a player from scoring a goal. It felt just as good stopping an offensive chance as it did putting on the red light."

Mohns could play a hard-hitting game, but on one occasion, it backfired on him. Playing against the Canadiens, Mohns noticed that Montreal defenseman Ian Cushenan had dropped his stick.

As Cushenan—nicknamed "Crash" for good reason—leaned over to retrieve it, Mohns pushed the stick away from him. Once again, Cushenan leaned over and again Doug used his own stick to shove it further away.

Then, Mohns skated blithely up the ice, figuring that Ian would be occupied for a while. But the Bruin had miscalculated, big-time.

The enraged Cushenan ignored his stick. Instead, he took off after Mohns, drew abreast of him, and, without bothering to remove his gloves in the time-honored tradition, he proceeded to crash his large, leather-armored hand against the side of Mohns' jaw with bone-shattering results.

Cushenan received a match misconduct penalty for his troubles, but only a $50 fine. NHL president Clarence Campbell ruled that under ordinary circumstances the fine would have been higher, but that in this case, Mohns had provoked the attack.

After the 1958-59 season, the Bruins slipped into a non-playoff funk that lasted through Mohns' final year in Beantown, 1963-64. On June 8, 1964, he was dealt to the Blackhawks for Reg Fleming and Ab McDonald.

"I was sorry to leave Boston," said Mohns. "I had spent fourteen years in the Bruins' organization. We had some good years when I first joined them, and one year we went to the Stanley Cup finals before losing to Montreal.

"But, frankly, I was getting despondent not getting into the playoffs year after year. Sometimes, in those last years with the Bruins, I had to talk myself into playing a good game."

In Chicago, Mohns was moved back to his original position at wing and thrived alongside Hall of Famer Stan Mikita and Ken Wharram. He was traded to the Minnesota North Stars in 1970-71 and to the Atlanta Flames for the 1973-74 campaign.

Mohns' final major league season was 1974-75, when he played seventy-five games for the Washington Capitals. Even then, he showed that his skills had not diminished very much, but he also knew that the time had come to call it a career.

Maybe he never did make it to the Hall of Fame, but Doug Mohns remains one of the few big leaguers to have played twenty-one seasons at a very high level.

A teen-aged Allan Stanley as a member of the Boston Bruins.

Allan Herbert "Snow Shoes" Stanley

Born: Timmins, Ontario; March 1, 1926

Position: Defense

NHL Teams: New York (R), 1948-54; Chicago, 1954-56; Boston, 1956-58; Toronto, 1958-68; Philadelphia, 1968-69

Awards/Honors: Hall of Fame, 1981

Allan STANLEY

Allan Stanley was meant to be a Bruin; the only trouble was that he went about it the hard way— very hard, as a matter of fact—and when he finally did land at Boston Garden, it was for an all-too-short period.

Nevertheless, his roots as a Bruin date back to the 1943-44 season, when he played for the Boston Olympics in the old Eastern Amateur Hockey League. Stanley was a mere seventeen-year-old at the time, but immediately impressed the bird dogs and lasted a total of three seasons with the Olympics before graduating to the Providence Reds of the American League. At that point, his career as a potential Bruin took a major detour and it would lead to humiliation and more humiliation before he finally was vindicated as a legitimate star for the black, gold and white.

Allan Stanley was bought from Providence of the AHL to play for the Rangers before he went on to be one of the Bruins' best defensemen.

chided as the "$70,000 Beauty," and then the "$70,000 Lemon." None of this would have happened had the Blueshirts been winners, but they hovered between mediocrity and melancholy.

Boucher, who had brought Stanley to New York, appreciated Allan's talents more than most and was upset by the fans' reaction. He decided to spare Stanley any more hurt by playing him only in away games, but that just left the Rangers with a rusty defenseman, and further increased the fans' hostility.

"They'd boo every time I touched the puck. Then they began to boo every time I got on the ice. Why, even the few games when I sat on the bench, they'd yell at me."

The agony went on for six years, with one brief break when the Blueshirts took the Detroit Red Wings to the seventh game of the 1950 Stanley Cup finals before losing. Lynn Patrick was the New York coach at the time and called Stanley his most valuable Ranger.

"Every summer," Stanley once recalled, "I'd think about improving my play the next year and winning the fans over to my side. I was always hoping that I'd play like Superman."

And so Stanley's agony went on, seemingly interminably, until a cool Wednesday in 1954, when the agony was stilled.

Boucher raced into the Ranger press office and announced with a mixture of anger and relief that he had traded Stanley and forward Nick Mickoski to the Chicago Blackhawks for Bill Gadsby, a high-quality defenseman, and Pete Conacher, a forward.

The trade was as sensational as the original deal for Stanley, since Gadsby was also considered a potential star. (As it happened, Gadsby played twenty years in the NHL, never skated for a Cup winner and was named to the Hall of Fame in 1970.)

Big Allan played two seasons in Chicago with little hint of martyrdom. In the fall of 1956, the Blackhawks gave up and general manager Tommy Ivan prepared to send him to the Hawks' minor-league affiliate in Buffalo.

The Bruins, in need of an extra defenseman, bought him from Chicago for something less than the waiver price of $15,000. It was one of the best buys since the NHL was created.

Stanley's impact was immediate and powerful. A season

Big Allan's saga began when the Rangers were desperate for defensemen in the years immediately following World War II. Stanley had become the property of Lou Pieri, owner of the Reds, and Rangers' boss Frank Boucher negotiated a deal for Stanley through the AHL boss.

To obtain Stanley, New York dispatched three pro players, cash and the rights held by the Rangers to the services of an amateur. The value was estimated at the time to be about $70,000. By today's fiscal standards, it would be close to $1,000,000.

"One night," said Stan Saplin, the Rangers' creative press agent, "Allan was a minor-leaguer in Providence, enjoying a postgame glass of beer with a few teammates at midnight. The next noon he was in Leone's restaurant and being acclaimed, in effect, as the savior of the downtrodden Rangers."

In no time at all, the "$70,000 Rookie" was being

earlier Boston was a fifth-place team in the six-team NHL. A year later—with Stanley a starting Bruins blue liner—the club had climbed to first place. Bruins general manager Lynn Patrick claimed that Big Allan was "one of the main reasons" for the resurgence.

"Stanley was playing a calculating brand of hockey," said Saplin, who had covered the defenseman when he had played in New York. "Almost every move was sound. His deliberate pace was deceptive, giving him an appearance of being slower and less effective than he actually was. His easy skating style made tough plays look simple, coupled with the fact that, by style, he was not a rushing defenseman but rather one who stayed back."

Needless to say, Stanley played some of his best games against the Rangers at Madison Square Garden. He played two seasons in Boston, and when the Bruins, figured Big Allan had had it, they traded him to Toronto for Jim Morrison. It was an awful move for the Bruins, although they were looking for a younger backliner. But Stanley was far from finished. Skating for Punch Imlach in Toronto, Stanley was just as good as he had been in his Boston prime. It was the kind of move that helped brand Imlach a genius.

Stanley skated just as deliberately in Toronto as he had with the Rangers. The difference was that he was now playing before a sophisticated Maple Leaf Gardens audience who appreciated his defensive gifts as much as his boss, Imlach.

It was no coincidence that the Leafs annexed four Stanley Cups with the big guy snowshoeing behind the blue line. Stanley's play had a blend of majesty and intelligence that was both hard and clean. Textbook defense, you might say, the kind that is as rare today as a nickel cup of coffee.

Could Big Allan have achieved the same distinction as a Ranger? Under the circumstances, it would have been a 50-1 shot.

The inescapable problem in New York was frustrated fans who would not—or could not—get off his back.

"There is always a nucleus of fans," said Saplin, "who pay their way in whether their team is a winner or not. They need an outlet, though, for the bitterness that grows within them as failure piles upon failure."

In the eyes of the Ranger faithful, Stanley was an abject failure, a skater who never fulfilled his notices, who would never cut it on Broadway and, needless to say, would never make it to hockey's Hall of Fame.

But he did, and part of Big Allan's endorsement was his excellent—albeit short—career as a Bruin.

One night the Rangers were playing host to Boston at Madison Square Garden. Stanley played brilliantly for the Bruins, who defeated the Rangers in that contest. Many New York fans had difficulty understanding how well the player they had booed out of The Big Apple was playing for the New Englanders.

As Stanley left the dressing room and walked out onto Manhattan's 49th Street after the match, a Rangers fan approached Big Allan. The New York rooter had a quizzical look on his face as he admonished the defenseman.

"You didn't play that way when you were with us," the fan said accusingly.

"Yes, I did," Stanley replied, a bit sadly. "Yes, I did!"

Mike Milbury in the middle of the action.

Michael James Milbury

Born: Brighton, Massachusetts; June 17, 1952

Position: Defense

NHL Teams: Boston, 1975-87

Coaching: Boston, 1989-91; New York (I),

1995-98

Mike MILBURY

As a defenseman for the Bruins, Mike Milbury was like an old, reliable automobile that won't win any beauty contests but will take you where you want to go.

There never was anything fancy about the Walpole, Massachusetts, native, not as a National Hockey League rookie in 1975-76 and not in 1986-87, his last in the bigs. But over a dozen seasons, this much could be said without equivocation: he got the job done.

Sometimes he did it with undue force and other times with an overdose of emotion. Rarely did he execute his job as a backliner with exquisite grace or grandeur. A Bobby Orr he was not, and yet when Milbury was out of the Bruins' lineup, the team invariably was the worse for it.

When you think about it, the mere fact that Mike played a single game as a Bruin is something of a minor miracle. Hockey hardly was uppermost on his mind when he attended Walpole High.

"I was pretty well occupied with my studies," said Milbury, "and playing four sports for Walpole at different times. I really didn't give professional hockey a thought, even after I went to Colgate. I just figured I wouldn't have a snowball's chance."

It was a reasonable assumption, considering that Mike first and foremost was a football star. At least that's what interested the recruiters at Colgate.

"They wanted me for football," Milbury recalled. "At least they did at the beginning but when my file went through the athletic office, (coach) Ron Ryan noticed my hockey record and asked me to play just in scrimmages. I started out as a forward and then moved back to defense. Eventually, I made varsity.

"We were horrendous. We'd play fifteen or sixteen Division One games a season and win maybe five. In a good year we'd finish third from the bottom. I was the captain

those days," Milbury remembered, "was that we didn't play nearly as many games nor get the same quality coaching in the early developmental stages."

Ironically, his coach in Boston was the ultimate Canadian chauvinist, Don Cherry who, somehow, took a liking to the local boy.

"Mike was good, strong and intelligent even as a rookie," Cherry remembered. "He played his position well."

Well enough to have played seventy-five games in the 1976-77 season. He was a stay-at-home defenseman who somehow grabbed headlines during the Bruins-Flyers playoff that year by scoring a game-winning goal in the third period, no less.

With the score tied, 1-1, Terry O'Reilly sent a pass to Mike. "I was turning as the puck got to me," Milbury said. "I just wanted to get wood on it, deflect it somehow. [Goalie] Wayne Stephenson was fooled by the speed of my shot. It was going so slow, end-over-end. It wasn't the prettiest goal."

But it was vintage Milbury and, more important, the winner. Ray Didinger of the *Philadelphia Bulletin* didn't

---

"I was very intense then. I took every loss hard. After the games I'd go around the locker room breaking sticks. I was very immature. I didn't know how to channel my frustrations."

—Mike Milbury

---

and I led the team in penalty minutes. That was my claim to fame. I didn't make All-American or All-Conference. I didn't even make player of the week.

"I was very intense then. I took every loss hard. After the games I'd go around the locker room breaking sticks. I was very immature. I didn't know how to channel my frustrations."

But he learned well enough to develop the kind of collegiate skills that capture the eyes of NHL bird dogs.

In time, hockey took over from football, and he was scouted by the Bruins and wound up playing in the American Hockey League for Rochester. After a few glitches here and there, he made the big team, alongside the likes of Brad Park, Dallas Smith and Gary Doak. He was an American playing a Canadian game at a time when it still was unusual to find Uncle Sam's skaters in the NHL.

"The main difficulty for American hockey players in

mince any words. "It was a Colgate kind of goal, a clumsy, off-balance swat that sent the puck fluttering over Stepenson's shoulder like a dazed butterfly."

Milbury blossomed into a dependable, throwback defenseman, although his awkward style occasionally evoked derison. One year *Boston* magazine singled him out as "The Worst Athlete in Boston."

Mike's reaction was reasonable, to say the least: "I didn't think they'd raise a monument for me on top of Bunker Hill. Naturally, I wasn't tickled about it but I was mature enough to realize that I happened to be a well-rounded athlete. The man who made that judgment about me must have looked at my scoring stats and saw I had no goals. But when you think about it, assuming that what he said was true, it certainly must be to my credit—my ability to adapt—that I was able to survive in the National Hockey League for twelve years. The funny thing was that year, I

Milbury always provided the ultimate effort.

got a Christmas present from my grand-aunt, who was a great lady, and she sent me a subscription to *Boston* magazine!"

Under Cherry, the rules for Milbury were very simple, "get the puck up the boards," and he did. Mike never won a Stanley Cup in Boston—hey, nobody has since 1972—but he gave the Boston Garden crowd value for their money.

His relationship with Cherry was priceless. The chemistry between the two was as good as it gets. Grapes could relate to Mike because Cherry himself had played the game a lot like his young defenseman, and Milbury appreciated the fact that his coach had so much confidence in him.

Cherry showed his affection for Milbury with many a complimentary turn of phrase in his autobiography, *Grapes*. One of the best Milbury-Cherry tales of them all involved a forlorn plant they detected during an automobile drive:

"Only Mike and I could fall in love with a lowly weed, but this actually happened during our drives to and from Boston Garden. As we were motoring along the highway one day, I noticed a single weed, about two feet high, growing through a crack in the concrete at the side of the road. Suddenly it dawned on me that this weed had great symbolic value. Although it was ignored by everyone and maligned as a mere weed, it had managed to survive storms, salt, spraying, blizzards and whatever else might have been dumped on it. Still it managed to stand tall and I offered this bit of insight to Mike.

"He immediately understood how I felt about this weed and I instantly knew that he, too, felt for the little shaft of green. 'Mike,' I said one day, 'that weed shows character. Any plant that can grow out of a crack in concrete and survive all the climatic indignities has to be something special. Our team has to have character like that.' Milbury agreed and, each day, we would acknowledge the weed as we headed for Boston.

"But one day a terrible thing happened. As we were driving to the Garden we noticed that a highway clean-up truck was grooming the side of the road *and was heading straight for our favorite weed.* 'Mike,' I said shouting, as if a human life was in danger, 'they're going to get our weed.'

"He slammed on the brakes, jumped out of the car and ran—dodging the rush-hour traffic—back in the direction of the weed. Several times I thought he was going to get killed as he raced to beat the cleaning truck to the weed. Sure enough, he got to it just in time, plucked it from the concrete crack and then zigzagged back through the traffic again until he safely reached the car. As he slammed the door, he said, 'Grapes, they aren't gonna get *our* weed. No way!' When I got home I took some fertilizer and planted the heroic weed in my backyard.

"Two days later, Rose was weeding the garden and came to our weed. She looked at it and thought, 'What's this old weed doing here?' She uprooted it and threw it in the garbage. I suppose there is a moral here, but I haven't figured it out yet."

The Cherry years were a delight for Milbury. He went to the Stanley Cup finals, won plenty of games and, in 1977, was on a team that came close to actually beating Montreal for the title.

A classic Milbury incident occurred at Madison Square Garden on December 23, 1979.

Milbury speeding out of his own end.

Stan Fischler Collection

It involved Mike and other Bruins clashing with Rangers fans. A photo that was widely circulated after the episode depicted Milbury, clobbering a fan with his shoe.

Milbury: "Looking back, it struck me as a genuine farce. I hope this doesn't sound insensitive of me but few people were aware of the facts behind the episode. All they remember is seeing me with a guy's shoe in my hand, standing over him and Milbury looking very much like the bully. If the truth be known, I was in a great mood that night. We had just come up with a dramatic win over the Rangers. As a rule I didn't like to spend too much time on the Garden ice because I never knew what's going to come flying out of the stands to hit me in the head. So, I rushed off the ice with our goalie [Gerry Cheevers] and traipsed into the locker room. All of a sudden I looked around and realized that there was nobody there but me and Cheesie. Then, I heard a roar from outside and that could mean only one thing—trouble. I dashed back to the rink and, whaddya know, there were our guys heading into the stands under attack from fans. My first reaction was 'Uh-oh, my friends are in trouble.' The weird thing about it was that I wasn't angry. I was happy and also a little confused. I didn't even climb over the glass. I just walked around into the stands and began climbing the stairs in the direction of Peter McNab, who was battling with a fan.

"At the time I didn't know what to think but there was a feeling uppermost at the time—camaraderie. I wanted Peter to know that I was with him in case any other fan showed up to start trouble. So, even though Peter had pretty good control of the fan I just grabbed him. Then, the guy started to kick at me and continued to kick. In defense, I grabbed his leg. He was wearing those cheap, flexible loafers and one of them popped off his foot and he kept kicking. So, I just took the loafer and whacked him once in the thigh; not in the head. It was as if to say, 'Okay, that's enough, you're fighting a losing battle.' But in the pictures and on the videotapes it looked much worse. The most amazing thing was that of the three of us (Bruins) who were involved and wound up with eight, six and six

game suspensions, respectively, not one of us threw a punch. To me, that was unbelieveable."

Milbury remained one of the top four Bruins defensemen through the mid-1980s. His teams never missed the playoffs and always had a winning record. As NHL players go, Milbury certainly would be rated an intellectual. He was a voracious reader and uninhibited about revealing his thoughts. While 99 percent of the members of the Players' Association went along with Alan Eagleson's leadership, Milbury was a lone voice critical of The Eagle. Years later, many of Mike's points were proven valid.

As Milbury's career wound down, his boss, Harry Sinden, began suggesting that Mike might have a post-playing career as an executive. The 1986-87 season was Milbury's last in the bigs—and one of his most depressing.

The club was having its problems and many in Boston Garden took out their frustrations on the hometown boy. The harder Milbury tried, the more the boos rained down upon him. He considered it one of the lowest points in his NHL life.

Years later, Milbury told Mike Smith, "I showed up every night, but there were nights I wasn't talented enough to get it done. I felt the boos were unfair. I felt betrayed. That was a tough time."

That it was, but Mike always displayed a high degree of resilience. In time he would become Bruins coach and a member of the high command. He left Sinden's organization in 1994 to become a television analyst at ESPN. When the New York Islanders offered him a coaching job, he moved to Long Island and eventually was named general manager. Despite several tumultuous—and losing—seasons, he held the job through the 1999-2000 season.

Sinden once said of Milbury, "I think of Mike as a person who is torn between wanting to live an intellecutal life and one as a job."

Bruins fans think of Milbury as a New England talent who gave their favorite club a decade's worth of hard work and intensity.

> Milbury remained one of the top four Bruins defensemen through the mid-1980s. His teams never missed the playoffs and always had a winning record.

Hall of Famer Leo Boivin checks Bobby Hull into the boards.

Leo Joseph Boivin

Born: Prescott, Ontario; August 2, 1932

Position: Defense

NHL Teams: Toronto, 1951-54; Boston, 1954-66; Detroit, 1966-67; Pittsburgh, 1967-69; Minnesota, 1969-70

Awards/Honors: Hall of Fame

Coaching: St. Louis, 1975-76, 1977-78

When historians refer to the art of "old-time bodychecking," it's commonplace for the name of Leo Boivin to be mentioned.

"Leo was very special," said erstwhile Bruins forward Ed Westfall, who played on Boston teams with Leo. "He was one of the few players for whom it could be said that bodychecking became an art form."

If nothing else, Boivin was favored by gravity. His body was squat, extremely low to the ice, so that his balance remained perfect when his 5' 7", 190-pound frame crushed an opponent.

More important, Boivin learned to synchronize his hip thrust in mid-ice collisions so that he was able to torpedo an enemy attacker amidships.

"For the most part," explained Westfall, "Leo's checks were hard but clean."

A native of Prescott, Ontario, Boivin premiered in the National Hockey League with Toronto in 1951 but was traded to Boston three seasons later. He became a fixture on Hub teams that regularly challenged for the Stanley Cup but never quite made it.

"We had a good club," said Boivin. "We had a fairly big club, a good skating club. I don't suppose there was a lot of talent on it, but there was a lot of work and hustle."

It was Boivin's—and the Bruins'—misfortune to peak at precisely the same time as Montreal's five-straight-Stanley Cup dynasty, from 1956 through 1960.

During that span, Boston played the Habs in two series, losing them both, but battling hard and well.

"For about four years," Boivin remembered, "we never changed a hockey player and we competed with the best of them.

"All of a sudden we change and we went right to the bottom."

From 1959-60 through the arrival of Bobby Orr in the mid-1960s, Boston was the NHL doormat, and Boivin suffered through those depressing years. One of his coaches was Phillipe Henri Watson, otherwise known affectionately to the media as "Phiery Phil."

Watson had coached the Rangers into the playoffs for three successive seasons in the late 1950s and then failed when his emotions got the better of him. Hired by the Bruins, Watson still was a wild man, and on at least one occasion, Boivin was the center-piece of a Watson episode.

During training camp, the Bruins coach was orchestrating a practice that emphasized getting the puck out of the defensive zone. Each line would attack, and one skater would take out the defenseman as the forward shot the puck.

Watson wasn't pleased with the execution, and at one point he screamed, "Come on, you guys. Don't you know how to take out a defenseman yet?"

> "We had a good club. We had a fairly big club, a good skating club. I don't suppose there was a lot of talent on it, but there was a lot of work and hustle."
>
> —Leo Boivin

With that, Watson decided to do it himself. Johnny Bucyk passed the puck to Boivin, who was at the point. Boivin then shot the puck.

"Phil came charging at him like a freight train," recalled Bucyk. "Phil went to take him out and Leo just braced himself. Phil hit him but it was like smashing into a stone wall. Phil just went head over heels straight backwards.

"He hit his head on the ice and just lay there, kicking the heels of his skates into the ice and counted to ten. The whole team just stopped and roared."

As good as he was on defense, Boivin was not averse to taking a turn up front.

During the 1963-64 campaign, the Bruins needed a hard-hitting, good-checking left wing, and since none were available at the time, coach Milt Schmidt asked Leo if he would try it.

"If it helps the team," said Boivin, "I'm for it."

He scored ten goals in sixty-five games that year, a career high, and was the Bruins' captain from 1963 through 1966.

A member of the Hockey Hall of Fame, Boivin was inducted in 1986. At the time, he had an unbroken 34-year association with The Game as player, coach and scout.

Unfortunately, his last years on Causeway Street were depressing. He remained a Bruin into the 1965-66 season and then was traded to the Detroit Red Wings. With the advent of NHL expansion, he moved on to the brand-new Pittsburgh Penguins and concluded his playing career in 1969-70 with the Minnesota North Stars.

Almost two decades of big-league play were aptly summed up by the Hall of Fame, which said that Boivin was "remembered as a rugged defenseman and premier bodychecker of his era."

One might say that was true not only of Leo's era but of all time.

Leo Boivin (left) wraps up the Red Wings' Gordie Howe.

Peter McNab focusing on a scoring opportunity.

Peter Maxwell McNab

Born: Vancouver, British Columbia; May 8, 1952

Position: Center

NHL Teams: Buffalo, 1973-76; Boston, 1976-84;

Vancouver, 1984-85; New Jersey, 1985-87

Why isn't this man in the Hockey Hall of Fame?"

The question was raised not long ago by someone who had closely studied the evolution of Peter McNab from a tall, gawky Vancouver Canucks rookie in 1973-74 to a starry member of the Bruins who twice reached the 40-goal plateau and was as good a playmaker as scorer.

In his Bruins heyday—the late 1970s and early 1980s—McNab's scoring proclivity was such that some observers, such as *Toronto Star* sports columnist Milt Dunnell likened Peter to erstwhile Boston scoring machine Phil Esposito.

"Ridiculous," laughed McNab. "Esposito was a superstar."

Some would say that McNab was too modest. Starting with a 38-goal year in 1976-77, he then proceeded to follow that with 41 goals, 35 and then 40. Granted, he never reached 40 goals again, but in 1980-81 he came up with 37 and a career points high of 83.

"Peter was an extremely accurate shooter," said Bruins boss Harry Sinden, who signed McNab as a free agent from Buffalo on June 11, 1976. "That's one of the things we liked about him from the start. Actually, there was a little bit of Espo in him. We realized he was not a good skater but his skating seemed to improve."

The Bruins acquired McNab in a curious manner. Andre Savard had been Boston's first draft choice in 1973, but by 1976 the club and Savard could not agree on money nor the duration of the contract. That's where Sinden got his managerial radar going.

"I found out that Buffalo had not signed McNab," Sinden explained. "His problem was that he wasn't getting enough time on the ice. So that's when we made the deal—Savard for McNab. And we had no trouble signing Peter."

Sinden also knew that Peter had come from solid hockey stock. Pete's father, Max McNab, had played for the 1950 Detroit Red Wings Stanley Cup-winning team and later became a top hockey executive.

Born in Vancouver, where Max once guided the minor league Vancouver Canucks, Peter later learned his hockey in balmy San Diego, when Max was running the pro team in Southern California.

"My father helped my shooting because when he was in the NHL just about everyone used the wrist shot, not the slapshot, so he helped me develop my wrist shot," Peter explained. "The other advantage I had in San Diego was free use of the rink when the team wasn't playing.

"I'd be alone there and the only thing I could do was practice shooting at the net. And that helped me develop accuracy."

Ironically, McNab won a baseball scholarship to Denver University, but made the varsity hockey team, playing well enough to attract NHL scouts. He was signed by Buffalo and alternated between the Sabres and Cincinnati in the American League in 1973-74. He latched onto a permanent big-league job the following year.

But it wasn't until he was dealt to Boston that McNab flowered into a major player. Fortuitously, he arrived in Beantown at the apex of Don "Grapes" Cherry's steward-

Once heralded as the next Phil Esposito, Peter McNab was just the kind of hulking center the Bruins needed. He was acquired from Buffalo in 1976.

Stan Fischler Collection

ship as coach, while some of the most gifted big-leaguers—such as Jean Ratelle, Brad Park, John Bucyk and Terry O'Reilly—were skating for the black, gold and white.

"I was lucky to be traded to Boston," McNab asserted. "The club had an excellent passing defense, which set up a lot of the plays. We also had wings who got the puck into the slot. That's where I got a lot of my goals.

"That's how Esposito used to work, too. I'm a little bigger than Phil but I didn't have his maneuverability."

Another element McNab lacked—at least early in his Boston career—was Esposito's confidence. Where Phil also knew that he could score goals, McNab was given to periods of self-doubt whenever he would hit a slump.

McNab: "One of my handicaps early-on was that my emotions would take over too quickly. If I played a good game, I would tell myself, 'Peter, you CAN play in the NHL.' But when I played a poor game, I would start questioning myself.

"'But as my game improved with the Bruins, my confidence climbed and I stopped feeling sorry for myself. Also, I discovered productive areas on the ice. It was what I called a 'floating slot.' On the power play, for example, I would move from post to post, depending on which point man had the puck."

Easygoing and amiable, McNab proved a challenge for the irascible, short-tempered Cherry. "I always knew he'd be a scorer," Grapes said. "When I was coaching in the AHL with Rochester, I watched Peter develop. Even then he had terrific accuracy with his shot."

The McNab wrist drive was as effective in the playoffs as it was during the regular season. In 1977-78, Peter tallied eight goals and eleven assists for nineteen points in fifteen playoff games. In the 1980 playoffs he scored eight goals in ten games.

Over a period of five winters, he had banged home 191 goals, which was a 38.2 clip. He had become as much a hometown favorite as O'Reilly and Park and was regarded as an ideal player in the dressing room. Obviously, he had learned well.

"When I came to Boston," McNab remembered, "I roomed with Johnny Bucyk at first. After I had been with the team for a week, it felt as if I had been with them for five years. Once you make the club, you become part of that 20-member group and that's what happened with me.

"I had become a Bruin. I was one of the guys and we went together, ate together, had fun together. And, most of all, we did our damnedest to win together."

Not that life was perfect for Peter in Boston. While Cherry handled him with kid gloves, Sinden was more abrasive. "Your checking, McNab, has not improved by one iota," Sinden shouted one day.

Cherry believed that the manager was making a mistake. "Anyone who knew Peter McNab realized that if you criticized him he would go into an absolute state of shock," said Cherry. "So, what happened after the Sinden incident was that Peter turned out to be useless for a month."

There was a humorous twist to the episode: for the rest of the season, Cherry called McNab "One Iota."

If nothing else, Cherry was correct about McNab's sensitivity. During the 1981-82 season, he started with fourteen goals in nineteen games. "It was my best start ever," said McNab. "Then, bang! I hit a wall."

He failed to score in eleven of his next dozen games and by Christmas had become exiled to the role of fourth-string center. Although nobody could say for sure at the time, in retrospect, it was the start of a long downhill side for McNab's Bruins career.

"I could see it coming," Peter reflected. "The team started losing confidence in me, then I began to lose confidence in myself, and pretty soon it all snowballed.

"It wasn't just the two hours during the game that hurt; it was the other twenty-two hours of the day. Those were the tough ones. That was when my mind started playing games."

Cherry had been succeeded by former Bruins goalie Gerry Cheevers, who did not take to McNab as easily as Grapes. One night in Quebec, Cheevers benched McNab until there were only ninety seconds left in the game.

McNab: "When I was on the bench that long I had a terrible problem with my feet going to sleep. This night they were asleep way up to my knees! But Cheesie sent me in, and I figured I had to do something to justify being there, so I started speeding around the net as fast as I could, although I'm not exactly the Montreal Express. Then I look up, and who's coming right at me? Moose Dupont. My feet

wouldn't move! I thought, 'Oh boy, he's gonna murder me.' Dupont just looked at me like he couldn't believe I was standing there. Then he realized I was out of control, so he ducked at the last second. Pow! My stick went into the stands, my gloves went flying and all the guys on the bench were cracking up. So there's always a funny side to things."

Nevertheless, McNab finished that season with a rather serious and respectable 76 points (36-40) and did just as well the following year when he posted 22 goals and a career-high 52 assists. But his buddy, Cherry, was long gone, and on February 3, 1984, he was dealt to the Vancouver Canucks for Jim Nill.

The move was not a total surprise. McNab's name had been heard in trade rumors for a couple of years and his declining production certainly didn't help, nor did his age. He played one full season in Vancouver (1984-85) before turning free agent once more.

When the Canucks released him, he was signed by—of all people!—Max McNab. Peter's father had become general manager of the New Jersey Devils, a club that was searching for scoring talent in the summer of 1985. When father McNab offered son McNab a contract, the offspring actually had to think about it for a few days before signing.

"I was worried about what other players and the fans might say," Peter admitted. "My wife finally told me, 'They'll think about it for one minute in a day. That's not a very big part of their lives.'"

His dad had a different perspective. "I've never scouted a player as thoroughly as I have Peter," said Max, who formerly had been general manager of the Washington Capitals. "When I added up the number of winning goals and winning assists he had against my team in Washington and against the Devils, it made me mad enough to sign him."

McNab concluded his NHL career with the 1986-87 season, retired from the ice and moved up to the broadcast booth, where he became the Devils' television analyst for SportsChannel, and more recently with the Colorado Avalanche and Fox Sports.

As for making the Hockey Hall of Fame, that won't happen but, really, it doesn't matter.

Peter McNab won the hearts of Boston hockey fans because he was a talented scorer, a hard tryer and, most of all, a genuinely nice guy. Sometimes that's better than being a Hall of Famer.

> "I had become a Bruin. I was one of the guys and we went together, ate together, had fun together. And, most of all, we did our damnedest to win together."
>
> —Peter McNab

The incomparable and irresistible Derek Sanderson.

Derek Michael "Turk" Sanderson

Born: Niagara Falls, Ontario; June 16, 1946

Position: Center

NHL Teams: Boston, 1965-72 and 1973-74; New York (R), 1974-75; St. Louis, 1975-77; Vancouver, 1977; Pittsburgh, 1977-78

Awards/Honors: Calder Trophy, 1968

*I*f ever there was a stickhandler whose sex appeal matched his considerable talents as a center man, Derek Sanderson was that man—with no runner-up in sight.

During an era in NHL history when teammate Bobby Orr was hockey's dominating personality, Sanderson managed to steal headlines on the strength of his brash behavior, which thoroughly enthralled the media from Boston to Baton Rouge.

In fact, Sanderson was the first big-league personality to gain attention in non-hockey areas because of his non-hockey exploits as much as his talent as a shooter and playmaker.

Sanderson, the hockey player, ranks among the most underrated of all time. He played both ends of the rink equally well. He terrorized the opposition with an assortment of legal and illegal checking tactics and, given the opportunity, could score and arrange goals with insightful passes. Further, Derek was the premier face-off specialist for the Bruins throughout his tenure in Beantown.

Unfortunately, Sanderson was cast in a second-fiddle role to Phil Esposito, the opportunistic scorer, who played a one-way game but managed to put more points on the board than Derek. It was Sanderson's lot in life to be cast as a checking forward simply because Espo obtained the glory assignments. Nevertheless, hockey purists knew from the get-go that Sanderson was the more comprehensive performer.

Before the 1969 East Division Cup final, the *Toronto Daily Star* put the two centers in perspective with a headline: "HABS FEAR SANDERSON MORE THAN ESPO."

The Canadiens recalled that Derek was the star in Boston's four-game sweep over Toronto. The Montreal forecast proved correct; Sanderson helped Boston to a 2-2 tie in games until a devastating check by John Ferguson disabled Derek for the remainder of the series.

It was no coincidence the Bruins folded in six games. Sanderson condoned Ferguson's check but frankly admitted he was going to get even sooner or later.

"Sure I'm a dirty player," he acknowledged. "I like playing dirty. Anyway, that's the way the game should be played. I like fighting. Maybe I'll get beat up a lot, but I'll get the guy eventually."

And he got some good ones: Terry Harper, Ted Harris, Dick Duff and Orland Kurtenbach for starters. He rated Kurtenbach of Vancouver the best fighter in the league and considered Gordie Howe one of the meanest players. He was warned to stay away from Howe, but scoffed at the suggestion.

"One theory I go on: I don't care who he is, his face will bleed just like mine, right?" he said. "That stick is a great equalizer. I've cut people so often I can't remember who or when. So has Howe."

Such irreverent pop-offs caused the Bruins' brass to shudder. Once when Derek delivered some choice remarks to Paul Rimstead, the former sports editor of *The Canadian* magazine, coach Sinden snapped, "Is he shooting off his mouth again?"

Sinden could say what he pleased, but Sanderson knew what he was after and he got the ink. During the non-hockey months, he was a continual item in Boston papers, sometimes on the fashion page, sometimes on the society page and sometimes on the sports page. But it was always Sanderson—and he made no bones about it.

"There are three things you need to make money in professional sports," he maintained, offering a superb clue to his philosophy. "One is talent. The second is points. The third is color. Orr has the talent. Esposito has the points. The only thing left for me is the color."

Sanderson's talent outshone his color during the 1970 and 1972 playoffs but, typically, he never got center stage. In 1970, for example, it was a crisp, centering pass by

Sanderson to Orr that enabled the onrushing defenseman to fire the Cup-winning overtime puck past St. Louis goalie Glenn Hall. Orr, deservedly, got the accolades, but Derek essentially was forgotten.

Likewise, in the 1972 finals against the Rangers, it was Sanderson's somewhat-to-the-left-of-legal checking that defused New York's top scoring threat, Rod Gilbert, enabling Boston to capture its second Stanley Cup in three years.

After that series, Rangers defenseman Brad Park ripped the Bruins in his autobiography, *Play the Man.* Park put it this way:

"On the road there's more lamb in the Bruins, except for Derek Sanderson. What bothers me most about Derek is his flakiness; at any given time on the ice he doesn't know what he's going to do and he has no concept of hockey ethics.

"Once when he'd been tripped and was sliding toward the boards, I put my gloves out to keep him from crashing headlong against the wood. So what does Sanderson do when he gets up? Thank me? Never. Instead, he shoves his stick between my skates and dumps me flat on my face."

Sanderson's belligerent style had more variety than anyone in big-league hockey. He could be tough with his coach, as well as with the president of the National Hockey League, and he had a very rough mouth. If Sanderson had been born forty years earlier and a Hollywood scout had discovered him, Derek certainly would have been signed with either The Dead End Kids or The Bowery Boys. Young Sanderson was tough almost from the time he began to walk in the small Canadian city of Niagara Falls, Ontario.

"I've heard a lot about tough neighborhoods," said Sanderson. "I know there's Hell's Kitchen in New York and the South Side of Chicago, and Boston has a few places that wouldn't quite qualify as dainty. But I'll stack our area of Niagara Falls against any of them. You had to be tough to exist there. And it wasn't very hard to get yourself in trouble if you watched what the older fellas were doing."

Sanderson was five years old when his father, Harold, put him on skates. Derek frequently mentioned how strong an influence his dad was in developing his philosophy toward life, toward hockey and toward just plain toughness. The fittest survive, and Derek made it plain in his autobiography, *I've Got to Be Me,* that was precisely what his father meant.

"If it's worth fighting over," Harold Sanderson told his son, "the fight is worth winning. So, if the other fellow is bigger than you, use something—a stick, a pipe, anything you want. Just make sure you beat him."

Not long after receiving that fatherly lecture, Derek played a game of hockey and was soundly licked in a fight on the ice. After the game, Harold took his son aside and said, "If you let a guy do that to you again, I won't talk to you."

The art of toughness, as practiced by the Sanderson clan, involved the development of an immunity to pain. Harold Sanderson began his lessons for his son when Derek was eight years old. Lesson One consisted of tossing a hard baseball at the youngster, rather than simply lobbing it to him. If Derek failed to catch the ball, it would either hit him or fly past him, which meant that he had to take a long walk to retrieve it. Neither of the choices was particularly appetizing to the youngster. He soon learned that catching the rock-hard ball was better than having to chase it down the block.

"After a while I got smart and began standing in front of a wall when he'd pitch to me," Sanderson recalled. "But he still fired it at me and I felt it."

When baseball season was over, Harold Sanderson would apply another toughness test, this one on the ice. It began one day after a puck slammed into Derek's head, opening a large, bloody wound. The kid skated to the sidelines expecting first-aid treatment from a doctor and commiseration from his dad. He got neither.

"You're all right, for Christ's sake," said Harold Sanderson. "Get back out there. The blood will dry. Shake it off."

Derek bled for the entire workout. An hour elapsed before his father took him to the hospital, where three stitches were required to close the wound. Before the week was up, Derek returned to the doctor to have the stitches removed. "Let me have them," said Harold Sanderson.

The surprised doctor handed the stitches over to Mr. Sanderson while his son looked on in amazement, wondering what his father had in mind. "When we got home," Derek recalled, "he put them in a little plastic box. He saved every one of my first 100 stitches and, pretty soon, I started to become proud of them. I'd come home after a tough game and say, 'Hi, Dad, eight more!'"

Aggression wasn't the only attribute Harold taught his son to focus on. He was a stickler for scientific hockey and had Derek work on several aspects of his game. By the time Derek was seven, he was turning both ways on his skates, to the left and to the right. "It may seem easy but it really isn't," said Sanderson. "Practically all kids who become professional hockey players tend to favor one side. Usually

Derek Sanderson surrounded by Blackhawks.

they turn to the left most easily because that's the way people turn in a skating rink. Harold would have none of that. He would watch while I skated fifty times around the rink, stopping on both feet, then on one foot, then on one foot on both sides."

Toughness also went beyond the threshold of physical pain to strength in mental attitude. Harold Sanderson taught his son to strive for the best he could achieve. "I don't want you to end up like me," he told young Derek. "I want you to have a shot at everything and then decide for yourself. Whatever you do, be something—a surgeon, a lawyer, dentist or writer.

"But preferably, be a hockey player."

The latter was clearly Derek's goal, but he was not going to be just any skater. He wanted to be known as a guy who would not back down, who worked for everything he got, and, like idol and Hall of Famer Ted Kennedy, one who could dominate on face-offs. "Winning face-offs means your team controls the puck, and when your team controls the puck it controls the game," said Sanderson. "Kennedy was something. He was so good at face-offs, it was like he had a string on the puck. I became fascinated by the way he moved his feet before he took the draw, and I said to myself, 'Man, I've got to try this.' From Kennedy, I copied the way he positioned his feet, his hands and his weight, and I copied his timing."

In *I've Got to Be Me*, Sanderson explained, with confidence, his prowess on draws:

"There's no question in my mind that I'm the best faceoff man in the league. This didn't come by accident. I began refining my technique to a point where I now expect to win without too much trouble about 90 percent of the faceoffs I engage in. The secret is concentration.

"Every so often there is the challenge of going up against a new man. Once the guys on our bench started bugging me. 'Watch it, Turk,' they said, 'you're going up against Tkaczuk tonight.' I laughed when they said that. 'Who's Walt Tkaczuk?' I said. 'Tkaczuk played against me for five years in junior hockey and never beat me. He's not going to beat me now.'

"In another game I won 38 faceoffs and lost one. The only reason I'll ever lose a faceoff is because I may experiment or gamble on an offensive play. But if I pull it back in the traditional way, there's nobody in the NHL who can beat me."

Sanderson made the step to the NHL at the age of 18 after a junior career in his native Niagara Falls. Derek felt when he stepped onto the ice at that first Bruins camp he had expectations to live up to and that he needed to prove himself. Not surprisingly, his first instinct was to fight.

"Anytime anyone came near me—smack!—I tried to hit him. I went after every single guy on the team," said Sanderson. "One of them happened to be Teddy Green, who is about as tough as they come. You just don't play games with Greenie if you know what's good for you. Except I didn't know that at the time."

So Sanderson hit him a few times. Green slashed him and Derek retaliated with a few slashes of his own. "Listen kid," Ted told him. "I hit you, you *don't* hit me! You got that straight? You don't ever hit me or you won't be playing in this league very long."

To which Sanderson replied, "The next time you do that, I'm gonna crunch your face."

Luckily for Derek, nothing happened. When he got back to the bench, his training camp roommate Don Awrey told him, "Don't antagonize him. He knows you're not scared of him now, so don't bother him."

After the first week, Green said, "You know, I *like* you. You've got guts."

Sanderson and Green went out together that night and became good friends. "Listen, kid," Ted told him. "Anytime you're in a jam, I'll be there."

Though Sanderson could take comfort in the idea of Ted in his corner, the rookie knew he also had to take care of himself. His first fight was against the big Canadiens defenseman Ted Harris, who was in a scrap with Bobby Orr at the time. Derek could tell that Orr was tired, so he stepped in and said, "Try me." Harris took a swing, but Sanderson got the jump on him.

Green loved that. He gave Derek a smile and said, "That's it. We're away. We've got another fighter."

"After that Greenie just married me," recalled Sanderson. "He'd say to anybody who wanted to mess with me, 'Listen, if you try to cut this kid you'll have to come through me.' I said, 'Thank you. See that, there's Greenie, my pal.'"

Fighting was not going to keep Sanderson in the league, and he knew it. He needed to score—and score he did. By mid-season he was leading the race for rookie of the year with 14 goals and 14 assists. At season's end, he captured the Calder Trophy, as well as the hearts of Beantown hockey fans.

"I wouldn't want to play in any other city. I love Boston," Sanderson said in *I've Got to Be Me*. "I like the guys who come to the games with two days' growth on their face; the gooks who scream their lungs out. I love them because they're good people who work hard. They never got a break in life, so their enjoyment is the hockey game. I dug the crowds in Junior Hockey, but Boston Garden is better, especially the 'Gallery Gods,' sitting up in the top section. These guys have been coming for 15, 20 years—it's like a private club up there. They throw chairs, beer bottles, whiskey bottles. It's wild, but it's a great atmosphere and, for my money, hockey fans are the greatest fans in the world."

If fans loved a player with a mouth, they found their god in Derek Sanderson. He was often criticized for his outspokenness, but that never stopped Turk. After the Bruins were eliminated from the East Division finals in 1969 by Montreal, he said, "The Canadiens don't have the team, the defense, the talent or the guts."

"I meant every word of it," said Sanderson. "In fact, I've seldom been sorry for anything I've ever said in my life."

Before Game Four of the 1970 Cup finals against the St. Louis Blues, Sanderson was up to his old tricks, this time telling a reporter, "We have tougher workouts in practice than we've had in our games with the Blues.

"Didn't bother me a bit," he continued. "I had great confidence in our team. In fact, I had developed such a confidence in my faceoff ability that my teammates would challenge me with bets. Once, while I was getting ready for a faceoff, Bobby Orr pulled me aside and said, 'I bet you can't win it.' Well, I won it, sent the puck to him in the corner and he got knocked down on top of it, which called for another faceoff.

"I won three straight faceoffs—and won three bets— and each time he got knocked down with the puck. 'Listen,' I finally said to him, 'if you want me to win these things, you've got to get the puck out of here.'"

The Bruins won Game Four in overtime on Orr's goal, and the scene in the dressing room afterwards was chaotic, to say the least. In the midst of the celebration and champagne, though, Sanderson took a moment to pay homage to the man who made his Stanley Cup dreams possible. He took the shiny silver hardware overflowing with bubbly spirits and emptied it over his father's head.

Not all of Sanderson's career was destined to be glitz and glamor, however. After winning two Cups with the Bruins, he said goodbye to the NHL in the summer of 1972. He signed what was reported to be a ten-year, $2,500,000 contract with the Philadelphia Blazers of the World Hockey Association.

"I might just buy myself the whole damn city," said Sanderson when he jetted to Philadelphia and signed the contract. The Blazers expected him to be the captain, sex symbol and first-class fighter. When president Jim Cooper mentioned the fighting aspect to Derek, the suddenly rich young man seemed unhappy. "Fighting," Derek replied. "I don't know about that. That was the image when I was 23, 22, 21. But I'm getting older now, you know. I'm 26 now. I'm getting too old for that kind of non-sense."

On opening night in Philadelphia, the ice-making machinery broke down and the game had to be canceled. It was a portent of things to come—all bad.

Sanderson's failure to lead, score or fight for the Blazers went down as one of the singular disappointments of professional sports. He returned to the Bruins that same season, where flakiness remained a major part of Derek's image. Instead of fitting neatly back into the Bruins' mold, Sanderson seemed as ill at ease as he had in Philadelphia. He was suspended mid-season during a road trip to California after engaging in a bitter fight with teammate Terry O'Reilly and then missing the team plane back to Boston. Coach Bep Guidolin said he wanted no part of Derek on the Bruins as long as he, Guidolin, was coach. Sanderson, in response, said he would play for the Bruins again but not as long as Guidolin was coach. The Bruins fired Guidolin in May 1974, and soon after, Derek was traded to the Rangers for Walt McKechnie.

After a brief stint in New York, the tide turned against Sanderson again. By 1978, the one-time highest-paid athlete in sports was flat broke. He lost all of his money in a haze of alcoholism and poor investments made by so-called friends who targeted his lack of financial shrewdness. In 1980, he checked himself into a rehabilitation clinic in St. Catharines, Ontario, and began to get his life back in order.

Sanderson made Brad Park a prophet when he said: "At any given time you don't know what Derek is going to do." Clean and sober, Derek landed on his feet and joined the Bruins in the broadcast booth from 1987 to 1997. Sanderson also took finance courses and received a license to sell securities. He made sure the financial hardships which befell him would not have to happen to other players.

Sanderson in his last days as a Bruin.

All things considered, Turk authored one of the most remarkable recoveries of any athlete who was on the ropes. Still witty and philosophical in 1999, he was able to reflect on a roller-coaster career that nearly killed him. He learned what it was like to be deceived and now delivers advice based on bitter experience.

"Athletes get suckered into all kinds of bad investments. They gravitate toward nightclubs and restaurants," said Sanderson. "They meet someone who is nice, and they equate that with trust . . . They always pick up the tab. I would order drinks at a bar, and the world would show up."

In March 1998, Sanderson and colleague Phil Kenner opened a special fund through State Street Research, a Boston-based money management firm. The fund, which caters to professional athletes and coaches only, has grown from a few thousand dollars in assets to $18 million in assets and represents 85 professional athletes.

At age 52, Sanderson was still a headline-grabber, but not simply in Boston. On May 27, 1999, Derek's picture made the front page of *The Dallas Morning News'* business section. The headline read, "Money Plays," and featured a story about Derek's idea about the athlete's fund.

"Sanderson travels around the country, giving presentations to teams and speaking to players and agents," wrote staff writer Bill Deener.

Three decades after he became a household name in New England, Derek Sanderson was as beloved a Boston athlete as ever strode along Causeway Street. And nobody had paid a stiffer price to earn those accolades.

John McKenzie's spunk made him a favorite of the gallery gods.

John Albert "Pie" McKenzie

Born: High Rover, Alberta; December 12, 1937

Position: Right Wing

NHL Teams: Chicago, 1958-59; Detroit, 1959-61; Chicago, 1963-65; New York (R), 1965-66; Boston, 1966-72

John McKENZIE

*H*is career was strange—and one might say even disappointing—until John Albert McKenzie arrived in Boston.

Poof! Instant hero. The David who takes on all the skating Goliaths. When Johnny McKenzie stepped on the ice, he was like a runaway grenade.

"My custom at the start of the games was to take a run at somebody on my first shift," said McKenzie. "I just wanted to stir things up and plant the idea that if a squirt like me can go after them—particularly if my target is a big star—then why not every-body? I tried to act the same way when we were sagging in a tight game."

How much did they love the man nicknamed "Pie"?

"Pie" McKenzie's shooting often was overlooked.

Assorted banners boosting "Pie" hung from the Boston Garden balcony. Automobile bumpers were sighted throughout New England with the message: "No matter how you slice it, Pie is the greatest."

Curiously, he was not idolized anywhere else, as his early career stats suggest. McKenzie, as a matter of fact, mucked through a rather undistinguished career from his junior hockey days in Medicine Hat, Calgary and St. Catharines up to his rookie season with the Chicago Blackhawks in 1958-59.

Bird dogs who watched him with the Detroit Red Wings between 1959 and 1961 were no more impressed. In fact, McKenzie was dropped to the minors in 1961 until Chicago retrieved him for two more seasons (1963-64, 1964-65).

The tenacious right wing could skate, to be sure, and he seemed to have scoring attributes, but the Blackhawks finally gave up on him, and in 1965-66, he played for the New York Rangers.

But on January 10, 1966, the Blueshirts' general manager, Emile Francis, figured that McKenzie's six goals in thirty-five games were not enough. Francis dealt Pie to Boston even-up for Reg Fleming.

The turnabout in McKenzie's game was immediate and arresting. In thirty-six games as a Bruin, Pie more than doubled his New York output while improving his playmaking ability as well.

It was a fortuitous time for both the player and his team. The Bruins were slowly and painfully lifting themselves out of the NHL's subterranean depths while adding tough, new players and, of course, Bobby Orr.

None was tougher than McKenzie. Standing 5-9, 178 pounds, Pie was thirty years old when he came to Causeway Street, but his enthusiasm bubbled like that of a ten-year-old. And this was just what attracted the native of High River, Alberta, to Boston Garden's blue-collar crowd.

Toronto sportswriter Bob Pennington commented on the adulation of McKenzie as "peculiar chemistry."

Veteran Boston hockey writer Leo Monahan noted that, had a popularity poll been taken in 1970 "Pie would rank just a cut below Bobby Orr, Derek Sanderson and Phil Esposito. Bruins fans took the bouncing winger to their hearts."

It was not merely McKenzie's bronco-busting style that endeared him to the balcony crowd. For whatever reason, the numbers that he couldn't put up in Chicago, Detroit and New York became evident in Beantown.

During the 1967-68 season, he came into his own with 28 goals and 38 assists. The 66 points were a personal high to that point in his career, but they would later be surpassed.

Pie worked alongside Fred Stanfield, the vastly underrated center, and John Bucyk, a future Hall of Famer.

"By 1970," said McKenzie, "we had been together three years. We got to know each other's moves."

and made a living punching cows in the off-season. At his horse-riding best, Pie would compete in rodeos like the Calgary Stampede until Bruins general manager Milt Schmidt ordered him to cease and desist.

"I didn't want him to get hurt doing something foolish in the off-season," said Schmidt.

Surprisingly, Schmidt didn't get an argument from his right wing. "I considered it a compliment," McKenzie admitted. "Let's face it, they had to be interested in me to show that kind of concern. It was nice to feel wanted. Besides, the most I had ever won was $150 in a wild-cow milking contest. I never did make $500 in a season, which would have qualified me for the Cowboys' Protective

---

"It really wasn't much as skull fractures go. Just a little bone where the nose is hooked onto the forehead. I looked like Frankenstein but it only hurt when I smiled at Ken Dryden in the Canadiens' nets."

—John McKenzie

The line was particularly effective during the Bruins' 1970 march to the Stanley Cup. "I remember a two-on-one breakaway against the Blackhawks," said Pie. "Their goalie, Tony Esposito, thought that Freddie was going to pass to me but I knew that he wasn't. I just knew, that's all, and he went in and scored.

"After a while, it got so that in any given situation, I knew where Fred was and we both knew what the Chief [Bucyk] had on his mind."

McKenzie's popularity was so intense that on one occasion, after it had been reported that he was being examined at Massachusetts General Hospital, more than 300 people found their way to his room within 24 hours.

"Eventually," said McKenzie, "security police had to be brought in."

Ironically, McKenzie, Stanfield, Esposito and another teammate, Ken Hodge, all were refugees from the Blackhawks who turned the Bruins into a powerhouse and what would be a two-time Stanley Cup-winning team.

"That's why beating Chicago was always so sweet for me," Pie added.

Despite his notorious roughhouse style, McKenzie's penalty minutes never reached triple figures—77 minutes in 1970-71 was his high point—but he always was intimidating.

The rambunctiousness in McKenzie was rooted in his youth. He was born in Western Canada's cowboy country

Association. But I did acquire the conviction that those rodeo cowboys were the best-conditioned athletes in all sport."

The rodeos were tough, but the NHL was even tougher. After all, it was not too many years earlier when major league hockey had nearly killed him. Literally.

In a game against Toronto, McKenzie charged through the China Wall defense of Bob Baun and Carl Brewer. He was skewered with a stick and suffered a ruptured spleen.

"The doctor said that if he hadn't patched me up right away, I'd have been a goner." The proof was a cruel-looking scar that ran down his abdomen.

Montreal writer Andy O'Brien thenceforth referred to McKenzie as "the man without a spleen who is all heart."

Milt Schmidt preferred calling him a "mood-setter." Snarly was the mood that best befit the Bruins when they began taking dead aim at the NHL's stratosphere. Derek Sanderson, Ted Green, Wayne Cashman and Ken Hodge all contributed to the club's aggressive image, but it was McKenzie who seemed to do the most as agitator-extraordinaire.

This splendidly negative mood was as real as they come. After Pie had scored the series-clinching goal against Chicago in 1970, players from both teams lined up for the traditional post-game handshake. But not McKenzie. He made a beeline for the locker room, avoiding any pleasantries.

Johnny "Pie" McKenzie often owned the boards.

"It wasn't that John hated anyone," a team official explained. "But he couldn't be bothered shaking hands with his own mother if she was on another team."

McKenzie was an integral part of both the 1970 and 1972 Cup-winning machines. His first Cup ring was obtained more than a decade after his NHL debut and made up for many frustrating years as a professional.

"Up until 1970," he recalled, "I never even got a smell of Cup money. Chicago traded me the year before the Blackhawks won the Cup in 1961."

In reviewing the McKenzie dossier, it strikes one as strange that supposedly savvy front office types such as Tommy Ivan in Chicago and Emile Francis in New York neglected to exploit Pie's assets.

"All I can say," McKenzie asserted, "is that the best break I ever got was being traded from New York. My game was a hitting game and I didn't fit into the Ranger picture.

"The Bruins liked to hit. When I came to Boston, I had a bonus for twenty goals. I scored only nineteen but Milt Schmidt gave me the bonus anyway. He said I played

okay for him."

More than okay. On what was the Gashouse Gang of hockey, McKenzie was a perfect fit. Irreverent, loquacious, just like so many of his teammates.

McKenzie: "When I got a shoulder separation in January 1971, I was sitting in agony stripped to the waist with a hunk of bone sticking up under the skin of my left shoulder. Just then the team came stomping into the dressing room at the end of the first period. Phil Esposito took one look and said, 'You won't be using your extra tickets for a while, can I have them?'"

"Then, Bobby Orr stopped to point at my shoulder and say, 'Hey, look at that cute bump!' Knute Rockne couldn't have worked with that bunch of guys."

During the harsh 1971 Canadiens-Bruins playoff, McKenzie suffered a seven-stitch cut across the bridge of his nose. He continued to experience headaches after the series had concluded and was invited in for Xrays. It turned out that he had a fractured skull.

"It really wasn't much, as skull fractures go," said Pie.

> "I remember a two-on-one breakaway against the Blackhawks. Their goalie, Tony Esposito, thought that Freddie was going to pass to me but I knew that he wasn't. I just knew, that's all, and he went in and scored."

—John McKenzie

"Just a little bone where the nose is hooked onto the forehead. I looked like Frankenstein but it only hurt when I smiled at Ken Dryden in the Canadiens' nets."

If you're wondering where the Pie nickname came from, McKenzie will tell you that it had nothing to do with the NHL. "I was playing for Buffalo in the American League (1962-63) and one of my teammates was Gerry Melnyk. He figured that my round face looked like a pie so I've been Pie ever since."

Opponents had other less genteel names for him. During the 1969 Boston-Montreal playoff, Canadiens' coach Claude Ruel fumed over McKenzie's rough style and denounced him as "Yellow."

When Brad Park was a Ranger and authored *Play the Man*, he was equally harsh on Pie. "McKenzie's bag is running people from behind," wrote Park. "No player really objects to getting hit straight on, but when a guy rams you from behind, that's bad news."

McKenzie never made any excuses about his frontier behavior. Once he was asked if it was true that he would have croaked his mother if she played for another team.

"Absolutely," he said. "If you don't throw the calf, it'll throw you!"

McKenzie threw the Bruins for a loss after they had won the 1972 Cup. Along with teammates Green, Sanderson and Cheevers, McKenzie jumped to the new, rival World Hockey Association.

During that spring of 1972 the Bucyk-McKenzie-Stanfield line had set an NHL playoff record with 53 points—breaking the record the same line had set in 1970.

Then, almost inexplicably, McKenzie was left unprotected by the Bruins in the Expansion Draft. When the New York Islanders chose Eddie Westfall, the Bruins filled with McKenzie.

Being exposed in the draft was a blow to McKenzie; he made no bones about it. "I'll have to wait until contract time to see where I stand," he told reporters.

By this time the WHA teams were making outrageous offers to many NHL stars, including Chicago's Bobby Hull, who jumped to the Winnipeg Jets. When the WHA's Philadelphia Blazers dangled the big money, McKenzie, who had three daughters, signed with Philly as player-coach. When the club moved to Vancouver, McKenzie went with them and bounced around the WHA from Minnesota to Cincnnati and, finally, the New England Whalers, playing out of Hartford.

Pie's playing career concluded in 1978-79 with the Whalers the year before the club was admitted to the NHL.

Had he remained a Bruin, it's conceivable that Boston might have won a Stanley Cup instead of being runner-up in 1974 when the Flyers eliminated them in the finals. The Beantowners did have Bobby Orr and Phil Esposito, but there was one missing person who could have made a difference—Pie McKenzie.

Tommy Williams

Thomas Mark "Tommy" Williams

Born: Duluth, Minnesota; April 17, 1940; died

February 8, 1992

Position: Center

NHL Teams: Boston, 1961-69; Minnesota, 1969-

71; California, 1971-72; Washington, 1974-76

Tommy Williams was not the first American-born player to land a contract with

the Bruins, but he was a very important one because of his timing.

A native of Duluth, Minnesota, Williams began pursuing a hockey career in the

post-World War II years, when America's hockey fortunes were at a terribly low ebb.

The National Hockey League had only six teams at the time, and competition for

jobs was never keener, especially for college kids.

Williams had spent a year at the University of Minnesota when he won a position

on the 1960 United States Olympic Team, which competed at Squaw Valley, California.

By any standards, Uncle Sam's sextet was an underdog among underdogs, yet it

defeated the Soviet Union, and then in the final match, Czechoslovakia, for the first-

ever Olympic gold medal in ice hockey for the United States.

Williams, who centered a line between Minnesota cronies Bill and Roger Christian, was one of the Squaw Valley stars and was signed to a pro contract by the Bruins.

He was assigned to their affiliate in Kingston, Ontario, playing for the Frontenacs of the Eastern Professional League. Williams played well but certainly wasn't outstand-

past the American League.

By contrast, Williams got better with age. In 1962-63 he scored a career-high twenty-three goals in sixty-nine games, and he was the only American.

"It meant a lot to me," Williams recalled. "Even though I wasn't scoring as much as a Gordie Howe, I could

---

> ## "I had a good time playing hockey. Most of the times were good. I really enjoyed my career. It was important for me that the players liked me and sometimes I would even compromise being a better player just to be a good guy."
>
> —Tommy Williams

---

ing. The Bruins were in no hurry to elevate him and Williams appreciated the patience.

"They let me learn the ropes," he recalled, "and get a feel of what it was like to play pro." The Bruins finally put Williams on the big team for 1961-62.

To some observers these days, it may not seem to have been a big deal, but back then it was looked upon as a meaningful move. Not that Williams was in as nearly a trying situation as Jackie Robinson when the latter broke the baseball color barrier, but Tommy once said that there was, for him, a feeling of aloneness because he was from the States.

"I was the only American-born player in the NHL for six or seven years," said Williams.

One must remember that this was a time when Yankees—whether they were New Englanders or anyone from south of the 49th Parallel—were not freely welcomed by many of the Canadian-born NHL players.

Williams scored two goals in his first game as a Bruin. That helped.

The fact that he had good speed, could pass decently and stickhandle on a big-league level made his transition somewhat easier. Only one other player from the 1960 gold medal team had any NHL impact, and that was goalie Jack McCartan.

Immediately after Squaw Valley, McCartan was signed by the New York Rangers and won his first big-league game at Madison Square Garden. He commanded considerable publicity, but it soon faded, and by the 1960-61 season, McCartan was in the minors to stay.

Defenseman Rod Paavola of the Olympic team also took a crack at minor pro hockey, but never made it

always say I was the only American and I was scoring." Williams showed he was a big-leaguer, even though his club missed the playoffs through the 1966-67 season when Bobby Orr became a teammate.

In his oral history, *Life after Hockey*, Michael A. "Mike" Smith, who later became an NHL general manager, interviewed Williams.

"I found Tom to be quite frank and candid," said Smith.

Asked by Smith to view his career, Williams responded: "I had a good time playing hockey. Most of the times were good. I really enjoyed my career. It was important for me that the players liked me and sometimes I would even compromise being a better player just to be a good guy."

In retrospect, Williams confessed to Smith that he suffered a lack of self-confidence when he was called to the NHL.

Williams told Smith, "Here I am going on a team that I didn't think I was good enough to play on, and I never thought I was good enough to play pro hockey. Then, I'm thrust on to an NHL team and playing. And before I even had a chance to grasp the impact of it all, I'm out there and, hey, I got two goals in my first game. I said, 'Holy Christ, this is more than I can stand!'"

When Orr became a Bruins rookie in 1966-67, the team began climbing toward respectability. Even though Williams was eight years older than Orr, Tommy couldn't help but be awed by the kid.

"Playing alongside Bobby was one of the greatest thrills I ever experienced in hockey," said Williams. "He was an outstanding player—as everyone knew—but he also was a greater person, and that meant a lot to me."

In 1967-68, Williams enjoyed his most productive season in Beantown. Over 68 games, he scored eighteen goals and thirty-two assists. In the playoffs, he tallied his one and only postseason goal.

Tommy played one more season for Boston, 1968-69, before being dealt to the Minnesota North Stars with defenseman Barry Gibbs for Minnesota's first-round draft choice (Don Tannahill) and Fred O'Donnell.

Life was not kind to Williams after that. His wife was found dead in a car in 1970. He was thirty years old at the time with five children. A couple of months later he was suspended by the North Stars because of a tiff with the general staff.

He later was traded to the California Golden Seals and completed his big-league career in 1975-76 with the Washington Capitals.

Williams remarried in 1979 and seemed to be getting his life back in order. When Mike Smith asked him during their book interview if he was satisfied with his current status, he allowed that he was. "If I died tomorrow," Williams told Smith, "I would say that I've been the luckiest guy in the world because I really worked at what I had to do and I did it and I would describe myself as being really successful. I've been fortunate."

He was, for a time.

At the age of twenty-three, Bobby Williams, one of his sons—and a Bruins prospect—died of an asthma attack on June 1, 1987.

Less than five years later, Tommy Williams passed away. On February 8, 1992, the likable Bruin—fifty-one years old—was the victim of a fatal heart attack.

"I wanted to be the best player in the world," was what Williams told Mike Smith, "but I came up short."

Perhaps, but over a span of eight seasons, Williams was a treat to watch, a treat to chat with and a symbol that, yes, Americans could make it to the top of the hockey heap.

Ken Hodge forechecking behind the net.

Kenneth Raymond Hodge

Born: Birmingham, England; June 25, 1944

Position: Right Wing

NHL Teams: Chicago, 1965-67; Boston, 1967-76; New York (R), 1976-78

*I*f nothing else, British-born Ken Hodge always can claim that he was a central figure in two of the best trades the Bruins ever made.

The native of Birmingham, England, launched his big-league career in Chicago, but after two seasons with the Blackhawks, Hodge was included in a deal that also brought Phil Esposito and Fred Stanfield to Boston.

The date was May 15, 1967, and it remains eternally significant to Beantown fans because the trade catapulted the Bruins from non-playoff also-rans to the NHL elite.

Of the three players sent to Chicago—Pit Martin, Gilles Marotte and Jack Norris—only Martin made an impact, and that was minimal. Meanwhile, the right wing Hodge was placed on a line centered by Esposito, with tall, rangy Wayne Cashman on the left side.

The trio became an instant terror to the opposition. Cashman was the enforcer, Esposito the playmaker and scorer, while Hodge offered something of both.

"I didn't have to elbow people," Hodge explained, "or spear them. I just used my assets—like size and strength."

One of the early major league power forwards, Ken had scored only six and ten goals, respectively, in his two seasons with Chicago. As a Bruin, he immediately rang up 25 goals (1967-68) and reached 45 red lights a year later.

Likewise, his linemates also thrived. In 1968-69 Esposito led the NHL in scoring (49-77-126) and the trio emerged as one of the most feared units in the league.

"We stood up for each other," said Hodge. "We never backed down when trouble came. As for me, I never looked for trouble, I just looked for the puck."

Usually, he found it. In 1970-71 and 1972-73, Hodge racked up 105 points. A check of the arithmetic revealed his versatility.

During the former campaign, he tallied 43 goals but added 62 assists; a testament to his playmaking ability. Yet in the latter season, he had a career-year, goal-wise, with 50, and 55 assists; which is about as balanced as a top forward can get on an NHL tightrope.

At 6' 2", 215 pounds, Hodge was one of the biggest forwards in the league and, at times, looked as if he was not skating as fast as the Boston Garden faithful would have liked, or coach Harry Sinden, for that matter. During the 1969-70 season, Sinden actually benched Hodge to send a message.

"He didn't feel that I was playing as capably as I could," Hodge remembered. "Maybe he was right, maybe he wasn't. But that's all past."

Hodge played on two Stanley Cup-winning teams (1970 and 1972). When the Bruins annexed the silverware in 1972, Hodge starred in over 15 playoff games, scoring nine and assisting on eight other goals.

He remained a key Bruin through the early and mid-1970s but his star began fading after his second 105-point season. A year later, his numbers had plummeted by 39 points, but an even more traumatic shock was Sinden's decision to trade Esposito to the Rangers in November 1975. That season Hodge registered a modest 25 goals and 36 assists while his stock among fans and management

After nine stellar seasons in Boston, right wing Ken Hodge was traded to the New York Rangers for budding star Rick Middleton on May 26, 1976.

continued to drop.

Meanwhile, Esposito—despondent over his trade to New York—lobbied Rangers general manager John Ferguson to obtain his buddy Hodge. Following the 1975-76 season, Ferguson relented. He dispatched young, gifted scorer Rick Middleton—then a discipline problem—to Boston for Hodge.

Ken had played nine full seasons with the Bruins and was the least-mentioned of the Causeway Street Gashouse Gang in terms of points produced. Esposito had been the bigger goal-scorer and more garrulous of the bunch, while Cashman was notorious for his policeman's work, as well as his point production. Hodge, on the other hand, was the poster boy for the line. He was exceptionally handsome—perhaps too good-looking for the Gallery Gods—and well-spoken.

Still, Ken looked like a wonderful acquisition for Ferguson, who was general manager of the Rangers in May 1976. "We needed winners," he explained, "and Hodge, already had two Stanley Cup rings in his collection."

Harry Sinden wanted the Rangers' rugged left wing Steve Vickers in exchange for Hodge but Ferguson was reluctant to part with what still looked like a promising prospect. Instead, Ferguson proposed Middleton, who had seemed on a treadmill to oblivion with the Rangers despite exceptional gifts as a shooter and stickhandler.

Hodge was ecstatic about the move to New York. "The way I look at it," he said, "I owe John Ferguson and the Rangers something. They wanted me, and went out and got me. That's a great vote of confidence. It's going to make me try that much harder."

The words sounded plausible. And for a short time,

Hodge in his matinee idol days.

Hodge played well for the Blueshirts. He had 21 goals and 41 assists in his first year as a Ranger. In Boston, Middleton's numbers were 20-22-42. Ken was a full twenty points better than Rick.

But that was as good as it got for Hodge in the NHL. A year later, he played only 18 games for the Rangers (2-4-6) before being shipped to the minors. He never returned to the NHL again.

There was, however, another Ken Hodge on the big-league scene. His son, also a forward, looked like a winner with the Bruins in 1990-91, scoring 30 goals and 29 assists. But his production immediately decreased, and after a brief fling with the Tampa Bay Lightning in 1992-93, the younger Hodge also departed the bigs.

There has been a tendency to diminish the contribution of the senior Hodge, but like many big, talented players over the years, he appeared to be doing less than was actually accomplished.

But over a period of nine years, he was a major force on the two Cup-winning teams at the start of the 1970s.

Andy Moog, is all concentration between the pipes.

Steve Babineau

Andy Moog

Born: Penticton, British Columbia; February 18, 1960

Position: Goaltender

NHL Teams: Edmonton, 1980-87; Boston, 1988-93; Dallas 1993-97; Montreal, 1997-98

Awards/Honors: William Jennings (shared with Rejean Lemelin), 1990

ndy Moog was deceptive.

His baby face; his calm demeanor and his less-than-commanding physique tended to obscure the tiger inside him.

This was a competitor with a capital C.

Never the best goaltender in the world, Moog nevertheless was very good, very often. From 1987-88 through 1992-93—five full seasons—the Penticton, British Columbia, native gave Beantown fans the kind of goaltending reassurance they had received in earlier years from the likes of Tiny Thompson, Frank Brimsek and Pete Peeters.

"He was a gritty little character," said Mike Milbury, who coached the Bruins when Moog was in Boston.

Andy got to New England by way of Edmonton, where he had become second fiddle to Grant Fuhr. Moog got fed up with the situation and in September 1987, he called a press conference in Edmonton to announce that he would join the Canadian Olympic team.

"I had as much confidence in Andy," said Oilers defenseman Kevin Lowe, "as I did in Grant. Andy was a great goalie. He had a kind of cockiness, a confidence that was one of his biggest assets."

It showed during the 1988 Olympics, when Moog posted a 4-0-0 mark, including a shutout of Poland. After the Games his persistence was rewarded when, on March 8, 1988, he was traded to Boston in exchange for Geoff Courtnall, Bill Ranford and a second-round pick in the 1988 draft.

In Boston, his alter-goalie would be Reggie Lemelin, giving the Bruins a compatible one-two combination. Moog settled in and, after two seasons of nearly equal sharing with Lemelin, took over the No. 1 job. He led his Bruins to the finals in 1990, where they lost, ironically, to Ranford and his former Oiler mates. Despite the loss, Moog became one of the more revered goalies in Bruins' history.

He also emerged as a low-key but high-intensity member of the NHL Players' Association and was as visible during the April 1991 strike as leaders Bryan Trottier, Mike Gartner and Doug Wilson.

The spotlight returned to Moog early in January 1993, when the Bruins hit a dreadful slump. Losses piled up and the Andy-Reggie tandem was history.

"We're playing wide open," Moog explained. "It's not the style of game that makes a goaltender relaxed, comfortable and confident. You may not be faced with a lot of shots, but the ones they get are good ones and they wear on your confidence."

During an interview with the author while Moog still was a Bruin, he offered the following insights into the business of goaltending.

How do the pressures of playing goal affect a goaltender's psyche?

"The fun or exhilaration of goaltending can also be the worst part of goaltending because you have to keep your team from losing or make your team win. Then comes that instance when it's you and nobody else; when the goal goes in, it's you and nobody else; and when the save's made, it's you and nobody else."

Why did you want to be a goalie?

"My father was a goaltender."

What advice did he give you?

"He told me to try and relax and be thoughtful about goaltending. He wouldn't necessarily say, 'Oh, you gotta make the glove save this way.' Or, 'You gotta kick the puck out that way.' He would try to help on certain areas. For instance, if I was beaten on a shot he thought I should have stopped, he would say, 'That was a bad goal—forget about it, you have the rest of the game to play.' When you're ten or 12 years old and you're learning these lessons, then you're ahead of the game.

Which was your favorite year in Boston?

"The year we went to the Stanley Cup finals after we won the President's Trophy for most points in the regular season (1989-90). I was also nominated for the Vezina Trophy."

Moog never achieved Hall of Fame status but he did attract the eye of netminding experts who acknowledged his qualities.

"Andy's style got simpler as the years went by," said Anaheim Mighty Ducks goalie coach Francois Allaire. "He eliminated a lot of unnecessary moves from his game. His biggest asset was that he knew his limits and played accordingly."

Moog was well-endowed with goaltending lore, being the son of a goaltender who had the courage to play professionally before the era of the mask.

"My father taught me when I was 13 or 14 years old and he emphasized that I should never get rattled," Andy remembered. "He taught me not to give the other team an advantage by reacting to what happens on the ice. Those pointers helped me."

Battered Don Moog was not a pleasant sight for his son to see. "His nose was a big piece of jelly," said Andy. "It was all over his face. His teeth—they were false." Eventually, Don concluded his hockey career and became a Greyhound bus driver. The old pads were placed in the basement of the family home and remained there with the gloves and other equipment.

By the time Andy was 10, he was invited to play hockey with his neighborhood chums. Where would he play? No question.

"I already had the equipment," he laughed, "so I became the goaltender."

The path toward professional goaltending went from Penticton to Billings, Montana, where Moog played for the Billings (Junior) Bighorns. He was named to the Second All-Star team in 1979-80. That induced the Edmonton Oilers to select him 132nd overall in the 1980 Entry Draft on their sixth pick.

He was sent to Wichita of the Central Hockey League a year later to ripen for the big time. All signs suggested that he was at least two or three years away from "The Show." But strange things were happening in Edmonton, where the goaltending was in a state of turmoil prior to the opening playoff round against the Montreal Canadiens.

Oilers coach Glen "Slats" Sather had two veterans, Eddie Mio and Ron Low, but neither was healthy, so he went with untested Moog.

Teammate Kevin Lowe, who later authored a book

about his Oiler experience, put it this way about Moog:

"Andy came in and stood on his head. While he was doing that, he got a little help from his friends. He needed it. In our earlier two games at Montreal we scored a grand total of one goal. No way Moog would win for us if we didn't score for him but our new kids obliged in a hurry. Glenn Anderson and Jari Kurri beat Richard Sevigny in the first, while Slats encouraged us to keep taking the play to them. He figured that the Habs could be had by throwing them on the defense. Slats figured that if we jumped into the lead and held it for a bit, the rabid Montreal crowd would turn on the Canadiens and screw them up even more.

"He couldn't have been more right. We beat them 6-3, and Moog kept making saves. The more saves he made, the more reassured we felt in front of him. We relaxed, realizing we didn't have to play defensive all the time and as we opened up, the Canadiens backed off. It was hard to believe that this wonderful Andy Moog had a 14-13 record with Wichita in the Central League and a 3.33 goals-against average. Overnight, he had become a Canadian national hero—except, of course, in Montreal.

"But could Andy Who do it again? The test came in Game Two and Moog passed it with as much ease as he had in the opener. Staked to a 2-1 lead after two periods (Coffey and Siltanen had scored for us, which shows you we had offense on the defense!), Moog shut the door on the Habs in the third. Kurri put the game away, thanks to Wayne Gretzky's pass late in the third, and we walked out of The Forum with an incredible two games to none lead.

"And to top it all, Montreal's goaltending was mediocre compared with the magnificent Moog. We dominated them in Game Three and Moog continued to play like Georges Vezina. 'Maybe I was in a daze,' said Andy, 'but who cares, it was working.'

"[Guy] Lafleur was invisible and Gretz was all over the place. Wayne scored a hat trick and we just cruised at the end, holding a 6-2 lead. Near the close, the fans began a countdown and went out of their minds. Actually, I couldn't help but feel sorry for the Canadiens. Guys like Lafleur, Larry Robinson, Rejean Houle, [Serge] Savard and Lapointe were names I revered growing up in Lachute— and they had just gone under.

"It was, as the *Edmonton Sun* proclaimed the next day, 'INCREDIBLE!'"

Moog became as much a fixture in Edmonton as Northlands Coliseum. In 1982-83 he played in 50 regular-season games and 16 playoff matches as the Oilers went to the Stanley Cup finals, where they were beaten in four by the New York Islanders.

On another team Andy would have been *the* goalie, but the Oilers also felt comfortable with a youngster named Grant Fuhr. In 1983-84 the battle for the top spot was all

tied up when Fuhr took the lead, as well as a Stanley Cup ring.

That was it. Fuhr had become the go-to guy, while Moog was, for all intents and purposes, the back-up. This was an intolerable situation for a professional who believed he was equally competent. After playing on Stanley Cup champs in 1984, 1985 and 1987, Andy asked to be traded.

Sather refused and Moog left Edmonton to play for the Canadian National team and the 1988 Canadian Olympic team. "I felt that I was not being challenged," Andy explained. "I was not developing as a player. It was time to move on."

The Oilers cooperated by trading Moog's rights to the Boston Bruins. In Beantown he became a hero of sorts through five seasons. In 1990, 1991 and 1992, he played 20, 19 and 15 playoff games, respectively. He became a favorite in the manner of past Bruins goalie heroes such as Frankie Brimsek, but there was one essential difference: when Brimsek played, there was no NHL Players' Association. Now there was, and Moog stood front and center as its vice-president. He was outspoken on labor issues to the point of angering his Bruins bosses. Still, it was difficult for general manager Harry Sinden to dump Andy. His record was too good.

In 1992-93 he finished with a career-high 37 wins and went 17-1 in his last 18 games with a 1.88 goals-against average. He was, as Dallas Stars' GM Bob Gainey said, "able to carry his team."

Carry them, that is, up until the playoffs.

Perhaps it was an overload of work; perhaps it was just bad breaks. Whatever it was, Moog played uncharacteristically poorly in the 1993 playoffs, but there were good reasons. Don Moog had been stricken with lung cancer and his life was ebbing. Andy, who previously had missed three regular-season games, returned to be at his father's side. "It was a very difficult time," Andy recalled. It was equally difficult for the Bruins. Andy was not in top form and Boston quickly lost the first-round playoff to Buffalo in four consecutive games. Moog started three games and lost them all. His average climbed to an unsightly 5.22.

That was just the lever Sinden required. He sent Moog packing to Dallas in June 1993 for Jon Casey. "Hockey is a humbling game," said Moog. "You have to earn respect for yourself every time out. Every night."

Respect was restored in Texas. Moog became one of the top stars on the Stars and one of the NHL's workhorses. After four seasons there, he signed as a free agent, ironically, in Montreal and played in his final campaign.

By the end of 1997-98 Moog had chalked up 18 big-league years and 47,603 minutes played. That was the equivalent of over 793 hours, or about 33 consecutive days.

Following the end of his playing career, Moog became president of the Ft. Worth Brahmas minor league team.

Roy Conacher was one of the most unobtrusive but effective Bruin snipers in the pre-World War II era.

Roy Gordon Conacher

Born: Toronto, Ontario; October 5, 1916; died
December 29, 1984

Position: Left Wing

NHL Teams: Boston, 1938-42, 1945-46; Detroit,
1946-47; Chicago, 1947-52

Awards/Honors: NHL scoring leader, 1949

Roy CONACHER

Mention the name Conacher to a Canadian sports historian and the chances are the first names to be heard in response will be Lionel and Charlie.

Each is a distinguished member of the Hall of Fame. Lionel, who was an all-sports star, was named Canada's Athlete of the Half-Century in 1950. Charlie, who packed one of the hardest shots in hockey, starred for Toronto's "Gashouse Gang" Maple Leafs in the 1930s and later became an NHL coach in Chicago.

Their kid brother, Roy, had never intended to be a hockey player. He was more interested in softball. "Yet, it was inevitable that the youngest of Canada's famous hockey family would eventually carry the name of Conacher into NHL stardom, just as his brothers had done," said Canadian sportswriter Vince Lunny.

But Roy hardly won raves in his early stickhandling years. As a matter of fact, he was a borderline failure, twice being invited to the Bruins' training camp in the late 1930s and twice being rejected.

Manager Art Ross refused to give up on the lad, knowing full well about the family's bloodlines, so Ross dispatched Roy to the Kirkland Lake Blue Devils, a powerful senior team in Northern Ontario.

With the necessary seasoning, Conacher earned another tryout at the Hershey, Pennsylvania, training camp. Pleased with the results, Ross signed Roy to an NHL contract and put him on a line with Mel Hill and Pat McReavy to start the 1938-39 season.

"We were together for a month," Roy remembered, "and why Art Ross kept us that long I'll never know. We certainly weren't getting any goals. As a matter of fact, we were pathetic. Then, Bill Cowley, who had been out of the lineup with an injury, came back to play and one center had to go. Pat McReavy was elected and Bill centered Mel and me."

The ingredients blended together as sweetly as sugar and coffee. Conacher suddenly looked like a superstar and finished the campaign with a league-leading 26 goals. The Cowley-Hill-Conacher line afforded the Bruins a spectacular attack to complement the Kraut Line of Milt Schmidt, Bobby Bauer and Woody Dumart.

"Roy for the first time in his life began to do more than was expected of him," said Vince Lunny. "He might have won the Calder Trophy as rookie-of-the-year but it went to the fellow on the team whose job it was to prevent scoring."

Conacher's 37 points was more than any of the Krauts could produce and second only to Cowley's 42 points. The

Roy Conacher as a Bruin.

Bruins were, in relative terms, one of the NHL's all-time powerhouses, finishing first by 14 points over the runner-up New York Rangers.

During the 1939 playoffs, Conacher and Hill finished with six goals each, second to leader Gordie Drillon of Toronto. In terms of importance—not to mention poignancy—Conacher's most important goal was scored in the fourth game of the Stanley Cup finals against the Leafs.

Boston was leading the best-of-seven series, two-games-to-one, with the pivotal Game Four at Maple Leaf Gardens, where only a few years earlier, Roy sold programs to get in to see Charlie strut his stuff.

Just past the two-minute mark of the first period, Bingo Kampman of Toronto was penalized. Cowley snared the puck at the face-off and skimmed a power-play pass to Hill inside the defense. Spotting the unchecked Conacher, Hill dispatched a pass and Roy rifled the puck past goalie Turk Broda.

The one-goal lead held until almost the 13-minute mark of the third period, when Hill relieved Toronto's Nick Metz of the rubber. Hill immediately sent another pass to Conacher, who clinched the game with another unerring drive. Final score: Conacher 2, Toronto 0.

"That was my biggest thrill in hockey," Conacher later allowed. "It wasn't so much that I was fortunate to score but because Charlie and Lionel were in the audience."

Others would argue that Roy was even better in Game Five at Boston Garden. With the Cup-clincher within the Bruins' grasp, Conacher set up Hill for the opening goal and then, after Toronto tied the count at 1-1, Roy beat Broda at 17:34 of the second period. It turned out to be not only the winning goal in the 3-1 verdict but also the Cup-winner.

Even at the very top of his game, Roy was a noticeably less flamboyant performer than his older brothers. "As a result of the reputations established by Lionel and by Charlie in a lesser way, young Roy found his name both a help and a handicap," said Lunny. "Much was expected of him and Roy did exhibit a flair for goal-getting."

The Bruins finished first again in 1939-40 and a year later. By this time Roy had established himself among the top forwards in the league.

In 1940-41, Conacher helped linemate Cowley to the NHL scoring championship and once again led the Bruins in goal-scoring with 24. He had only nine penalty minutes, which included a fight that he won. At 6-1, 180 pounds, Roy could handle his fists but was disinclined to fight unless suitably provoked. As it happened, he was only involved in two fights as a Bruin and won each easily.

Then came a bigger fight, World War II. He volunteered for service in the Royal Canadian Air Force following the 1941-42 season, as did several other Bruins. Roy was posted overseas as a physical training instructor and was stationed at an air force base in Durham, England.

At first, Roy had decided he had had it with hockey, but when teammate Milt Schmidt—also with the RCAF at Durham—asked him to join the air corps hockey team, he agreed.

The armed forces stint took three of the best years from Conacher's hockey life, and how much it affected it is anyone's guess. But when he did return to Boston, the club's attitude toward him had changed.

Roy played only four games for the Bruins in 1945-46, scoring twice with one assist, before being traded to Detroit for Joe Carveth. He spent a season in the Motor City and then moved on to Chicago, where Roy played for brother Charlie, who then was coach.

Clearly, his hands had not lost their skill. In 1948-49 he was the leading scorer in the NHL (60 games, 30-24-54) and performed splendidly for Chicago until the 1951-52 campaign, when he skated in a dozen games and managed three goals and an assist.

Roy retired following the 1951-52 campaign, not quite as memorable as his brothers, Lionel and Charlie, but a star nonetheless.

Any Boston hockey fan who watched him deliver a Stanley Cup at Boston Garden in 1939 will vouch for that.

> "As a result of the reputations established by Lionel and by Charlie in a lesser way, young Roy found his name both a help and a handicap. "Much was expected of him and Roy did exhibit a flair for goal-getting."
>
> —Vince Lunny

Mel Hill went from obscure third-liner to playoff hero.

John Melvin (Mel "Sudden Death") Hill

Born: Glenboro, Manitoba; February 15, 1914;

died April 11, 1996

Position: Right Wing

NHL Teams: Boston, 1937-41; New York (A),

1941-42; Toronto, 1942-46

*H*e played only three full seasons as a Bruin, but he became a legend.

And for good reason, because Mel Hill to this day is the only National Hockey

League player to have earned—really and truly earned—the nickname "Sudden Death."

It all happened in his first full campaign in Beantown. In 1937-38, he was pro-

moted from the American Hockey League's Providence Reds to the big club and played

six games for Art Ross. The manager was mildly pleased as Hill scored two goals in his

brief rookie run.

For the 1938-39 season, Hill had been named a regular right wing on a line with

Roy Conacher and Gordie Pettinger. Over 46 games, he scored ten goals and ten assists.

There was nothing to suggest what would evolve in the playoffs.

The only man with the nickname "Sudden Death"—Mel Hill.

was a sharpshooter extraordinaire and worked well with Cowley. Logic dictated that if the Rangers suspected that Cowley would skim his passes to Conacher, then Hill might be overlooked by the New Yorkers.

This thought also entered the mind of Bruins' coach Art Ross, who finally passed the suggestion on to Cowley. Sure enough, late in the third sudden-death period, Cowley entered Rangers territory, carefully stickhandling the puck.

Meanwhile, Hill found an unguarded piece of ice near the goal crease. Cowley drifted into the corner of the Rangers zone and then dispatched a crisp feed to Hill. Mel's shot eluded goalie Davey Kerr and Boston had gained the important first win of the series.

Hill was a hero, to be sure, in Beantown but the best was yet to come—at Boston Garden. Game Two was fought to a draw again after three periods, but this time the overtime end came quickly; courtesy of Mel Hill and Bill Cowley.

In a remarkable case of déjà-vu, Cowley again orchestrated the play—this time it was a drop pass inside the New York zone—and Hill supplied the winner, which was a relatively long (40-foot) shot past the embattled Kerr.

If Hill wasn't the toast of Boston by this time, it was only because there also were players like Eddie Shore, Frankie Brimsek and Milt Schmidt on the roster. They combined to dispose of the Rangers, 4-1, in Game Three, thereby setting the stage for a four-game sweep.

Whether it was overconfidence or simply a Rangers club that would not lie down and die, the series would not be easily wrapped up by the Bruins. New York valiantly rallied, winning Games Four, Five and Six, forcing a seventh and final match.

The date was April 2, 1939, and to no one's surprise, Boston Garden bulged for the climactic encounter. Until this point in NHL history, no team had ever won the first three games of the playoffs and then lost the next four straight. Yet that was the fate that confronted the Bruins if they couldn't dispatch the Rangers in yet another overtime match.

Hill's heroics had fans awaiting the start of the third extra session. They wondered who would be the hero—if there was to be one—among the home skaters. Schmidt, perhaps. Conacher the sharpshooter, or maybe even the indomitable Eddie Shore. Or could anyone imagine Mel Hill rescuing the Hub skaters yet again?

It was then that Hill suddenly emerged as a phenom. It was a situation where everything fell into place for the heretofore third-stringer. In fact, if one were to have scripted the Hill scenario in advance, it would have seemed too implausible to have really happened.

But it did in the memorable Spring of 1939. On March 21, 1939, to be specific, the Bruins faced their bitter rivals from Manhattan at Madison Square Garden. The Rangers—like Boston—were a team on the rise and loomed as a formidable foe.

The even quality of play was reflected in the score after three periods of regulation hockey. It was 1-1, and the count remained that way through the first, then the second and into the third sudden-death overtime period.

During the extra sessions, Hill—he had scored ten goals during the 1938-39 campaign—hardly was a standout. But he was playing on a line with a pair of superior forwards, Bill Cowley and Roy Conacher, either of whom was capable of breaking open the game.

As center, Cowley instinctively would keep his eyes out for Conacher as the likely recipient of his passes. Roy

> *Camping on his favorite acreage in front of the Rangers' crease, Hill did not have to wait long. Cowley quickly distributed the puck, and before Gardiner could properly react, Hill scored the biggest goal of his young hockey life. When the red light flashed, not only had Boston won the series, but Mel Hill had a nickname for the rest of his NHL life— "Sudden Death."*

As the minutes ticked by in the third session, no result was in sight. Then, as the seven-minute mark was about to give way to eight, Eddie Shore prepared a Boston counterthrust. He skimmed the biscuit to Conacher, who fired a heavy shot at the Rangers' netminder.

Bert Gardiner was forced to extend himself, but he did make the save and kept play alive by tossing the puck into his own end zone. His assumption was that a teammate would recover and move back into the Bruins zone.

This time, however, the Rangers' defensemen were slow and outhustled by Cowley, who snared the rubber behind the net. By now Hill knew what he had to do—and he did it.

Camping on his favorite acreage in front of the Rangers' crease, Hill did not have to wait long. Cowley quickly distributed the puck, and before Gardiner could properly react, Hill scored the biggest goal of his young hockey life.

When the red light flashed, not only had Boston won the series, but Mel Hill had a nickname for the rest of his NHL life— "Sudden Death."

His career never was the same after that, especially in Boston, where his numbers never matched the expectations of fans or, for that matter, the management.

During the 1940-41 season, Hill was dispatched briefly to the American Hockey League, where he played a total of six games with the Hershey Bears and Springfield Indians. On June 27, 1941, Hill was traded by Boston to the Brooklyn Americans for cash. He tallied 14 goals and 23 assists in his first and only season with the Americans before being acquired by the Toronto Maple Leafs in 1942. He spent four years in Toronto, where he played some of his most productive hockey. In his first season with the Leafs, he scored a career-best 44 points in 49 games, with 17 goals and 27 assists. Hill was also a key member of the 1944-45 Toronto squad that captured a Stanley Cup, registering two goals and five points in 13 playoff games.

In 1946, Hill was again demoted to the minor leagues, where he played the final six seasons of his career with the Pittsburgh Hornets and the Regina Caps. He retired in 1952.

Leo Labine—he could score, he could intimidate and he could talk a blue streak.

Leo Gerald "The Lion" Labine

Born: Haileybury, Ontario; July 22, 1931

Position: Right Wing

NHL Teams: Boston, 1951-61; Detroit 1961-62

Leo **LABINE**

*I*f there was a Derek Sanderson before Derek Sanderson played for the Bruins, his name was Leo Labine.

Brash, irreverent, tough, funny. You name it, if the term fit Sanderson, it fit Labine as well during a nine-year career on Causeway Street that was filled with incidents.

More important, it should be established that the native of Haileybury, Ontario, was first and foremost an awfully good hockey player. But, like Sanderson, he never quite reached the greatness level which some observers believed was within his grasp.

At a time during the 1950s when the National Hockey League was filled with starry right wings such as Maurice Richard, Gordie Howe and Bernie Geoffrion, Labine was right behind them.

"Leo was a great team player," said his coach, Lynn Patrick. "He would never let up."

But ever since he had been a kid player in Northern Ontario, Labine was known as a prankster, if not a buffoon. The Montreal Canadiens invited Leo to their camp in 1948 and managing director Frank Selke, Sr. called Labine the best prospect they had.

"Unfortunately," Selke explained, "Labine caused so much trouble needling our veterans and generally making a nuisance of himself that I had to put him straight. Leo ended up telling me how to operate the club. I told him that life was too short for the likes of him and I released him."

Selke's loss was Boston's gain. He eventually signed on with the Bruins' farm team in Barrie, Ontario, and made his Bruins debut in 1951-52. "Leo could dish it out in those days," said Montreal hockey writer Vince Lunny, "but he couldn't take it. He parted the hair of Chicago's Gus Mortson with his stick and otherwise got himself into deep trouble."

Lynn Patrick impressed upon his prodigy the need for discretion and Leo learned. One night in Toronto, the Maple Leafs agitator Eric Nesterenko broke a hockey stick over Labine's head. "You shouldn't do such things," said Leo. "You'll get a penalty."

Sure enough, Nesterenko was whistled off while Leo spent the next two minutes laughing.

Labine's clashes with Rocket Richard were headline-makers. During the 1952 playoffs, Leo nearly killed the Rocket with a blindside check. On the other hand, Richard—a prominent francophone—took issue with Labine in print because he felt that Labine was a French name and yet Leo was ignoring his heritage.

"Labine is ashamed to admit he can speak his native tongue," chided Richard.

Incensed by the charge, Labine shot back, "My mother is Irish and my father's family has been in Ontario for years. The only thing French about me is my name. I can't speak the language."

That night when the Bruins took the ice against the Canadiens at The Forum, Labine whizzed by the Rocket. *"Comment ca va, mon vieux?"* he asked in perfect French, carefully coached by teammate Réal Chevrefils. *"Prenez guard ce soir."* (Translated: "How are you, old man? Watch yourself tonight.")

Later in the game Richard jammed his stick butt into Labine's ribs. Leo barked, "Look, Rocket, you've got 32 teeth. Do you want to try for 16?"

> **"If nature had endowed Leo with the attributes of a left winger—instead of his competing on the right side with Gordie Howe and Rocket Richard—he would have emerged as an All-Star."**
>
> —Sportswriter Vince Lunny

By this time Labine had become so efficient that Lynn Patrick told the press that he wouldn't even trade Labine for The Rocket. "Leo had become the most popular player to come into the league in ten years," said Patrick. "The only player I'd consider trading him for is Jean Beliveau."

The sad truth is that Labine never came close to achieving those lofty goals. He never scored more than 24 goals in a season (1954-55) nor more than 47 points (18-29 in 1956-57). At a time when it appeared that he had a chance for All-Star status, his star abruptly plummeted.

He was traded to the Detroit Red Wings with Vic Stasiuk for Gary Aldcorn, Murray Oliver and Tom McCarthy in January 1961. Just as his counterpart in Boston, Lynn Patrick, had high hopes for Labine, so too did Jack Adams in Detroit.

Sadly, Leo's production was so insignificant that the Red Wings dropped him after the 1961-62 season and Labine played his last five seasons with the Los Angeles Blades in the Western Hockey League.

Reflecting on his career, Labine chuckled, "I was lucky to get out of the game alive."

Well, he did accumulate 730 penalty minutes over 643 games played but, if nothing else, he was a thorn in the side of opponents, especially Les Canadiens.

"I made a lot of Frenchmen famous by losing to them," Labine concluded. "I just wish we had better players on our teams."

On the other hand, Leo made a lot of Bostonians happy because of the upbeat manner in which he treated hockey and because of the talent he displayed.

Writing in *Sport* magazine, Vince Lunny commented, "If nature had endowed Leo with the attributes of a left winger—instead of his competing on the right side with Gordie Howe and Rocket Richard—he would have emerged as an All-Star."

Leo Labine (center) battles Edgar Laprade of the Rangers for the elusive puck.

Johnny Peirson and his magic stick.

John Frederick Peirson

Born: Winnipeg, Manitoba; July 21, 1925

Position: Right Wing

NHL Teams: Boston, 1946-58

Johnny **PEIRSON**

The National Hockey League was not in John Frederick Peirson's sights while he served in the Canadian Army during World War II. Education was primary in the Winnipeg native's mind. He had attended McGill University in Montreal and could have pursued a business career right then and there.

However, a chance meeting with a Canadian Army acquaintance started Peirson on the road to Boston. One day after his discharge he met Don Penniston, who was coaching the Bruins farm team in Hershey.

Penniston invited his Army pal to Hershey where he impressed the Bruins' scouting staff. He was signed to a contract and made the varsity in the fall of 1946.

It was the start of a distinguished—if not sensational—career, although there were bumps at the beginning.

Johnny Peirson (#23, back row) was the "go-to" guy for the Bruins from 1948-49 through 1953-54.

The right wing broke his wrist in a preseason practice game and returned to Hershey for more experience. A season later he was recalled for the final fifteen games of the 1947-48 season and scored four goals and two assists. He followed that with five playoff games, averaging a point a game (two goals, three assists).

"I had decided to give pro hockey an opportunity for a year or two," Peirson recalled. "The money they were paying in the NHL at the time was not very substantial, but I could save some, and if I didn't get too far, I could always quit and go back to school."

But Peirson's goal-scoring talent ensured his varsity status. He often played alongside Paul Ronty and Ken Smith, giving the Bruins one of the league's better offensive units. In three seasons, the black-haired sharpshooter scored 68 goals.

"I considered myself an above-average but not great player," said Peirson. "I used the term 'above-average'

because I was a better-balanced player, a forward who knew how to backcheck. I had some defensive skills as well as being able to find the net."

From 1948-49 through 1953-54, Peirson was the go-to guy, scoring 20 or more goals in four seasons during an epoch when a 20-goal scorer was roughly equivalent to a .300 hitter in baseball.

"The older I got, the better I played," said Peirson, who played a major part in the Bruins 1952-53 playoff success. Johnny totaled three goals and six assists for nine points in eleven games. His six assists ranked him second-best— teammate Fleming Mackell was first with seven—of all playoff performers.

During Peirson's decade in Beantown, the Bruins usually were in the playoffs, although they never won a Stanley Cup. "We never had a powerhouse," he explained, "but we had some representative teams. Nobody blew us out of the building."

At 5-11, 170 pounds, Peirson never could run over the opposition but he played the game hard. In retrospect, he once told author Frank Pagnucco in the book *Heroes* that he regretted not having fortified his physique more than he had.

"I wish I had worked more diligently on my upper-body strength because I would have been a better player," said Peirson. "I lost a lot of battles and wasn't able to do what I would like to have done from the viewpoint of strength."

He was strong enough to last a decade in the bigs, playing for only one team, the Bruins. In 1951 he married the former Barbara Hunt of Wellesley. Following the 1957-1958 season, John retired and joined his father-in-law's furniture business.

In addition, Peirson became a journalist of sorts, as an analyst on Bruins' telecasts. He remained a popular figure throughout New England not merely because of his excellence as a Bruin, but also as quite simply a nice guy who became a credit to the community.

Rick Middleton, deft with the disk.

Rick "Nifty" Middleton

Born: Toronto, Ontario; December 4, 1953

Position: Right Wing

NHL Teams: New York (R), 1974-76; Boston, 1976-88

Awards/Honors: Lady Byng, 1982

Rick **MIDDLETON**

*I*t is a measure of the esteem with which Rick Middleton was held by hockey sages that he was recommended as a candidate for the Hall of Fame.

Middleton didn't make it, but he permanently endeared himself to New Englanders with a brand of artistry that helped provide balance to a roster sprinkled with tough guys, characters and the irrepressible coach, Don "Grapes" Cherry.

Originally a New York Ranger, Middleton arrived in Boston for the 1976-77 season precisely when Cherry was reaching his apex on Causeway Street.

After a so-so (20-22-42) opening season with the Bruins, Middleton blossomed under Grapes' coaching and soon was being called "Nifty" around Boston Garden.

One day somebody asked why he was nicknamed "Nifty". Forward Keith Crowder had an immediate answer: "Just watch him."

What they saw was a dazzling skater who was fulfilling the potential that the Rangers believed he had when they brought him to the NHL for the first time in 1974-75. He could shoot with the best, skate even better and create plays in the manner of a Jean Beliveau.

"I've seen them all," said Brad Park, a Hall of Famer who was Middleton's teammate, "and Nifty was the best one-on-one player in hockey at the time. You could take anyone in the league, give Nifty the puck and 90-percent of the time he'd turn the other guy inside out."

When he was Rangers general manager, John Ferguson dealt Middleton to Boston in exchange for Ken Hodge. Fergie insisted that he was forced into the deal by Phil Esposito, who was languishing on Broadway and wanted Hodge, his former linemate, to skate with him again. In retrospect, Ferguson called it the worst deal he had ever made.

While Hodge lasted only one and a quarter seasons with the Rangers, Middleton spent a decade with the Bruins, most of the time as a star. Writing for *Sports Illustrated*, Mike DelNegro observed that Nifty combined "superb quickness and stickhandling with unusual balance and instinct."

Cherry employed him in every conceivable job from penalty-killing and power-playing as well as taking a regular turn. At 5-11, 170 pounds, Middleton was not an impressive physical presence but his numbers certainly were awesome.

In 1979-80 he had a team-high ninety-two points on forty goals and fifty-two assists. A year later he topped the century mark (47-58-105), which was remarkable, considering the mucking-type game employed by the Bruins.

"Boston had a backward team in those days," said an NHL coach. "Except for Middleton, they got almost no offense from their forwards. Except for Middleton, they got their offense from the defense. It should have been the other way around."

His best season was 1983-84, when he reached 105 points (47-58), although his primary mentor, Cherry, had long gone.

"Don changed my whole philosophy about hockey," Middleton explained. "I became a complete player because of Don. I always knew how to carry the puck and play offensive hockey, but Grapes taught me how to be in the right position so I wouldn't waste any steps. It was amazing how things worked out when I learned how to do it his way. Even just by backchecking I got a lot of offensive opportunities."

Cherry: "I have to hand it to Middleton. When he came over from New York, he had a reputation as a free spirit. From the way people were talking, you would have thought he had committed everything short of murder. But for me he did everything I asked of him."

Middleton never earned a Stanley Cup ring, but he put up impressive numbers along the way. "It was no secret," said Rick. "I didn't have to fly up and down the rink to be effective. I just went with the flow, waited for an opening and then pounced."

One of Nifty's most memorable games—and one of the most arresting in Bruins annals—was Game Seven of the 1979 playoff against the Montreal Canadiens. Over a span of eleven playoffs games, Rick scored four times, including a memorable goal in that game.

After Les Canadiens had stormed back to tie Boston, 3-3, late in the game, Nifty beat Ken Dryden with only minutes remaining to give Boston a one-goal lead and what seemed at the time to be a certain berth in the Stanley Cup Finals. Suddenly, a too-many-men-on-the-ice penalty left the Bruins shorthanded. Guy Lafleur tied the score and Montreal won in overtime.

"I never felt so mentally and physically drained over a period of a few weeks as after that series," Middleton confessed. "The intensity was greater in that series than it had been in the two Cup finals that we had lost to them the two previous years. After a couple of weeks I would start to get over it, but then I would think about it some more and still get depressed."

When the Bruins dealt penalty-killing specialist Greg Sheppard to Pittsburgh, it opened up an area of the game that Nifty had not been accustomed to as a Ranger. "In New York," he remembered, "my job had always been to go to the net, to score. Before I came to Boston, if anybody ever told me to cover some player on the other team, I honestly couldn't remember that happening."

Cherry's insistence on a total game made a keen impression on Nifty, although the transformation into a

> "I have to hand it to Middleton. When he came over from New York he had a reputation as a free spirit. From the way people were talking you would have thought he had committed everything short of murder. But for me he did everything I asked of him."
>
> —Don Cherry

total performer took a while. "It came step by step," he said. "In late games I suddenly found that I was still on the ice. I got a whiff of confidence. I started to see how playing defense led into playing offense. It was weird, but checking made things happen. It opened up the ice. I'd get passes at the blue line, not at the circle."

By 1983-84 Middleton was ranked among the NHL's top forwards. The term "Nifty" was now accepted throughout the league as a signature of greatness by friend and foe alike. "He was the most exciting one-on-one player in hockey when he was in his prime," said Wayne Cashman, a teammate for most of Middleton's NHL career.

Were it not for Sinden's sagacity and Cherry's patience, historians today might consider the Hodge-Middleton deal a wash. But Sinden understood what he had obtained and was less surprised than others by the excellent results.

"We knew how good he was at least three or four years before those who started raving about him later on," said Sinden. "He had a great presence of mind and uncanny hands."

His feet also were a bit different from those of ordinary hockey players. Because of them, he had what one writer described as an "ankles-in, chop-chop, power-shift-here-we-go style of skating." It invariably put so much stress on Middleton's blades that they had to be secured to the boot with special copper studs instead of conventional steel rivets.

"If it wasn't for the copper studs, he would have torn the blades off every game," said Bruins equipment specialist Dan Canney. "We only had one other guy who we had to do that for and that was Bobby Orr."

One of Nifty's teammates and roomates during their Boston heyday was Peter McNab, who was the beneficiary of many a Middleton pass. "If you went to a spot," said McNab, now a television analyst in Denver, "you might not know when or how the puck would come but it would come. And if I was ready for it, I was going to have a great scoring chance."

Middleton's last big year as a Bruin was 1986-87 when he hit for sixty-eight points (31-37) in seventy-six games. His accuracy was the talk of goaltenders such as Rogie Vachon, who played both against and with Nifty.

Nifty checking out the scene.

"Even in warm-ups, he was able to pick the corners," said Vachon. "When I faced him, I knew that I couldn't stay back in the crease. He was so quick and never panicked. It was very tough for a goaltender to outguess him."

Middleton: "I would watch the goalie and let him move first. If he came out—which was the way I liked it—I would fake around him. If he stayed in or backed up, I would pick a corner. I usually went for the top corners."

He closed out his NHL career in Boston. The year was 1987-88 and the production was down. In fifty-nine games he had only thirty-two points (13-19), but he never lost the respect of fans, teammates and management.

Rick Middleton always was—how do they say it?—Nifty.

"Sugar Jim" Henry in his prime as a Bruins goalie.

Samuel James "Sugar Jim" Henry

Born: Winnipeg, Manitoba; October 23, 1920

Position: Goaltender

NHL Teams: New York (R), 1941-42, 1945-48;

Chicago, 1948-49; Boston, 1951-55

Jim HENRY

With his hair slicked back neatly around a part on the side, Jim Henry was deserving of the nickname "Sugar Jim."

He was a sweet guy and a sweet goaltender in the most positive sense of each word.

Henry also was a fighter who managed to survive all manner of injuries during an era when goaltenders played without masks and with gloves that looked more like fruit baskets than hockey equipment.

Longtime Boston fans remember the battling Bruins' goalie best for a moment at the conclusion of a fierce series against Les Canadiens in the 1951-52 season.

In this classic photo, Henry (left) pumps Richard's hand.

The series was tied at three games apiece—thanks in large part to Henry's goaltending—and on the morning of the final game, Sugar Jim was not in the best of physical shape. His nose had been smacked by a puck in the preceding game, and when he got off the train in Montreal, he couldn't see, except straight ahead. His eyes were almost shut tight.

For three and a half hours he stretched out on the rubbing table in the Bruins' dressing room while trainer Hammy Moore alternately applied hot and cold applications to get the swelling down and the eyes open.

Sugar Jim was determined to play, and play he did, holding the Canadiens to a tie until late in the third period, when Maurice "Rocket" Richard scored a spectacular goal to beat Henry and win the series for the Habs.

By game's end, Henry was a physical wreck. His eye was totally black and his head filled with wounds covered by dried blood. Even his goalie pads had been torn.

A photo taken on the shake-hand line immediately after the Bruins loss shows Henry pumping the hand of Richard, who had scored the winning goal against him half an hour earlier. Later in the dressing room, someone mentioned to Henry that he had a lot of courage playing with impaired vision.

"After coming this far," he replied, "you can't quit. No matter what, I wanted to stay in there to the bitter end. That's how I felt. Nothing was going to keep me out of that game."

Another time he was asked about his profession.

"When it came to goaltending," Henry remarked, "I always used to say, 'You don't have to be crazy, but it helps!'"

Henry made his NHL debut with the Rangers at the start of World War II and led New York to a first-place finish in 1941-42. He then enlisted in the Canadian armed forces and returned to the Blueshirts in time for the 1945-46 season.

By that time, the seventh NHL club, the New York Americans, had folded, and players were distributed among the six other teams. American goalie Chuck Rayner—a close friend of Henry—was awarded to the Rangers, giving the Big Apple sextet two topflight netminders.

Rayner eventually was given the full-time job, while Henry bounced from the Chicago Blackhawks to the Bruins, starting with the 1951-52 season. Sugar Jim was 31 years old at the time, and not much was expected of him since Henry already had spent two years in the minors with Omaha, Kansas City and Indianapolis.

Amazingly, Sugar Jim played every single one of Boston's seventy games in 1951-52 and put together a handsome 2.51 goals-against average. The club finished fourth during the regular campaign and then faced the mighty Montreal Canadiens in the semifinal round.

The series went a full seven games before the Habs

edged Boston 3-1, but Henry was considered the Bruins' playoff hero—and a very modest one at that. "He was humble and he was thankful for his chance to play with the Bruins," a Boston reporter noted. "He was thankful for the help his mates gave him, and for the way the Boston fans received him. But it should have been the other way around because without Henry the Bruins might never have come so close to providing a major upset."

Nobody appreciated Henry's work more than Bruins president Walter Brown. At the conclusion of the 1952 playoffs, Brown shook Henry's hand at the breakup party and said, "You had a great season, Jim. Do you think you could please have another one next year?"

Henry smiled and blinked through his discolored eyes. "Just have me back," he said sincerely.

Sugar Jim was delighted to be a Bruin for many reasons, but he emphasized that in his long career he had never played on a team with more harmony and more spirit. Part of the credit belonged to coach Lynn Patrick, son of Lester Patrick, who had originally signed Henry to a Rangers contract at the start of the 1940s.

"I never tried to tamper with Sugar Jim's style or technique," said Lynn Patrick. "Why should I? He knew the business, which was keeping the puck out of the net."

However, in the first playoff game of the 1952-53 Stanley Cup semifinals between Boston and Detroit, Henry's game fell apart. The Red Wings, who were heavy favorites to win the series, played to form and crushed the Bruins. The final tally was 7-0.

Sugar Jim was ridiculed by the Motor City media. Reporters made him the "goat" of the game and implied that he would be a soft touch for the rest of the series.

"Henry, who hid his actual feelings behind a habitual smile, absorbed the ridicule—and sizzled inwardly," said Roger Barry, who covered the Bruins for the *Quincy Patriot-Ledger*. "For the remainder of that historic series, he was wonderful."

Although the Red Wings were loaded with such aces as Gordie Howe, Ted Lindsay and Terry Sawchuk, the Bruins rebounded to win Game Two 5-3. Henry followed that outstanding effort by beating Sawchuk, 2-1, in a match

that wasn't settled until Jack McIntyre fired the winner at 12:29 of the first sudden death.

Red Wings coach Tommy Ivan was the first to praise Sugar Jim. "You can't say it was the Boston defense that did it," said Ivan, "for we took a lot of shots at Henry. It was the goaler who really hurt us the most."

High-scoring defenseman Red Kelly, one of the best of the Red Wings, shook his head. "Sugar Jim was just great," he said.

Boston won the series in six games, capping one of the most unlikely upsets big-league hockey has ever known. "There are undoubtedly ways of beating the Bruins," said Roger Barry, "but one of them was not by belittling Jim Henry."

A year later, during the 1953-54 season, a similar episode took place. This time Maple Leafs boss Conn Smythe suggested Henry was losing his touch. Sugar Jim's answer was to toss a shutout at the Leafs.

"Smythe was supposed to be a keen hockey man," said Sugar Jim, "but he must have been slipping by then. He said that I wasn't using my hands anymore; that I was blocking shots with my body. It surprised me to hear that from such an authority, since I never used my hands much in all the years I was playing goal.

"What any goaltender knows is that some nights we seem to miss everything and other nights we just can't miss. Every shot, no matter how good, seems to come right at us."

Injuries began taking their toll on Henry's body. After the 1953-54 season, he frankly observed, "I don't know how much longer I can keep going. I'm not getting younger and I'm starting to feel that way."

His buddy from Ranger days, Chuck Rayner, already had retired because of injuries, but Sugar Jim decided to continue. He played 26 regular-season games in 1954-55 and three playoff games in a losing semifinal round against his nemesis, *Les Canadiens*.

For Henry it was a relatively short career as a Bruin, but as noble as they come. And the photo of the battered goaltender shaking hands with the warrior-scorer, Rocket Richard, remains a testimony to the guts of the man known as Sugar Jim.

"I never tried to temper with Sugar Jim's style or technique. Why should I? He knew the business, which was keeping the puck out of the net."

—Lynn Patrick

Willie O'Ree as a Bruins rookie.

William "Willie" O'Ree

Born: Fredericton, New Brunswick;

October 15, 1935

Position: Left Wing

NHL Teams: Boston 1957-58, 1960-61

Willie
O'REE

The Bruins had the distinction of breaking big league hockey's "color barrier" in 1958 when forward Willie O'Ree was signed by Boston.

Since then, many people have tried to portray O'Ree as "The Jackie Robinson of Hockey." This is understandable, although somewhat overstated. O'Ree has frequently—and earnestly—played down this aspect of his lengthy professional hockey career. Willie understood from the moment the first comparisons were made that there was a key distinction between the baseball hero and himself.

Robinson not only opened the door for his race, he also immediately emerged as a superstar whose feats would become legendary far beyond his home at Ebbets Field in Brooklyn.

The fact that O'Ree played a total of only 45 NHL games for the Bruins should not be minimized. Based on ability alone, he could have enjoyed a decade-long career. He skated effortlessly, shot accurately and possessed a sharp radar for The Game's other nuances. But he was restricted in an area that had nothing to do with his color but everything to do with his physical grasp of his ice surroundings. By the time he had entered the NHL, O'Ree had lost sight in his right eye because of an accident he had sustained in junior hockey.

Can you imagine Jackie Robinson coming to the Dodgers in 1947 and then competing as a big-leaguer with only one eye? Yet one-eyed Willie O'Ree was able to surmount hockey's vast physical and emotional challenges to reach the top league in his sport.

Many who saw O'Ree perform, this author included, believe that he was a capable NHLer who could skate with the best of them. Thus, it was with some amazement that NHL observers learned that O'Ree had not returned to The Show after the Bruins released him in 1961.

He seemed better than many of his peers and certainly faster. What happened? Only recently have pieces of this mysterious puzzle fallen into place.

For starters, nobody knew about his optical limitations when O'Ree became a Bruin. It was accepted that he was blessed with two good eyes, like every other NHL performer.

Although Willie doesn't know this for a fact, it is likely that once Bruins management became aware of O'Ree's defect, they consulted an NHL bylaw that specifically forbids any team to employ a player who is afflicted with hampered vision, such as O'Ree.

It certainly didn't limit Willie's style. Despite the setback, he continued his pro career in what was then a powerful Western Hockey League. "He became one of the most popular and productive players in pro," says Max McNab, who operated the WHL's San Diego Gulls when O'Ree was there.

In spite of his relatively brief NHL career, O'Ree emerged as a significant pro hockey personality because he was a pioneer. What was it like for him? During a visit to New York, O'Ree met with the author at the NHL's Manhattan offices. Articulate, energetic and forthright, O'Ree expounded on his remarkable career.

Fischler: Describe your route to the NHL.

O'Ree: I am the youngest of 12 children. I started skating at age three, started playing hockey at age five. I was born and raised in Fredericton, New Brunswick, Canada. Naturally, in the wintertime everything freezes over: the streets, ponds, lakes, rivers, you name it. I used to skate to school. We lived in an area with a good-sized backyard. My dad used to scrape it out, throw the hose on it and there was a rink. And I used to skate for hours there, skate to school, skate back from school. I was on the ice every

opportunity I had. I never played on an indoor rink until I was 15 years old.

SF: Who was *your* team?

WO'R: Montreal Canadiens.

SF: Why?

WO'R: They were winning Stanley Cups in the '50s. Maurice Richard stands out in my mind, Doug Harvey, Geoffrion. Everyone in the New Brunswick area was a Montreal fan. There were some Toronto Maple Leaf fans, but I would say 70/30 Montreal. I used to listen to Foster Hewitt on the radio. I would run home on Saturday night and turn it on, and Mom and Dad would be there, just ears to the radio, and listen to Foster Hewitt and the games.

SF: When did you realize that you could be a professional?

WO'R: It was my first year of junior. I was scouted by Phil Watson. I was playing for the Fredericton Capitals in the New Brunswick Senior League. I was 16 or 17. And Phil came and scouted me, and said, "I am putting a team together, the Quebec Frontenacs. I think you'd be an asset to our club. I have watched you play the last couple of years, and how would you like to come away to Quebec?"

I talked to my mom and dad, and then told him, "Phil, I am going to stay and play here and finish my education." And he said, "Willie, you are missing a great opportunity. I have seen other players, other black players." This was after Manny McIntyre, but he says, "I really feel you could be the first of your race to play in the National Hockey League. You have everything: you can skate, shoot, stickhandle, handle yourself, you have the size. There is only one thing, your color. There hasn't been a black man in the NHL." So I went away to Quebec. I played with Phil. He convinced me.

SF: How old were you?

WO'R: Seventeen. I think the Montreal Junior Canadiens beat us out in the playoffs. I had a good year, but the thought entered my mind about playing in the National Hockey League. I was in Quebec, playing on a team, having a heck of a year.

SF: How did the opposition treat you when you were with Quebec?

WO'R: Not good. I played in Quebec, but in some of the other cities, most of the guys were French, and they would have the name-calling and stuff. I used to do a lot of fighting when I first started, when I first went with Phil. He warned me, "Will," he said, "you are going to get an awful lot of crap. You are going to get guys calling you stuff. Don't let it bother you. You have my solid promise that anything you do on the ice has 100 percent backup from me. Anything you do on the ice, if it is for the good of the team, don't worry about it. If you have to fight every game, fight every game. If it's in the best interest of the club, then go ahead and do it."

SF: So you went back after Quebec?

WO'R: No, that was it. The next year, I got a letter from the Canadiens saying, "Your contract has been acquired by the Montreal Canadiens. You will report to the Kitchener Junior Canucks." Nice letter, Montreal letterhead. So I went and played in Kitchener. I was playing on a line with Walter Bradley and Stan Baloo. We had a hell of a line, scored a lot. We were called the BOB line: Baloo, O'Ree, Bradley.

SF: What was it like?

WO'R: I was playing with guys who could score goals, skate, shoot. My coach, Jack Stewart, told me the same thing. He said, "Willie, you are probably going to get a lot of smack, but I have watched you play in the last two years. I have read about you. You can excel above a lot of these hockey players." He also told me, "You could be the first one of your color to play in the National Hockey League." Well, again, it kind of went in one ear, out the other. All I knew was that I was on a team.

And then, unfortunately, we were playing in Guelph one night. Kent Douglas, a big, burly guy who eventually played for the Toronto Maple Leafs was a teammate of mine. He and I have the puck behind the net. I go in, the defenseman comes in and crosschecks me and I go up against the boards. Then the other defenseman comes in behind the net and runs at me and I step aside, get the puck and see Kent Douglas out in the slot. So I pass the puck out to him. Then I go out in front of the net to position myself, the defenseman comes around the other way and crosschecks me across the back of the head. As he does, he swings my body around. I try to look to see where the puck is coming, and as I bring my stick down, Kent just shoots the puck. It hits a defenseman on the shoulder and comes over and hits me flat here in the face and breaks my nose.

That is what caused 97% damage in my right eye. I was still conscious, but I remember I had dropped to my knees. They took me to the hospital and they did surgery. I was in the hospital about four or five days, and when I opened my eyes, I could see just a light out of my good eye, and I couldn't see anything out of my right eye. And I thought I was blind.

So a few days later, more sight came back into my eye, and more sight, and then I had 20/20 in the left eye, but couldn't see anything out of the right. I was out eight weeks from hockey. I will never forget when Dr. Henderson said, "Mr. O'Ree, I'm sorry, but you won't be able to play hockey anymore." I said, "What do you mean?" And he said, "There was considerable damage to the back of your retina." And he said at that time that there was no operation that could heal this. So I said, "But I was just getting started."

After eight weeks I could still see out of my left eye, up and down, to the side. "I am going to start skating again with the club," I told people. So I go out and start skating, handling the puck again. Then I started passing a little bit.

And then I started playing again. I was a left-handed shot playing left wing. Consequently, all my passes were coming from my right side. Usually, I could be looking this way and pick the puck up. But I couldn't see it, so I had to turn my head more to pick it up with my left eye. Consequently, I was getting hit a lot more by guys who never could catch me before. It was because they were coming on my blind side. But I kept at it. Pucks were going under my stick or across, and I was thinking, "Oh, God, I never used to do this."

That was my last year. I didn't know what I was going to do. I went home, and I told my mom and dad, "Well, that's it, I played my last game in junior. I don't know if I am going to get a shot at a pro contract or not." I took my mother to Bridgetown, Nova Scotia, to visit my sister. We're there three or four days, and all of a sudden there is a knock on the door. My sister answers the door, and I am in the other room, and my sister says, "Yes, Willie is here. May I ask who is calling?"

"Punch Imlach."

So I go out, and say, "Mr. Imlach!" And he said, "Hi, Willie, how are you doing? I found that you were here, and I wanted to come over. I have watched you play the last couple of years and I would like to talk to you about signing a pro contract." And I said, "I don't know. I was going to school and..." After a few days, he came back and he said, "Willie, I am putting a team together in Quebec called the Quebec Aces in the strong Quebec Senior League and I think you would be an asset to the team."

I went to camp and Punch wanted to sign me to a contract. So I told my mom. Punch had a contract for $3,500. That was my playing contract, and he gave me $500 for signing. Back in 1956, I was just 19 years old. So I said, "Well, I dunno Punch, that isn't a lot of money."

"Well, yes," he said. "I have some guys here who have played pro four or five years making $6,000." He is telling me this, and I said, "Wait a minute. I can score 25 goals in this league if I don't get hurt. If I score 25 goals, I would like a bonus of $300. And you say you are putting a championship team together. Well, if we get in the semifinals, I want $200. And if we win everything, I would like $500." And he said, "No, no, no . . . $200 to $100." Well, to make a long story short, I signed. And we won everything that year, including the Duke of Edinburgh Trophy.

I played with the Aces one year, then Punch wanted to sign me to a two-year contract. He said, "I'll give you X amount of dollars for so-and-so. You know, Willie, I'll treat you right." Then he was the third person who told me, "You could be the first of your race to play in the National Hockey League. You've got everything."

Punch told me this and I played in '57, came back in '58 and he said, "You could be the first." Sure enough, they get a call: "The Bruins want you in Montreal. They had a couple of injuries."

SF: How did your eye improve?

WO'R: It didn't improve. I saw five or six specialists and they all told me the same thing: when the puck hit me, it caused so much damage to the retina, there was nothing they could do. I accepted that for a while until, all of a sudden, I started getting these tremendous pains in my eye. So the doctor prescribed some drops, which I put in my eye four times a day. That helped for a while, but then it started to get worse. So they prescribed other drops. It got to the point where I saw this specialist, and he said, "Willie, it seems these drops are not doing any good. There are two alternatives. We can inject a serum into the eye, which would deaden the eye." In other words, I would be looking at something, turn my head and it would take a few seconds until the eye actually moved. "Or," he said, "we can remove the eye. There will be no more pain. It is a choice you'll have to make." So I talked it over, and I said, "I can't see out of it and there's this continual pain. I am going to have it removed."

He showed me the charts and he said, "This is what the operation entails." So I had my eye removed and then he introduced me to a Dr. Colbert, who made prostheses. Now I go back and get my eye checked. It's just like a contact lens, only a little bigger. And what I do is, I have to take my eye out every now and then, and there's a solution that I use to clean it. I've had no more pain.

SF: When you were playing for Imlach, you only had sight in one eye?

WO'R: That's right.

SF: Nobody knew that.

WO'R: I knew.

SF: That's a miracle. That is just the most fantastic thing I've heard!

WO'R: Even several people today don't know that I played my 21 years pro with one eye. Even when I went up with the Bruins. And I think that's the reason why I didn't go back with the Bruins. You'll notice in the documentary, when they interviewed Milt Schmidt and Milt said, "Well, in those days, you know, anybody with an eye injury couldn't play in the National Hockey League."

So I went to their camp twice, in 1957 and '58. And after we went to their camp, then we went back to Quebec and played. But nobody ever asked me, "Are you blind? Can you see?" When I left Kitchener, it was like a forgotten thing. I'd go try out for these clubs. I'd make the clubs. I'd go and play.

And Milt said, "Oh, the rascal, he didn't tell us he had one eye."

SF: So you're with Quebec . . .

WO'R: Three years.

SF: Where were you when you got the call?

WO'R: Quebec. Got a call: "Willie, the Bruins want you in Montreal." I don't know if they called me that day, the 18th. That's when I played. So I met the Bruins in Montreal.

SF: What did you feel like? Were you scared?

WO'R: I wasn't scared. We'd played the Canadiens four or five times in exhibition games and I had played in The Forum three times when I was with the Aces. The only difference was when I stepped on the ice January 18, 1958. I had a Boston Bruins jersey on. Number 22. Same building, same ice, same everything. I had the butterflies because it was the first time I realized I'm playing in the National Hockey League. I'm playing in the Montreal Forum, against the Montreal Canadiens. But after a couple of shifts...

SF: Do you remember who you played with? Who was on your line?

WO'R: Tom McCarthy and Charlie Burns, and then I also played with Don McKenney. We beat the Canadiens 3-0 that night. I never got a point or an assist or anything, but just going into Montreal. Then we got on the train...

SF: Wait, wait, wait. Did anybody make a big deal about it?

WO'R: Nah, nothing, zilch, nada. I never knew. It really didn't register to me that I was the first black player to play in the National Hockey League. I was just excited about playing and beating the Canadiens. So we get on the train that night, go to Boston and we play the Canadiens on Sunday. They beat us 5-3 and the next day I'm on the train back to Quebec. I finished the rest of 1958 out, then I was traded next year to the Kingston Frontenacs of the Eastern Quebec Hockey League. Then in '61, I was up with the Bruins for 43 more games.

SF: That wasn't a very good Bruin team. Why didn't you stay?

WO'R: I think they found out about my eye. When I left the Bruins after the season, I was in the office with Milt Schmidt and Lynn Patrick and they said, "Willie, go home, have a good summer, look forward to coming back with the Bruins. We were impressed with your play." I mean, I was about that high off the ground. When I got home, I told my mom and dad, "I'm going back with the Bruins." I told all my friends, "I'm going back with the Bruins."

I was home six weeks and I got a phone call. My mom answered the phone and says, "It's a gentleman from the *Telegraph Journal.*" I took the phone and he said, "Mr. O'Ree, what do you think about the trade?" And I said, "You have me at a disadvantage. What trade are you referring to?" He said, "You've been traded to the Montreal Canadiens. It's come over the teletype. So how do you feel about playing with the Montreal Canadiens?" I say, "Well, to be honest with you, I don't know if I'll be playing with the Montreal Canadiens. I will probably be playing with one of their farm teams."

I didn't get any notification from the Bruins. I did get a nice letter from the Montreal Canadiens on a letterhead, saying, "Your contract has been acquired by the Montreal Canadiens. You're to report to the Hull-Ottawa Canadiens and so on and so forth. So I think I played 15 games for them, had 12 goals and some assists.

So I come into practice one morning. We're supposed to be on the ice at 10:00, but I get there about 8:10, because I like to get there early, check my equipment and that. The trainer is there and he says, "Sammy Pollock wants to see you in his office." So I go up and he is sitting at the desk like this [head in his hands] and he just waves, "Come in, come in." He's got his head down. I come over and I stand in front of his desk for a few seconds and I say, "Mr. Pollock, sir, you wanted to see me?" "Oh yes, yes. We've been very impressed with your play. You're one of our top goal-getters. We've had to make a trade. We've traded you to the Los Angeles Blades of the Western Hockey League." He gave me an envelope and said, "Here is your plane ticket and expenses. Get to Los Angeles tomorrow and contact George Agar, the Blades' coach. Your plane leaves at 12:50."

I go downstairs and their trainer is there with one other player and I said, "Well, I've been traded to Los Angeles." "Oh, you're going out there with the movie stars." Shook hands with the trainer, grabbed my skates and sticks, went back to the apartment, went to the bank, got some money, got on the plane. I step off the plane at 6:25, November 12. It's 75 degrees in L.A. and I had a top coat on, a scarf and everything.

Then I go over the next morning to meet George Agar and the players. We practice that morning. The next night we beat the Calgary Stampeders 5-3. I get a couple of goals, a couple of assists and the paper says, "O'Ree Sparks Blades." So I played there for six years.

SF: What was your single biggest kick as a player?

WO'R: Well, I think the first one was when I scored my first NHL goal for the Bruins.

SF: Really? Against who?

WO'R: Against the Canadiens. It turned out to be the winning goal. It was in Boston, 1961. It was New Year's night. I remember it like it was last night.

SF: How did they treat you in Boston?

WO'R: Great. Well, I didn't live right in Boston. I have a cousin who lives in Roxbury, an area that was predominantly black. So I used to take the train. It was about a half-hour ride from North Station. But I can remember to this day that I was treated very well by the Boston fans. I never heard one racial remark from the fans. The guys I played with were 100 percent behind me on and off the ice.

SF: What about the opposition?

WO'R: Ehh . . . It was a problem. Chicago was bad, Detroit. A lot of racial remarks. Back then they were made every game, and there was nothing I could do about it. But again, in one ear, out the other. I was determined to just play.

SF: What was New York like?

WO'R: Not bad. I had some racial remarks, but nobody really tried to physically attack me or anything like that. But Chicago was bad, on and off the ice.

SF: They tried to assault you?

WO'R: Yeah, some of the fans in the stands. Back then, there weren't the partitions that they have now that would separate the players from the fans.

SF: Where was the best treatment?

WO'R: Montreal and Toronto. I played junior in both cities.

SF: Did you ever wonder what would have been if you hadn't had the injury?

WO'R: Yeah, it was unfortunate. But I said to myself, "I can't quit, I can't quit." I really would only have quit if the other eye had been hit.

SF: Your biggest regret?

WO'R: Well, probably not having the strength to stand up to some coaches and let them know how I felt. But I knew I couldn't change my color, I just wanted to be another player, not black or white. And this is what I want to teach today's kids. There isn't any bitterness, though.

SF: When you see black guys like Anson Carter or Mike Grier playing in the NHL, what do you feel?

WO'R: It makes me feel good. I opened doors for black players when I played for the Bruins. And maybe now, more will be able to play. The way has been paved for them; the door has been opened.

Willie O'Ree's NHL career actually resumed long after his retirement from the ice. Under the aegis of commissioner Gary Bettman, the league organized a Diversity Task Force. In 1995, O'Ree was named Director of Youth Development for the Task Force. Well into his sixties, he crisscrossed the continent giving clinics and guidance to youthful stickhandlers, and still does.

"Even several people today don't know that I played my 21 years pro with one eye. Even when I went up with the Bruins. And I think that's the reason why I didn't go back with the Bruins."

—Willie O'Ree

Anson Carter battles a Canadien.

Anson Carter

Born: Toronto, Ontario; June 6, 1974

Position: Center

NHL Teams: Washington, 1996-97;

Boston, 1997-Present

First Willie O'Ree and now Anson Carter. The Bruins can boast that, A. They were the first National Hockey League team to sign a black player (O'Ree) and, B. They have in Anson Carter potentially the best black stickhandler to skate in the bigs.

A full four decades after O'Ree graced Boston Garden ice as a Bruin, Carter became a member of the Beantowners, although each took a distinctly different route to Causeway Street.

While O'Ree labored through the minor leagues for years before getting his break in Boston, Carter took the university route. He played four years in the Central Collegiate Hockey Association for Michigan State, where he was twice named a CCHA First-Team All-Star. He also was a finalist for the Hobey Baker Trophy as the top college hockey player in the country.

Carter, a native of Toronto, totaled 102 goals and 68 assists for 170 points over a four-year collegiate run. The numbers were enough to persuade the Quebec Nordiques (now Colorado Avalanche) to select him with their tenth pick—220th overall—in the 1992 NHL Entry Draft.

For reasons best known to the Avalanche, the Colorado general staff chose not to retain Carter. He was traded to the Washington Capitals for a 1996 fourth-round pick (Ben Storey) on April 3, 1996. It was a superb deal for the Caps who dispatched Anson to their Portland American League farm club for twenty-seven games in 1996-97.

While in the minors, he compiled thirty-eight points in twenty-seven games. It was enough to persuade the Washington general staff to realize that they just might have a good one in their midst.

And they did—but there were problems in Washington late in the 1996-97 season. The Caps were in a desperate playoff drive and opted for veterans to turn the season around for them. Carter was part of the decision. He was dealt, along with Jason Allison, Jim Carey and a 1997 third-round draft pick (Lee Goren), for Adam Oates, Bill Ranford and Rick Tocchet on March 1, 1997.

Carter only played 19 games for Boston at the tail end of a non-playoff season but impressed by averaging almost a point a game. Then, Pat Burns took over as coach and the ambience changed at Fleet Center. Carter not only had become a regular but a meaningful member of the offense.

"He became a power forward with great hands," said teammate Joe Thornton.

His numbers still were less than overwhelming in 1997-98, but he did play in 78 games and impressed Burns. He also was welcome enough to earn a nickname—"A.C."

"You haven't yet seen the best of Anson Carter," said Burns.

Actually, nobody saw the best of Carter in the early part of the 1998-99 season. A salary dispute caused him to leave the Bruins for a temporary stint in the International League. Once that was resolved, he returned to Boston at a time when Burns' club was in the throes of a playoff drive against the New York Rangers, Carolina Hurricanes and Pittsburgh Penguins.

Carter's game rose right along with the pressure. "A.C. took charge," said team captain Raymond Bourque. "He raised his game. It was a matter of sustaining it and being consistent, bringing it to the rink every day."

> "He's got size, speed, good balance, doesn't get knocked off the puck, and he's a fast, strong skater. He's a good scorer and he's going to get better."
>
> —Bruins' President/G.M. Harry Sinden

As the Rangers and Bruins battled for the remaining playoff berth, the teams clashed at Madison Square Garden on March 12, 1999. It was a Friday night and the Bruins were nursing a two-point lead over New York. As the clock ticked past the 15-minute mark of the third period, the Rangers appeared to have secured the two points. The Blueshirts led 4-3 and Mike Richter had grown stronger in goal.

There now were less than three minutes to play when Carter simply turned the entire game around by himself. He beat Richter at 17:13 to tie the score and take the crowd out of the game.

The Rangers were just hoping to get to the overtime and then regroup, but they never had the opportunity. Just 19 seconds after his first goal, Carter stole the puck from rookie Manny Malhotra and beat Richter again. It proved to be the winning goal and lifted Boston to a four-point lead over New York with 16 games remaining.

It was a defeat that torpedoed the Rangers' playoff hopes. They soon dropped out of sight, while the Bruins, energized by the victory, cruised into the postseason derby.

Perhaps it was appropriate, then, that gazing down at Carter's locker at Fleet Center are the faces of two Boston hockey legends—Woody Dumart and Phil Esposito. They must have been smiling at his pre-playoff heroics.

"It's kind of scary knowing that those two are looking down at me," Carter chuckled one day when reminded about Woody and Phil. "Sometimes, when we're winning, it's nice. When we're losing, I think they are looking down on me, kind of mad."

Really, one finds it difficult to get angry at Anson. His disposition is upbeat and always has been since his days growing up in Toronto's Scarborough suburb. At age eight, he promised his mother, Valma, that he would attend an American university and become an orthopedic surgeon.

Hockey got in the way of medicine, but nobody is complaining. Carter's dedication and game plan have always been evident and certainly impressed his collegiate coaches, Ron Mason and Tom Newton.

"Anson was a businessman at the rink," said Newton. "He worked hard, pushed himself and forced himself to get better."

He probably would have improved even more with the Capitals, but his chances in Washington were uncertain, a fact that didn't exactly sit well with Carter. "My chances with the Caps were limited," he averred. "On the other hand, the Bruins gave me every opportunity."

Bruins' president/GM Harry Sinden on Carter: "He's got size, speed, good balance, doesn't get knocked off the puck, and he's a fast, strong skater. He's a good scorer and he's going to get better."

And he did get better in 1998-99. Once he shook off the rust from his IHL sabbatical, Anson became a notable Bruin. In 55 regular-season games he tallied 24 goals, including six on the power play, as well as six game-winners. His 16 assists gave him a total of 40 points.

He continued to excel in the 1999 playoffs, which began with a grueling opening-round series against Carolina. A.C. helped dispose of the troublesome Hurricanes with three goals in six games,

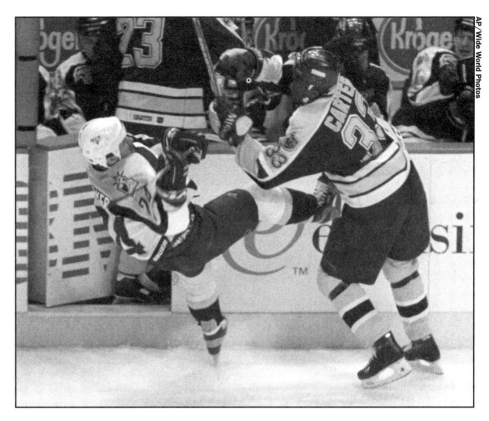

Carter's strength gives him a checking advantage.

including a game-winner in double overtime. Over the two series in which Boston was involved, he delivered seven points in a dozen games.

As his popularity rose, so too did media coverage, with extensive attention to the fact that his parents are from Barbados and he was born in Canada following their move North. Carter also has been keenly aware of O'Ree's contributions, as well as those of the other African-Canadian players who have made an impact on the NHL.

After meeting O'Ree, Carter became friends with the veteran. In an interview with the *New York Times'* Joe Lapointe, Carter explained his kinship with O'Ree: "He's a great guy," he said. "A really good guy. He's awesome. I couldn't ask for a better role model than Willie O'Ree. The fact that he was the first colored player to play in the NHL, here in the city of Boston, it just adds to it. Every time I get a chance to speak with him, he relays some great stories about playing. His love for the game hasn't dwindled at all, regardless of all the tough things he's been through."

To Carter, the use of the phrase "African-American" in the States strikes him as odd. "I'm Canadian-Caribbean or something," he said. "I hear 'African-American' all the time and it doesn't really apply to me."

As for the racial issue, vis-a-vis the NHL, Carter

offered interesting insights: "I guess things have been said, but I don't really hear anything. If I was thinking something like that wouldn't happen, I'd be dumb, because it happens in the real world. In sports, athletes sometimes live in a bubble. It still exists. But it doesn't faze me. I know who I am and I am comfortable with who I am and I wouldn't want to change who I am. Therefore, if they call me racial slurs, it's going to fall on deaf ears. I'll turn and laugh.

"I heard the stereotypes when I was traded here. My parents said to me, 'Be careful when you go into Boston. We've heard a lot of negative things about black athletes' experiences there.' But I came in with an open frame of mind, just like I did when I went to school. Sure, people at Michigan State never saw a black hockey player before, and here I was, cast right in the spotlight. The people here in Boston, they couldn't have treated me better than I've been treated so far. I've been treated with a lot of respect and a lot of class."

All of which indicates that Carter's ambition to become an orthopedic surgeon will be on permanent hold. Which should make both Sinden and Boston fans happy several times over.

Both sides are aware that the best is yet to come from A.C.

Jason Allison—potential superstar.

Jason Allison

Born: North York, Ontario; May 29, 1975

Position: Center

NHL Teams: Washington, 1993-97;

Boston, 1997-Present

Jason
ALLISON

*I*t is a measure of Jason Allison's potential that when he slumped during the 1999 Stanley Cup playoff series against Buffalo—which the Bruins lost, four games to two—president-general manager Harry Sinden publicly ripped his big forward.

The boss questioned the "dedication" and "sacrifice" of his top-scoring center. He also claimed that Allison had become a fat cat; that his multi million-dollar contract had diminished his drive.

The criticism, which some observers considered excessive, nevertheless demonstrated that the 6-3, 205 pounder from North York, Ontario, commands attention and if he isn't scoring to Sinden's standard, it's worthy of comment.

On paper at least, the boss had little to complain about either in 1997-98 or 1998-99, when it came to performance.

In his first full year as a Bruin (1997-98), Allison averaged more than a point a game (81 games, 33-50-83), which led the team in scoring. Jason not only established career season highs in all categories but finished ninth overall in the scoring race. It marked the first time a Bruin had reached that level since 1993-94.

He continued to excel during the 1998 playoffs with two goals and six assists in six games. "There was nothing Jason did that year by accident," said his agent Bob Gerow, who then proceeded to negotiate a robust new deal for his client.

One reason for the big bucks was Allison's impressive rate of improvement. During his last year (1996-97) as a Washington Capital, he looked more like a bud that might never blossom. His five goals and seventeen assists in fifty-three games persuaded Caps GM David Poile to include Jason with Anson Carter, Jim Carey and a 1997 third-round draft pick (Lee Goren) for Adam Oates, Rick Tocchet and Bill Ranford.

In his first full campaign with Boston, Allison registered the most improvement of any NHL player with a plus-55 differential. Bruins' assistant GM Mike O'Connell was so impressed with the production, he said he hoped some of Jason's magic would rub off on another prodigy-in-the-works, Joe Thornton.

"We should take a film of Allison and show it to Thornton and say, 'See what you're going to be if you get your act together.'"

Jason got his act together after a couple of indifferent seasons with the Caps because he finally was given the chance to play, something that was not always apparent in Washington.

Those who remember Allison as a youth growing up in the Greater Toronto area worried that his inferior skating ability would deter him from reaching the top. One of his early colleagues was Sabres captain Michael Peca, who played on the Canadian World Junior team in 1994 along with Allison's current teammate, Anson Carter.

Peca: "Jason had the same reputation his whole life. He was a kid who always was the best player on his team, yet everyone said he wouldn't make it because of his skating. He'd go from one team to another and always be the best."

It all got serious for Allison when he gained a varsity spot on the London, Ontario, junior club. In the 1993 NHL Entry Draft he was selected 17th overall by the Capitals—Washington's second pick—and then proceeded to lead the Ontario Hockey League in scoring during the 1993-94 season. He also was named Canadian Major Junior Player of the Year.

The kudos notwithstanding, Allison continued to be twitted over his slow skating, and for a time it seemed like a legitimate complaint—until he arrived at Fleet Center.

Under new coach Pat Burns, Allison's game leaped to a higher level and the Bruins climbed with him.

The exceptional first year in Boston proved a contract catalyst. Allison came out of it with a three-year pact with a base salary of $2.25 million as well as incentive clauses. Jason responded with 23 goals and 53 assists for 76 points in 82 games.

Whether or not he played to his abilities always will be a matter of debate, but there was no debating what coach Burns thought of him. "By 1998-99 Jason had become our number one center," said Burns. "Our team will play as well as our number one center."

Allison has never ducked big games. "I usually play my best when there's a lot of pressure on us."

He performed well enough to help the Bruins beat Carolina in the 1999 opening round, but the loss to Buffalo and the ensuing tirade by Sinden raised hackles, if not doubts. Some players would accept the gibes and get on with their off-season, but not Jason. He invoked the free speech amendment and fired a few verbal volleys in return.

"What Sinden said—that being given the big money is why I didn't play well—well, that's a crock. Maybe that's his way of covering himself. I don't know. But I do know that I didn't think the comments were called for.

"This is a tough situation for me because, on the one hand, I'm upset and I don't want to say something I don't want to say. Yet on the other hand, I want to express myself. I think I deserve to express myself after his comments."

Jason also put his money where his feet are, in the sense that he took the criticism about his speed seriously. Immediately after the Bruins were eliminated he signed up with two-time Canadian Olympic speed skater Kevin Scott. The two devised a dual on-ice and off-ice program featuring three or four skating sessions and up to ten off-ice workouts per week.

"It shows that Jason has a lot of dedication to excellence," said Scott. "What drives an athlete like him to the next level is that he's willing to work harder than other people. For him to put a month aside for this shows how badly he wants to get better."

Scott insisted that Allison was faster than his critics contended. To the skating coach, it was a classic case of the big hockey player appearing to be slower than he actually was, and all because of his size.

"Jason has such long legs," said Scott, "that people look at him and think, 'Geez, he's not skating that hard.' But because his legs are so long, he's not going to have the frequency of, say, a Theo Fleury. His speed is deceptive. He can take one stride and go as far as another guy goes in two."

Allison: "I realize that if I'm going to play 22 to 25 minutes a game, I really have to reach another level of conditioning. I can't play my best if I'm out there tired. It's something I want to do on my own, conditioning-wise, and get a smoother skating stride."

Were it not for Allison, the Bruins would not even have gained a playoff berth in 1998-99. From February 21-27, 1999, when the Bruins and Rangers were vying for the remaining playoff berth, Allison delivered three goals and six assists over four games. It ignited a four-win, one-tie roll that thrust Boston back into the race at a time when the club appeared destined for oblivion.

Stephen Harris of the *Boston Herald* noted: "His 1-2-3 performance in a 4-3 victory over the Capitals included Allison deflecting a shot out of the playing surface while Boston was two men short, plus two last-minute face-off victories over Adam Oates after Washington pulled its goalie.

"One game later, in a 3-2 victory over Phoenix, Allison didn't score a point. He juiced up his teammates, however, by dropping his gloves and battling Coyotes captain Keith Tkachuk, who had cross-checked Allison in the back before blind-siding longtime teammate and linemate Anson Carter."

At age 25, Allison still had not fully matured as a big-leaguer. Only two full seasons in Boston under Burns was hardly enough to qualify as more than basic training under the moustachioed coach. If nothing else, the man behind the bench was both patient and perceptive about his key pivot.

"Jason does things we don't see," said Burns. "It's not merely a matter of how many points he puts on the board; you have to look at everything else he does for the club."

Unquestionably, the 1999-2000 season will be pivotal for Allison. Sinden will be watching closely, but if one were to ask his teammates about Jason, the responses would be unquestionably supportive.

Allison patrolling the wing.

"Jason's a hungry player," said Bruins goaltender Byron Dafoe. "It's not easy for him to be satisfied with himself. Obviously, he was very happy with what he did last year (1997-98), but he still felt he could be better. For the first half of this season he had good numbers, but for him, it wasn't where he wanted to be. It's great to see him step up at crucial times. We need him to win hockey games, and he's been there when we need him."

All things considered, Allison has done the job well for two seasons. He is respected by friend and foe, particularly the one foe who knows him better than most, captain Peca of Buffalo.

"Jason's game is to bring things to his level," Peca explained. "He likes to slow things down and lull people to sleep. He can get guys to overcommit to him. Like all great centers, he has the ability to draw defenders to him, open things up and find the open man."

Did you catch those words, "like all great centers"?

Great? Maybe not in Harry Sinden's eyes, but Jason Allison is in good position to get there.

Sergei Samsonov, Boston's Russian Rocket.

Sergei Samsonov

Born: Moscow, USSR; October 27, 1978

Position: Left Wing

NHL Teams: Boston, 1997-Present

Awards/Honors: Calder Trophy, 1998

When the Bruins approached the 1997 Entry Draft, media attention was focused on Boston's first selection, which just happened to be first overall in the annual NHL whiz-kid rodeo.

Virtually everyone connected with hockey assumed that the Hub brain trust would select 18-year-old, 6-4, 220-pound Joe Thornton with the primary pick. Thornton had been touted for more than a year as the second coming of Eric Lindros or thereabouts.

But Harry Sinden had a second selection in the first round, which was eighth overall, and he had many possibilities. Matt Zultek was one and Marian Hossa was another, but the general staff was fascinated with a 5-8, 184-pound left wing from Moscow, Russia.

Samsonov—small but rugged.

nineteen-year-old."

When he was seventeen, he played for the Red Army Elite team and then jetted to North America, where he was signed by the Detroit Vipers of the International Hockey League. Then, as now, the IHL featured a number of older, former NHL players who were wise to the ways of the game.

Sergei made the adjustment to American pro hockey without missing a step. He played in seventy-three games and totaled twenty-nine goals and thirty-five assists. In six playoff games, he averaged over a point a match with two goals and five assists.

He was The I's rookie of the year and a primary reason why the Vipers annexed the Turner Cup, emblematic of the IHL's championship.

Gerry Callahan, who profiled Samsonov for *Sports Illustrated*, described the minuscule Russian as having "the cool, hard look of a soldier and the intensity of a man who is playing to pay the mortgage."

That explains why the Bruins had no compunctions about drafting him as high as they did. What remained to be seen at the start of the 1997-98 season was whether Samsonov had the goods to survive in the bigger, faster NHL.

The signs were positive at training camp in Wilmington, Massachusetts, where, at one point, the crowd at Ristuccia Center erupted in spontaneous applause after Samsonov dipsy-doodled down the ice and scored.

"The kid had them doing that all week," Bruins vice-president and Hall of Famer Tom Johnson mentioned to a reporter who had just arrived. "He looks special. He's the best young talent we've had in training camp in decades."

Sinden tended to be conservative in his talent estimates, especially when it came to unproven rookies. Nevertheless, the boss could hardly remain unmoved by Samsonov's speed.

Granted, his size appeared to be against him in an era of towering forwards, but Sergei Samsonov had gifts that could not be ignored. He could skate like the wind, pick corners as if there was radar in his stick and handle the rough stuff when necessary.

"Sammy is like an old-time Russian hockey player," said Ted Donato, who was his teammate in Samsonov's rookie year, 1997-98. "He's intense, driven and has a purpose to everything he does. He's a great kid. When he came to the Bruins, I called him more of a traditional

"He showed the most speed we have ever had in a camp," said Sinden. "In every drill, he finished first. I was excited when we drafted him, but having watched him in Boston, I was more excited than ever."

Samsonov's early-season play as a rookie was not exactly out of Gang Busters, but he showed enough skill and endurance to remain a regular. In the second half of 1997-98, Sammy's game simply took off. While Thornton struggled to find himself, the Russian became a serious candidate for the Calder Trophy as NHL rookie of the year.

"Joe was still a kid," said Sinden, "and still kind of giddy about the whole thing. Sergei was all business. I don't think he was giddy about anything."

Certainly, Samsonov gave that impression to interviewers. Media types, both home and away, were impressed by his serious air, which suggested a player ten years older. He was remarkably articulate for one who had only been away from his homeland for three years, and very accommodating.

The Bruins had signed Russian players in the past, and Sinden had a first hand knowledge of stickhandlers from the Soviet Union, having coached Team Canada in the classic 1972 Summit Series.

"Sergei reminded me of the great Russian players of twenty years ago," said Sinden. "Most of their forwards were built like this kid. Short. But strong, quick and with a wonderful knack for making plays."

Sammy played eighty-one games in his freshman year and totaled forty-seven points (22-25), which was good enough for him to win the Calder. Thus, he became the

Samsonov scores! Again!

first player ever to be named IHL rookie of the year in one year and the Calder in the next.

In his first-ever Stanley Cup playoff round, Sergei responded to the pressure as well as any Bruin. His six-game run resulted in two goals and five assists. More than that, he demonstrated that the wear and tear was not enough to cause him to miss more than one game, and that was due to the flu.

"We were concerned about his size at first," Sinden allowed. "Yes, he's short, but he's big. He's a man."

As a sophomore in 1998-99, he played in two less regular-season games, but tallied four more points than in the previous year. The totals were 25-26-51, but the arithmetic never tells the full tale.

"He's an exciting player," said former Bruins goalie and coach Gerry Cheevers. "That's the best way to describe him—exciting."

Samsonov has used captain Raymond Bourque as his role model. From time to time, the veteran defenseman has driven the kid from Russia to the rink. Some insiders believe that Bourque's philosophy and hockey ethic have already rubbed off on Sammy.

"I see Ray working hard as hell in practice and he's been in the NHL for twenty years," said Samsonov. "That tells me that I have to do the same."

So far, so good. Nobody is saying he will be as productive as Pavel Bure or as stylish as Sergei Fedorov, but if Samsonov continues to mature at the rate he has in just two seasons as a Bruin, he could be an All-Star in the 21st century.

"The kid had them doing that all week. He looks special. He's the best young talent we've had in training camp in decades."

—Bruins V.P. and Hall of Famer Tom Johnson

Don Sweeney, the consummate compact defender.

Don Sweeney

Born: St. Stephen, New Brunswick;

August 17, 1966

Position: Defense

NHL Teams: Boston, 1988-Present

*H*e has done his job with such quiet efficiency that it's often hard to believe that Don Sweeney has played defense for the Boston Bruins for more than a decade.

Not only that, but he has survived the NHL grind in an era when players who resemble brontosauruses are more appreciated than compact types such as Sweeney, who usually checks in at 5-10, 184 pounds.

In the case of the St. Stephen, New Brunswick, native, it clearly has been a case of brains over brawn.

"Some people have it in their minds that you have to be a certain size to play defense in this league, but I can't do anything about that," Sweeney explained. "It's important to have players with speed to neutralize players on the other team who have speed."

Sweeney deflates a Capital.

Numbers have never been that important to Sweeney, whether they are goals, assists or the controversial plus-minus stat.

"The plus-minus can be a very misleading statistic," said Sweeney. "You can be totally uninvolved in a play, but there's a breakdown someplace else and the puck's in your net. Then again, you could be the sole cause of a goal against your team, but everyone else on the ice with you has to share it.

"Nobody likes to be a minus player, though. It's frustrating to pick up a stat sheet and see that. You want to take pride in that statistic and I always try to."

Milbury, who has since become general manager of the New York Islanders, has remained a Sweeney booster.

"The best thing about him is his reliability. You know what you're going to get from him every night; which is plenty of effort.

"His name comes up a lot when I talk to people around the league. Don is liked for a lot of reasons.

"He's almost never standing still. And you've got to be moving to pass effectively. When he gets it, if there's no pass there, he takes the conservative route."

Granted that point production never has been Don's top priority, but he has put up commendable numbers, considering his style. Point-wise, his best season was 1992-93, when he tallied seven goals and twenty-seven assists for thirty-four points. He played in a career-high eighty-four games that year.

"Earlier in my career," said Sweeney, "Mike Milbury made me a better player. He made me smarter, making me see what was going on out on the ice all that much clearer."

In 1993-94 Don led the Bruins in plus-minus at plus-29. A year later, two of his three goals were game-winners, and in the season after that, three of his four goals were game-winners. Sweeney's durability was evidenced in the 1995-96 season, when he played his 500th NHL game on February 14, 1996.

Sweeney always has played a relatively clean game for a defenseman, never exceeding 74 penalty minutes (1991-92) but usually hovering around the 60-minute mark. In 1998-99, he accumulated sixty-four penalty minutes in eighty-one games. His twelve points (2-10-12) were relatively low for Don, but he finished with a commendable plus-fourteen rating and was an efficient force during the 1999 playoffs.

Playing in the shadow of future Hall of Famer Raymond Bourque throughout his major league career, Don Sweeney has earned considerably fewer headlines, but nonetheless, has earned his spurs as a Bruins' Bruin.

After completing four years at Harvard, Sweeney made his NHL debut in 1988-89. He had been the Bruins' eighth pick (166th overall in the 1984 Draft), but it wasn't until the 1990-91 season that Sweeney completely established himself as a Bruins full-timer. He played 77 games and totaled 8-13-21. In 19 playoff games that spring, Sweeney added another three goals. His coach at the time, Mike Milbury, singled out Sweeney's virtues.

"Don's a guy with a lot of heart, is very steady and he always keeps himself in great shape," said Milbury. "He's small by NHL standards, sure, but he does the things to help himself in other areas, like maximizing his quickness and the experience he has gained in his years in the league."

Sweeney always played a cerebral game ever since he was a top defenseman for four years at Harvard. He helped lead the Crimson to the NCAA finals in 1986, where they bowed to Michigan State. He was named an NCAA East All-American in 1987-88 in addition to earning first-team ECAC All-Star honors, as he had 6-23-29 totals in 30 games.

Guess who scored? Don Sweeney.

Lord Byron (Dafoe) of the Crease.

Byron Dafoe

Born: Sussex, England; February 25, 1971

Position: Goaltender

NHL Teams: Washington, 1992-95; Los

Angeles, 1995-97; Boston, 1997-Present

Few hockey reclamation projects have been as impressive as the one that has seen Byron Dafoe turn from a never-was to a has-been to a star in the space of eight years. And then an agonizing holdout in the Fall of 1999.

To say that the native of Sussex, England, had his hockey life renewed by the Bruins would be roughly equivalent to claiming that the automobile made good use of an invention called the wheel. Then, the wheel went flat early in the 1999-2000 campaign.

But the fact remains that Dafoe hardly was outstanding first as a member of the Washington Capitals and their farm teams and later with the Los Angeles Kings in the two years he played in Tinseltown.

The turnabout began on August 29, 1997, when he was traded to Boston with Dimitri Khristich for Jozef Stumpel, Sandy Moger and a 1998 fourth-round draft pick (Pierre Dagenais).

A brief respite for goalie Dafoe.

His first season in Boston, 1997-98, inspired a surprising number of ooohs and ahhhs. This was not a mediocre, second-string goalie Bostonians were watching but rather a composed, confident young man who looked every bit a winner.

When the dust had cleared in the spring of 1998, Dafoe had won thirty games, lost twenty-five and tied nine. His goals-against average, 2.24, was laudable, and his six shutouts were more than any Bruins fan could have expected.

Such neat numbers notwithstanding, there remained a nagging suspicion that Dafoe's big season was merely a one-shot; a fluke that would not be repeated in 1998-99. It was a reasonable—albeit skeptical—assumption that could only be resolved by the test of time.

Game by game, week by week, month by month, Dafoe disposed of the doubters in the most basic manner known to goaltending: stopping pucks. On Causeway Street, Dafoe was called "Da-fortress." He was better than good, leading the Bruins through a pulsating homestretch run against the New York Rangers, who supposedly had better goalkeeping with the veteran Mike Richter.

"Byron is above the level of a number-one goalie

now," said Bruins boss Harry Sinden.

What made the Dafoe saga so delightful was the goaltender's persona. He's a warm, intelligent, amusing character who never is too busy for the media or the fans. Unlike other goalies, who seem burdened by tons of mental baggage, Dafoe treats his profession with joy.

While other goalies nervously shun day-of-game interviews, Dafoe inevitably was available and amiable. Unquestionably the man appreciates life because he has suffered through difficult times in his climb to the top.

"Some people act as if I've had nothing but success," Dafoe explained. "By the 1998-99 season, I was into my eighth pro year. For me to become a regular did not happen overnight."

There were disappointments and there were those nearby to help him around the detours. One night in Los Angeles, when Dafoe was backup to Kelly Hrudey, he was given some advice from the veteran: "You never give up, no matter what the score. All you worry about is making the next save. And you can never stop fighting for yourself because once you do stop, they'll know you've given up."

It is possible that Dafoe never would have found his way to Boston had it not been for an earlier Bruins hero,

Gerry "Cheesy" Cheevers. A Hall of Famer and broadcaster, Cheevers had been one of the best and most combative goalies who ever graced Boston Garden. Cheesy had a keen eye for the crease, and one night he happened to be watching a minor league game in Baltimore when he noticed Dafoe in action. His eyes were caught by the young man's performance. Cheesy made a mental note to check him out a few more times in the future, which he did.

When Cheevers was convinced that Dafoe could be an asset in Boston, he passed on the information to his bosses. It was enough to convince Harry Sinden & Co., who eventually traded for Byron.

There was no suggestion at the time that Dafoe would be numero uno. After all, the Bruins already had dealt for Jim Carey, who had a Vezina Trophy on his mantle. Besides, that very same Carey had edged Dafoe out of the top goaltending job in Washington.

But now Pat Burns was coaching the Bruins. According to Burns, the goaltending slate would be wiped clean, and the number one for 1997-98 would earn his job on merit. And that is precisely how Byron ascended to the top position.

Of course, there have been games played by Dafoe that come under the heading of Bummers, but the likeable Dafoe had rebounded smartly from enemy strafing. Once in November 1997, the Florida Panthers put six of a dozen shots past him in a 10-5 loss. It was the kind of night that would have traumatized a less strong-willed goalie.

Dafoe was justifiably uneasy when he showed up at the dressing room on the morning after the debacle. Burns read the situation and calmly pulled his goaltender aside.

"Do you see that yellow star up there?" said Burns. "That's the sun and it came out today. Don't worry about it;

you're going back into the nets."

Dafoe responded to the vote of confidence in the best way possible: by delivering wins to his coach.

"Byron has improved with time," said Burns. "That's the way it is with goalies. Look at Dominik Hasek. Seven, eight years ago, Hasek couldn't be the backup in Chicago. You have to give a guy some time and Byron is biding his time, playing well and getting people noticing."

Getting noticed has been difficult. In 1998-99 *The Hockey News* listed Dafoe at number nineteen—Richter was six—but when it came time for the All-Star ballot, Dafoe's name was not even on it.

"I was very disappointed," Byron allowed. "My numbers proved that I should have been on the ballot."

Interestingly, Richter, who was listed far ahead of Dafoe, failed to make the playoffs for the second straight year. By contrast, Dafoe guided the Bruins into the postseason and past Carolina in a closely played opening playoff round. The Boston Express finally was derailed by Hasek and the Buffalo Sabres, who defeated the Bruins and went on the the finals.

"Byron's personal goal is to compete with Hasek," said Bruins defenseman Kyle McLaren. "Any goalie in the league wants to compare himself with the best, and Byron has done that."

When Dafoe launched his contract holdout in October 1999, the Bruins responded by using two less-experienced goaltenders, Robbie Tallas and John Grahame. After a shaky start, the Bruins found their footing and played commendable hockey until Dafoe finally relented. By the beginning of November, Lord Byron was back in the fold and all was right with Boston's goaltending world again.

Hal Gill

Hal Gill

Born: Concord, Massachusetts; April 6, 1975

Position: Defense

NHL Teams: Boston, 1997-Present

Hal **GILL**

The local-boy-makes-good scenario—as it applies to Boston hockey—dates back to Myles J. Lane's Bruins' stint from 1928 to 1930.

More recently, the likes of Mike Milbury and Ted Donato demonstrated that New Englanders could not only crack the Bruins lineup but make meaningful contributions.

The latest to join that distinguished line is Concord-born defenseman Harold Priestley Gill III, better known to the public as Hal Gill.

In the manner of Milbury and Lane, Gill originally starred as a football player. He was a quarterback at Nashoba Regional High School, and was offered scholarships to play college football at schools like Northeastern, the University of New Hampshire and Boston College.

"Best quarterback in the state," Bruins GM Harry Sinden told *The Hockey News* .

Only one school, Providence College, recruited him to play hockey. Gill was forced to weigh the prospect of being a fourth-string quarterback with the chance to play hockey on a regular basis.

"It was a tough decision," he said. "Where I went to high school, hockey was played but it wasn't played at a really high level. I played for fun. I was prepared to stick with football from my junior year on."

Football may have been in his blood, but hockey was also part of Gill's hemoglobin mix. The scouts at Providence College must have known it, because he was given a full scholarship to trade in his cleats for a pair of skates.

He spent four years skating defense for the Friars in Hockey East and was a member of the Hockey East championship squad in 1995-96. The Bruins must have seen the same assets that attracted Providence, because in June 1993—before he moved to Rhode Island—Boston drafted him on the Bruins' eighth pick (207th overall).

On draft day, Gill was watching the proceedings at home in Concord with his mother. When Bruin officials called to notify him that he had been selected, he was convinced that it was actually one of his brothers playing a practical joke. Rumor had it that former coach Mike Milbury scouted Gill during the young man's senior year at Nashoba Regional High School, but Hal never expected that his hometown Bruins had taken a serious interest in him.

"I never thought it could happen," said Gill. "I was caught between disbelief and being really excited.

"The Bruins were the only team I watched growing up. I used to watch with my brothers. Guys like Ray Bourque, Ted Donato—I grew up watching those players, so to play with them was really amazing."

He graduated from Providence College in 1997 and, remarkably, was in the Bruins lineup on November 17, 1997, for a game against the Canucks. The Bruins were on a West Coast trip, and Gill was the seventh defenseman. His NHL debut lasted all of two shifts—not very good ones, either—and he played in one of only ten games before being assigned to the Providence Bruins of the American Hockey League.

Though Gill's stay in the minors lasted only four

Hal Gill uses his size to his advantage.

games, he said it was a necessary basic training to prepare him for the pace of the big league. Once recalled to Boston, he remained a member of the varsity at Fleet Center.

All things considered, Gill's rookie NHL year was most positive. He recorded two goals and four assists in 68 games with the Bruins, along with 47 penalty minutes.

Clearly, the Bruins' high command liked what they saw in the 6-7, 240-pounder, and in 1998-99, Hal confirmed their confidence in him. He was routinely used to kill penalties, matched up against opposing teams' top lines and often paired with Beantown mainstay Raymond Bourque.

"Ray plays hard, he never gives up, and he'll do whatever it takes to win," Gill said of his sometime defense partner-mentor. "He goes out and gives one hundred percent in practice, in the weight room, and in the games."

Gill learned by watching the captain and listening to the coach.

Bruins goalie Byron Dafoe summed up the 23-year-old's talents succinctly: "His size and strength are his biggest assets by far."

"Gill has no illusions why he's made it," noted Mark Brender of *The Hockey News*. "He knows if you're 6-foot-7 and weigh 240 pounds and want to play in the NHL, being big is a fine area in which to excel."

Few could imagine that one like Gill, with such a shallow hockey background, could orbit to the NHL so fast. But Boston sportscaster-agent-attorney Mark Witkin knew from the get-go that Hal was an exception.

"The thing that stands out in my mind," said Witkin, "was his athleticism. He obviously was well-coordinated. You could see that when he was at the point, or taking a shot. It was almost like a golf swing. Very fluid. There was a much higher percentage of shots on net, and he had a cannon for a shot."

Likening Gill to a young giant—Kjell Samuelsson but with greater offensive potential—Witkin suggested that Gill could revolutionize the role of the big defenseman in much the same way as Magic Johnson revolutionized the position of point guard in the NBA.

"I would love to see him play in front of the net on the power play," said Witkin. "Coming from nowhere, the

way he did, coaches told him to keep it simple, just stick to playing sound defense. But as time goes by, I think you will see him expand his game."

Though Gill fondly remembers his first NHL goal—a one-timer that beat St. Louis netminder Grant Fuhr off a feed from Rob DiMaio on November 13, 1998—he might be most proud of his outstanding defensive play against Pittsburgh Penguins superstar Jaromir Jagr.

"I would say that Gill is the first defenseman I just cannot beat," said Jagr, when asked to name his toughest opponent. "Whatever I do, Gill is just stronger than me. I have got to figure out something."

So frustrated by Gill's defensive work was Jagr that, on one occasion, he took a swing at the hulking Bruin. A friend mailed Gill a photograph of the incident.

"He was very frustrated," said Gill. "To see that frustration—I just got a picture of him pushing me in the head. That's probably the highlight of when I play."

"The other telling moment," added Witkin, "was in the first day of training camp. Someone was trying to make the team as an enforcer, and he went after Hal. Who won or lost didn't matter. What mattered was that Hal was prepared. He has an extremely bright future."

Byron Dafoe also recalled Gill's training camp debut. "All I saw was this big guy," the goalie remembered. "He wasn't sure on his feet, wasn't sure of his hands."

"I think it's natural that a guy like me would get a lot of grief about playing," Gill added. "There's a lot of people who said, 'What the hell's this kid doing here?' I'm not an offensive weapon. I mean, I can shoot it hard, but I don't know where I'm shooting."

That Hal had reached a meaningful level of competency in only his second NHL year still comes as a source of surprise to those who remember him best from the gridiron.

But the pigskin is part of his past. His eyes are only on the puck, and it is reasonable to expect that the eyes of Bostonians will be on Harold Priestley Gill III for many years to come.

> "Gill has no illusions why he's made it. He knows if you're 6-foot-7 and weigh 240 pounds and want to play in the NHL, being big is a fine area in which to excel."
>
> —Mark Brender, *The Hockey News*

Boston BRUINS

The Best, Worst and Most Unusual in Boston Hockey

Best Losing Overtime Game in Bruins History

The fifth game of the first round of the Boston-Toronto series at Maple Leaf Gardens would decide the series. It began on Monday, April 3, 1933, and concluded on Tuesday, April 4, 1933. It was that long.

The arena was jammed with 14,450 rooters for the finale that pitted Toronto's goalie Lorne Chabot against his Beantown counterpart, Tiny Thompson. Each was at the peak of his career, and it showed.

Neither team scored during regulation time. Chabot was beaten once by Boston's Alex Smith, but the play was nullified by an offside. Finally, the match went into overtime and neither goalie would give an inch.

It was still 0-0 after the first overtime and remained the same after the second sudden-death session. By the time the third extra session had begun, it was well past midnight.

"Morning papers appeared in the rink," said Maple Leafs publicist Ed Fitkin, "and were sold as fast as they were produced. Fans both in and out of the rink were apparently determined to see it through. The players on the ice were dog-tired and near exhaustion."

Bruins defenseman Eddie Shore played for the first sixty consecutive minutes and then took only brief respites during overtime. Other players were equally gallant. "There wasn't a weakling out there," said Fitkin. "The fans knew it and began talking about the inhumanity of letting the game go on."

During the fourth overtime, it appeared as if Joe Primeau of Toronto had beaten Thompson, but the whistle had blown for an offside. Neither team scored during the remainder of the fourth overtime. During the intermission, the respective managers, Art Ross of Boston and Conn Smythe of Toronto, convened and decided that a coin toss should determine the winner. But when they told their players about it, neither the skaters nor NHL president

Frank Calder agreed. "The game," said Calder, "must be fought to a finish, no matter how long it takes."

Leafs forward Harold Cotton almost scored in the fifth overtime, circling the net and then stuffing the puck between Thompson's skate and the goalpost, but the goalie covered up in time.

The fifth overtime ended with the score still 0-0. It was now 1:30 a.m.

In the sixth overtime, Shore was totally fatigued but continued to play. Finally, he needed a rest and tried an offside pass to stop play. He saw Joe Lamb in the clear and slid the puck toward him.

But Toronto's Andy Blair intercepted the pass and sent the puck to his tiny linemate, Ken Doraty, who took it in stride. Doraty skated for a couple of seconds and then shot the puck past Thompson.

"At first," said Fitkin, "the fans seemed unable to comprehend the fact. When they did, however, bedlam broke loose and Doraty was mobbed by his teammates."

The time was 1:55 a.m. The puck had gone in at 4:46 of the sixth overtime after a total of 104 minutes and 46 seconds of overtime had been played. Up until that point, it was the longest NHL game in history—a record that held for three years.

Worst Suspension

A lifetime suspension is as bad as it can be for a professional hockey player, no matter what the infraction. And Billy Coutu of the Bruins found that out firsthand.

It happened in 1927 in an Ottawa-Boston playoff game during which Coutu made three mistakes:

1. He slugged referee Jerry Laflamme, knocking him down to the ice 2. He knocked down linesman Bill Bell with a flying tackle 3. He did it all right in front of NHL president Frank Calder.

The NHL boss fined Coutu—often known as Couture—$100 and added the lifetime suspension.

Interestingly, few leaped to the Bruin's defense. The ten-year veteran had established himself as a mean-tempered individual with both opponents and teammates.

Five years later Coutu's suspension was lifted, but by then, he was too old to return to the NHL.

Most Unusual Present From One Rival to Another

By far one of the most bitter front-office rivalries in the NHL's early years involved the Bruins and Maple Leafs. To put it mildly, their respective bosses—Art Ross in Boston and Conn Smythe in Toronto—hated each other.

Once, Ross accused the Maple Leafs as a team and Smythe as an individual of lacking class. The next time his club visited Boston, Smythe bought ads in the Beantown dailies urging Bruin fans to come to Boston Garden "and see the team with class—the Maple Leafs."

Still not satisfied with that ploy, Smythe rented a tuxedo, replete with top hat and tails, and wore it to the game that night. Smythe had been acutely aware that his arch-rival, Ross, was recovering from an operation for hemorrhoids. En route to the rink, the Toronto impresario got a brainstorm the moment he saw a vendor selling flowers.

Smythe purchased a bouquet of roses with thorns the size of cacti. On the accompanying card, Smythe added a note, inscribed in Latin: "INSERT THESE UP YOUR YOU-KNOW-WHERE." When he reached the Maple Leafs dressing room, Smythe handed the roses to his defenseman King Clancy and told Clancy to hand deliver the flowers to Ross prior to the game. As it happened, Ross was sitting acros the ice with some blue-blooded Bostonians when Clancy skated over with the roses.

Ross was taken aback by Smythe's seemingly gentle gesture and was further touched by the note, particularly since Ross could not read Latin. It just looked good. The woman sitting with Ross graciously accepted the gift until she looked at the note inviting her to shove the flowers up her derriere. Ross discovered, only too late, his companion could read Latin! As Smythe added in a postscript: "Every place Ross and I met, we fought!"

Best Feud between Bruins

Considering that each is a tempestuous individual cut from the same cloth, it was inevitable that Harry Sinden, the general manager, and Don "Grapes" Cherry, the coach, would clash once they were united on the same team.

It was Sinden who originally hired Cherry to coach the Bruins in 1974 and, for a time, it was a high command marriage made in hockey heaven.

Cherry made the Bruins into the lovable Lunchpail

A.C. and always was available to liven up a postgame media session. The Bruins won with "Grapes," but the more they won, the more outrageous he became.

By the end of the 1978-79 season, Sinden had had it with Cherry's bombast and braggadocio. Grapes left Beantown and took over as coach of the Colorado Rockies for the 1979-80 season.

Cherry remained bitter about his rupture with the Bruins and at every opportunity would toss a needle at Sinden. By contrast, Harry stayed as far away from the feud as possible although from time to time, a journalist would phone to elicit a comment about one of Grapes' gibes.

Mutual friends would, occasionally attempt to mediate an armistice, but two decades after the nastiness had begun, Cherry and Sinden were as far apart as ever.

Worst Luck for a Bruins Defensman

Gord Kluzak was Boston's top selection in the 1982 Entry Draft and had superstar written all over him. He made his debut in the 1982-83 season and impressed friend and foe alike with his size and smarts. But a crippling series of injuries limited his effectiveness and, by 1990-91, his career was over.

Most Unusual Theme Song for a Hockey Team

Most NHL teams—or, at least, The Original Six—have had sensible theme songs. For Detroit, it's "Pretty Red Wing" and for the Blackhawks, it's "Chicago, Chicago." For Montreal, it has been "Canadian Capers." The Bruins' song, oddly enough, was called "Paree." The tune, written by Leo Robin with music by Jose Padilla, had been a hit tune when the Bruins went on a European barnstorming trip in the late 1920s. They were in Paris when "Paree" was being played everywhere and brought the tune home with them. Boston Garden organist John Kiley would always play a chorus of "Paree" when the Bruins would step on the ice at the start of a home game.

Best Animal Mascot

Bruins coach Don Cherry's beloved pet was a dog named Blue. At every opportunity, Grapes would regale players and journalists with tales of his bull terrier. He also used Blue to inspire his players. "Once," said Cherry, "I used Blue as a role model. I told Stan Jonathan, John Wensink and Al Secord that they should maintain eye contact with the enemy the way Blue did. I'd say, 'After you hit somebody, don't skate away with your head down. That's like saying the coach sent you out to make the hit so don't get mad at me.' Then I brought Blue into play and pointed out that even though I was her master and she loved me, if I had eye contact with her, she'd come at me. Jonathan, Wensink and Secord got the point."

Worst Bruin with the Most Laughs

During the 1934-35 season, the Bruins employed a defenseman named Jean Baptiste Pusie. According to Bruins legend Milt Schmidt, Pusie did some ridiculous things when he was in Boston.

"When he was with us," said Schmidt, "Pusie once bet $10—which was a lot of money in 1936—that he would get all his hair cut off. Nobody would believe that a hockey player would do that in the middle of the season but Pusie took the ten bucks and came back—bald!

"Another time he was awarded a penalty shot, which is a serious matter. But it wasn't to Jean. The first thing he did was skate to the enemy goalie, pat him on the back, wish him well and then return to center ice for the shot."

Former Bruins president Walter Brown once recalled an incident from the 1933-34 season while Pusie was playing for the Boston Cubs of the Canadian-American League. During one game, Pusie was served a major penalty and his yapping at the referee cost him an additional ten-minute misconduct.

Assuming Pusie was tucked away in the penalty box, the referee continued with the game. A few minutes later, he looked toward the box, but Pusie was gone and nobody knew where he was.

"It seemed that Pusie had become a bit thirsty during his rest in the penalty box," said Canadian author Bill Roche. "He had quietly eased out of the box and strolled along the runway to the dressing room to get a drink. When he was next seen, Jean was on his way back, leisurely peeling and eating an orange."

Pusie's problem never was his sense of humor; it was his lack of big-league ability. After his one season as a Bruin, Jean bounced to the Canadiens in 1935-36 and then passed out of the NHL forever.

Most Unusual Reaction to a Fire Alarm

Frank Brimsek earned his epaulets as a Bruins star before World War II. He was a sensational goaltender, fully deserving the nickname Mister Zero.

During the war, Brimsek served in the U.S. Coast Guard, and upon the conclusion of his service, he returned to Boston. Unfortunately, the years away from the NHL had dulled his skills. He never was the same sharp goalie he had been in his younger days. Finally, the Bruins dealt him to the Blackhawks, where his play got even worse and his nerves even more frayed.

One tale about Brimsek had it that on a road trip with the Blackhawks, his team stopped over in Boston. Before

the game, Frankie was walking along a Beantown street with a teammate when they approached a corner that had a fire alarm box.

In those days each fire stanchion was topped by a red globe that flashed whenever there was an alarm in any part of the city.

Unfortunately, the fire box globe bore a distinct resemblance to the goal light behind Brimsek's net. As Frankie and mate reached the corner, Mister Zero noticed the flashing red light atop the fire box. He grabbed his teammate by the arm and shouted, "GOAL! GOAL! GOAL! GET ME OUTTA HERE!!!"

Best Underrated Bruin

Bobby Orr, Phil Esposito, Milt Schmidt, Eddie Shore and Frankie Brimsek are among the best-known Boston hockey heroes, and deservedly so. But one Boston skater who deserves to be ranked among them—and never seems to get the mention—is Bill Cowley. He entered the NHL during the 1934-35 season with the St. Louis Eagles, but became a Bruin to stay the following year. He starred for the Boston sextet through the 1946-47 season. Smaller than Schmidt, Cowley relied on guile more than strength, emphasizing subtlety over Schmidt's accent on sock. Many critics believe that if Cowley had been blessed with linemates such as Woody Dumart and Bobby Bauer, who complemented Schmidt on the Kraut Line, then Cowley would have been by far the most productive Bruin. As it stands, he remains the most underrated.

Worst Reason for Delaying a Bruins Home Game

Pearl Harbor Day was December 7, 1941—"[The] day that will live in infamy"—when the Japanese bombed the American naval, army and air force bases in a sneak attack that mobilized the country. But war was not immediately declared. However, on December 9, 1941, the Bruins had a game against Chicago at Boston Garden. The contest was delayed for twenty-eight minutes as players and fans listened to President Franklin Delano Roosevelt announce to the nation that war had been declared. Shortly thereafter, several Bruins—including Milt Schmidt, Bobby Bauer, Woody Dumart and Frank Brimsek—enlisted in the armed forces.

Most Unusual Position for a Bruins Forward

During the NHL's one-goalie era, it occasionally was necessary to replace the starting netminder with a substitute if the regular puck-stopper was seriously injured during a game. Usually, a "house" goalie assigned by the NHL would take over but this was not the case on October 6, 1960. When regular Bruins goalie Don Simmons was wounded on the ice and removed for treatment in a game against the Detroit Red Wings, forward Jerry Toppazzini went between the pipes. Topper didn't get hurt because only a minute remained in the game. Besides, Boston lost the game to Detroit, 4-1.

Best Bruins Nicknames
(In Alphabetical Order)

Carl "Buddy" Boone; Frank "Mr. Zero" Brimsek; John "Chief" Bucyk; Gerry "Cheesie" Cheevers; Don "Grape" Cherry; Aubrey "Dit" Clapper; Pat "Boxcar" Egan; Johnny "Black Cat" Gagnon; Lloyd "Gabby" Gronsdahl; Doug "Hawk" Halward; Robert "Red" Hamill; Fern "Curley" Headley; "Long" John Henderson; Murray "Moe" Henderson; Gord "Red" Henry; "Sugar" Jim Henry; Mel "Sudden Death" Hill; Jim "Dede" Klein; Joe "Duke of Paducah" Klukay; Al "Junior" Langlois; Jeff "Lazar" Lazaro; Reggie "Rifle" Leach; "Horse Face" Harry or "Apple Cheeks" Lumley; Nevin "The Kid" Markwart; Gilles "Captain Crunch" Marotte; "Slick" Rick Middleton; Chris "Knuckles" Nilan; Jim "Peggy" O'Neill; Eric "Cowboy" Pettinger; Jacques "Jake the Snake" Plante; Walter "Babe" Pratt; Ed "Rags" Reigle; Vladimir "Rosie" Ruzicka; Derek "Turk" Sanderson; Ed "Sandy" Sandford; Glen "Slats" Sather; "Big" Al Secord; Eddie "The Entertainer" Shack; Albert "Babe" Siebert, Reginald Joseph "Hooley" Smith; Pat "Whitey" Stapleton; Nelson "Old Poison" Stewart; Bill "Red" Stuart; Cecil "Tiny" Thompson; Jerry "Topper" Toppazzini; Zellio "Topper" Toppazzini; Mike "Shaky" Walton; Grant David "Knobby" Warwick; John "Wire" Wensink; Jim "Ripper" Wiemer.

Worst Non-Playoff Run

Before their glory days in the 1970s, there were the dark ages of the 1960s. From the 1959-60 season through 1966-67, the Bruins missed the playoffs for seven consecutive seasons.

Derek Sanderson's Four Bests as a Player

1. He was the most underrated of the Big, Bad Bruins who won Stanley Cups in 1970 and 1972. 2. He was the first NHL player to pose seminude in *Life* magazine. 3. He was the first NHL player to co-author two autobiographies—*I've Got to Be Me* (Dodd Mead) and *The Derek Sanderson Nobody Knows* (Follet)—within three years. 4. He was the first NHL defector to the World Hockey Association to purchase a Rolls-Royce.

Most Unusual Hobby

When Bobby Orr and the Big, Bad Bruins were winning Stanley Cups in 1970 and 1972, Ed Westfall was neutralizing the enemy ace with magnificent aplomb, while managing to score a few himself. In his spare time, he was also a licensed pilot.

Gunilla Knudson, "the Noxzema Girl," shares a laugh with Derek Sanderson on the set of his Boston-based television show, circa 1971.

Boston BRUINS

A Chronology of Fifty Momentous Events in Bruins History

1. *February 9, 1924* — The city of Boston is granted a National Hockey League franchise. Owner Charles F. Adams decides to name it the Bruins.

2. *December 1, 1924* — Boston's baby Bruins defeat the Montreal Maroons, 2-1, in their first game. It is the inaugural game at Boston Arena.

3. *April 7, 1927* — The Bruins are in their first Stanley Cup final, facing the Ottawa Senators. The score was 0-0 at Boston Arena. The game was called with one minute remaining in the second overtime because the ice was too rough to continue. Ottawa would win the series, two games to none, with two ties.

4. *November 20, 1928* — Boston Garden on Causeway Street opens to an overflow crowd as fans knock down the doors to see the Bruins meet Les Canadiens. Montreal wins, 1-0, before an estimated 17,000 fans.

5. *March 29, 1929* — After beating the Rangers, 2-0, at Boston the day before, the Bruins defeat New York, 2-1, at Madison Square Garden to win their first Stanley Cup. Bill Carson scored the winning goal at 18:02 of the third period.

6. *March 18, 1930* — Bruins goalie Tiny Thompson wins his first Vezina Trophy with a league-leading 2.23 goals-against average.

7. *March 22, 1931* — For the second consecutive year, the Bruins win the NHL's American Division race with a record of 28-10-6.

8. *March 23, 1933* — Boston defenseman Eddie Shore totals eight goals and twenty-seven assists for thirty-five points in forty-eight games to win his first Hart Trophy as the NHL's Most Valuable Player.

9. *November 6, 1937* — The Kitchener Kids—also known as the Kraut Line—composed of Milt Schmidt, Bobby Bauer and Woody Dumart, make their debut as a unit.

10. *April 19, 1938* — Eddie Shore captures his fourth Hart Trophy and goaltender Tiny Thompson wins his fourth Vezina Trophy.

11. *November 27, 1938* — Tiny Thompson plays his last game in a Bruins uniform. He beats the New York Americans, 8-2. He is then sold to the Detroit Red Wings and replaced by rookie Frank Brimsek.

12. *December 1, 1938* — Brimsek takes over in goal and loses to Les Canadiens, 2-0, but then returns with a 5-0 shutout over Chicago followed by a 2-0 blanking of the Blackhawks. Next was a 3-0 decision over the Rangers. In three weeks Brimsek would have six shutouts in seven games and would be dubbed "Mister Zero."

13. *April 2, 1939* — Mel Hill scores his third overtime goal in the Boston-Rangers best-of-seven series at Boston Garden. The goal at eight minutes of the third overtime gives the Bruins a four-games-to-three victory in the semifinals and sends them on to the finals against Toronto.

14. *April 16, 1939* — The Bruins win the Stanley Cup, defeating Toronto, 3-1, at Boston Garden. Roy Conacher scores the winning goal as the Bruins romp, four games to one.

15. *April 23, 1939* — Rookie goalie Frank Brimsek wins both the Calder and Vezina Trophies.

16. *March 17, 1940* — Members of the Kraut Line — Milt Schmidt, Bobby Bauer and Woody Dumart—finish one-two-three in NHL scoring. Schmidt has 52 points while the others are tied at 43 points. Following them is teammate-center Bill Cowley with 40 points.

17. *April 12, 1941* — Sweeping the Detroit Red Wings, four games to none, the Bruins win their second Stanley Cup in three years. The final game, at Detroit's Olympia Stadium, is won on a three-goal Bruin rally in the second period. Bobby Bauer scored the winning goal in the 3-1 decision.

18. *January 8, 1947* — Aubrey "Dit" Clapper puts a signature on a sensational career by scoring his 200th NHL goal. Clapper, who broke in during the 1927-28 season, played the first half of his career as a forward and the latter half as a defenseman.

19. *April 5, 1953* — One of the biggest upsets in playoff history is completed, as underdog Boston defeats heavily favored Detroit, four games to two. Led by Jack McIntyre, who scored the sudden-death winner in Game Three, the Bruins beat Detroit, 4-2, at Boston Garden for the clincher. Sugar Jim Henry outgoals Terry Sawchuk in the nets and elderly Woody Dumart checks Gordie Howe to a standstill.

20. *June 3, 1955* — A blockbuster Bruins-Red Wings deal sends Ed Sandford, Real Chevrefils, Warren Godfrey, Norm Corcoran and Gilles Boisvert to Detroit. In return, Boston receives Terry Sawchuk, Vic Stasiuk, Marcel Bonin and Lorne Davis.

21. *January 15, 1958* — After serving a long stint in the minors, Willie O'Ree is promoted to the Bruins. He becomes the NHL's first black player.

22. *October 19, 1966* — Heralded as the savior of a woeful Boston sextet, Bobby Orr graduates from junior hockey and makes his NHL debut. The defenseman is an instant hit.

23. *May 9, 1967* — Fulfilling his notices, Bobby Orr wins the Calder Trophy as rookie of the year and is named a defenseman on the Second All-Star Team.

24. *May 15, 1967* — General manager Milt Schmidt makes the deal of a lifetime. He trades second-string center Pit Martin, disappointing defenseman Gilles Marotte and minor league goalie Jack Norris to Chicago for centers Phil Esposito and Fred Stanfield, as well as right wing Ken Hodge. The trio becomes the offensive nucleus of Stanley Cup winners in 1970 and 1972.

25. *December 2, 1967* — Left wing John Bucyk passes Milt Schmidt to become the Bruins' all-time leading goal scorer.

26. *May 17, 1968* — Bobby Orr—only nineteen years old—emerges as the dominant defenseman of his era, winning the first of eight straight Norris Trophies.

27. *March 30, 1969* — Phil Esposito sets an NHL record for points (126) and assists (77).

28. *March 30, 1969* — With 303 goals, the Bruins become the first team in NHL history to score more than 300 goals.

29. *May 10, 1970* — For the first time since 1941, the Bruins win a Stanley Cup. Bobby Orr beats St. Louis Blues goalie Glenn Hall at forty seconds of overtime to clinch the four-game sweep. Orr wins the Conn Smythe Trophy as the playoffs' most valuable player.

30. *April 4, 1971* — Phil Esposito sets a new NHL record for goals with 76, while Bobby Orr breaks the record for assists with 102.

31. *April 18, 1971* — The Bruins Express, rolling toward a second straight Stanley Cup, is derailed in the opening round. Les Canadiens, behind rookie goalie Ken Dryden's outstanding work, defeat the Bruins, 4-2, at Boston Garden to win the series, four games to three.

32. *May 11, 1972* — In a hard-fought six-game series, the Bruins clinch their second Stanley Cup in three years with a 3-0 win over the New York Rangers at Madison Square Garden. Bobby Orr scores the winning goal at 11:18 of the first period. Orr also wins the Conn Smythe Trophy for the second time in three years.

33. *October 30, 1975* — John Bucyk becomes the seventh player to net 500 career goals. He scores a goal in his 1,370th game for a 3-2 Boston win over St.Louis.

34. *November 7, 1975* — In a stunning trade among bitter rivals, the Bruins send onetime hero Phil Esposito and defenseman Carol Vadnais to the Rangers for defenseman Brad Park, center Jean Ratelle and defenseman Joe Zanussi. Boston is shocked by the deal.

35. *May 24, 1976* — Jean Ratelle, who is making Bostonians forget Phil Esposito, wins the Lady Byng Trophy. Coach Don Cherry wins the Adams Award.

36. *May 26, 1976* — The Bruins trade right wing Ken Hodge to the Rangers for right wing Rick Middleton. In time, this would prove to be the most one-sided one-on-one deal—in Boston's favor—ever made in the NHL. Hodge flops in New York. Middleton stars with the Bruins.

37. *June 24, 1976* — The Bobby Orr era ends in Boston. Guided by his agent, Alan Eagleson, Orr signs with the Chicago Blackhawks as a free agent.

38. *May 10, 1979* — Leading Game Seven of the Montreal-Boston semifinals, 4-3, late in the third period, the Bruins are caught with too many men on the ice. On the ensuing power play, Guy Lafleur scores and Don Cherry's team—which looked good enough to win the Stanley Cup—is eliminated on a Habs goal in overtime.

39. *August 9, 1979* — With the eighth pick overall in the NHL Entry Draft, Boston selects Raymond Bourque. The defenseman from Verdun of the Quebec Major Junior League would become the Bruins' cornerstone through the end of the 20th century.

40. *May 30, 1980* — Raymond Bourque wins the Calder Trophy, launching an award-filled career that in many ways would equal that of defense icons Eddie Shore and Bobby Orr.

41. *December 11, 1980* — Brad Park becomes only the second defenseman in NHL history to get 500 assists. Like Jean Ratelle, Park emerges as an ex-Ranger-turned-Boston-hero.

42. *February 3, 1983* — Wayne Cashman, one of the most popular forwards in Boston hockey history, plays in his 1,000th NHL game.

43. *September 17, 1985* — Raymond Bourque is named co-captain of the Bruins, along with Rick Middleton. Bourque would become full captain in the 1988-89 season.

44. *November 15, 1986* — Rick Middleton—nicknamed "Nifty"—scores his 900th NHL point.

45. *December 3, 1987* — In an emotional ceremony at Boston Garden, Raymond Bourque removes his number seven jersey and presents it to Phil Esposito to retire Espo's number. Bourque then reveals his new number seventy-seven uniform.

46. *March 8, 1988* — The Bruins acquire goaltender Andy Moog from the Edmonton Oilers for Geoff Courtnall, Bill Ranford and a second-round draft choice.

47. *May 8, 1988* — A Bruins-Devils game at Byrne-Meadowlands Arena in New Jersey is delayed because of a court injunction. The Devils had protested the NHL suspension of coach Jim Schoenfeld. After a local judge supported the hockey club, Schoenfeld went behind the bench for Game Four of the series. However, the regular referee, Dave Newell, and linesmen Gord Broseker and Ray Scapinello refused to officiate. Three off-ice officials replaced them, wearing yellow sweatshirts. The Mother's Day game was dubbed Yellow Sunday because of the shirts. New Jersey won the game, 3-1.

48. *May 14, 1988* — Probably the best-ever save made by a Bruins goalie is pulled off by Reggie Lemelin in the first period of Game Seven of the Boston-New Jersey series. With the score tied, 0-0, and the first goal expected to be the winner, Pat Verbeek of the Devils took a pass in front of the net. Far out of position, Lemelin appeared helpless as Verbeek shot at the gaping net. Somehow—nobody quite knows how—Lemelin stretched his glove, pad and stick and deflected the puck to the side. Boston won the game, 6-2, and the series.

49. *May 24, 1988* — A major electrical breakdown occurs at Boston Garden during Game Four of the Oilers-Bruins Stanley Cup finals. With the game tied, 3-3, and the arena in a state of near-chaos, play is suspended by NHL president John Ziegler and the fans sent home.

50. *March 28, 1999* — Raymond Bourque scores his 385th career goal in a game against Toronto at Air Canada Centre, tying him with Paul Coffey for the regular-season record among defensemen.

The 1924-25 Bruins were America's first NHL team.

Boston BRUINS

Oral History: Ed Sandford and Myles J. Lane

Ed Sandford

He is still seen around Bruins home games, a tall distinguished figure who epitomizes Boston hockey both past and present.

Ed Sandford can be described as a pure Bruin, first as a player and more recently as an off-ice official at home games.

In the following oral history, which originally appeared in Heroes and History: Voices from the NHL's Past, *co-authored by Shirley Fischler, Sandford details what hockey life was like in Boston. The era covered spans the years 1947-55. It was an uncomplicated time, when Sandford was one of big-league hockey's most productive players.*

Where I grew up, in Toronto, everybody inherited a pair of skates and I was no different. We had an outdoor rink nearby where everybody skated—the neighbors, the kids, everyone. Of course, there was a competitive team, and when I was about 11, I made the team. From that point on, I was playing plenty of hockey.

In those days all the games were played outdoors at night, against teams from neighboring towns. At the time, I had no idea I was going to be a professional hockey player. Sure, I was interested in the game, and we all listened to Foster Hewitt broadcast the Maple Leafs games every Saturday night.

When spring came and the ice melted, I switched to lacrosse, which was very popular where I came from. Other places had baseball as the big warm-weather sport, but not us; it was lacrosse, which was a wonderful conditioner for hockey.

At that time, junior hockey was extremely popular in Ontario, and the Ontario Hockey Association's Junior A League was the top of the line. If you could reach that level, you knew you had a chance to turn pro, because a whole bunch of guys from the OHA had made it to the NHL over the years.

I was very fortunate. I kept improving and finally made it to Saint Michael's College, which was a Catholic boys' school in Toronto. St. Mike's was renowned for its terrific hockey teams, so I considered myself in very good company. Grade nine was my first semester at St. Mike's, and I remained there right up until I joined their Junior A club.

We had a wonderful team and one year actually won the Memorial Cup. By that time I knew that pro scouts were looking at us, but I still had no thoughts of an NHL career. My first thought was about getting a good education—not that I had anything against hockey.

World War II was at its peak then and I was getting very close to being drafted. My father worked in a munitions plant, so you can imagine that the war was uppermost in our minds. In 1944 the Allies invaded France [D-Day] and, thank goodness, the war began to swing in our favor. Meanwhile, I was still playing hockey and getting better at it all the time.

There were lots of top players in juniors then. Tod Sloan, who later became a big player with the Maple Leafs, was with us at St. Mike's, and Gus Mortson, who was a very good Maple Leafs defenseman, and Jimmy Thomson as well. Red Kelly, who eventually made it to the Hockey Hall of Fame, was also a St. Mike's grad. In fact, I played defense with Red in juniors.

Then, right out of the blue, I got an offer to play for the Bruins—contract and all. At first I wasn't sure that I wanted to go to Boston. The idea of giving up school weighed on me, and then there was the possibility of taking night courses. I finally decided to give the Bruins a shot, and am I ever grateful that I made that decision. It was one of the best moves of my life.

It wasn't easy to break into the big-time that year because of all the players who had come back from the armed forces. Only five or six centers broke in that whole year that I made the Bruins. It was a very competitive field and I was lucky to get a spot on the varsity.

The Bruins didn't have a championship team when I came down in 1947, but they were good. Frankie Brimsek was our goalie. His nickname was "Mister Zero" from all the shutouts he got when he came to Boston as a rookie.

Frank had reached his peak when World War II broke out, and then he joined the U.S. Coast Guard. Brimmie was one of the guys who suffered from a long stint in the service, but he still had some good goaltending in him (2.80 goals against). He was a marvelous athlete who kept himself in excellent shape. He had one concern and that was spotlights or flashing lights anywhere near him at any time of the day of a game, even hours before the game. In the dressing room he would sit with his head covered with a towel because he didn't want the lights of the room bothering his eyes. Brimsek was always concerned about not being able to see as well as he wanted. When I joined the club, he had a pretty good defense in front of him.

Our veterans were Pat Egan, whose nickname was "Boxcar," because that's what he was built like, and Johnny "Jack" Crawford. Jack was a piece of work, let me tell you. He was the only player in the league to wear a helmet at the time, but it had nothing to do with protecting his head. Jack was completely bald and he was so embarrassed by it that he decided to wear the headpiece. The best young defenseman on the club was Fernie Flaman, out of Saskatchewan. Flaman had played for our minor league club in the Eastern League, the Boston Olympics, and he was a tough customer.

Up front, I had some good forwards to work with, including Milt Schmidt and Woody Dumart, who were two-thirds of the Kraut Line. Among the younger guys was Johnny Peirson, who was from Montreal and had gone to McGill University for a year. John was the right wing on my line. He was an astute hockey player; a smart, right-hand shot and a good skater who played his position well. I'd call him a thinking man's hockey player—always watching to see what the other guy was doing and trying to offset him. I liked playing with Peirson because I knew pretty well what he was going to do when we were on the ice.

In my first full season, 1947-48, I scored 10 goals and 15 assists over 59 games. We finished third, behind Toronto and Detroit, and then played the Leafs in the opening playoff round. They had a powerful club that year with three great centers: Max Bentley, Syl Apps and Ted Kennedy. We almost beat them in the opening game at Toronto, but they won it in overtime and then took the next two. We finally beat them once in Boston before they knocked us out in five games.

A year later we finished second and I scored 16 goals and 20 assists in 56 games. As luck would have it, the Leafs, who finished a poor fourth—under the .500 mark—got hot at the right time. They beat us four games to one in the first round and then swept Detroit in four straight to win the Stanley Cup for the third straight time, which was a league record.

When I think back, the real negative in my career is that I never played on a Stanley Cup-winner. The

Canadiens were the power team right after the war, then the Maple Leafs won three straight Stanley Cups up to 1949, and in 1950 the Red Wings, with Ted Lindsay, Sid Abel and Gordie Howe, won the Cup.

We kept getting to the semifinals, but not beyond. In 1951, for example, we played the Leafs and looked like we might take them. The opening game was in Toronto and we came out on top, 2-0. Our goalie was Jack Gelineau, who was rather unique in that we got him straight out of McGill University. If we had won the second game—also in Toronto—I think we could have won the series. As it happened, the second game was a real oddity. In those days, the City of Toronto had what they called a blue law, which meant that you couldn't play a professional sport on Sundays. That was when Toronto was a very conservative town.

Well, the second game was on March 31, 1951, which was a Saturday night. That was no problem, except that the score was tied 1-1 after three periods, and we went into overtime.

Into the extra session we went and still there was no score, except that now it was getting closer and closer to midnight—and Sunday, when no pro hockey could be played. Finally, the game was stopped at midnight, a 1-1 tie and a washed-out game. But the law was the law, so we headed for Boston and Game Three on April Fool's Day. Turk Broda, who was Toronto's elderly goalie—but a great one in clutch playoff games—shut us out 3-0, and then Toronto beat us again on our home rink, Boston Garden, 3-1. We lost the next two, 4-1 and 6-0, and we were out again.

We had a very competitive team, but we just couldn't get over the hump. Our coach was Lynn Patrick—father of Craig Patrick, general manager of the Penguins—and he really knew his stuff. He had coached the Rangers when they went all the way to the seventh game of the Stanley Cup finals against Detroit in 1950, and then he came over to Boston.

In 1951-52 we finished fourth and then had a terrific semifinal playoff series with Montreal, who had finished second. They took the first two games at home by big scores [5-1, 4-0] but then we bounced back and won the next three in a row. Game Six was in Boston, and if we win that, we go to the finals.

This was a dandy. The game was tied 2-2 at the end of regulation. We played a whole overtime without a goal, and then they beat us a little more than seven minutes into the second overtime. So, the seventh game was in Montreal and they won that, 3-1, and we were out again.

We finally made it to the finals in 1953, but only after a terrific upset over the Red Wings in the opening round. Detroit had a powerhouse in 1952-53. Gordie Howe was at the top of his career; they had a fine defense, and young

Terry Sawchuk was in goal.

They trounced us 7-0 in the opening game at Detroit and everyone figured that they'd run right over us. But we came right back and won 5-3 in Game Two at Detroit and, all of a sudden, a lot of things were going right for us. The line I played on—with Johnny Peirson and Fleming Mackell—got hot and we defensed very well against Howe and Lindsay.

Our old-timers—Milt Schmidt and Woody Dumart—were terrific. Lynn Patrick assigned Dumart to guard Howe and he did a terrific job shutting him down. Our reserves, particularly a fellow named Jack McIntyre, came through for us big-time. We came home to Boston Garden and beat Detroit 2-1 in overtime, and all of a sudden the hockey world was going wild, especially after we beat them again, 6-2, at home.

We returned to Detroit and they came up big, 6-4, at old Olympia Stadium, but we knocked them off 4-2 in Game Six at Boston and that was that, one of the biggest upsets in hockey history.

I got six goals in that series and my linemates got two or three, so we carried the team offensively and that put us up against the Canadiens—Montreal had beaten Chicago four games to three in the other semifinal—in the finals.

It was the closest I ever came to winning a Stanley Cup. Montreal beat us 4-2 in the opener and then we rebounded for a 4-1 win at the Forum, of all places. After that it was all downhill. They took us 3-0, 7-3 and 1-0 to wrap things up. The last game was tied 0-0 after three periods, but before the overtime was two minutes old, Elmer Lach scored on a Maurice Richard pass and we were done.

That wasn't my last playoff; I had two more with the Bruins but never got to the finals again. I stayed a Bruin until June 1955, when I was traded to Detroit. It was quite a deal; Real Chevrefils, Norm Corcoran, Gilles Boisvert and Warren Godfrey, all from the Bruins, went to the Red Wings. In return, Boston got the great Sawchuk, as well as Marcel Bonin, Vic Stasiuk and Lorne Davis.

Ed Sandford taking flight.

Steve Babineau

I only played four games for the Red Wings and then got dealt to Chicago for Metro Prystai in October 1955. The 1955-56 season was my last in the NHL and I finished playing 57 games for Chicago, getting a dozen goals, nine assists and 21 points.

All in all, I had a very enjoyable career, and I was fortunate to remain connected to hockey and to have been able to follow the game in the 37 or so years since I played in the NHL.

Comparing today's game with that when I played is interesting. The NHL players now are bigger and stronger than we were, and much faster than I ever was. The game itself has changed enormously and I doubt that our Bruins line [Mackell-Peirson-Sandford] would be able to contain any of today's big lines. They skate faster today and they shoot the puck harder. The one thing we could do better was pass the puck. Really, we're talking about two different eras. It's like trying to compare the earlier baseball players to the current players.

It was a completely different style. We only used straight-bladed sticks—no curves or hi-tech stuff like they have now—and virtually nobody used the slap shot. We traveled from city to city by train and we had more time with each other.

Another difference was the birthplace of the players. Nearly all of us were Canadians. There was a sprinkling of Americans in the NHL, guys like Frankie Brimsek, who came from Minnesota, but nearly everybody came from Canada and, of course, there were no Russians at all, although there was a Finn—fellow named Pentti Lund—who played for the Rangers and Bruins for a while.

I can remember the first time I saw the Russians playing at the Boston Garden. It was about 25 years ago. They played Harvard and, to be honest, they didn't look all that good to me.

What I recall was that I wanted very much to see them practice, and they were always very guarded about those things. They would never tell you when they were going to practice. They'd have a practice scheduled for noon, and then you'd find out that the scrimmage was another time.

I finally did get to see them practice, and what I noticed was that they borrowed some of the best techniques of our prewar teams, like the old Rangers, who were so good at passing the puck and stickhandling. That was what Bill and Bun Cook and Frank Boucher had done so well when the Rangers were winning Stanley Cups in the late 1920s and early 1930s. The Russians had improved on these methods and were using them in their practices. That's how they got so good to where they could compete against the NHL All-Stars in 1972.

Getting back to my own hockey life, I retired in 1958 and got a job with an investment company in the Boston area, a small brokerage firm. In 1967-68 I became an off-ice official with the NHL, except in those days we were called "minor officials."

As a result, I've been fortunate to have seen a lot of hockey and to have witnessed the evolution of the game. When I played, the shots were so much slower; now the slap shot is very, very prominent. I look back to the years when Phil Esposito led the NHL in scoring and I don't even think he ever slapped the puck. Maybe once or twice. Same with Gordie Howe.

Now the slap shot is dominating, but I don't think it should be as prominent as it is, because it is so hard to be accurate with it.

When I played for the Bruins, Clarence Campbell was president of the league and remained so long after I retired. I became an off-ice official while Campbell still was president and I've worked through the John Ziegler administration and now under the commissioner, Gary Bettman.

Big-league hockey is a whole new ball game nowadays, and the accent is more on entertainment than it was when I played. In the late 1940s and early 1950s, we weren't thinking of ourselves and of marketing and things like that. We just thought that hockey was an interesting game for people to watch. Those of us who came down from Canada found that we were in competition with many other sports, such as basketball, baseball and football, not to mention a whole lot of other things, but we did well. At the time we didn't think it was necessary to market our game, to encourage people to come and watch it.

Times have changed, and now they look at it differently, what with television and ratings and competition. Now the NHL is doing an effective job after some troubled times.

I believe that if the NHL can educate the people in the southern states, hockey will become even more popular, although it is not an easy task. But I'm convinced that the game is moving in the right direction.

Certainly, it has done well by me, and proof that I still love it is the fact that I have remained connected with the sport for all these many years—all in Boston.

When I think back, I can assure you that I wouldn't have changed many things, other than the fact that I would have loved to have played for just one Stanley Cup-winner.

Otherwise, if I had to do it all over again, I would do it about the same—although I would want to be a faster skater!

Myles J. Lane

No other former Bruin could make this statement—he played defense in the National Hockey League and later became a justice on the New York State Supreme Court. That honor belonged to Myles J. Lane, who not only was a hockey star and a scholar, but also an All-American football player at Dartmouth. A native of the Boston area, he played for both the New York Rangers and the Bruins. In his own words he told Stan Fischler what it was like to grow up in the Boston area and eventually become a member of the Bruins.

Lots of places across the United States could qualify as "the hockey capital of the nation," but my choice is Melrose, Massachusetts—my hometown. Even before I grew up, hockey was the number one sport there and some really fine players learned the game in our neighborhood.

Many people in the States know the name Hobey Baker, since he's one of the few Americans in the Hockey Hall of Fame, but we had a fellow in Melrose, "Bags" Wanamaker, who in those days was the next best thing to Baker. He wasn't the only top-notch skater around. Hago Harrington, later a big man in Boston hockey, was also from our area and, like me, played on the big pond in the middle of town whenever it was frozen.

I was about six years old when I got my first pair of skates and it was something awful trying to learn on them. I attempted to play with the big boys, but could hardly stand up on the blades and was so small my hockey stick would be taller than I was and end up around the faces of my bigger friends. In other words, I was high-sticking at the age of six.

We had hockey little leagues in grammar school then, just as they have in Canada and in parts of the United States now. And, don't forget, this was back in the early twenties.

It took a bit of time, but I soon started to improve my skating, and when I reached my teens was good enough to play defense for our high school team. That was really something. Ours was the best hockey team in the state; we won something like 23 games and lost only one during a single season, and that was because we were physically exhausted.

I'll tell you just how good we were. We once scrimmaged with Harvard, the intercollegiate champions, and although they beat us 2-1 in a 60-minute game, it was quite a feather in the cap of Melrose High. That same year we defeated Boston College.

Even though I was playing defense for the high school team, I liked rushing and did quite a lot of puck-carrying; I continued to rush right through my college playing career since nobody said "don't do it." Meanwhile, I played against some really first-rate competition. When I was still in high school, I can remember being permitted to play for a team that took on a bunch passing themselves off as amateurs but who later became the Pittsburgh Yellow Jackets. They were really pros but nobody said anything about it.

All of this gave me terrific experience. Here I was, only 16 years old, going up against fellows who were professionals. It provided quite a head start for my college tryout and, in retrospect, it made playing college hockey as easy as rolling off a log. When it came time for me to select a college, I went up to Hanover, New Hampshire, to look over Dartmouth. I had already received three or four football scholarships elsewhere but liked the looks of Dartmouth and decided to go there, although they didn't give any hockey scholarships.

College hockey was very big in those days. We played Harvard, Yale, Princeton, Toronto, Boston University and M.I.T. Whenever we played in Boston against Harvard or Yale, the Garden would be packed and, usually, the proceeds for those games went to a charity.

At the time, my heart was set on graduating from Dartmouth and then going to law school. I didn't think I wanted to be a professional athlete for the simple reason that a top-notch hockey player couldn't stay in the NHL for more than eight or ten years but one could have a lifetime career by going into law, finance, or some other business.

I also figured only the really big stars made the big money. I knew I was taking something of a gamble, but my target was law school, not the NHL. Then, in my senior year, our team went up against the University of Toronto, managed by Conn Smythe, who soon left the university to become boss of the Maple Leafs. Apparently, he liked the way I played, because he contacted me to say he'd like me to join the Toronto Maple Leafs.

Naturally, I was flattered but told Smythe I wanted to go to law school; and if I was going to pursue hockey, I would do it with a team in the United States. That way, I could continue my law studies and still play hockey. In those days if a representative of an NHL team talked with you, it meant your name was automatically put on that team's list and no other team could negotiate with you.

So, I wound up with my name on the Toronto Maple

Leafs' negotiation list. I've since heard that Boston had wanted to sign me too because I was a local boy—Melrose is only about seven miles outside Boston—but they couldn't deal with me on account of Smythe. After a while, I convinced Smythe that I didn't want to go to Toronto, so the Leafs swapped my name with the New York Rangers and Toronto took a player from the New York list.

The Rangers didn't own me; I was still in college and hadn't signed with them. In fact, I didn't talk to anybody connected with the Rangers until after I had made a trip South that spring with the Dartmouth baseball team. We had gone down to Atlanta and were heading home when I got a wire from Colonel Hammond, the Rangers' president. He said he wanted to see me in New York, which was okay with me since we were stopping off at Philadelphia for a game against the University of Pennsylvania.

After the game, I came up to New York and sat down with him. The first thing he said was that he wanted me to sign, but I replied nothing doing. At the time I just wasn't sure that I wanted to go into hockey. There were other things on my mind, other offers.

One was an opportunity to teach at the Taft School in Connecticut, and I couldn't decide whether I wanted to play one year of hockey or teach one year at Taft, then go to law school. I spoke to Mr. Taft and he said something to me I've never forgotten.

"Mr. Lane, the job is yours, if you want it. But, don't fool me!"

I asked, "What do you mean?"

He answered, "Don't come here for one year and then leave me. It's a good position if you want to teach for the rest of your life. But don't fool with me. Let me know if you intend to stay with me or just want to make it a one-year proposition."

"Mr. Taft," I told him, "I can't fool you and I can't give you an answer. I have in the back of my head a desire to go into the law business so I'm not certain whether I'd stay one year or more than one."

Right then and there with that exchange I decided to accept the Rangers' hockey proposition. In September, I contacted Colonel Hammond and signed with New York, got a bonus and made a lot more money than any of my college classmates did.

When I joined the Rangers, they had four defensemen led by Ching Johnson and Taffy Abel. The third man was Leo Bourgault, a little fellow about 5'8" and 140 pounds. Leo was a rushing defenseman but too small to do much checking. I was the fourth man. Strangely enough, coach Lester Patrick started me out with Ching.

I'll never forget my first game at Madison Square Garden. I was thrown off the ice three times with penalties and Ching finally came over to me and said, "If you don't cut this out you're going to be the bad man of hockey instead of me."

But my penalties were the result of inexperience more than anything else; after all, I was just a rookie. Then, after the game, a funny thing happened.

A fellow by the name of Eddie O'Neill was covering hockey for the Associated Press at the time and he came into our dressing room and started interviewing me. His first question was: "How did you feel out there tonight in your first game as a professional?"

I replied, "Well, it wasn't really too bad out there."

Eddie said, "No, give me an angle. Look, I'm like you —I'm a college man. Was there anything different out there from the kind of hockey you experienced at Dartmouth?"

"Look, Eddie," I told him, "that's a silly question because you know as well as I do that there's no comparison between college and professional hockey. It's an entirely different game, like the difference between minor league baseball and major league ball."

O'Neill went on. "Let me ask you a couple of questions," he said. "Did you ever play a college game in which you were a lot more tired than you are tonight?"

I said, "Of course I did," and he asked why.

"When I played college hockey," I replied, "I played as much as 60 minutes without relief. If you're in a daisy chain for 60 minutes, you'll get tired of walking around. But out there tonight I'd get relief every three or four minutes, so I wasn't so tired afterwards."

"Wasn't it rough?" O'Neill asked.

"Sure," I said, "it's rougher than the college game, but I wasn't tired because of the relief I got."

When O'Neill was finished, I got dressed, returned to my hotel and went to bed. The next morning I went downstairs for breakfast and ran into the desk clerk, a friend of mine. He asked if I had seen the *Times* that morning and when I replied no, he said, "Here, take a look."

So I picked up the paper and saw a headline across the sports page that read, "LANE SAYS PROFESSIONAL HOCKEY A CINCH COMPARED TO THE COLLEGE BRAND."

That was really something. Worse still, I had to report to the Garden later that day, since it was customary to check in with the club on a daily basis. When I walked into the dressing room there were all those Canadian players— and me just an American collegian—and you could have cut the silence with a knife.

I simply told them the headline was a complete fabrication; I had never made such a claim. And that was that, as far as the players themselves were concerned.

Not long after, we took a trip to Montreal to play the Maroons. This was the English team that represented Montreal in the NHL; and they were big, husky and tough. When we arrived in town, I picked up a paper and read an article exhorting the populace to come down to the game and watch this upstart American collegian get his comeuppance. The paper went on to say how I had told a reporter what a simple game this Canadian hockey was, and so forth.

As expected, the people came streaming into the Forum that night looking for blood, and I knew it. On the very first rush I made down the ice, two Maroons came at me and tried to put me right over the sideboards. One of them went off with a penalty.

I rushed down the ice three times and on those three rushes, three Montreal players went into the cooler. The game got rougher and rougher as it went along. Later on, Ching Johnson skated down the ice and was whacked hard by one of the Maroons. He lost his balance and slid into the backboards. Though he threw both his feet up to break the slide, unfortunately his skate got caught in the boards and his ankle twisted around and broke. He was through for the season.

After that happened, Taffy Abel made a rush down the ice and someone stepped on his foot. He needed 13 stitches to close the wound. That left Leo Bourgault and myself out on the ice. I was about 6'1" and 195 pounds and I remembered what Ching had told me at the start: "The first lesson in this game is to protect yourself. Make sure when you bump somebody that your stick is right up in front of you so they don't give you a stick in the face. When you hit them, hit them hard; hit them clean if you can, but always protect yourself, because in this game there are no medals for bravery."

So, whenever I bumped somebody, I remembered Ching's advice and never got into much trouble. I got put off the ice quite a bit but never had to drop my gloves and punch. And, after that first incident, I was never really needled about being a collegian. On the whole the guys were very fair.

When I was with the Rangers, my boss was Lester Patrick, a fine man who treated me fairly—there was no question about it. After a while he suggested that I be sent down to Springfield for some polishing up in the minors. And he was right. If I'd been going to make a career of hockey, I would have said yes and gone to Springfield, but I wasn't in it for life; I was in it to get enough money for law school. Of course, the Rangers didn't know that until Lester suggested I go to Springfield. He wanted me there for a month or two and I said I'd go, but on only one condition —that I get my full share of money if the club won the Stanley Cup.

He said he couldn't agree to that and maintained I would have to go down to Springfield. It was February and the season was almost over. "Oh, no," I told Lester, "I don't have to go because if you insist that I do, then I'll just quit hockey."

The next thing I knew, I was traded to the Boston

Bruins, right there in my first year of NHL hockey. That was fine with me because Boston had a strong team; I came from the Boston area and liked the players on the club.

Tiny Thompson was the goaltender. Eddie Shore and Lionel Hitchman were the first-string defensemen, with George Owen and myself as second-stringers. Up front we had Harry Oliver, Perk Galbraith, Cooney Weiland and Dutch Gainor.

Dutch was the only man I ever saw in hockey who had a double shift. He'd come at a man, fake it one way, fake it the other, and then walk right through.

Shore was the best of all. He was a lot like Ted Williams in that he could help a teammate if you wanted help. Eddie was very fair about things; if you asked him how to play this or that man, he'd tell you. He didn't withhold advice. Personally, I liked Shore. He was the greatest hockey player I ever saw. He could skate like Bobby Orr did in a later era and he could shoot, and he was a great defenseman who could hit. He was a dynamic person who could really lift a team.

One night we took off for a game in Montreal; it was a wintry night, snowing and all that. What happens—Shore misses the train. The rest of the club was rolling up to Montreal, snug on the train, while Shore got hold of a Cadillac from a friend of his and drove all night through the mountains in blizzards and then into the next day and arrived in Montreal about an hour before the game. He got into a uniform and we beat the Canadiens 2-1. Shore scored both goals.

I know some people have said Shore was a vicious player, but I don't believe they saw him play too much. Let's say he was a tough, rough player who could give it out as well as take it without complaining.

Having players like Shore and Hitchman on defense meant that I didn't play all that much, since they kept the stars out there most of the time—and rightly so; after all, it was a money game.

Needless to say, my own personal schedule was different from the other players', since I was going to law school. On Monday the team would practice from twelve to one and I'd practice with them after coming from morning classes. Then I'd go back to school in the afternoon.

Tuesday night was game night in Boston and I wouldn't have any practice that day. I'd study all day long, and at six in the evening I'd have my dinner; then at 7:30 I'd go down to the Garden, only a few blocks away, dress and play the game.

Myles J. Lane—Scholar-defenseman.

On Wednesday, there'd be a twelve-to-one practice or maybe one-to-two and the same on Thursday. Occasionally, we'd play in New York on Thursdays and the team would leave in the morning while I was at school and I'd take the noon or one o'clock train. I'd study all the way down to New York, get off and go to Madison Square Garden, play the game and come back with the team on the midnight train and get into Boston in the early morning, then go to classes.

We always had games on weekends, so I'd usually catch the nine o'clock train on Fridays for Montreal, Ottawa or Toronto, depending on where we happened to be playing that Saturday night. Wherever we were, I'd stay in the hotel all day with the books, then go to the game at night and take the nine o'clock train back to Boston on Sunday morning.

Every so often, there was a conflict between my hockey schedule and law school. Once, we had a game in Detroit when I was supposed to be taking my mid-year exams. The solution was supplied by the law school, which let me take my exams at the University of Detroit. They sent the exam out ahead, and when the team departed for the next game in Chicago, I was left behind in Detroit. I took the exam on a Friday, and Detroit University sent the papers back to Boston while I got the train to Chicago. They were very cooperative that way.

From time to time, people would ask me whether it was difficult concentrating on the books. Actually, playing was an incentive, and I was doing quite well in the NHL. We knocked off the Canadiens in the first round of the Stanley Cup playoffs, then took the Rangers in four straight to win the Cup. I wound up getting that full share of the playoff cut I had demanded of Lester Patrick. But then I had an unfortunate accident that affected my hockey career.

During the summer after my rookie season in the NHL, I was playing baseball on Cape Cod. One day a bunch of us were in a car, driving to a game, when the car was forced off the road. I came out of the accident with a broken bone in my knee and three fractured vertebrae in my spine. That kept me out of hockey for a whole year and I could never again skate as fast as I did before the accident.

To compensate for the loss of speed, I began concentrating more on my defensive play than on rushing with the puck. During my year out of action, a few good things happened to me. I was still going to law school and doing well there and at the same time was coaching football at Harvard.

Meanwhile, I had a good chance to study the Bruins as a team and to think about hockey in general. Art Ross was running the Boston club at the time,, and he was really a tough one, although I had no complaints with him. He was a strict taskmaster but a good hockey man. In those days the club was known as "The Bruising Bruins," and I think the reputation they had as a rough, tough hockey team stemmed from Ross. They hit and hit hard; that's just the way he wanted it.

I'm sure Ross knew I'd eventually quit hockey to go into law. But that didn't matter to him, and he did get some work out of me the year I was out with an injury.

Those were the days when the Bruins had a farm club called the Boston Cubs. They were a good minor league team in need of a manager, so Ross put me in charge; it turned out to be a very rewarding experience. When I took over, they were in last place, and by season's end, we were on top.

The Cubs consisted of a bunch of young fellows going up to the NHL and a group of veterans who had come down. There was a fellow on the team named Joe Geroux who was a little firecracker and nobody could handle him,

not even Ross. Here I was, the collegian with a broken back, running this club, trying to control Geroux and attempting to bring them up from last place.

For some reason I was determined to work with Geroux and help him, even though everybody else had dropped him because he was so wild. I knew he was a great hockey player; all he needed was a little balance. Well, I hadn't been with the Cubs too long, when Joe came to me with a problem.

He said, "You know those penalties I get for sometimes losing my head; well, I don't mind them so much but the $25 fine is cutting into my income. How can I stay on the ice without getting fined!"

I began to think to myself, "How am I going to keep him in the game?" I started playing for time and finally inquired, "Joe, why are you asking me that question?"

He replied, "Myles, you're going to law school. You know all the answers!"

I said I wished I did but knew I had to give him some advice, so I said, "Well, Joe, I'll tell you what you have to do —the next time anybody whacks you out on the ice, count ten before you do anything else."

Joe looked at me and said, "Why ten?"

"Because," I told him, "one of two things will happen. Number one: if the man you hit hasn't broken a leg, he'll skate out of reach, so should you swing that stick at him, you'll miss him. Number two: at the end of the count you'll be all over your mad, so you'll stay on the ice. Right?"

"Well, I'll try it," he said, and for the next month he was the star of the league. Then, it happened.

We went to play a game against New Haven at their rink, and they had a Polish fellow on their team by the name of Dutkowski. As the game moved along, I could see Joe's temper was rising because Dutkowski was bothering him. With only eight or ten minutes left, we were leading by one goal, however, and I was hopeful everything would be all right.

Dutkowski, a former Chicago Blackhawk, skated near Joe and, suddenly, Joe hit him over the head with his stick with such a clout that it looked as if a geyser of blood was coming out of Dutkowski's head. They carried him off the ice and there was almost a riot. A special platoon of police was called in and Joe was put off with a match penalty. Then New Haven scored two goals and beat us.

Later that night we were on the train back to Boston, and I was sitting and fuming about the incident when in comes Joe, acting like a big St. Bernard. He just sat there watching me and finally asked, "Myles, what's the trouble?"

"Are you kidding?" I said. "Look, Joe, I've been treating you like a brother. I figured to send you back to the major leagues. I've built you up all year long; that's all right, it's part of my job. But you came to me, wanting to know all about my law experience. You asked me how to stay on the ice—and, what do you do, Joe? You disgraced me out there."

"Disgrace you! How?" he said.

"You went out there," I said, "and hit some guy over the head, fractured his skull and we lost the game. I feel like you've let me down."

He said, "Myles, I didn't let you down."

"Joe," I asked, "what did I tell you to do?"

"You told me to count to ten, didn't you?" he said.

I said, "Yes."

"And you said I could swing my stick," he told me.

I agreed but added, "You didn't count to ten."

"Yes, I did," he insisted.

I said, "Joe, look, when you got into that bumping with Dutkowski, I started to count and got to five and then you let that stick go."

He replied, "Myles, I forgot to tell you one thing. You know I was born in Poland and came over to Canada when I was seven or eight years old. Whenever I get mad, I forget to count in English, so I did it in Polish and count twice as fast. When I was bumping Dutkowski, I counted to ten in Polish, let the stick go and he was in the way!"

What could I say to that? We had a good team, and after my year of recuperation I was ready to return to the NHL. One night I'll never forget was the Eddie Shore-Ace Bailey incident.

We were playing Toronto at Boston Garden and the local papers had more or less played up the game as a grudge match. As far as Ace was concerned, though, he was one of the nicest men ever to play hockey. On this night Shore had rushed down the length of the ice and Red Horner of Toronto, no shrinking violet himself, pushed Shore into the boards and really hit him hard. Shore struck his head and down he went.

Horner got the puck and went up the ice while Bailey dropped back on the Toronto defense. To this day I really believe Shore was so dizzy getting up that he thought the man in front of him was Horner, not Bailey.

As he went by Ace, Shore just dragged his stick. He didn't bump Ace, he just took the skates out from under him. Not expecting it, Ace fell backwards and struck his head on the ice, and suddenly he started to shudder.

Meanwhile, Shore skated back and stood there on defense, dazed. Horner skated up to him, took his gloves off, wound up like a pitcher would before throwing a fastball and hit Shore on the chin. Shore fell backwards, hitting his head on the ice.

Bailey was taken into the Toronto dressing room normally used by the Cubs. The Cubs' trainer, Joe Gilmore, had enough presence of mind to get chopped ice to encase Bailey's head. He looked like a mummy, but I think the ice saved his life; he was bleeding inside, and that ice kept the bleeding down. He had a double fracture of the skull, one on each side.

In the Bruins dressing room it took 18 stitches in Shore's head and he was out, too, although few people knew that. Bailey was rushed to the hospital, where Dr. Munroe, a famous brain surgeon, operated on him. They put two silver plates in his head. Of course, we didn't know what would happen to him but we still had the schedule to fulfill and went to New York for a game two nights later.

Shore was suspended for the rest of the year, and as far as the Bruins were concerned, they might as well have quit—they were finished. They couldn't play anymore, but they had to. I remember that night in New York; we were getting regular reports on Bailey's condition which was quite serious. They didn't think he was going to live, and he remained on the danger list for quite a while. Ace eventually recovered but never played hockey again. Shore came back a season later and was still a great player.

As for me, I finally finished my law studies and quit hockey. I wanted to come to New York, so I said, "Goodbye, NHL, you've helped me a lot. I'm never going to be a star; I've got a broken back. Thanks again for everything."

Boston BRUINS

The Greatest Bruins Team of All Time

There are those who believe that the 1972 Stanley Cup-winning Boston Bruins outfit was the greatest hockey team ever iced. It boasted the most prolific scorer in the history of the game to that point in Phil Esposito, the most accomplished high-scoring defenseman in Bobby Orr and a well-balanced lineup that frequently featured goals by third-stringers when they were most needed.

The Bruins probably had the best group of players ever assembled. It was a great team because it won the big games and it also won important matches on the road.

One need only examine the 1971-72 campaign to understand what a remarkable club was based at Boston Garden.

"Whenever we get careless," a member of the Boston Bruins remarked before the start of the 1971-72 season, "there's always the specter of April 1971 to put us back on the right track."

April 1971 is a black month in the history of Boston hockey. That was when the heavily-favored Bruins were dispatched from the first round of the Stanley Cup playoffs by the upstart Montreal Canadiens and their rookie goalie, Ken Dryden. It was an upset that was not supposed to happen; yet it did. Now, the Bruins had a whole new season in which to make amends.

It would not be easy. To begin with, the Stanley Cup-champion Canadiens would deliver an emphatic challenge, and then there were the improved and determined New York Rangers, Boston's traditional rivals.

The teams opened their battle on October 10, 1971, at Boston Garden and the Bruins were surprised by a 4-1 Ranger win. Obviously, coach Tom Johnson's club was not playing its game. "We weren't hitting," said Johnny McKenzie, "and we let them roam free."

The Rangers had already gained a psychological edge, and there were those who wondered whether the Bruins were still reeling from their 1971 playoff disaster. The answer to this vital question, which would eventually decide the final standings, was supplied when the teams next collided in Madison Square Garden on October 13.

A victory for the Rangers could have convinced them —and the Bruins—that the October 10 Boston Garden adventure was not a fluke. It might seriously impair the Boston sextet's confidence in its ability to handle the well-balanced New Yorkers.

Fortified with All-Star defenseman Brad Park and crack center Jean Ratelle, the Rangers believed they would be able to counteract the one-two punch of Bobby Orr and Phil Esposito.

It wasn't to be. From the opening face-off, the Bruins skated much better than the neutralized New Yorkers and, naturally, Orr orchestrated the attack—and defense. In fact, everything!

"Bobby can skate circles around me," said Park. "Because of his speed, he's always got that extra split second to do something special with the puck."

Rangers defensive forward Glen Sather, who was assigned to disrupt Orr, couldn't summon adequate adjectives to describe Boston's ace. "He doesn't beat you because he's Bobby Orr," Sather said. "He beats you because he's the best. If he came out in disguise with a wig on his head and different numbers on his back, he'd still beat you."

Rangers general manager-coach Emile Francis couldn't contain himself. "Orr," said Francis, "is one of the greatest players our game has ever seen."

The New York men seemed to realize that as long as Orr skated for Boston, the Rangers were dead. And they were correct in their assessment.

Not only did the Rangers fail to win another regular-season game from the Bruins, they rarely came close. On December 16 the Rangers were more or less chased out of Boston Garden, 8-1. In New York on January 2, 1972, Boston prevailed, 4-1. Back at Madison Square Garden again on February 2nd, the Bruins repulsed the Rangers' best effort and shut out the New Yorkers, 2-0. The regular-season series between the teams ended on March 23 in the Hub with the Bruins on top, 4-1. "Let's face it," said goalie

Ed Johnston, "every big game we had, we won."

But they had to win more than just their games against the Rangers. During the first half of the schedule, Boston failed to pull away from the Broadway Blueshirts in the standings. It was primarily a matter of coordinating their attack, as well as compensating for the loss of their defenseman, Don Awrey, who was hospitalized with a leg injury. However, by mid-season, coach Tom Johnson had fit all the pieces into place and the Rangers were left behind and stayed in second place.

The Bruins were now a really great team. It was a great team not only because of Orr and Esposito but even more important, because it had depth. For example, Dallas Smith, even though overshadowed by Bobby Orr, was an extremely able defenseman.

Another essential cog was goliath right wing Ken Hodge, who did the heavy work for Phil Esposito in the corners. Hodge missed 20 games with an ankle injury but returned to top form in the homestretch after some discouraging near-misses around the goalmouth.

A hulking six-foot-one, 216 pounds, Hodge epitomized the burly, contemporary Bruins who rolled over the opposition. "He's very big, and strong and rough," said Montreal Canadiens coach Scotty Bowman. "He's got lots of room when he comes in over the blue line. That's the big feature of his line with Esposito and Wayne Cashman. They just barge into your zone and defy you to do anything with them."

Once the Bruins had established their superiority over the Rangers and clamped a lock on first place in the East Division, their prime handicap could be overconfidence, as attested to by Derek Sanderson's statement, "We have difficulty getting 'up' for games against Buffalo and Vancouver."

As a result, Boston was occasionally derailed in most unusual fashion from time to time. Typical was an 8-2 defeat hung on the Bruins by the lowly Buffalo Sabres; a game which snapped a seven-game winless situation for the Sabres and ended a six-game Bruins winning streak.

Coach Johnson took immediate steps to isolate the basis of such complacency.

He informed one and all, "You can never be satisfied

Tom Johnson, Hall of Famer.

in this game and you can never feel really comfortable, because that's when things start happening to you. If we keep playing our game, we should win everything this year."

Heeding their coach's advice, the Bruins pulled so far ahead of the second-place Rangers that the battle for the Prince of Wales Trophy (awarded to the first-place winner in the East Division) became academic and something less than pulsating.

"If the race had been close," said Phil Esposito, "it would have been different. Remember how it was a couple of years ago when Chicago beat us out on the last day of the season—how we all hung around the radio listening to the end of that game. But this clinching of the division title had been pretty much inevitable."

Equally inevitable was Esposito's finish atop the scoring race. The deft center accumulated 66 goals and 67 assists for 133 points. He was followed by Bobby Orr who compiled an amazing 37 goals and 80 assists for 117 points. Amazing in many ways, especially for a defenseman. The Bruins' lead over New York at season's end was a comfortable 10 points. They entered the Stanley Cup playoffs determined to erase the ignominy of 1971.

Each Bruin realized that winning the Prince of Wales Trophy was only one step toward the Stanley Cup, although a most impressive step. But the knowledgeable and demanding Boston fans wanted more than that and the applause that accompanied the first-place finish was as fragile as the next defeat.

"All that cheering can turn the other way when you're not playing well," warned coach Johnson. "We've got a great team, but the better we play, the more perfection the people want. I've seen teams get nervous playing at home simply because they're afraid to do poorly. They have to get on the road before they can loosen up. I know some of our guys get nervous playing at home."

Then before the 1972 Stanley Cup playoffs actually began, Bruins' right wing Johnny McKenzie once again reminded one and all that the Boston sextet still felt the sting of their 1971 upset defeat at the hands of Montreal's Canadiens in the opening playoff round.

To reach the gold at the end of hockey's rainbow the Bruins first had to dispose of the fourth-place Toronto Maple Leafs. It seemed an easy enough chore after the first game at Boston Garden. A pair of goals by Phil Esposito and singles from McKenzie, Don Marcotte and Fred Stanfield provided the Bruins with an easy 5-0 victory.

The Leafs, however, were not about to play dead. They spotted Boston a two-goal lead in the second match at Boston Garden and then regrouped to tie the score, 3-3, sending the teams into sudden-death overtime.

Less than three minutes of the overtime had elapsed when big Toronto center Jim Harrison powered a shot past goalie Gerry Cheevers. The Leafs had tied the series at one apiece. "It was," said former Bruins coach Harry Sinden, "one of the finest comebacks and major upsets in Stanley Cup play."

Stunned to the core, the Bruins now had to contend with two consecutive games on hostile Maple Leaf Gardens ice. The pivotal third contest was a defensive classic that remained tied, 0-0, until the 18-minute mark of the second period. Darryl Sittler of Toronto took a minor penalty for holding Bobby Orr, and coach Tom Johnson promptly sent his power-play specialists onto the ice. Within five seconds, Orr passed the puck to Mike Walton, who blazed a shot past goalie Bernie Parent. Orr scored the game's second and last goal early in the third period and the Bruins' big machine was revved up once more.

Paced by Ken Hodge's pair of goals in the third period, Boston won the fourth game 5-4, leaving Toronto staggering on the ropes. The Leafs fought bravely and well in the fifth game, holding Boston to a 2-2 draw as late as seven minutes of the third period. Finally, the Bruins' power prevailed. Hodge shot a ten-foot drive past Parent to put Boston ahead to stay. "I got the puck," said Hodge, "and just rammed it as hard as I could. There was some tremendous passing by Wayne Cashman and Phil Esposito, and Parent didn't react as quickly as he had been doing earlier in the game."

With Toronto out of the way, coach Tom Johnson's sextet was now confronted with the St. Louis Blues, a club which traditionally had been easy pickings for Boston. This series was to be no different.

The Bruins won the first two games on home ice, 6-1 and 10-2, and made the West Division team look like a collection of minor leaguers. "I think our young team is awed by the Bruins," said St. Louis coach Al Arbour. "We're playing in a trance. We're mesmerized. We see Orr and Esposito and Bucyk and the rest of them out there and we wonder what we're doing playing on the same ice with them."

Skating on their home ice, the Blues lost 7-2 in the third game. St. Louis made a battle of it in the fourth game, although they never managed to take the lead. When the final buzzer sounded, Boston was on top, 5-3, with a record Stanley Cup total of 28 goals for a four-game sweep.

That was all well and good, but the Bruins, to a man, were pointing to the finals and their arch enemies, the New York Rangers. "None of us want another summer like 1971," said McKenzie on the eve of the first game against the men from Manhattan.

"If Ace Bailey played regularly," one of his teammates said before the Stanley Cup finals began, "he'd be a 30-goal man, at least."

Bailey, the Boston Bruins' blond, fourth-string center, gave a measure of truth to this statement by coming off the bench to score the winning goal against New York in the 6-5 opening game of the Cup finals on April 30 at Boston Garden. At the time, Bailey was replacing Derek Sanderson, who was recuperating from a colitis and virus attack.

There were fewer than three minutes remaining in regulation time and the score was tied, 5-5, when Bailey made his dramatic move. A double pass from Mike Walton and Ed Westfall sent the 23-year-old Bailey careening along the left boards. Only the Rangers' back pedaling defenseman Brad Park separated Bailey from New York goalie Ed Giacomin.

"I thought I had him," said Park, who was probably the most-hated Ranger in Boston. "I figured I had him by the boards and there was no way he could go around me."

Bailey just barely circled Park and approached Giacomin from a near-impossible angle, almost on a direct line with the goal crease. The Ranger goalie prematurely dropped to his knees and tried to poke the puck off Bailey's stick. However, Bailey flipped the puck over Giacomin's shoulder and into the short side of the net.

Bailey's winner was the culmination of a roller-coaster game in which the Bruins overcame Ranger Dale Rolfe's opening goal to take a 5-1 lead on scores by Sanderson and Fred Stanfield and a hat trick by Ken Hodge.

Most embarrassing to the Rangers was the fact that Sanderson's goal and one of Hodge's were scored during a first-period Ranger power play.

Then, just when it appeared that the Rangers were ready to expire, they revived and tied the score.

"We knew they weren't out of the game," said Boston's John McKenzie.

Rod Gilbert made it 5-2 at 11:54 of the second period. Then Vic Hadfield, Walt Tkaczuk and Bruce MacGregor successively beat Boston goalie Gerry Cheevers before the third period was half over.

"Losers quit," said Hadfield. "We didn't."

The Rangers, who had not won the Stanley Cup since 1940, appeared ready to capture the game on their momentum.

Bruins on a penalty-kill: (Left to right) Ed Westfall, Derek Sanderson, Gerry Cheevers, Bobby Orr, Dallas Smith.

In the final 10 minutes, however, their attack fizzled and Ace Bailey applied the "coup de grace."

Concealing their despair, the Rangers talked of a moral victory in defeat. "We're happy," said Hadfield. "Not happy that we lost, but that we could sure score goals against them."

The Bruins thoroughly outmuscled the smaller Rangers and Bailey personally dispatched Ranger forward Ron Stewart to the hospital with a fractured jaw. It didn't stop there. The Rangers had been humiliated by the Bruins.

When the score was 5-5, Rod Seiling of the Rangers lay prone on the ice as the whistle stopped play. A second later, Sanderson skated directly to Seiling, stopped short and sprayed ice flakes into the Ranger defenseman's face. Not a Ranger lifted a finger to Sanderson. That action seemed to symbolize the Bruins' disdain for the Rangers.

As for the quality of hockey, the 14,995 fans in Boston Garden witnessed some splendid offensive play by Tkaczuk, Bobby Orr and Hodge. Unfortunately, they also saw atrocious goaltending by Giacomin and Cheevers.

The perplexing question was which club would ultimately benefit most from the roller-coaster opener? The answer would provide the best clue as to the eventual Stanley Cup-winner.

In defiance of the law of averages, the Boston Bruins beat the New York Rangers on May 3 for the seventh straight time, 2-1, to take a 2-0 game lead in the National Hockey League's Stanley Cup finals. A power-play goal by Ken Hodge at 11:53 of the third period while New York had two men in the penalty box gave Boston the decision before a tumultuous crowd at Boston Garden.

Bruce MacGregor and Walt Tkaczuk of the Rangers were sitting out penalties when Mike Walton of the Bruins spotted Hodge camped in front of the New York net. Walton's pass was crisp, and Hodge deflected the puck past goalie Gilles Villemure.

Replacing Ed Giacomin, who was bombed in the series opener, Villemure got a piece of most of the 25 shots Boston hurled at him. His only other mistake was fanning on Johnny Bucyk's first-period power-play shot at 16:15 while Gary Doak was sitting out a penalty. That gave Boston a 1-0 lead.

Checking more vigorously than in the series opener, New York tied the score at 7:23 of the second period when Vic Hadfield relieved Ed Westfall of the puck in Bruins territory and passed off to his open right wing, Rod Gilbert. Without hesitation, Gilbert found an opening behind goalie Ed Johnston. From then on, the Rangers held fast until Hodge broke the tie in the third period.

"The first two games could have gone either way," said Hadfield. "Considering how well we played, there's no reason why we can't come back."

The best reason was the fact that Boston pounded the lighter New York players at every turn. They neutralized such scorers as Bobby Rousseau and MacGregor as they overwhelmed the smaller Ranger defensemen. Boston's goaltending in the second game was also superior to the Rangers' net work.

New York center Jean Ratelle, having failed to regain prime condition after an ankle injury, played only part-time. As a result, center Tkaczuk was worked overtime, killing penalties and skating the power play. Without a doubt, he was the outstanding Ranger forward.

"Tkaczuk is a superstar," said Bruins center Derek Sanderson. "He's among the top five centers in the league."

Tkaczuk overshadowed Boston's Phil Esposito, who was harassed by several New Yorkers, not the least among them being Tkaczuk. At times, the two big centers appeared close to coming to blows. However, when it came to winning face-offs, Esposito, Sanderson and Fred Stanfield were unbeatable.

In this game the Rangers successfully contained high-scoring defenseman Bobby Orr, but they were unable to penetrate the beefy Boston backline led by Don Awrey. He spent a good part of the evening sending Rangers headfirst to the ice. By comparison, the New Yorkers' defense was genteel.

Having lost five straight games to Boston during the regular season and now, two more in the playoffs, New York appeared destined to psych itself right out of the Cup finals in straight games unless it found the winning formula at friendly Madison Square Garden.

"The team that's going to win," said Hodge, "is the team that makes the big play when it's needed."

Up through the second game, it was only the Bruins who had made that very important play.

Mustering their strongest total performance against Boston in eight months, the Rangers defeated the Bruins,

5-2, at Madison Square Garden on May 4. The victory reduced Boston's lead in the best-of-seven series to 2-1. It was also the Rangers' first win over the Bruins all season on Madison Square Garden ice.

A frantic and frequently deafening crowd of 17,250 was treated to superlative efforts by New York right wing Rod Gilbert and defenseman Brad Park. Each scored twice and played vigorous hockey throughout the entire game. Peter Stemkowski scored the other Ranger goal, while Mike Walton and Bobby Orr produced goals for Boston.

The pattern of the game was established in the opening minute, when New York center Walt Tkaczuk captured the face-off and sped past the Boston defenders for a crisp shot at goalie Gerry Cheevers. In the process, defenseman Dallas Smith tackled Tkaczuk, taking a two-minute penalty.

The Rangers revved up their power play and took the lead at 1:22 on a dynamic 50-foot blast past Cheevers by Brad Park.

"Only the day before," said Park, "the coach told us we weren't getting enough shots on our power play. So I had it in mind to take more shots."

Soon the Bruins began generating shots. A spate of three straight New York penalties brought on the awesome Boston power plays before the 10-minute mark. A combination of vigilant goaltending by Ed Giacomin, superb penalty-killing by Tkaczuk and Bill Fairbairn and a bit of luck enabled the Rangers to blunt the Bruins' attack.

"In Tkaczuk and Fairbairn," said Gilbert, "we have the best penalty-killers in hockey."

Boston's penalty-killing was less effective. Two more Bruin penalties in the first period led to goals by Gilbert and Park (his second) for a 3-0 Ranger lead.

New York began losing its attack momentum late in the first period.

Walton's shot from the lip of the goal crease fooled Giacomin at 14:04 of the first. Orr scored as he was being tripped before the second period was two minutes old.

Reeling and apparently ready to blow the game, the Rangers were rejuvenated by Gilbert's second goal at 3:46 of the middle period on feeds from Park and Bobby Rousseau.

"It was a good shot," said Cheevers, "but I didn't play it the way I should have."

Reinforced with a two-goal lead, New York traded blow-for-blow with Boston in a game that grew progressively more hostile as the second period ended.

The more devastating clashes occurred between Ted Irvine and Carol Vadnais, Glen Sather and John McKenzie, Gene Carr and Bobby Orr, and Carr and Ed Westfall.

By the end of the second period, the Rangers had lost defenseman Jim Neilson, who left the game with a strained knee, and defenseman Ab DeMarco, who was carried off the ice on a stretcher. He suffered a deep skate gash in a

Esposito (left) and Orr banter during a charity game.

corner crash with Garnet Bailey, leaving New York with three back-liners, Brad Park, Dale Rolfe and Rod Seiling.

However, Stemkowski's goal late in the second gave New York a 5-2 lead which the Rangers nursed through the third, bolstered by Giacomin and his checking forwards.

The Bruins were not sanguine about possible defeat. Wayne Cashman, who, late in the season, had been suspended for menacing Dennis Hextall of Minnesota with his stick, nearly beheaded one Ranger as a teammate put a hard headlock on Park. Referee John Ashley didn't call a penalty.

"Tell Park," snapped Sanderson, "that we'll get him next."

If the Rangers were concerned, they didn't betray much emotion.

"We were more physical than I thought we would be," said Stemkowski. "This is the way to play the Bruins."

Several times members of the audience tried very hard to get into the act. One fan stormed the Bruins' bench

with beer bottle in hand, only to be intercepted by Garden police. Another grabbed McKenzie's stick and invited him outside to fight.

When the final buzzer sounded, the Bruins covered their heads with their hands as they left the ice under a hail of garbage.

"Those Ranger fans made a fine spectacle of themselves tonight," carped Cashman.

In a more positive sense, the Rangers did, too, for a change.

On May 7 the Bruins removed the New York Rangers from their brief flight of winning fantasy and returned them to the real world of thumping and bumping. The Bruins scored a 3-2 victory and took a commanding 3-1 lead in the Cup finals.

A capacity crowd was hoping the Rangers would tie the series that afternoon, but their cheers were turned to numb silence early in the first period when two successive goals by Boston defenseman Bobby Orr set the tone for the contest.

The Rangers were able to contain NHL leading scorer Phil Esposito, but Orr's rushes were irrepressible.

"You have to play a good forechecking game so as not to let him wheel out of his end with the puck," said Emile Francis in delineating the anti-Orr play. "You can't let him lug that mail out. He's too dangerous."

Unfortunately for the Rangers, there wasn't a New Yorker capable of putting the manacles on Prince Bobby often enough.

Francis' strategy backfired at the 5:26 mark of the opening period. He sent defenseman Jim Dorey onto the ice for the first time since his injury late in the regular season. Orr promptly broke past Dorey for the key first goal.

With his second goal, Orr set a playoff record of 21 points by a defenseman, one more than the mark he had set two years before.

For the Rangers now, it was all uphill against the Bruins' sextet. The men from Boston were determined to prove that their May 4 defeat on Madison Square Garden ice was a fluke. They smashed the Rangers at every turn. Fights were the order of the day. When the first period ended, referee Bruce Hood had whistled 76 penalty minutes.

Playing without regular defensemen Jim Neilson and Ab DeMarco, the Rangers appeared stale and off-balance. When the New Yorkers had a man advantage in the second period, it was Orr who fed penalty-killer Don Marcotte for the third Boston goal. That goal appeared to break the Rangers' backs.

Finally, at 18:38 of the middle period, the Rangers managed to score. Ted Irvine sped through the Boston defense for a 15-foot blast past goalie Ed Johnston.

Following Marcotte's goal, the Bruins scrapped their offensive drives for a more defensive posture, harassing the Rangers with saturating forechecking. It worked perfectly until Irvine scored.

The best Ranger effort was a long shot by defenseman Rod Seiling that beat Johnston with less than two minutes remaining in the game. Nevertheless, the leg-weary Rangers couldn't translate that goal into more energy. Once again they failed to obtain the tying score. Johnston had shut the door.

The Rangers had hoped to emerge from the fourth Cup match with a 2-2 series split. Instead, they came away with a 1-3 deficit and the knowledge that the next game was in Boston Garden, where Orr played better than he did in New York.

Just the thought of it was enough to dash New York playoff hopes.

Carefully primed for burial by the Boston Bruins,

Emile Francis' obstinate New York Rangers struggled back to life May 9 with a gripping 3-2 triumph over the Hub sextet in the fifth game of the Stanley Cup finals.

The Bruins' defeat, speeded by Bobby Rousseau's two goals, stunned the primed spectators in Boston Garden who had anticipated a gala Cup-clinching fiesta. Instead, the Bostonians were left with a tenuous 3-2 lead in the series and were now threatened by a persistent New York club that could almost smell championship champagne.

"We never thought we were dead," said the Rangers' husky left wing, Ted Irvine, the architect of Rousseau's winning goal. "We figured we could go all the way."

For two periods it appeared that the favored Bruins would go all the way to the championship. First-period goals by Wayne Cashman and Ken Hodge offset Ranger defenseman Dale Rolfe's score. Boston opened the third period nursing that one-goal margin.

At this point, Francis played his limited reserve strength to rare advantage. Rousseau, who had previously played pitifully against Boston, was called off the bench as center between Irvine and Peter Stemkowski.

The helmeted Rousseau immediately moved to the attack and bombed a 50-footer past defenseman Carol Vadnais, who screened goalie Ed Johnston. The puck ricocheted off Johnston's arm and into the net at 2:56, tying the game.

"We seemed tight," said goalie Johnston, who previously had thwarted the Rangers. "Maybe a little overconfident."

If so, the Bruins' ballooning overconfidence was definitely deflated at 12:45 by the ubiquitous Rousseau.

The winning goal was set in motion by Irvine, who skimmed the puck along the boards behind the Bruins' net. Boston defensemen Dallas Smith and Bobby Orr appeared to be having a high-level conference over just who owned the puck. Meanwhile, Irvine solved the problem by capturing the disk.

"I was all alone with the puck," said Irvine. "Then I noticed Bobby [Rousseau] alone in front of the net."

Irvine's pass had eyes, and Rousseau's shot had radar, as it bounced off defenseman Smith and swept past Johnston.

"It was a wrist shot," said Rousseau.

"I saw it coming," said Johnston, "until it hit Smith and changed direction."

There were less than eight minutes remaining for the Bruins to counterattack. New York goalie Gilles Villemure, who had kept the Rangers alive for two periods, blunted Boston's best shots until the final seconds of play, when a wild scramble developed outside the goal crease.

Villemure was pulled to the right side of the net as the puck slithered toward the left corner. Defenseman Brad Park slid into the breach, plugged the hole and the Rangers were home free.

"The turning point," said Bruins coach Tom Johnson, "was late in the second period when we had a two-man advantage and didn't score."

Gary Doak and Walt Tkaczuk of New York had been penalized within 32 seconds of each other, but somehow the Bruins' scoring machine was impotent. At one point, Park broke in alone on Johnston, but his shot hit the crossbar after beating the goalie.

Having weathered the double power play, the Rangers gathered momentum in the third period and produced the tying and winning goals while the champagne bottles languished in the Bruins' dressing room for the victory party that wasn't to be. At least not on the night of May 9.

In the professional hockey confrontation that seemed to be made in heaven for its fans, Boston's big, bad Bruins defeated the light-horse New York Rangers, 3-0, on May 11 to win the Stanley Cup, four games to two.

Bobby Orr, the league's best defenseman, scored one goal and assisted on another, while goalie Gerry Cheevers, in the nets, mesmerized the frustrated Rangers, thereby providing Boston with its second title in three years. New York had not won the Cup in 32 years.

The Rangers skated head to head with the Bruins in this viciously played contest until 11:18 of the first period. Then, Orr seized a power-play opportunity and delivered a potent shot from the right point following passes from Johnny Bucyk and Ken Hodge.

New York goalie Gilles Villemure appeared mummified as the puck blew into the open side to his left.

"I couldn't see the puck," said Villemure, "with all those guys in front of me."

With 17,250 fans at Madison Square Garden frantically cheering for a New York goal, the Rangers received a rare opportunity for three minutes and 12 seconds in the middle period when a spate of Boston penalties gave the Rangers a one- and then a two-man advantage.

New York's strategy, which ultimately proved fruitless, was to persistently feed center Walt Tkaczuk in the keyhole. But the big center, whose shot often was weak, fired either wide of the net or off the body of a Bruin. In between, Cheevers made a few saves of his own.

"I knew I could beat the Rangers," said Cheevers, who also had been in the horseracing business. "I felt like Riva Ridge."

Having defused the major Rangers' power play, Boston escaped from the second period with a fragile 1-0 lead. However, the Bruins had decisively weakened their foe with punishing bodychecks. The fights that broke out did nothing to help the Rangers.

In one event Derek Sanderson took Rod Gilbert off the ice. Ken Hodge almost decimated Vic Hadfield. A less convincing bout featured Tkaczuk and Wayne Cashman.

The Rangers' last gasp was taken early in the third period, when the fast-tiring New Yorkers delivered a few threatening drives at Cheevers.

Then, with 3:20 gone, defenseman Dale Rolfe was penalized for draping Phil Esposito along the left boards and the Boston power play once more asserted itself. Just 10 seconds before Rolfe was to return, Orr accepted Esposito's face-off pass and fired the puck along the same route as his first-period drive, only this time Cashman directed it past Villemure.

"I saw Orr wind up and shoot," said Villemure, "and I had a clean try for the puck. But then it hit Cashman, went off the post and in."

The time was 5:10 and it signaled the flagging of New York's attack. If there was any doubt about the Bruins' right to the championship, it was supplied at 18:11 by Cashman, who converted Esposito's pass on a two-on-one breakaway after Villemure managed to get a piece of the puck.

From then on, Boston defensemen such as Don Awrey, Dallas Smith and Orr threw a checking blanket over the Rangers until the final buzzer officially signaled Boston's return to Stanley Cup glory.

"It was great to beat them on their own ice," said John McKenzie. "We're the best team and we wanted to show it here."

The Big, Bad Bruins' show of strength could not have been more convincing, nor the Rangers' congenital failure so obvious to the witnesses.

"We had our chances," said Rangers coach Emile Francis, underlining his club's failure, "but could not put the puck in the net."

The Bruins could, which explained why, for the fifth time in the club's history, Boston became king of the hockey world. It would also mark the last time the New Englanders would win the Stanley Cup.

Boston BRUINS

The Great Debate: Brad Park vs. Bobby Orr

As individual hockey rivalries go, few were better than the one involving Bobby Orr and Brad Park. Ironically, these two great defensemen of the 1970s would briefly be teammates on the Boston Bruins in 1976 before Orr left for Chicago.

But when Park was a Ranger and Orr a Bruin, their clashes gripped hockey fans everywhere for many years. The following is a depiction of the Orr versus Park rivalry.

It was early in the evening of January 25, 1972, at Metropolitan Sports Center in Bloomington, Minnesota. The cream of the National Hockey League crop began drifting into the East Division dressing room for the annual East-West All-Star Game.

For one evening, at least, all hatreds between opponents were to be suspended. Vic Hadfield of the New York Rangers joked with Phil Esposito of the Boston Bruins. Frank Mahovlich of the Montreal Canadiens enjoyed a pleasant conversation with Paul Henderson of the Toronto Maple Leafs. It was a lovely truce among the ice warriors— except for one corner of the room, where First All-Star defenseman Brad Park of the Rangers unloaded his gear.

At the time, Park, a chunky, baby-faced hitter who was affectionately known as "Huckleberry Finn on skates," was rated second to the other First All-Star defenseman, Bobby Orr of the Bruins. Blond, handsome and as tough as Park, Orr often was regarded as the greatest hockey player of all time. And still is, to many experts.

The warmth that surrounded Mahovlich, Esposito, Henderson and Hadfield stopped short of Park's cubicle. One observer remarked that when he approached Park, he could cut the tension with a knife. "The temperature was 30 below zero outside the rink," said hockey writer Red Burnett of the *Toronto Star*, "and the air around Park in the dressing room when Esposito, Orr and Johnny McKenzie of the Bruins went past him was 50 below and dropping."

Significantly, Esposito, Orr and McKenzie all skated for the Bruins, a club which had been mauling the Rangers for decades. Orr, a native of Parry Sound, a village in Northern Ontario, had entered the NHL with blaring

fanfare in 1966 and then proceeded to demolish all records held by defensemen, as if the job done were child's play.

By contrast, Park quietly became a big-leaguer two years after Orr's entrance. Several months elapsed before the Rangers' defenseman began to be recognized as one of the game's greatest. From the beginning, Brad was number two, but he did try harder, and his perseverance paid handsome dividends. By the start of the 1971-72 season, he not only was being favorably compared with the gifted Orr, but some critics rated him almost on a par with Bobby.

"Park is defensively sounder than Orr" said Detroit Red Wings manager Ned Harkness. "Brad's a great one. By comparison, Orr is more offensive-minded."

Vancouver Canucks executive Hal Laycoe, who once played for both Boston and New York, also favored Park over Orr and predicted that the Rangers' defenseman would outlast the Bruins ace because Orr was more susceptible to injury. "Park is tough and aggressive," said Laycoe. "He's likely to have a longer and more productive career than Orr."

Although Park himself had suffered injuries as a young player, Orr's gimpy knees were regarded as the problem that could abruptly end his career at any moment. Yet Orr continued to play a freewheeling game, frequently carrying the puck from one end of the rink to the other, setting up forwards or scoring goals himself. Park, too, could skate with power and speed, but Brad's strong suit was his ability to manipulate the puck in and around his skates with a magical now-you-see-it-now-you-don't quality. Having outwitted the enemy with his adroit stickhandling, Park usually would pass the puck to a free wingman or his fellow defenseman. Then he'd skate to the opponent's blue line and await a potential return pass for a hard shot on goal. Park and Orr could both fire shots of close to 100 miles per hour.

So in January 1972, Park and Orr were almost—but not quite—equals as performers. But others in that All-Star group were equally talented at their positions. Why should there have been a special rivalry between Orr and Park?

The answer was that the Ranger ace had carried his battle against Orr and the Bruins out of the playing area. The Boston players wanted to freeze out the New York defenseman because they believed that Park had burned them as a team, and particularly Orr, in print.

The Bruins had just read Park's autobiography, *Play the Man*, and bubbled with anger over statements Brad had made about Orr. "I hated sharing the dressing room with that creep," said Orr's teammate and friend Johnny McKenzie. "Park's presence took all the joy out of being an All-Star."

What angered Orr and his teammates were Brad's words on page 67 of his book: "Orr doesn't like to get hit, and sometimes he'll throw a cheap shot at one of our guys. A man of his ability needn't revert to such stuff, but he does."

Park's anti-Orr barrage set off explosions throughout the NHL. One headline shouted: "BRUINS ARE BUSH, BRAD PARK WRITES." Another alluded to Park's concern about retaliation: "AUTHOR EXPECTS TO BE A MARKED MAN."

No doubt Park was a marked man in the All-Stars' dressing room, but once on the ice that night he was promised a temporary truce by Orr and his Boston friends. Park responded by skimming a perfect pass to McKenzie late in the second period, enabling the Bruin to tie the game. Phil Esposito scored in the final period to give the East team a 3-2 edge over the West Division stars. But once the match had ended, the truce melted in the heat of anger. Park became a marked man in both Boston Garden and his own Madison Square Garden whenever the Rangers and Bruins played.

The Bruins had the toughness—and some said the meanness—to retaliate against Park. "They're not called 'The Big, Bad Bruins' for nothing," said former NHL defenseman Carl Brewer. "Boston has brutalized the game of hockey. On the other hand, Park plays the game hard but clean, the way it's supposed to be played."

Park was right. The Bruins were rough and often dirty. Orr frequently would erupt in anger if cleanly hit. More often, revenge was left to his teammates. Once when Toronto defenseman Pat Quinn nailed Bobby with a legal bodycheck, it appeared that the entire Boston team would try to assassinate Quinn.

"The Bruins," said former NHL forward Brian Conacher, "like the gang-warfare style of hockey. And they have the guys to play that kind of nasty game."

Unfortunately for Park, his Rangers were not equipped for Boston's heavy body play and angry stick-swinging. Park and clean-playing center Jean Ratelle epitomized the New Yorkers' Boy Scout style of hockey. It all made Brad's best battle against Orr and his Bruins' mates that much more difficult.

> "Park is defensively sounder than Orr. "Brad's a great one. By comparison, Orr is more offensive-minded."
>
> —Ex-Detroit Red Wings manager Ned Harkness

In Boston Garden, Orr's army of fans deafened Park with hostile barbs whenever he stepped on the ice. But the young Ranger shrugged off the boos and played his usual competent game. "They never loved me in Boston anyway," Park explained, "so it shouldn't have made much difference. Anyway, I'm not paid to like people. What I said in the book about Orr and the Bruins describes the way I feel."

Orr himself rarely took on Park either physically or verbally. But his teammates were plenty willing. Both Johnny McKenzie and Ted Green went after Brad and, each time, Park punished them with a flurry of punches. Nevertheless, the Bruins kept coming back, determined, it seemed, to edit Park's "heretic" book on the ice. And yet Park continued to tear away at Orr's image.

"One of the myths of hockey," said Park, "is that Orr is unstoppable. Some people have written, and rightly so, that Orr can be held in tow by forechecking him in his own end of the rink before he has a chance to get up a head of steam, and by taking advantage of the big openings he leaves when he takes off on one of his many rushes into enemy territory."

Such barbs continued to peck away at Orr's ego. But Bobby refused to reply in kind. Time and again newspapermen attempted to get Bobby to answer, but he played the questions as coolly as he would intercept an enemy forward on the ice. "I'll do my talking during the games," he insisted.

Brad seemed to revel in the controversy. "Somebody called me an egoist," he said, "but heck, the book is *my* book." While Park talked endlessly with newsmen, Bobby would frequently stay in the privacy of the Bruins' trainer's room to avoid the questioners. When Orr was cornered, he would duck the direct answer to a direct question.

"I never think of myself as an idol," said Orr. "I'm a hockey player. I enjoy hockey. The money? I never think about becoming a millionaire, or anything like that. When I quit hockey, it will be because I don't enjoy it anymore."

"Throughout it all," said author Tom Dowling, "Orr remains remote and circumspect, a little abashed at all the furor unloosed in his name."

Perhaps Park's literary onslaught would have been casually ignored by Orr had Brad been a mediocre player. But the Ranger was the prince, if not the king, of

Orr: Artistry in rhythm.

As the Park-Orr feud worsened in the 1970s, observers wondered just what kept prompting Park to explode with so many headline-grabbing statements that infuriated some of Brad's own teammates as well as the Bruins. "I said what I felt," Park insisted. "I'm not paid to love the Bruins nor their fans. I know that what I've said arouses them. And I'm sure they are more interested in seeing me get licked than anything else. It's all part of the game."

Some thought that Park spoke out because he did not receive the recognition he thought he deserved. It was easy for Orr to be a well-known hockey superstar in Boston, which is the most avid hockey town outside of Canada. But it was more difficult for Park to be a hero in giant New York City, where hockey often is a stepchild to the more popular basketball and where celebrities from all fields seem to be a dime a dozen. Even after Park had reached the heights in his profession, he still was hardly recognized off the ice in his team's hometown.

"Stop people on the streets of New York," noted *Sports Illustrated*, "and ask them about Brad Park, and the answer will sometimes be confusing. Brad Park is a playground in The Bronx. Brad Park is a botanical garden over in Brooklyn. Brad Park is a garage near the 59th Street Bridge.

"But mention that name on Ste. Catherine Street in Montreal or on Boylston Street in Boston. 'Brad Park,' goes the response, 'is Bobby Orr disguised as a New York Ranger.'"

Even the Boston fans came to appreciate Park's fighting spirit. Whenever the Bruins would attempt to bully the Rangers, Park seemed to arrive on the scene, ready and willing to take on all comers. Twice during the 1971-72

defensemen. More than that, he seemed to have obtained a keen insight into the Orr style, one which apparently eluded many viewers.

"Another myth about Orr," Park went on, "is that he's a gentlemanly and clean player. Actually, Orr can be a hatchetman just like some of his Boston teammates. This makes opponents more wary of him. Sometimes Bobby pulls off the cheap shots that really aren't necessary under any conditions."

season, Park tangled with Bruins players on Boston ice. Each time Brad so thoroughly outpointed the home skater that a second Bruin was compelled to intrude and save his teammate.

One time when Park was fighting McKenzie, one of his favorite Boston targets, Phil Esposito rushed in to rescue his mate. Surprisingly, Park approved. "Esposito is a terrific team man," said Brad. "He stepped in when it looked like McKenzie and I were going toe-to-toe. I'm a few inches taller and heavier, and logically I should take McKenzie . . . so Espo came into it. A good team man does something like that."

No matter what he did, Park still couldn't obtain recognition throughout the NHL that he was in Orr's class. A few critics thought so, but even some of Brad's friends admitted that Bobby was better. "Brad is a very good

approached Brad and began asking him questions. Ranger star Rod Gilbert leaned over and quipped sarcastically, "Go ahead, Brad, and tell him something that will make another team mad at us. We haven't got enough people sore at us now."

Orr's Bruins ultimately finished first in the East Division in the 1971-72 season, ten points ahead of Park's Rangers. Bobby also topped Brad in scoring—117 points to 49. But the New Yorkers would get their opportunity for revenge in the 1972 Stanley Cup finals.

The 1972 Stanley Cup collision marked the high point of the Boston-New York rivalry. It was the first time that the two foes had met in the finals since 1929. The natural competition between the teams was even further inflamed by Park's comments, which by this time had been so well-circulated they were on the lips of fans from Boston

---

"I never think of myself as an idol. I'm a hockey player. I enjoy hockey. The money? I never think about becoming a millionaire, or anything like that. When I quit hockey, it will be because I don't enjoy it anymore."

—Bobby Orr

---

defenseman," said Harry Howell, who once teamed with Park on the New York defense. "Second to Orr. Bobby is the best I've ever seen."

"I don't mind being Number Two," Park insisted. "It's a challenge. If I think the guy is better than me, I have to try harder. If I work harder, I play better—better than anybody."

Translating the words to action was not always easy. Two months after Orr and Park had confronted one another at the 1972 All-Star Game, they met again at Boston Garden. This time the Bruins won the match 8-1. Park played capably, to be sure, but his teammates appeared lost. Many of the Rangers privately complained that Brad's book had done them as much harm as the Boston sticks.

"There's no doubt," agreed Bruins executive Tom Johnson, "that Park's book helped us more than it's helped the Rangers. It gave our guys extra incentive to beat them. I wonder, though, if Brad even realizes how much the things he said in the book can hurt him and the Rangers. He's certainly entitled to his opinions, but he's lost respect among his fellow players for the things he wrote."

Brad had expected to antagonize Orr and the Bruins, but he never expected hostile reactions from his own buddies. After that 8-1 shellacking, a newspaperman

to Bangor. But Orr and his Bruins won that battle, four games to two.

But the Orr-Park rivalry was far from over. Before the 1972-73 season began, Orr had an operation on one of his bad knees. He returned for the 1972-73 campaign a slower skater than before, and it appeared that Park might finally become the number one defenseman.

Like many Orr-watchers, Park noticed the change in Bobby's style. And once again, he couldn't keep his mouth shut. "Last year," he said, "when Bobby hit our blue line he was accelerating. Now he's just moving regularly when he hits the line. What that means is that we—the defensemen—can angle Orr against the boards because he does not have the spurt to go around us."

But Park got his comeuppance in November 1972, when his bad knee was injured in a collision with Philadelphia defenseman Ed Van Impe. Another collision a month later worsened the condition, and Park lost a step in the process.

"I had to readjust my style because of it," Brad admitted. "It was frustrating. I could take a full stride with the left leg but only a half a stride with the right; it gave me a gimpy effect. I couldn't rely on my reflexes enough. I had to out-think guys coming at me, try to head them off at the pass. And if I made a mistake, I couldn't always recover quick enough and too often the guy was gone."

Even with the injuries, Park and Orr stood head and shoulders above other defensemen most of the time and led their teams into a head-to-head confrontation once more in the playoffs. "Our Day Will Come," sang Park before the opening face-off and, this time, he was right.

Although the 1973 series opened on Boston Garden ice, Park never was better, and the Rangers seemed to take heart from his performance. Pushing the Bruins aside as if they were plastic table hockey players, the Rangers stunned Boston with a 6-2 defeat and followed that with a 4-2 decision. After two games at home, the mighty Bruins were down two games to none.

Oddly enough, the Bruins came to life in New York in the third game, winning 4-2. But it had become apparent that Orr could be stopped, and when Orr was stopped, the Bruins were dead.

"We watched films of Orr in action," said Rangers goalie Ed Giacomin. "After studying the films we decided that the best way to keep him from hurting us was to flood his side. We kept throwing the puck in and making him go back and chase it. If that's done to anyone, the player will get tired. That's what happened to Orr, and it hurt his game."

This was obvious in the fifth game of the series, at Boston. Orr moved as if he were skating in mud, while Park flitted around the rink as if he had wings on his boots. The Rangers easily won the match, 6-3, and eliminated the Bruins.

Park unquestionably was the hero, outplaying Orr in every phase of the game, including Bobby's forte, scoring. In the five games, Park collected two goals and four assists for six points, right behind team leader Bill Fairbairn, who had eight points. Virtually helpless against the New York defenses, Orr managed only one goal and one assist.

That round went to Park, but Orr was heard from again in May 1973 when the All-Star ballots were counted. The votes kept the Bruins star on top, giving him a spot on the First Team for the sixth consecutive year. Park, who had been a First All-Star twice, was relegated to the Second Team.

From all indications "number two" would remain second best to Orr as long as Bobby's knees were able to carry him at top speed.

Inge Hammarstrom of the Toronto Maple Leafs, who had played in the top European leagues against the foremost Russian, Czechoslovakian and Finnish aces, summed up the majority opinion about the Orr-Park argument. "There are many stars, fine skaters, stickhandlers and playmakers and scorers," said Hammarstrom, "but none can control an entire game like Orr.

Brad Park

Bruce Bennett Studios

He amazes you the way he sets the tempo of the game from fast to slow and back again."

In 1973-74 Bobby led the Bruins back to the top of the East Division, while Park's Rangers remained in close pursuit. The two defensemen had matured considerably since their early days in the majors. Both had married. Both had emerged as unquestioned leaders of their respective teams and were counted among the most exciting personalities in hockey history.

If Orr kept his edge over Park on the ice, Park remained the more colorful of the two as he continued to strive for the coveted number one position.

"Brad knows that Bobby is the greatest player *at the moment*," said a close friend of Park's. "But he also knows that if Orr's knees ever go, the best defenseman in the world will be Brad Park. In the meantime Brad remains the best-selling defenseman-author."

That was true. Meanwhile, the bitterness was still evident whenever Brad encountered the Bruins. "It happens whenever the Rangers play the Bruins," said Hugh Delano of the *New York Post* during the 1973-74 season. "The Bruins fans won't let the Rangers' defenseman forget their anger at what he wrote about their heroes."

"Everything I put in the book," said Park, "reflected the way I felt. I have no regrets about it. After all, I can't say everybody's a good guy."

Then, a pause and a wink: "But I'll say that Bobby Orr is a great hockey player. Maybe even better than me!"

Not very long after that, Park was traded to Boston. In no time at all, Bobby and Brad became pals as well as teammates. And for one brief season, the Bruins featured two of the best defensemen in history. But no one doubted that, in the end, Orr was *the* greatest.

Boston BRUINS

The Best Front-Office Characters

Art Ross

The Bruins would not be where they are today without Arthur Howey "Art" Ross.

He was the franchise's first manager and coach, imported by new owner Charles Adams when the National Hockey League invaded Boston in 1924.

Described as a "crusty, dour Scot," Ross also was a creative executive steeped to his neck in hockey knowledge.

A native of Naughton, Ontario, Ross had been a defenseman for Westmount, Brandon, Kenora, the Montreal Wanderers and the Ottawa Senators before calling it a playing career in 1918.

It was growing up playing street shinny in Montreal's Westmount area that Ross would encounter the Patrick brothers, Lester and Frank, for the first time, in what would be a lifelong relationship.

"One of the 'refined' kids who showed up to play ball one summer afternoon was a cocky ten-year-old named Art Ross," wrote Eric Whitehead in his book *The Patricks: Hockey's Royal Family*. "This was a name that would dog the Patricks for most of the next half century in a strange mix of bitter rivalry and warm friendship. It was a name that would come to mean to the Boston Bruins almost what the name Lester Patrick would be to the New York Rangers."

Art and Lester began their competition early in life, nearly exchanging blows in an on-ice scrap. The fight would certainly have taken place had Mother Nature not intervened.

Frank Patrick recalls: "There was this one game in Haileybury—not really unusual in that northern Ontario mining country—when it was 25 below zero, with a bitter wind that made it seem much colder than that. We had to wear mittens to keep our hands from dropping off, and Art Ross, the Haileybury captain, wore a pair of fur gloves and a woolen toque rolled down over his face with peep holes cut out for the eyes. He looked the very devil himself, and he played as mean as he looked.

"There was one funny incident when Art went after Lester with his stick, clubbed him on the jaw, and Lester retaliated. Art—I think he was just looking for a good scrap just to keep from freezing to death—backed off, took off his gloves and tossed them onto the ice. He made a few gestures with his fists and then suddenly turned and scrambled to retrieve his gloves and get them back on again. Lester burst out laughing, and the fight was called off. Called on account of cold."

The relationship between Ross and the Patricks would bring them together in the NHL after Art was hired to run the Bruins by Charles Adams. Whitehead wrote, "Ross thus became the first grad of the old Westmount street gang to move into a position of power. Stuck with a motley first-year Boston roster, Ross was already on the prowl for quality players. As he well knew, many of these were out in the Western Canada League, so what better than to contact his old chums, the Patrick brothers.

"He wrote to Frank to say that he was in the market for some good hockey players and would appreciate anything Frank might do along that line. Frank wrote back a nice, polite letter that said, in effect: Not yet. Ross did not push the proposition, but did suggest that they get together in maybe a year or two to talk things over. That was fine with the Patricks, who were already plotting survival with honor, plus a few dollars cash."

After icing a mediocre Hub club in 1924-25, Ross gradually built on a talent foundation that would bring Stanley Cups to Boston in both 1929 and 1939.

The turnabout in the Bruins' fortunes began in Montreal's Windsor Hotel in 1925. As it happened, Frank and Lester Patrick were there, about to dissolve their Western Hockey League.

Whitehead: "Ross walked in, struck up a friendly conversation and then casually inquired about the health of a few Western League players. He seemed particularly solicitous about the well-being of Eddie Shore, Duke Keats and Frank Frederickson.

"He expressed a special admiration for Frederickson.

"'No deal,' Frank said, smiling.

"'I haven't suggested any,' Ross replied. 'But I will.'

"No deal was made at that time, but the wheels had begun turning and Frank had an important ally. Ross listened to the sale plan, agreed that there might be some benefit there for his Bruins and said he would help swing the $300,000 deal. He seemed quite confident that it could be done.

"'Let me say right now,' Frank explained, 'that without Ross's support from there on in, we never would have succeeded.'"

Ross, who was inducted into the Hockey Hall of Fame in 1945, also was inventive. The official NHL puck, "the Art Ross puck" and the official goal net, "the Art Ross net," were not named after the former Boston Bruins manager for nothing. One of the more creative minds in hockey, Ross redesigned the rubber puck—which formerly had sharp edges that caused painful cuts—had the edges beveled and improved the game. Pre-Ross nets were simple devices with sloping flat rear sections that frequently inspired pucks to bounce out of the twine as fast as they went in. Ross's improvement became the NHL-approved net with a double half-moon interior built to retain pucks shot into the webbing.

But Ross did considerably more than that. His major accomplishment was building the Boston Bruins into a dynasty in the late twenties and constantly rebuilding the Bruins so they remained the class of the NHL for most of Art's life. He developed such aces as Eddie Shore, Frankie Brimsek, the Kraut Line, Bill Cowley and Dit Clapper. He also acquired the great Frank Frederickson in 1927.

"[Frederickson] was not only great on the ice but also enlivened the team's train trips with impromptu concerts on his violin, often performed in the middle of the night," wrote Eric Whitehead. "Sometimes, just for variety, he switched to the ukulele and sang a little.

"The Bruins' fearless defenseman, Eddie Shore, was also musically inclined. He considered himself to be pretty good on the tenor saxophone, although he was just learning to play the instrument. He occasionally took his sax on the road to practice, and what with Frank on the fiddle and Eddie on the horn, the night rides through the hitherto peaceful wilds of New York, Maine and Quebec at times became just too much for manager Art Ross. No lover of fine music, Ross banned musical instruments from all road trips, and thus the first brave pioneer road company of the Boston Pops was no more."

Ross also was a cantankerous sort, who frequently feuded with his managerial colleagues, but especially with Conn Smythe of the Maple Leafs. Smythe claims the feud started because Ross duped him first. It happened when

Smythe had bought the Toronto franchise in the late twenties and was on the lookout for talent. Ross recommended a player named Jimmy "Sailor" Herberts. Smythe bit, paid $18,000 for Herberts, and then learned that he had purchased a dud.

According to Smythe, Ross's chief goal in life was to make a fool of him. "Once," said Smythe, "Ross stationed two longshoremen near our bench in Boston Garden and their instructions were to goad me into a fight. Ross wanted to have me put in jail."

Sure enough, the longshoremen pushed and shoved Smythe as he was heading for the dressing room after the game. Smythe snarled at them and then noticed Ross in the background, apparently ready to charge at Smythe. "My assistant, a little guy named Frank Selke, saw Ross coming and dove at him with a flying block that knocked Ross down," Smythe recalled. "We got out of there fast, but not before I yelled at the longshoremen, 'When your boss gets up tell him I can't waste my time with anybody that a man as small as Selke can lick.'" All Smythe had done was pour gasoline on the flames of his feud with Ross. Each man eagerly awaited the opportunity to go one up—or two or three up, if possible—on the other.

During a Bruins slump, Smythe bought four columns of space in all of the Boston newspapers. Addressed to the fans, the ad read: "If you're tired of what you've been looking at, come out tonight and see a decent team, the Toronto Maple Leafs, play hockey,"

Livid, Ross demanded that league president Frank Calder fine Smythe $3,000 for conduct detrimental to the NHL. He snapped that Smythe was nothing more than "the big wind from Lake Ontario."

Ross didn't get his way, and subsequently, Smythe went at him again. This time, when the Leafs returned to Boston, Conn rented a tuxedo and pranced haughtily around Boston Garden, tipping his hat and waving to the Bruins' fans as if he were the city's official greeter. A bouquet of roses were dispatched to Ross as the added fillip.

Smythe always respected Ross's hockey ability, and following World War II, they patched up their feud. According to the Toronto boss, it was *his* idea, based on Ross's sons' participation in the armed forces. "His two sons served overseas," Smythe explained, "and had excellent records. I figured anybody who could rear two boys like that must be all right."

By the end of the 1930s, Ross had become a legend in Boston. The development of Milt Schmidt, Bobby Bauer and Woody Dumart, along with Roy Conacher and Flash Hollett, enabled the Bruins to finish first in the 1939-40 season. Schmidt led the scoring race, followed by Bauer and Dumart in a tie for second and Bill Cowley behind them.

Ross's coaching stints were twice interrupted. Frank Patrick took over for two seasons (1934-35, 1935-36), and Cooney Weiland ran the bench for the 1939-40 and 1940-

41 campaigns.

From 1941-42 through the 1944-45 season, Ross coached for the last time. In 1945-46 he gave the reigns, to Dit Clapper and concentrated on front-office duties.

In the post-World War II years, Ross's Bruins remained competitive, but would not win another Stanley Cup until 1970, after he was gone. One of his best moves in that time, though, was luring Lynn Patrick to Boston as coach. The son of onetime rival Lester Patrick, Lynn arrived during the summer of 1950.

Despite the fact that he was the nephew of the coach Ross had fired after a harsh, lengthy quarrel, Lynn had only praise for Ross.

"He was the greatest boss I ever had," said Lynn. "I loved the guy, and I think the feeling was mutual. He personally groomed me to take over as general manager, and he never at any time did anything to harass me or undermine my authority. The matter of Uncle Frank never came up between us, nor was it broached by anyone else in town."

During the 1949-50 season, Patrick had guided the underdog Rangers to the seventh game of the Stanley Cup finals with Detroit. Not surprisingly, when Patrick came to Boston, the Rangers' fortunes went down and the Bruins' went up. New York missed the playoffs consecutively from 1951-55, while Boston emerged as a postseason contender.

After leading the Bruins for more than three decades, Ross eventually retired in 1954 and passed away ten years later at the age of 81.

Don Cherry

Unquestionably the most colorful coach in Bruins history, Don "Grapes" Cherry also could pass for the most colorful in NHL annals. Period.

Grapes earned the opportunity to coach the Boston Bruins after two seasons as Coach of the Year in the American Hockey League. His Rochester clubs, with no major-league affiliations, still managed to challenge for the Calder Cup and finished first in 1973-74 in the divisional race.

His job with the Bruins was a difficult one, especially for a man who played in only one NHL game. He led men like Bobby Orr and Phil Esposito, top stars for years, with only a minor-league background. But it was a background which included four minor-league championships in his last five years as a player.

Cherry's popularity in Boston was instant and intense. He turned the Bruins into the Lunchpail A.C. as well as a constant playoff threat.

He was the media's darling, not only in Boston but throughout the hockey world. To say that there wasn't a microphone Grapes didn't like would be the understatement of the past half century.

But he also had his enemies. One was ex-Bruin Ed Westfall, who became New York Islanders captain in 1972 and one of Cherry's prime foes.

"After I left the Bruins in '72," Westfall recalled, "I came into Boston with the Islanders and Cherry resented the fact that I was getting all this ink. One night in Boston he had Stan Jonathan chase me, but I hammered Jonathan in front of the Bruins' bench. Then, I turned to Don and said, 'Cherry, you keep sending these guys after me, why don't you try me? You've got 16 guys sitting on the bench and not one of them likes you.'"

Naturally, Grapes offered another version. "In my first NHL coaching year, Eddie told the papers, 'The Bruins don't look like they're in shape.' I, of course, was the guy responsible for putting them in shape. It made me look bad. Next season I had Jonathan and John Wensink chase him around. There was a time-out with the face-off in front of our bench. I leaned over and said, 'What kind of bleeping shape are we in now, Eddie?' I don't mind people calling me names—racist, pig, cretin, redneck—but to call me a wimp, never!"

Cherry's last stint in Denver took a turn for the worse after Grapes had a disagreement with Mike McEwen and settled it by grabbing the defenseman by the neck.

"Right after that," Westfall remembered, "the Rockies came to Long Island and the word was out that Don would soon be fired. I ran into him in the corridor and he put his hand out and said, 'Eddie, I got to talk to you. Remember all that bullshit we went through in Boston? Well, I would like to bury it. As you probably realize, I need all the friends I can get.' I said, 'You got that right.'"

Within two seasons behind the Bruins' bench, Cherry had become the people's choice. He was the Gallery Gods' favorite and turned seemingly ordinary players such as Terry O'Reilly and Don Marcotte into civic heroes. When Rick "Nifty" Middleton arrived from the Rangers for Ken Hodge, Cherry made Nifty into a star.

And when Brad Park and Jean Ratelle were dealt to Boston in a controversial trade with the Rangers, Cherry not only eased their passage onto the Bruins Express but made them tops at their respective defense and center positions.

"When all was said and done, the big deal saved my career," Cherry said. "I give Harry [Sinden] full marks for a lot of guts on the deal. He knew we were in trouble and went out and did something, even though he knew it would be unpopular with the players, the fans and the media. Park, who was supposed to be out of shape and possibly at the end of his career because of his knee problems, played sensationally for me, as did Ratelle. Of course, at the time we had no way of knowing that it would work out so well, and a number of players on the Bruins suffered grave doubts. Phil [Esposito] and Vad [Carol Vadnais] were popular with their teammates and Park was high on the Bruins' hate list. He had written a book as a Ranger, *Play the Man*, in which he was severely critical of some of the Boston players, inspiring intense resentment among the guys. Nobody had feelings either way about Ratelle, who was always considered a quiet and classy guy."

Ironically, Cherry received as much attention for a *faux pas* he pulled behind the Bruins' bench as he did for all the good works. This was in the 1979 playoffs with Montreal. Boston nursed a one-goal lead late in the third period and seemed to have the game in the bag when the officials caught the Bruins with a minor penalty for too many men on the ice.

In his autobiography, *Grapes*, Cherry explained: "The time of the penalty was 17:26. How did it happen? Why did it happen? I have asked myself these questions so many times!

"For starters let me say for now and for an eternity that *I* accept full responsibility for the blunder of blunders. When a team gets caught with too many men on the ice at that stage in a hockey game, it has to be the coach's fault. I deserved to be court-martialed.

"The confusion was rooted in the fact that Marcotte had stayed on left wing through three shifts. The other guy was nervous and got carried away. When he finally came back to the bench after [John] D'Amico whistled the penalty, he had tears in his eyes. So did my son, Timothy, who had been watching the game at bench level. I imagine I would have been crying, too, but, at that point, I suspect that all my bodily functions had gone on strike. At that moment I took a look at the Canadiens' bench. They looked like a pride of lions about to jump a wildebeest.

The Wrath of Grapes.

There was only one thing to do. I called a time-out.

"Were we ever in a mess. My trainer, Frosty Forristall, had tears in his eyes and two Bruins fans sitting next to our bench were bawling like babies. I wanted to cry myself but I couldn't. (That would come later.) I told the guys that we had to stop [Guy] Lafleur, to stay between him and the net as much as possible.

"Okay. The time-out was over. There was a face-off and the puck was in motion. I couldn't believe what a terrific job we were doing of killing the penalty. A minute had gone by and we still had the lead. Now it was 70 seconds elapsed and we were *still* ahead.

"But the Canadiens mounted a counterattack. Jacques Lemaire, one of the most underrated players on that Montreal team, took a pass near our blue line. Lafleur was moving down the right side like the Japanese Bullet Train. Lemaire dropped the pass over to Lafleur. I figured he was going to try to move in on [Gilles] Gilbert, try a few dekes and get into a really good scoring position.

"He was way over to the right, far, far out, sort of where I wanted him. A shot from there would be desperate, but he drew his stick back. He *was* desperate. For a split second I almost felt reassured. Then, his stick swung around the big arc and the blade made contact with the puck.

"I can't tell you precisely how fast that puck traveled but anything faster than that shot had to break the sound barrier. Almost in the same moment Lafleur slapped the rubber, it bulged the twine in the left side of the net behind Gilles [Gilbert]. There went the lead. *Boom!* Just like that.

"We left the ice tied 4-4 at the end of regulation time. The way my players plodded into the dressing room you would have thought that they had just finished a trek across the Sahara Desert—in uniform. I have seen teams throughout my career that were down, but none as thoroughly subterranean as this one.

"I knew that getting them to even a reasonable state of battle readiness for the overtime would be the chore of my life.

"Before going into the room I had to get my frustrations out. It does no good for the players to see the coach upset, or for the coach to take his frustrations out on the players. So I left them alone for a while. Then I took a deep breath and walked into the room.

"It was like a morgue. No jokes this time. I said to

them, 'Look, when we were down two games to none in this series going back to Boston, if I could have said to you, "Would you be happy to go into overtime of the seventh game?" What would you have said?' And they all yelled, 'YES!'

"I didn't know if I believed it, but they did and that's most important. They were banging at the doors to get going. There never was, nor ever will be, a better bunch of guys. I love them.

"And before you knew it, the buzzer was sounding for the start of sudden-death overtime.

"To my surprise, we came out with more drive than I thought we had in us. Marcotte took a pass from (Terry) O'Reilly when [Ken] Dryden had one knee down on the ice. Marcotte shot it for the upper corner and started to raise his stick in celebration, as if the puck was going in. But Dryden, who was so damn big, got his shoulder in front of the puck—more by accident than by skill—and my heart was still in my mouth. The rebound came out to O'Reilly and, with an open net waiting to greet his shot, the puck bounced over his stick.

"Back and forth the play whirred at a dizzying pace. The clock ticked past the nine-minute mark and there still was no tie-breaker. My guys—particularly the older ones—were struggling. [Brad] Park, Bobby Schmautz and [Wayne] Cashman had blood running into their underwear but they kept on going.

"At last, Lafleur was off the ice and it seemed as if we might have a respite, but [Scott] Bowman had some excellent infantrymen. One of them was a kid named Mario Tremblay who had gone into orbit along the right boards. Another was Yvon Lambert, who always looked as if he had two left feet until he put the puck behind your goalie.

"Al Sims was alone on defense, with Park coming back, and I could see the fear in Al's eyes as Lambert sped to the goal crease while Tremblay, tantalizingly, waited for the precise moment to deliver the pass. Lambert eluded Park, accepted the puck at the lip of the net and pushed it past Gilbert before the goalie could slide across the crease.

"The pain I felt when the red light flashed behind our goal cannot be measured in traditional human terms. To say

that a pile-driver applied to my stomach would not have created a deeper hurt would simply be minimizing the ache.

"A lot of people—and I know that they don't have sadistic tendencies but it feels like they do—ask, 'What were your feelings at that exact moment?' I tell you, it was sorrow for my players, especially those who had been given shots of Novocain before the game. The goal doesn't flash in my mind, but somebody's underwear, with blood mixed with sweat, does.

"I felt disgusted with myself for letting it happen. Sometimes when you have too many men on the ice it's the players' fault. But not this time. I hadn't spelled out the assignments plainly enough.

"Strangely, I didn't even think of my job until a reporter asked me, 'Do you think this will cost you your job?' I said, 'My friend, after this loss, I don't really care one way or the other,' But I knew I was gone. I had known I was gone as far back as Christmas. There was a slight chance of me staying if we had won the Cup, but at that moment I really couldn't have cared less."

Cherry and Harry Sinden never signed an armistice, which meant that someone had to go. It was the coach. Grapes departed Boston with a lucrative contract to coach the dismal Colorado Rockies.

That was the last coaching job he would work in the NHL. Cherry clashed with the Rockies' general staff and left the NHL to become an analyst for "Hockey Night in Canada."

Working with Ron McLean on "Coaches Corner," Cherry became the most popular—and controversial—off-ice hockey personality in North America.

He's also one of the smartest and, through the 1990s, continued to be hockey's foremost personality.

"To be an expert you have to be in the game for 40 years, you have to play for 16, you have to be Coach of the Year in the NHL, AHL, and coach Team Canada in the Canada Cup and then coach kids to a championship in a high school when I was in Rochester. So if I'm not an expert, and I watch at least 10 games a week, and if I'm not an expert, I don't know who is."

Neither do we!

Harry Sinden

It is a measure of Harry Sinden's value to the Boston Bruins that 33 years after he began working for the franchise Sinden was told by owner Jerry Jacobs, "You can stay as long as you want—even another 27 years!"

Few executives in the history of sports could lay claim

to such a vote of confidence.

Jacobs was not merely blowing smoke; he meant every word of it.

Since coming to Boston as Bruins head coach in 1966, Sinden has served the organization in many capacities, and one constant has marked each level: success.

His teams have won the Stanley Cup, six conference titles and 12 division crowns.

For Sinden, the trip to Beantown actually began in 1961 as a player-coach in Kingston, Ontario, and later as coach of Boston's minor league team in Minneapolis. He then moved to Oklahoma City as a player-coach, guiding that team to the 1965-66 CHL championship with eight straight victories.

Sinden was the right man in the right place at the right time when the Boston Bruins handed him their coaching reins at the start of the 1966-67 campaign. The Bruins had finished dead last five times in the previous six seasons, and the city was hungry for a winner. It didn't happen immediately. The Bruins finished sixth in Harry's first year on the job, but a hotshot rookie named Bobby Orr provided plenty of consolation. A year later, Derek Sanderson arrived, along with Phil Esposito, Kenny Hodge and Fred Stanfield, and suddenly nobody laughed at the Bruins anymore. For the first time in eight years they made the playoffs, and two seasons later they captured Boston's first Stanley Cup in 29 years.

The whole town was just wild about Harry. But in the midst of the grand celebration, Sinden abruptly quit Boston—publicly charging the brass with underpaying him—and began a new career in the modular home industry. By the start of the 1972-73 season, the firm he was working for went into bankruptcy. Meanwhile, the Bruins, who had added another Stanley Cup in his absence, were rapidly coming apart at the seams. Defections to the upstart World Hockey Association, injuries to veterans and subpar performances by formerly dependable players all took a toll on the Bruins. In September 1972, Sinden coached Team Canada to its stirring victory over the Soviet national team. When a new owner bought the Bruins, the first move was to bring Sinden back, hoping he was the man to put Humpty Dumpty together again in 1972-73.

A young Harry Sinden.

Just three years after he had left town as a conquering hero of sorts, Harry returned to a less-than-heart-warming welcome. He was introduced as the team's managing director, a strange title that did not hide the fact that he was actually replacing one of the most popular personalities on the Boston sports front, Milt Schmidt.

Schmidt, who had been general manager during Harry's successful coaching stint, was given the new title of executive director, but everybody knew Milt had been relegated to mere window dressing in the front office. Sinden caught the full force of the backlash from the sympathy extended to Schmidt by both the press and the public. Understandably, Harry was slow to assert himself.

Except for replacing coach Tom Johnson with Bep Guidolin, Harry walked softly through his first year at the post. "I intend to get a lot closer to the players in the future," he said. "I'm going to try opening up our lines of communication." He then rolled up his sleeves and went to work. After the 1974 playoff loss to Philadelphia, Sinden dropped Guidolin and hired Don Cherry as coach. As manager, though, Sinden still had not proven he was as competent as he was coaching. His Bruins were rapidly wiped out of the playoffs in 1975.

The Cherry hiring was inspirational, until the two egos clashed irrevocably during the later 1970s. Grapes left the team in 1979, creating a furor in Beantown, but Sinden weathered the storm and twice went behind the bench until he could hire a coach in whom he believed.

In 1988, Harry was named team president while retaining the general manager's portfolio—a position he continues to hold. A member of the Hockey Hall of Fame in the Builder's category, Sinden remained a powerful voice in NHL circles through the turn of the twenty-first century.

And if Jerry Jacobs has anything to say, this voice will be heard for years to come.

Pat Burns

It's never easy to quantify precisely how much a particular coach contributes to a team's success, but there are some guidelines.

In the case of Pat Burns, one can simply say he rejuvenated a maudlin Bruin team that had missed the playoffs for the first time in 30 years.

If ever there was a perfect coach for the perfect team, Burns was the man. The evidence was there on the ice as well as on the stat sheets. The Bruins became playoff contenders once more while the mustachioed Irishman provided the brand of *joie de vivre* behind the bench that had been missing since the golden years of Don Cherry.

Some seasoned sportswriters detected a remarkable similarity between Burns and football's Bill Parcells. Others commented that if Burns were a corporate executive, he would be one of those CEOs who reshapes a crumbling conglomerate into a money-maker faster than you can say Chase Manhattan.

"He took the Canadiens and Maple Leafs when they were both down, turned them around and now he's done it again with the Bruins," said ex-NHL-coach-turned-broadcaster Harry Neale. "The man does the job everywhere he goes."

Bulldog blunt and Seinfeld comedic, Burns fit Boston as snugly as Parcells did when he took New England's Patriots to the Super Bowl in 1997.

"Pat and Bill are really the same guy," said WEEI-Boston broadcaster Dale Arnold. "They're both no-nonsense, straight-shooters who'll go to the wall for their players. And they're both winners."

As a rookie coach of the year, Burns pushed the Habs to the 1989 Stanley Cup finals. In 1993, the Burns-led Leafs surprised the hockey world by reaching the conference finals before being knocked out in seven by Wayne Gretzky's Kings.

"There's no coach better at instantly recognizing which of his players are going and which aren't, and adjusting his lineup to suit the situation," said Neale. "Once Pat sees a guy is hot, he plays the life out of him. A lot of coaches lack that talent."

After Boston missed the playoffs for the first time in 30 years, Burns was imported in 1997 to resuscitate a comatose franchise. Pat provided the kind of pizzazz you get from a just-opened seltzer bottle, except that Burns' fizz lasts longer.

Presumed dead before the 1997-98 season began, the Bruins deked the undertakers, finishing second in the Eastern Conference (39-30-13-91), precisely 30 points better than the Hub's last-placers of 1996-97. The reasons were multiple—Ray Bourque's A-1 defense and Byron Dafoe's airtight tending—but the common denominator was Burns, the quintessential players' coach.

"I wouldn't want to play for anyone else," said forward Anson Carter, who found himself as a major leaguer under Burns. "Pat makes the game fun, but when we lose he's tough. And that's exactly how it should be."

Although he was never an NHL player, Burns has impeccable intuition when it comes to discerning what his skaters are thinking. Even one of the most cerebral of Bruins, Ken Baumgartner, once admitted that.

"Pat realizes that players are highly paid athletes and will tune out an intense coach," said Baumgartner. "He picks his spots, and when he turns the intensity on, it's very effective. He's intelligent and adapts to the game as it changes. Losing is unacceptable to him and now to us."

As routine as exhaling, Burns not only revived jaded veterans like Baumgartner, Grant Ledyard and Dave Ellett but turned them into meaningful assets. Ellett, for example, not only played solid defense but helped develop young backliners such as Hal Gill. "Pat was demanding when I had him in Toronto," said Ellett. "He preached hard work and his players always put the team first because of that. The only way he's changed since coming to Boston is that his fuse is a little longer."

Burns' toughness is as legendary as it is controversial. While coaching *Les Canadiens*, Pat disapproved of Claude Lemieux's dives. Once, after Lemieux went down, contorted in pain, Burns restrained his trainer from helping the forward. Eventually, Lemieux came to his senses and limped to the bench without help. Few questioned Burns' resolute —if not macho—refusal to show sympathy for Lemieux.

No less controversial was Burns' reaction to Ted Donato, a Harvard-educated, Boston-bred Bruin. Donato had been a valuable goal-scorer under other Beantown coaches until a game against the New York Islanders on December 20, 1997.

Unexpectedly, the usually composed Donato smacked tough defenseman Rich Pilon on the head with the shaft of his stick. Teddy had fallen to the ice after the swipe, at which point Pilon angrily charged the helpless Bruin. Instinctively, Donato raised his skates—more for protection than in anger—and grazed the furious Islander.

The episode inspired a league-imposed three-game suspension for Donato and what seemed to be a permanent turnoff from Burns. Donato's ice time fell from regular to erratic, and soon prompted requests for a trade. The Bruins finally obliged, ironically dispatching him to Pilon's Islanders for enforcer Ken Belanger.

Few doubt there was a direct connection between Donato's misdeed and his permanent entrance into Burns' doghouse, although the coach never explicitly reamed Donato in public. To this day, Donato is mystified.

"I could waste a lot of time thinking about what happened as far as my situation went," said a diplomatic Donato. "The bottom line is that Pat deserves a lot of credit for putting Boston in the playoffs after what had happened the year before."

Burns usually speaks softly and carries a big stick, but if the case merits otherwise, he'll raise the decibel level and carry a big fist. Mathieu Schneider can vouch for that. The Rangers' defenseman played under Burns for three years and once literally got Pat up in arms.

Burns: "I wouldn't lay a hand on a player on the bench, but the dressing room is another story. I did it to Schneider right in the dressing room when we were in Boston. We'd been through a tough run of injuries and had about six or seven AHL players up with us. I remember saying to myself, 'Pat, you'd better be a good coach tonight.' We actually won the game and played really well, but later in the game Matty cross-checked a guy from behind—which was completely ridiculous—and took a stupid penalty. What I mean is he didn't have to do it, and we even stressed before the game the need to avoid getting dumb penalties, and there Schneider does that, which really upset me. So, after the game, he walked past me in the dressing room and I sort of grabbed him—and two coaches wound up pulling me off Matty."

Schneider never bore a grudge against Burns. Following the clash, the young defenseman would regularly chat with his coach and eventually got the drift of what Pat wanted from him.

"I was trying to make him realize at that point in time that, 'Hey you're a young kid in this business and a marquee player. You're gonna have to listen and do things for the team, not yourself.'"

"He was very tough on me but that's the way he motivates guys—as a disciplinarian," said Schneider, "and he's had a lot of success doing it. He teaches a strict system and, in retrospect, his teams always play his system. It's a team-oriented game under him, with no room for individuals."

The Burns philosophy is rooted in his Montreal childhood home, not far from the Forum. Pat was the youngest of six children to an anglophone father and a francophone mother. Typically sardonic, Burns explains, "My mother couldn't speak English and my father couldn't speak French, but they must have been able to communicate because they made six of us kids."

He spent seventeen years as an Ottawa cop, including a stint as a detective before turning to full-time work as coach of the Hull Olympiques. "The police work helps his coaching because Pat has heard all the excuses from his job as a cop," said goalie-turned-TV analyst Chico Resch. "He's not going to be swayed and players know that they are not going to be able to snow him."

Which explains why, in francophone Montreal, he survived run-ins with such favorites as Claude Lemieux, Stephane Richer and Stephan Lebeau. But Burns had Hall of Famers Larry Robinson and Bob Gainey in his corner and, when the Habs made him the highest-paid coach in hockey in 1991, Pat insisted he wanted to stay in Montreal "for the rest of my life."

The more colorful and outspoken he became, though, the more Burns collided with a Montreal media eager to eviscerate a politically incorrect coach. Once, he told French-speaking magazine *L'Actualite* that it would be discomfitting for him to have a known homosexual in his club. Another time, after Shayne Corson was involved in a barroom incident, Burns told a francophone interviewer, "As far as I'm concerned, Shayne Corson can eat s—."

After four successful regular seasons in Montreal, Burns abruptly resigned from the Habs to ink a four-year deal with Toronto at $400,000 a season. While conducting his orderly retreat, Burns protested that he had to defend every coaching move in Montreal because of the daily media third degree. "I could no longer function effectively," he explained. "After four or five years in the same town, even if you have a lot of success, it's time to move on unless you win the Stanley Cup every year."

He didn't win a Cup in Toronto, but he pushed the Leafs to the finals in 1992-93 and, in the process, pushed around hitherto untouchable favorites such as Wendel Clark. The result was Clark's best-ever (10-10-20) playoff scoring.

"Throughout Wendel's career he never was told a lot of things," said Burns. "He was never advised, 'Well you can't do this and you can't do that.' I sat him down and told him you fight if you have to fight, but I didn't want him running around from one board to another, just running people and getting hurt. He understood."

The supposedly tough Toronto media took Burns to its collective bosom, partly because Pat is one of the most press-friendly coaches of all time. "He's the most intelligent and accommodating coach there is," said *Toronto Sun* columnist Steve Simmons.

Sometimes he can be the most deceptive. After the Bruins blew a 4-0 lead and settled for a 5-5 tie with the Florida Panthers at the Fleet Center, Burns sounded more like St. Francis of Assisi than a fire-breathing NHL leader. "You seem disappointed that I'm not yelling and you see s— going down a hole. I'm not going to put on a show and embarrass myself. The players are responsible for their actions and have to be accountable. When they hold management up for more money, they have to go out and earn it."

Or study their coach, who has earned his salary wherever Pat Burns has worked.

Burns certainly has earned it after two years at the FleetCenter. He not only pumped life into a fading franchise but delivered two straight playoff berths. Not only that, but Pat emerged as one of the precious few coaches who fans come to see—and hear!

Boston BRUINS

A Day in the Life of Ray Bourque

Along with Bobby Orr, Raymond Bourque is the most significant Bruin of the post-World War II era.

Reams have been written about Captain Ray over his two-decade career. Usually, the stories deal with the defenseman's on-ice heroics. But little has been detailed about a day in the life of Ray Bourque.

Ask any Bruin employee—the trainers, equipment people, media—and they'll tell you that Bourque is one of the lowest-maintenance hockey players. He rarely asks for anything, and when he does, he is thankful and polite.

To get another view of the office and on-ice Bourque, Fischler Hockey Service reporter Eric Reich traced the captain's moves during the 1999 Bruins-Sabres playoff, which began at Buffalo. The chronology follows:

Morning Skate

10:42 a.m. Bourque arrives at the visitors' dressing room at Marine Midland Arena in preparation for the Bruins' morning skate.

11:04 a.m. Dressed in shorts and t-shirt that he'll wear under his equipment, Bourque closely examines his sticks. The Bruins order two dozen custom sticks for Bourque each game. Of the twenty-four, Bourque chooses three or four of his favorites that will be used in the game. The remaining twenty sticks are either sent to charities, given to stick boys and other players or returned to the manufacturer.

11:36 a.m. During the morning skate, Bourque works on skills or strategy with younger players. Today, Kyle McLaren receives a lesson in clearing the slot.

12:06 p.m. Bourque leaves the ice. After showering, he returns to the hotel, where he will eat a high-carbohydrate pasta meal. That is followed by a nap, a little television watching and some phone calls.

Pre-Game

5:17 p.m. The Bruins slowly file into the dressing room. After a look at his sticks, Bourque has a brief conversation with coach Pat Burns and the coaching staff.

6:44 p.m. Bourque steps onto the ice for a pre-game warm-up period. Bourque leads most of the drills and is one of the first out of the dressing room.

6:52 p.m. Standing at his bench, Bourque changes sticks. During the warm-up, he will finalize his stick selection from those he used at the morning skate.

7:03 p.m. Using a pile of pucks, Bourque experiments with the ice surface at Marine Midland Arena. Each NHL ice surface plays a bit differently, so Bourque investigates each rink prior to each road game. Tonight, he shoots pucks around the boards, testing for the speed and softness of the dasher, as well as testing the glass for partition gaps and problem areas.

7:16 p.m. Pat Burns is giving his pre-game address. Each player is sitting quietly at his locker. Bourque analyzes a chalkboard that lists all of Buffalo's line combinations and tendencies.

7:27 p.m. Tonight's game will begin the same way that each game does for Ray, listening to the anthem at his self-designated spot, at the intersection of the boards and the blue line, opposite his bench. Unlike many players, Bourque respectfully refuses to begin skating until the anthem is completed.

1st Period

19:50 1st per. Only ten seconds into the game, Bourque is forced to take a penalty on a Buffalo player in good scoring position. Buffalo scores on the ensuing power play. Boston's penalty-killers seem lost without Bourque leading the unit for the full two minutes.

12:34 1st per. For the first time in the game, Bourque changes his gloves on the bench. During each game, he will change his gloves two or three times a period, in order to keep them dry and light. The Bruins' equipment staff assists Bourque in rotating five pairs. When not in use, the gloves are put on a hair dryer-type contraption behind the Boston bench.

6:16 1st per. Buffalo, on the power play, is unable to get any shots on goal, because of Bourque. Most times, Bourque himself does not clear the puck, but his impeccable positioning in his own zone leads to bad passes or shots that sail wide.

First Intermission

Bourque has his hands taped exactly five minutes prior to the next period by the Boston training staff.

2nd Period

14:51 2nd per. On the bench, Bourque tries to drink as much water as possible, at the recommendation of the Bruins' training staff. When you play thirty minutes a night, it is easy to get dehydrated.

7:32 2nd per. With the Bruins attacking three-on-two, Bourque wisely skates to the bench for a line change. The simple mechanics of changing-on-the-fly are often overlooked. Each season, teams allow goals as a result of defensemen making bad changes. Bourque, who rarely gets caught out of position on the ice, knows when to get off.

2:04 2nd per. The Sabres are offside. As the teams change lines, an exhausted Bourque slowly skates toward the Bruins' bench. After a few seconds, referee Paul Stewart waits for Bourque to make his decision before signaling for last change. As Bourque leaves the ice, he smiles at Stewart. Another player might have been ordered to stay on the ice, but not Bourque. After twenty years, he receives almost regal consideration and respect from league officials.

Second Intermission

Annoyed by subpar play and a lackluster effort, Bourque makes what goaltender Byron Dafoe calls a "short but passionate speech" to the team.

3rd Period

17:21 3rd per. With Bourque on the ice prior to a neutral zone face-off, Buffalo coach Lindy Ruff uses his home-ice advantage and last change to send out the Sabres' checking line. Bourque, knowing that he is needed to play more against the top Buffalo lines in the third period, quickly heads to the bench immediately after the face-off.

13:16 3rd per. After Buffalo scores a goal which Dafoe has no chance to stop, Bourque skates to his goaltender to tap his pads and give him some much-needed encouragement.

4:59 3rd per. The play is beginning to get more physical, and with only five minutes to play, Bourque uses a stoppage of play to hold an impromptu conference at the Boston bench.

Post-Game

10:32 p.m. Bourque steps out of the shower and is immediately surrounded by reporters. He politely asks that he be interviewed after he dresses. After twenty years in the NHL, Bourque knows that it is more professional to answer questions on television in a suit rather than in a towel.

10:48 p.m. A reporter asks the obligatory question to Bourque regarding his future and his intentions for the following season. As the unquestioned team leader, Bourque refuses to answer the question, knowing the distractions that could result. He smiles and simply says that he will honor his contract.

10:51 p.m. After finishing with the media, Bourque escapes to the training room, where he will call his family in Boston from a cellular phone.

11:03 p.m. Before leaving, Bourque enters the equipment room, where countless items sit for him to autograph. Items have been left from sponsors, agents and even the opposing team, all of whom know that Bourque's career could end any year. Even in defeat, Bourque will sign each stick, each sweater and each puck.

11:10 p.m. Finally, Ray leaves the dressing room. On the way to the team bus, he will greet and walk with some of the people who have waited for him, including other players, autograph seekers and team officials.

Boston BRUINS

Greatest Bruins Career Statistics by Player

Jason Allison

Regular Season

Year	Team	League	GP	G	A	PTS	PIM
1991-92	London	OHL	65	11	19	30	15
1992-93	London	OHL	66	42	76	118	50
1993-94	London	OHL	56	55	87	142	68
	Canada	Wrld. Jr.	7	3	6	9	2
	Portland	AHL	-	-	-	-	-
	Washington	NHL	2	0	1	1	0
1994-95	London	OHL	15	15	21	36	43
	Canada	Wrld. Jr.	7	3	12	15	6
	Portland	AHL	8	5	4	9	2
	Washington	NHL	12	2	1	3	6
1995-96	Portland	AHL	57	28	41	69	42
	Washington	NHL	19	0	3	3	2
1996-97	Washington	NHL	53	5	17	22	25
	Boston	NHL	19	3	9	12	9
	Totals		72	8	26	34	34
1997-98	Boston	NHL	81	33	50	83	60
1998-99	Boston	NHL	82	23	53	76	68

Playoffs

Year	Team	League	GP	GA	A	PTS	PIM
1991-92	London	OHL	7	0	0	0	0
1992-93	London	OHL	12	7	13	20	8
1993-94	London	OHL	5	2	13	15	13
	Portland	AHL	6	2	1	3	0
1994-95	Portland	AHL	7	3	8	11	2
1995-96	Portland	AHL	6	1	6	7	9
1997-98	Boston	NHL	6	2	6	8	4
1998-99	Boston	NHL	12	2	9	11	6

NHL Totals:

Regular Season

GP	G	A	PTS	PIM
268	66	134	200	170

Playoffs

GP	G	A	PTS	PIM
18	4	15	19	10

Bobby Bauer

Regular Season

Year	Team	League	GP	G	A	PTS	PIM
1935-36	Boston	NHL	1	0	0	0	0
1936-37	Boston	NHL	1	1	0	1	0
1937-38	Boston	NHL	48	20	14	34	9
1938-39	Boston	NHL	48	13	18	31	4
1939-40	Boston	NHL	48	17	26	43	2
1940-41	Boston	NHL	48	17	22	39	2
1941-42	Boston	NHL	36	13	22	35	11
1945-46	Boston	NHL	39	11	10	21	4
1946-47	Boston	NHL	58	30	24	54	4
1951-52	Boston	NHL	1	1	1	2	0

Playoffs

Year	Team	League	GP	G	A	PTS	PIM
1936-37	Boston	NHL	1	0	0	0	0
1937-38	Boston	NHL	3	0	0	0	2
1938-39	Boston	NHL	12	3	2	5	0
1939-40	Boston	NHL	6	1	0	0	2
1940-41	Boston	NHL	11	2	2	4	0
1945-46	Boston	NHL	10	4	3	7	2
1946-47	Boston	NHL	5	1	1	2	0

NHL Totals:

Regular Season

GP	G	A	PTS	PIM
328	123	137	260	36

Playoffs

GP	G	A	PTS	PIM
48	11	8	19	6

Leo Boivin

Regular Season

Year	Team	League	GP	G	A	PTS	PIM
1949-50	Port Arthur	TBJHL	18	4	4	8	32
1950-51	Port Arthur	TBJHL	20	16	11	27	37
1951-52	Toronto	NHL	2	0	1	1	4
	Pittsburgh	AHL	30	2	3	5	32
1952-53	Toronto	NHL	70	2	13	15	97
1953-54	Toronto	NHL	58	1	6	7	81

			GP	G	A	PTS	PIM
1954-55	Toronto	NHL	7	0	0	0	8
	Boston	NHL	59	6	11	17	105
	Totals		66	6	11	17	113
1955-56	Boston	NHL	68	4	16	20	80
1956-57	Boston	NHL	55	2	8	10	55
1957-58	Boston	NHL	33	0	4	4	54
1958-59	Boston	NHL	70	5	16	21	94
1959-60	Boston	NHL	70	4	21	25	66
1960-61	Boston	NHL	57	6	17	23	50
1961-62	Boston	NHL	65	5	18	23	89
1962-63	Boston	NHL	62	2	24	26	48
1963-64	Boston	NHL	65	10	14	24	42
1964-65	Boston	NHL	67	3	10	13	68
1965-66	Boston	NHL	46	0	5	5	34
	Detroit	NHL	16	0	5	5	16
	Totals		62	0	10	10	50
1966-67	Detroit	NHL	69	4	21	25	0
1967-68	Pittsburgh	NHL	73	9	22	31	74
1968-69	Pittsburgh	NHL	41	5	18	23	26
	Minnesota	NHL	28	1	7	8	16
	Totals		69	6	25	31	42
1969-70	Minnesota	NHL	69	3	15	18	30

Playoffs

Year	Team	League	GP	G	A	PTS	PIM
1949-50	Port Arthur	TBJHL	5	0	3	3	10
1950-51	Port Arthur	TBJHL	13	3	6	9	28
1951-52	Pittsburgh	AHL	10	0	1	1	16
1953-54	Toronto	NHL	5	0	0	0	2
1954-55	Boston	NHL	5	0	1	1	4
1956-57	Boston	NHL	10	2	3	5	12
1957-58	Boston	NHL	12	0	3	3	21
1958-59	Boston	NHL	7	1	2	3	4
1965-66	Detroit	NHL	12	0	1	1	16
1969-70	Pittsburgh	NHL	3	0	0	0	0

NHL Totals

Regular Season

GP	G	A	PTS	PIM
1150	72	250	322	1137

Playoffs

GP	G	A	PTS	PIM
54	3	10	13	59

Ray Bourque

Regular Season

Year	Team	League	GP	G	A	PTS	PIM
1976-77	Sorel	QMJHL	69	12	36	48	61
1977-78	Verdun	QMJHL	72	22	57	79	90
1978-79	Verdun	QMJHL	63	22	71	93	44
1979-80	Boston	NHL	80	17	48	65	73
1980-81	Boston	NHL	67	27	29	56	96
1981-82	Boston	NHL	65	17	49	66	51
1982-83	Boston	NHL	65	22	51	73	20
1983-84	Boston	NHL	78	31	65	96	57
1984-85	Boston	NHL	73	20	66	86	53
1985-86	Boston	NHL	74	19	58	77	68
1986-87	Boston	NHL	78	23	72	95	36
1987-88	Boston	NHL	78	17	64	81	72
1988-89	Boston	NHL	60	18	43	61	52
1989-90	Boston	NHL	76	19	65	84	50
1990-91	Boston	NHL	76	21	73	94	75
1991-92	Boston	NHL	80	21	60	81	56
1992-93	Boston	NHL	78	19	63	82	40
1993-94	Boston	NHL	72	20	71	91	58
1994-95	Boston	NHL	46	12	31	43	20
1995-96	Boston	NHL	82	20	62	82	58
1996-97	Boston	NHL	62	19	31	50	18
1997-98	Boston	NHL	82	13	35	48	80
	Canada	Olympics	6	1	2	3	4
1998-99	Boston	NHL	81	10	47	57	34

Playoffs

Year	Team	League	GP	G	A	PTS	PIM
1977-78	Verdun	QMJHL	4	2	1	3	0
1978-79	Verdun	QMJHL	11	3	16	19	18
1979-80	Boston	NHL	10	2	9	11	27
1980-81	Boston	NHL	3	0	1	1	2
1981-82	Boston	NHL	9	1	5	6	16
1982-83	Boston	NHL	17	8	12	20	10
1983-84	Boston	NHL	3	0	2	2	0
1984-85	Boston	NHL	5	0	3	3	4
1985-86	Boston	NHL	3	0	0	0	0
1986-87	Boston	NHL	4	1	2	3	0
1987-88	Boston	NHL	23	3	18	21	26
1988-89	Boston	NHL	10	0	4	4	6
1990-91	Boston	NHL	17	5	12	17	16
1991-92	Boston	NHL	19	7	18	25	12
1992-93	Boston	NHL	12	3	6	9	12
1993-94	Boston	NHL	4	1	0	1	2
1994-95	Boston	NHL	13	2	8	10	0
1995-96	Boston	NHL	5	0	3	3	0
1997-98	Boston	NHL	6	1	6	7	2

NHL Totals:

Regular Season

GP	G	A	PTS	PIM
1372	375	1036	1411	1033

Playoffs

GP	G	A	PTS	PIM
168	35	116	151	137

Frank Brimsek

Regular Season

Year	Team	League	GP	W	L	T	SO	AVG
1938-39	Boston	NHL	43	33	9	1	10	1.58
1939-40	Boston	NHL	48	31	12	5	6	2.04
1940-41	Boston	NHL	48	27	8	13	6	2.13
1941-42	Boston	NHL	47	24	17	6	3	2.45
1942-43	Boston	NHL	50	24	17	9	1	3.52
1945-46	Boston	NHL	34	16	14	4	2	3.26
1946-47	Boston	NHL	50	26	23	11	3	2.92
1947-48	Boston	NHL	50	23	24	13	3	2.80
1948-49	Boston	NHL	64	26	20	8	1	2.72
1949-50	Chicago	NHL	70	22	38	10	5	3.49

Playoffs

Year	Team	League	GP	W	L	SO	AVG
1938-39	Boston	NHL	12	8	4	1	1.50
1939-40	Boston	NHL	6	2	4	0	2.50
1940-41	Boston	NHL	11	8	3	1	2.09
1941-42	Boston	NHL	5	2	3	0	3.20
1942-43	Boston	NHL	9	4	5	-	3.54
1945-46	Boston	NHL	10	5	5	-	2.71
1946-47	Boston	NHL	5	1	4	-	2.97
1947-48	Boston	NHL	5	1	4	-	3.79
1948-49	Boston	NHL	5	1	4	-	3.04

NHL Totals:

Regular Season

GP	W	L	T	SO	AVG
514	252	182	80	40	2.70

Playoffs

GP	W	L	SO	AVG
68	32	36	2	2.56

John Bucyk

Regular Season

Year	Team	League	GP	G	A	PTS	PIM
1955-56	Detroit	NHL	38	1	8	9	20
1956-57	Detroit	NHL	66	10	11	21	41
1957-58	Boston	NHL	68	21	31	52	57
1958-59	Boston	NHL	69	24	36	60	36
1959-60	Boston	NHL	56	16	36	52	26
1960-61	Boston	NHL	70	19	20	39	48
1961-62	Boston	NHL	67	20	40	60	32
1962-63	Boston	NHL	69	27	39	66	36
1963-64	Boston	NHL	62	18	36	54	36
1964-65	Boston	NHL	68	26	29	55	24
1965-66	Boston	NHL	63	27	30	57	12
1966-67	Boston	NHL	59	18	30	48	12
1967-68	Boston	NHL	72	30	39	69	8
1968-69	Boston	NHL	70	24	42	66	18
1969-70	Boston	NHL	76	31	38	69	13
1970-71	Boston	NHL	78	51	65	116	8
1971-72	Boston	NHL	78	32	51	83	4
1972-73	Boston	NHL	78	40	53	93	12
1973-74	Boston	NHL	76	31	44	75	8
1974-75	Boston	NHL	78	29	52	81	10
1975-76	Boston	NHL	77	36	47	83	20
1976-77	Boston	NHL	49	20	23	43	12
1977-78	Boston	NHL	53	5	13	18	4

Playoffs

Year	Team	League	GP	G	A	PTS	PIM
1955-56	Detroit	NHL	10	1	1	2	8
1956-57	Detroit	NHL	5	0	1	1	0
1957-58	Boston	NHL	12	0	4	4	16
1958-59	Boston	NHL	7	2	4	6	0
1967-68	Boston	NHL	3	0	2	2	0
1968-69	Boston	NHL	10	5	6	11	2
1969-70	Boston	NHL	14	11	8	19	0
1970-71	Boston	NHL	7	2	5	7	6
1971-72	Boston	NHL	15	9	11	20	0
1972-73	Boston	NHL	5	0	3	3	4
1973-74	Boston	NHL	16	8	10	18	0
1974-75	Boston	NHL	3	1	0	1	0
1975-76	Boston	NHL	12	2	7	9	0
1976-77	Boston	NHL		5	0	0	0

NHL Totals:

Regular Season

GP	G	A	PTS	PIM
1540	556	813	1369	497

Playoffs

GP	G	A	PTS	PIM
124	41	62	103	42

Anson Carter

Regular Season

Year	Team	League	GP	G	A	PTS	PIM
1991-92	Wexford	MJHL	42	18	22	40	24
1992-93	Michigan St.	CCHA	34	15	7	22	20
1993-94	Michigan St.	CCHA	39	30	24	54	36
	Canada	(WJ, Pool A)	7	3	2	5	0
1994-95	Michigan St.	CCHA	39	34	17	51	40
1995-96	Michigan St.	CCHA	42	23	20	43	36
1996-97	Washington	NHL	19	3	2	5	7
	Portland	AHL	27	19	19	38	11
	Boston	NHL	19	8	5	13	2
	Canada	(Worlds, Pool A)	11	4	2	6	4
	NHL Totals		38	12	7	18	9
1997-98	Boston	NHL	78	16	27	43	31

Playoffs

Year	Team	League	GP	G	A	PTS	PIM
1997-98	Boston	NHL	6	1	1	2	0

NHL Totals:

Regular Season

GP	G	A	PTS	PIM
116	27	34	61	40

Playoffs

GP	G	A	PTS	PIM
6	1	1	2	0

Wayne Cashman

Regular Season

Year	Team	League	GP	G	A	PTS	PIM
1964-65	Boston	NHL	1	0	0	0	0
1967-68	Boston	NHL	12	0	4	4	2
1968-69	Boston	NHL	51	8	23	31	49
1969-70	Boston	NHL	70	9	26	35	79
1970-71	Boston	NHL	77	21	58	79	100
1971-72	Boston	NHL	74	23	29	52	103
1972-73	Boston	NHL	76	29	39	68	100
1973-74	Boston	NHL	78	30	59	89	111
1974-75	Boston	NHL	42	11	22	33	24
1975-76	Boston	NHL	80	28	43	71	87
1976-77	Boston	NHL	65	15	37	52	76
1977-78	Boston	NHL	76	24	38	62	69
1978-79	Boston	NHL	75	27	40	67	63
1979-80	Boston	NHL	44	11	21	32	19
1980-81	Boston	NHL	77	25	35	60	80
1981-82	Boston	NHL	64	12	31	43	59
1982-83	Boston	NHL	65	4	11	15	20

Playoffs

Year	Team	League	GP	G	A	PTS	PIM
1967-68	Boston	NHL	1	0	0	0	0
1968-69	Boston	NHL	6	0	1	1	0
1969-70	Boston	NHL	14	5	4	9	50
1970-71	Boston	NHL	7	3	2	5	15
1971-72	Boston	NHL	5	4	7	11	42
1972-73	Boston	NHL	5	1	1	2	4
1973-74	Boston	NHL	16	5	9	14	46
1974-75	Boston	NHL	1	0	2	2	0
1975-76	Boston	NHL	11	1	5	6	16
1976-77	Boston	NHL	14	1	8	9	18
1977-78	Boston	NHL	15	4	6	10	13
1978-79	Boston	NHL	10	4	5	9	8
1979-80	Boston	NHL	10	3	3	6	32
1980-81	Boston	NHL	3	0	1	1	0
1981-82	Boston	NHL	9	0	2	2	6
1982-83	Boston	NHL	8	0	1	1	0

NHL Totals:

Regular Season

GP	G	A	PTS	PIM
1027	277	516	793	1041

Playoffs

GP	G	A	PTS	PIM
145	31	57	88	250

Gerry Cheevers

Regular Season

Year	Team	League	GP	W	L	T	SO	AVG
1961-62	Toronto	NHL	2	1	1	0	0	3.50
1965-66	Boston	NHL	7	0	4	1	0	6.00
1966-67	Boston	NHL	22	5	11	6	1	3.33
1967-68	Boston	NHL	47	23	17	5	3	2.83
1968-69	Boston	NHL	52	28	12	12	3	2.80
1969-70	Boston	NHL	41	24	8	8	4	2.72
1970-71	Boston	NHL	40	27	8	5	3	2.73
1971-72	Boston	NHL	41	27	5	8	2	2.50
1972-73	Cleveland	WHL	52	32	20	0	5	2.84
1973-74	Cleveland	WHL	59	30	20	6	4	3.03
1974-75	Cleveland	WHL	52	26	24	2	4	3.26
1975-76	Cleveland	WHL	28	11	14	1	1	3.63
	Boston	NHL	15	8	2	5	1	2.73
1976-77	Boston	NHL	45	30	10	5	3	3.04
1977-78	Boston	NHL	21	10	5	2	1	2.65
1978-79	Boston	NHL	43	23	0	10	1	3.16
1979-80	Boston	NHL	42	24	11	7	4	2.81

Playoffs

Year	Team	League	GP	W	L	SO	AVG
1967-68	Boston	NHL	4	0	4	0	3.75
1968-69	Boston	NHL	9	0	4	3	1.68
1969-70	Boston	NHL	13	12	1	0	2.23
1970-71	Boston	NHL	6	3	3	0	3.50
1971-72	Boston	NHL	8	6	2	2	2.61
1972-73	Cleveland	WHL	9	5	4	0	2.41
1973-74	Cleveland	WHL	5	1	4	0	3.56
1974-75	Cleveland	WHL	5	1	4	0	4.60
1975-76	Boston	NHL	6	2	4	1	2.14
1976-77	Boston	NHL	14	8	5	1	3.08
1977-78	Boston	NHL	12	8	4	0	2.87
1978-79	Boston	NHL	6	4	2	0	2.50
1979-80	Boston	NHL	10	4	6	0	3.10

NHL Totals:

Regular Season

GP	W	L	T	SO	AVG
418	230	94	74	26	2.89

Playoffs

GP	W	L	SO	AVG
88	53	34	8	2.69

Aubrey Victor "Dit" Clapper

Regular Season

Year	Team	League	GP	G	A	PTS	PIM
1927-28	Boston	NHL	40	4	1	5	20
1928-29	Boston	NHL	40	9	2	11	48
1929-30	Boston	NHL	44	41	20	61	48
1930-31	Boston	NHL	43	22	8	30	50
1931-32	Boston	NHL	48	17	22	39	21
1932-33	Boston	NHL	48	14	14	28	42
1933-34	Boston	NHL	48	10	12	22	6
1934-35	Boston	NHL	48	21	16	37	21
1935-36	Boston	NHL	44	12	13	25	14
1936-37	Boston	NHL	48	17	8	25	25
1937-38	Boston	NHL	46	6	9	15	24
1938-39	Boston	NHL	42	13	13	26	22
1939-40	Boston	NHL	44	10	18	28	25
1940-41	Boston	NHL	48	8	18	26	24
1941-42	Boston	NHL	32	3	12	15	31
1942-43	Boston	NHL	38	5	18	23	12
1943-44	Boston	NHL	50	6	25	31	13
1944-45	Boston	NHL	46	8	14	22	16
1945-46	Boston	NHL	30	2	3	5	0
1946-47	Boston	NHL	6	0	0	0	0

Playoffs

Year	Team	League	GP	G	A	PTS	PIM
1927-28	Boston	NHL	2	0	0	0	2
1928-29	Boston	NHL	5	1	0	1	0
1929-30	Boston	NHL	6	4	0	4	4
1930-31	Boston	NHL	5	2	4	6	4
1932-33	Boston	NHL	5	1	1	2	2
1934-35	Boston	NHL	3	1	0	1	0
1935-36	Boston	NHL	2	0	1	1	0
1936-37	Boston	NHL	3	2	0	2	5
1937-38	Boston	NHL	3	0	0	0	12
1938-39	Boston	NHL	11	0	1	1	6
1939-40	Boston	NHL	5	0	2	2	2
1940-41	Boston	NHL	11	0	5	5	4
1941-42	Boston	NHL	5	0	0	0	0
1942-43	Boston	NHL	9	2	3	5	9
1944-45	Boston	NHL	7	0	0	0	0
1945-46	Boston	NHL	4	0	0	0	0

NHL Totals:

Regular Season

GP	G	A	PTS	PIM
833	228	246	474	462

Playoffs

GP	G	A	PTS	PIM
86	13	17	30	50

Roy Conacher

Regular Season

Year	Team	League	GP	G	A	PTS	PIM
1933-34	W. Toronto	OHA	6	0	1	1	0
1934-35	W. Toronto	OHA	9	4	3	7	8
1935-36	W. Toronto	OHA	10	12	3	15	11
1936-37	Toronto	OHA Sr.	8	3	3	6	4
1937-38	Kirkland	NOHA	12	12	11	23	2
1938-39	Boston	NHL	47	26	11	37	12
1939-40	Boston	NHL	31	18	12	30	9
1940-41	Boston	NHL	41	24	14	38	7
1941-42	Boston	NHL	43	24	13	37	12
1942-43	Saskatoon	City Sr.	20	13	8	21	2
1943-44	Dartmouth	City Sr.	3	9	2	11	4
1944-45	Dartmouth	City Sr.	4	1	2	3	0
1945-46	Boston	NHL	4	2	1	3	0
1946-47	Detroit	NHL	60	30	24	54	6
1947-48	Chicago	NHL	52	22	27	49	4
1948-49	Chicago	NHL	60	26	42	68	8
1949-50	Chicago	NHL	70	25	31	56	16
1950-51	Chicago	NHL	70	26	24	50	16
1951-52	Chicago	NHL	12	3	1	4	0

Playoffs

Year	Team	League	GP	G	A	PTS	PIM
1935-36	W. Toronto	OHA	5	4	2	6	4
1936-37	Toronto	OHA Sr.	4	3	0	3	2
1937-38	Kirkland	NOHA	1	1	0	1	0
1938-39	Boston	NHL	12	6	4	10	12
1939-40	Boston	NHL	6	2	1	3	0
1940-41	Boston	NHL	11	1	5	6	0
1941-42	Boston	NHL	5	2	1	3	0
1942-43	Saskatoon	City Sr.	3	2	2	4	0
1945-46	Boston	NHL	3	0	0	0	0
1946-47	Detroit	NHL	5	4	4	8	2

NHL Totals:

Regular Season

GP	G	A	PTS	PIM
490	226	200	426	90

Playoffs

GP	G	A	PT	PIM
42	15	15	30	14

Bill Cowley

Regular Season

Year	Team	League	GP	G	A	PTS	PIM
1934-35	St. Louis	NHL	41	5	7	12	10
1935-36	Boston	NHL	48	11	10	21	17
1936-37	Boston	NHL	46	13	22	35	35
1937-38	Boston	NHL	48	17	22	39	8
1938-39	Boston	NHL	34	8	34	42	2
1939-40	Boston	NHL	48	13	27	40	24
1940-41	Boston	NHL	46	17	45	60	16
1941-42	Boston	NHL	28	4	23	27	6
1942-43	Boston	NHL	48	27	45	72	10
1943-44	Boston	NHL	36	30	41	71	12
1944-45	Boston	NHL	49	25	40	65	12
1945-46	Boston	NHL	26	12	12	24	6
1946-47	Boston	NHL	51	13	25	38	16

Playoffs

Year	Team	League	GP	G	A	PTS	PIM
1935-36	Boston	NHL	2	2	1	3	2
1936-37	Boston	NHL	3	0	3	3	0
1937-38	Boston	NHL	3	2	0	2	0
1938-39	Boston	NHL	12	3	11	14	2
1939-40	Boston	NHL	6	1	0	1	7
1940-41	Boston	NHL	2	0	0	0	0
1941-42	Boston	NHL	5	0	3	3	5
1942-43	Boston	NHL	9	1	7	8	4
1944-45	Boston	NHL	7	3	3	6	0
1945-46	Boston	NHL	10	1	3	4	2
1946-47	Boston	NHL	5	0	2	2	0

NHL Totals:

Regular Season

GP	G	A	PTS	PIM
549	195	353	548	174

Playoffs

GP	G	A	PTS	PIM
64	13	33	46	22

Byron Dafoe

Regular Season

Year	Team	League	GP	W	L	T	SO	AVG
1988-89	Portland	WHL	59	29	24	3	1	5.32
1989-90	Washington	(Friendship Tour)	2	—	—	—	0	3.00
	Portland	WHL	40	14	21	3	0	5.11
1990-91	Portland	WHL	8	1	5	1	0	5.94
	Prince Albert	WHL	32	13	12	4	0	4.05
1991-92	Baltimore	AHL	33	12	16	4	0	3.87
	New Haven	AHL	7	3	2	1	0	3.63
	Hampton Roads E	CHL	10	6	4	0	0	2.78
1992-93	Washington	NHL	1	0	0	0	0	0.00
	Baltimore	AHL	48	16	20	7	1	4.38
1993-94	Washington	NHL	5	2	2	0	0	3.39
	Portland	AHL	47	24	16	4	1	3.34
1994-95	Phoenix	IHL	49	25	16	6	2	3.70
	Washington	NHL	4	1	1	1	0	3.53
	Portland	AHL	6	5	0	0	0	2.91
1995-96	Los Angeles	NHL	47	14	24	8	1	3.87
1996-97	Los Angeles	NHL	40	13	17	5	0	3.11
1997-98	Boston	NHL	65	30	25	9	6	2.24

Playoffs

Year	Team	League	GP	W	L	SO	AVG
1988-89	Portland	WHL	18	10	8	1	4.45
1992-93	Baltimore	AHL	5	2	3	0	5.48
1993-94	Washington	NHL	2	0	2	0	2.54
	Portland	AHL	1	0	0	0	6.79
1994-95	Washington	NHL	1	0	0	0	3.00
	Portland	AHL	7	3	4	0	4.18
1997-98	Boston	NHL	6	2	4	1	1.99

NHL Totals:

Regular Season

GP	W	L	T	SO	AVG
162	60	69	23	7	2.99

Playoffs

GP	W	L	SO	AVG
9	2	6	1	2.14

Woody Dumart

Regular Season

Year	Team	League	GP	G	A	PTS	PIM
1933-34	Kitchener	OHA	12	8	3	11	12
1934-35	Kitchener	OHA	17	17	11	28	10
1935-36	Boston	NHL	1	0	0	0	0
	Boston	Can-Am	46	11	10	21	15
1936-37	Boston	NHL	17	4	4	8	2
	Providence	AHL	32	4	7	11	10
1937-38	Boston	NHL	48	13	14	27	6
1938-39	Boston	NHL	45	14	15	29	2
1939-40	Boston	NHL	48	22	21	43	16
1940-41	Boston	NHL	40	18	15	33	2
1941-42	Boston	NHL	35	14	15	29	8
1942-43	Ottawa	OHA Sr.	6	6	5	11	—
1943-44	MILITARY SERVICE						
1944-45	MILITARY SERVICE						
1945-46	Boston	NHL	50	22	12	34	2
1946-47	Boston	NHL	60	24	28	52	12
1947-48	Boston	NHL	59	21	16	37	14
1948-49	Boston	NHL	59	11	12	23	6
1949-50	Boston	NHL	69	14	25	39	4
1950-51	Boston	NHL	70	20	21	41	7
1951-52	Boston	NHL	39	5	8	13	0
1952-53	Boston	NHL	62	5	9	14	2
1953-54	Boston	NHL	69	4	3	7	6
1954-55	Providence	AHL	15	2	2	4	0

Playoffs

Year	Team	League	GP	G	A	PTS	PIM
1933-34	Kitchener	OHA	3	1	3	4	0
1934-35	Kitchener	OHA	3	3	1	4	2
1936-37	Boston	NHL	3	0	0	0	0
1937-38	Boston	NHL	3	0	0	0	0
1938-39	Boston	NHL	12	1	3	4	6
1939-40	Boston	NHL	6	1	0	1	0
1940-41	Boston	NHL	11	1	3	4	9
1941-42	Ottawa	City Sr.	19	21	14	35	10
1945-46	Boston	NHL	10	4	3	7	0
1946-47	Boston	NHL	5	1	1	2	8
1947-48	Boston	NHL	5	0	0	0	0
1948-49	Boston	NHL	5	3	0	3	0
1950-51	Boston	NHL	6	1	2	3	0
1951-52	Boston	NHL	7	0	1	1	0
1952-53	Boston	NHL	11	0	2	2	0
1953-54	Boston	NHL	4	0	0	0	0

NHL Totals:

Regular Season

GP	G	A	PTS	PIM
771	211	218	429	99

Playoffs

GP	G	A	PTS	PIM
88	12	15	27	23

Phil Esposito

Regular Season

Year	Team	League	GP	G	A	PTS	PIM
1963-64	Chicago	NHL	27	3	2	5	2
1964-65	Chicago	NHL	70	23	32	55	44
1965-66	Chicago	NHL	69	27	26	53	49
1966-67	Chicago	NHL	69	21	40	61	40
1967-68	Boston	NHL	74	35	49	84	21
1968-69	Boston	NHL	74	49	77	126	79
1969-70	Boston	NHL	76	43	56	99	50
1970-71	Boston	NHL	78	76	76	152	71
1971-72	Boston	NHL	76	66	67	133	76
1972-73	Boston	NHL	78	55	75	130	87
1973-74	Boston	NHL	78	68	77	145	58
1974-75	Boston	NHL	79	61	66	127	62
1975-76	Boston	NHL	12	6	10	16	8
	Rangers	NHL	62	29	38	67	28
1976-77	Rangers	NHL	80	34	46	80	52
1977-78	Rangers	NHL	79	38	43	81	53
1978-79	Rangers	NHL	80	42	36	78	14
1979-80	Rangers	NHL	80	34	44	78	73
1980-81	Rangers	NHL	41	7	13	20	20

Playoffs

Year	Team	League	GP	G	A	PTS	PIM
1963-64	Chicago	NHL	4	0	0	0	0
1964-65	Chicago	NHL	13	3	3	6	15
1965-66	Chicago	NHL	6	1	1	2	2
1966-67	Chicago	NHL	6	0	0	0	4
1967-68	Boston	NHL	4	0	3	3	0
1968-69	Boston	NHL	10	8	10	18	8
1969-70	Boston	NHL	14	13	14	27	16
1970-71	Boston	NHL	7	3	7	10	6
1971-72	Boston	NHL	15	9	15	24	24
1972-73	Boston	NHL	2	0	1	1	2
1973-74	Boston	NHL	16	9	5	14	25
1974-75	Boston	NHL	3	4	1	5	0
1977-78	Rangers	NHL	3	0	1	1	5
1978-79	Rangers	NHL	18	8	12	20	20
1979-80	Rangers	NHL	9	3	3	6	8

NHL Totals:

Regular Season

GP	G	A	PTS	PIM
1282	717	873	1590	887

Playoffs

GP	G	A	PTS	PIM
130	61	76	137	135

Fernie Flaman

Regular Season

Year	Team	League	GP	G	A	PTS	PIM
1944-45	Boston	NHL	1	0	0	0	0
1945-46	Boston	NHL	1	0	0	0	0
1946-47	Boston	NHL	23	1	4	5	41
1947-48	Boston	NHL	56	4	6	10	69
1948-49	Boston	NHL	60	4	12	16	62
1949-50	Boston	NHL	69	2	5	7	122
1950-51	Boston	NHL	14	1	1	2	37
	Toronto	NHL	39	2	6	8	64
1951-52	Toronto	NHL	61	0	7	7	110
1952-53	Toronto	NHL	66	2	6	8	110
1953-54	Toronto	NHL	62	0	8	8	84
1954-55	Boston	NHL	70	4	14	18	150
1955-56	Boston	NHL	62	4	17	21	70
1956-57	Boston	NHL	68	6	25	31	108
1957-58	Boston	NHL	66	0	15	15	71
1958-59	Boston	NHL	70	0	21	21	101
1959-60	Boston	NHL	60	2	18	20	112
1960-61	Boston	NHL	62	2	9	11	59

Playoffs

Year	Team	League	GP	G	A	PTS	PIM
1946-47	Boston	NHL	5	0	0	0	8
1947-48	Boston	NHL	5	0	0	0	12
1948-49	Boston	NHL	5	0	1	1	8
1950-51	Toronto	NHL	9	1	0	1	8
1951-52	Toronto	NHL	4	0	2	2	18
1953-54	Toronto	NHL	2	0	0	0	0
1954-55	Boston	NHL	4	1	0	1	2
1956-57	Boston	NHL	10	0	3	3	19
1957-58	Boston	NHL	12	2	2	4	10
1958-59	Boston	NHL	7	0	0	0	8

NHL Totals:

Regular Season

GP	G	A	PTS	PIM
910	34	174	208	1370

Playoffs

GP	G	A	PTS	PIM
63	4	8	12	93

Frank Frederickson

Regular Season

Year	Team	League	GP	G	A	PTS	PIM
1913-14	Winnipeg	MIHL	11	13	0	13	—
1914-15	Winnipeg	MIHL	8	10	0	10	—
1915-16	Winnipeg	MHL Sr.	6	13	3	16	14
1916-17	Winnipeg	MHL Sr.	8	17	3	20	40
1917-18	MILITARY SERVICE						
1918-19	MILITARY SERVICE						
1919-20	Winnipeg	MHL Sr.	9	22	5	27	12
	Canada	(Olympics)	3	10	10	11	—
1920-21	Victoria	PCHA	21	20	12	31	3
1921-22	Victoria	PCHA	24	15	10	25	26
1922-23	Victoria	PCHA	30	39	16	55	26
1923-24	Victoria	PCHA	30	19	8	27	28
1924-25	Victoria	WCHL	28	22	8	30	43
1925-26	Victoria	WHL	30	16	8	24	89
1926-27	Detroit	NHL	16	4	6	10	12
	Boston	NHL	28	14	7	21	33
1927-28	Boston	NHL	41	10	4	14	83
1928-29	Boston	NHL	12	1	3	4	24
	Pittsburgh	NHL	31	3	7	10	28
	Totals		43	4	10	14	52
1929-30	Pittsburgh	NHL	9	4	7	11	20
1930-31	Detroit	NHL	24	1	2	3	6
	Detroit	IAHL	6	0	1	1	2
1931-32	Winnipeg	MJHL	DID NOT PLAY - COACHING				

Playoffs

Year	Team	League	GP	G	A	PTS	PIM
1914-15	Winnipeg	MIHL	1	1	0	1	2
1919-20	Winnipeg	MHL Sr.	6	22	5	27	6
1922-23	Victoria	PCHA	2	2	0	2	4
1924-25	Victoria	WCHL	8	6	3	9	8
1925-26	Victoria	WHL	8	2	3	5	16
1926-27	Boston	NHL	8	2	4	6	22
1927-28	Boston	NHL	2	0	1	1	4

NHL Totals:

Regular Season

GP	G	A	PTS	PIM
161	37	36	73	206

Playoffs

GP	G	A	PTS	PIM
10	2	5	7	26

Hal Gill

Regular Season

Year	Team	League	GP	G	A	PTS	PIM
1992-93	Nashoba	HS	20	25	25	50	—
1993-94	Providence	HE	31	1	2	3	26
1994-95	Providence	HE	26	1	3	4	22
1995-96	Providence	HE	39	5	12	17	54
1996-97	Providence	HE	35	5	16	21	52
1997-98	Providence	AHL	4	1	0	1	23
	Boston	NHL	68	2	4	6	47
1998-99	Boston	NHL	80	3	7	10	63

Playoffs

Year	Team	League	GP	G	A	PTS	PIM
1997-98	Boston	NHL	6	0	0	0	4
1998-99	Boston	NHL	12	0	0	0	14

NHL Totals:

Regular Season

GP	G	A	PTS	PIM
148	5	11	16	110

Playoffs

GP	G	A	PTS	PIM
18	0	0	0	18

Ted Green

Regular Season

Year	Team	League	GP	G	A	PTS	PIM
1956-57	St. Boniface	MJHL	17	1	2	3	76
1957-58	St. Boniface	MJHL	23	1	4	5	97
1958-59	St. Boniface	MJHL	25	5	11	16	120
1959-60	Winnipeg	WHL	70	8	20	28	109
1960-61	Boston	NHL	1	0	0	0	2
	Kingston	EPHL	11	1	5	6	30
	Winnipeg	WHL	57	1	18	19	127
1961-62	Boston	NHL	66	3	8	11	116
1962-63	Boston	NHL	70	1	11	12	117
1963-64	Boston	NHL	70	4	10	14	145
1964-65	Boston	NHL	70	8	27	35	156
1965-66	Boston	NHL	27	5	13	18	113
1966-67	Boston	NHL	47	6	10	16	67
1967-68	Boston	NHL	72	7	36	43	133
1968-69	Boston	NHL	65	8	38	46	99
1970-71	Boston	NHL	78	5	37	42	60
1971-72	Boston	NHL	54	1	16	17	21
1972-73	New England	WHA	78	16	30	46	47
1973-74	New England	WHA	75	7	26	33	42
1974-75	New England	WHA	57	6	14	20	29
1975-76	Winnipeg	WHA	79	5	23	28	73
1976-77	Winnipeg	WHA	70	4	21	25	45
1977-78	Winnipeg	WHA	73	4	22	26	52
1978-79	Winnipeg	WHA	20	0	2	2	16

Playoffs

Year	Team	League	GP	G	A	PTS	PIM
1956-57	St. Boniface	MJHL	7	0	0	0	10
1957-58	St. Boniface	MJHL	23	3	5	8	70
1958-59	St. Boniface	MJHL	9	1	5	6	32
	Winnipeg	MJHL	16	2	6	8	50
1960-61	Kingston	EPHL	5	1	0	1	2
1967-68	Boston	NHL	4	11	1	12	11
1968-69	Boston	NHL	10	2	7	9	18
1970-71	Boston	NHL	7	1	0	1	25
1971-72	Boston	NHL	10	0	0	0	0
1972-73	New England	WHA	12	1	5	6	25
1973-74	New England	WHA	7	0	4	4	7
1975-76	Winnipeg	WHA	11	0	2	2	16
1976-77	Winnipeg	WHA	20	1	3	4	12
1977-78	Winnipeg	WHA	8	0	2	2	2

NHL Totals:

Regular Season

GP	G	A	PTS	PIM
620	48	206	254	1029

Playoffs

GP	G	A	PTS	PIM
31	4	8	12	54

Jim Henry

Regular Season

Year	Team	League	GP	W	L	T	SO	AVG
1941-42	Rangers	NHL	48	29	17	2	1	2.98
1945-46	Rangers	NHL	11	1	7	2	1	3.95
1946-47	Rangers	NHL	2	0	2	0	0	4.50
1947-48	Rangers	NHL	48	17	18	13	2	3.19
1948-49	Chicago	NHL	60	21	31	8	0	3.52
1951-52	Boston	NHL	70	23	34	13	7	2.51
1952-53	Boston	NHL	70	28	29	13	7	2.46
1953-54	Boston	NHL	70	32	28	10	8	2.59
1954-55	Boston	NHL	26	8	12	6	1	3.09

Playoffs

Year	Team	League	GP	W	L	T	SO	AVG
1941-42	Rangers	NHL	6	2	4	0	1	2.17
1951-52	Boston	NHL	7	3	4	0	1	2.41
1952-53	Boston	NHL	9	5	4	0	0	3.06
1953-54	Boston	NHL	4	0	4	0	0	4.00
1954-55	Boston	NHL	3	1	2	0	0	2.62

NHL Totals:

Regular Season

GP	W	L	T	SO	AVG
405	159	178	57	27	2.87

Playoffs

GP	W	L	SO	AVG
29	11	18	2	2.79

Mel Hill

Regular Season

Year	Team	League	GP	G	A	PTS	PIM
1934-35	Sudbury	City Sr.	10	90	4	13	8
1935-36	Sudbury	City Sr.	10	7	6	13	15
1936-37	Sudbury	City Sr.	15	18	5	23	10
1937-38	Boston	NHL	8	2	0	2	2
	Providence	AHL	40	13	10	23	0
1938-39	Boston	NHL	44	10	10	20	16
1939-40	Boston	NHL	37	9	11	20	19
1940-41	Boston	NHL	41	5	4	9	4
	Hershey	AHL	5	1	5	6	4
	Springfield	AHL	1	0	0	0	0
1941-42	Americans	NHL	47	14	23	37	10
1942-43	Toronto	NHL	49	17	27	44	47
1943-44	Toronto	NHL	17	9	10	19	6
1944-45	Toronto	NHL	45	18	17	35	14
1945-46	Toronto	NHL	35	5	7	12	10
	Pittsburgh	AHL	13	7	8	15	0
1946-47	Pittsburgh	AHL	62	26	36	62	42
1947-48	Pittsburgh	AHL	63	10	22	32	14
1948-49	Regina	WCSHL	43	23	30	53	11
1949-50	Regina	WCSHL	50	17	21	38	16
1950-51	Regina	WCSHL	22	3	5	8	6
1951-52	Regina	SSHL	17	7	11	18	16

Playoffs

Year	Team	League	GP	G	A	PTS	PIM
1933-34	Saskatoon	City Jr.	3	4	0	4	0
1934-35	Sudbury	City Sr.	5	2	1	3	0

1936-37	Sudbury	City Sr.	16	9	14	23	6
1937-38	Boston	NHL	1	0	0	0	0
	Providence	AHL	7	4	2	6	0
1938-39	Boston	NHL	12	6	3	9	12
1939-40	Boston	NHL	2	0	0	0	0
1940-41	Boston	NHL	10	1	1	2	0
1942-43	Toronto	NHL	6	3	0	3	0
1944-45	Toronto	NHL	13	2	3	5	6
1945-46	Pittsburgh	AHL	6	1	2	3	0
1946-47	Pittsburgh	AHL	12	3	6	9	6
1947-48	Pittsburgh	AHL	2	0	0	0	2
1948-49	Regina	WCSHL	8	4	6	10	4
1951-52	Regina	SSHL	3	1	0	1	4

NHL Totals:

Regular Season

GP	G	A	PTS	PIM
323	89	109	198	128

Playoffs

GP	G	A	PTS	PIM
43	12	7	19	18

Ken Hodge

Regular Season

Year	Team	League	GP	G	A	PTS	PIM
1961-62	St. Catharines	OHA	31	4	3	7	6
1962-63	St. Catharines	OHA	50	23	23	46	97
1963-64	St. Catharines	OHA	56	37	51	88	110
1964-65	St. Catharines	OHA	55	63	60	123	107
	Chicago	NHL	1	0	0	0	2
	Buffalo	AHL	2	0	2	2	
1965-66	Chicago	NHL	63	6	17	23	47
1966-67	Chicago	NHL	68	10	25	35	59
1967-68	Boston	NHL	74	25	31	56	31
1968-69	Boston	NHL	75	45	45	90	75
1969-70	Boston	NHL	72	25	29	54	87
1970-71	Boston	NHL	78	43	62	105	113
1971-72	Boston	NHL	60	16	40	56	81
1972-73	Boston	NHL	73	37	44	81	58
1973-74	Boston	NHL	76	50	55	105	43
1974-75	Boston	NHL	72	23	43	66	90
1975-76	Boston	NHL	72	25	36	61	42
1976-77	Rangers	NHL	78	21	41	62	43
1977-78	Rangers	NHL	18	2	4	6	8
	New Haven	AHL	52	17	29	46	13
1979-80	Binghamton	AHL	37	10	20	30	24

Playoffs

Year	Team	League	GP	G	A	PTS	PIM
1961-62	St. Catharines	OHA	6	1	0	1	6
1963-64	St. Catharines	OHA	13	6	19	25	28
1964-65	St. Catharines	OHA	5	3	7	10	8
	Buffalo	AHL	4	0	0	0	4
1965-66	Chicago	NHL	5	0	0	0	8
1966-67	Chicago	NHL	6	0	0	0	4
1967-68	Boston	NHL	4	3	0	3	2
1968-69	Boston	NHL	10	5	7	12	4
1969-70	Boston	NHL	14	3	10	13	17
1970-71	Boston	NHL	7	2	5	7	6
1971-72	Boston	NHL	15	9	8	17	62
1972-73	Boston	NHL	5	1	0	1	7
1973-74	Boston	NHL	16	6	10	16	16
1974-75	Boston	NHL	3	1	1	2	0
1975-76	Boston	NHL	12	4	6	10	4
1977-78	New Haven	AHL	15	3	4	7	20

NHL Totals:

Regular Season

GP	G	A	PTS	PIM
879	328	472	800	777

Playoffs

GP	G	A	PTS	PIM
97	34	47	81	130

Flash Hollett

Regular Season

Year	Team	League	GP	G	A	PTS	PIM
1932-33	Syracuse	IAHL	19	0	2	2	16
1933-34	Toronto	NHL	4	0	0	0	4
	Ottawa	NHL	30	7	4	11	21
	Totals		34	7	4	11	25
	Buffalo	IAHL	13	5	4	9	8
1934-35	Toronto	NHL	4	10	16	26	38
1935-36	Toronto	NHL	11	1	4	5	8
	Syracuse	IAHL	4	2	1	3	8
	Boston	NHL	6	1	2	3	2
	NHL Totals		17	2	6	8	10
	Boston	Can-Am	18	6	15	21	24
1936-37	Boston	NHL	47	3	7	10	22
1937-38	Boston	NHL	48	4	10	14	54
1938-39	Boston	NHL	47	10	17	27	35
1939-40	Boston	NHL	44	10	18	28	18
1940-41	Boston	NHL	42	9	15	24	23
	Hershey	AHL	5	4	2	6	2
1941-42	Boston	NHL	48	19	14	33	41
1942-43	Boston	NHL	50	19	25	44	19
1943-44	Boston	NHL	25	9	7	16	4
	Detroit	NHL	27	6	12	18	34
	Totals		52	15	19	34	38
1944-45	Detroit	NHL	50	20	21	41	39
1945-46	Detroit	NHL	38	4	9	13	16
1946-47	Toronto	OHA Sr.	DID NOT PLAY - COACHING				
1947-48	Kitchener	OHA Sr.	15	6	11	17	24
1948-49	Toronto	OHA Sr.	31	6	15	21	20
1949-50	Toronto	OHA Sr.	42	7	27	34	29

Playoffs

Year	Team	League	GP	G	A	PTS	PIM
1932-33	Syracuse	IAHL	6	3	0	3	9
1934-35	Toronto	NHL	7	0	0	0	6
1936-37	Boston	NHL	3	0	0	0	2
1937-38	Boston	NHL	3	0	1	1	0
1938-39	Boston	NHL	12	1	3	4	2
1939-40	Boston	NHL	5	1	2	3	2
1940-41	Boston	NHL	11	3	4	7	8
1941-42	Boston	NHL	5	0	1	1	2
1942-43	Boston	NHL	9	0	9	9	4
1943-44	Detroit	NHL	5	0	0	0	6
1944-45	Detroit	NHL	14	3	4	7	6
1945-46	Detroit	NHL	5	0	2	2	0
1948-49	Toronto	OHA Sr.	20	5	13	18	15
1949-50	Toronto	OHA Sr.	14	1	8	9	14

NHL Totals:

Regular Season

GP	G	A	PTS	PIM
565	132	181	313	378

Playoffs

GP	G	A	PTS	PIM
79	8	26	34	38

Eddie Johnston

Regular Season

Year	Team	League	GP	W	L	T	SO	AVG
1962-63	Boston	NHL	49	11	27	11	1	4.08
1963-64	Boston	NHL	70	18	40	12	6	3.01
1964-65	Boston	NHL	47	12	31	4	3	3.45
1965-66	Boston	NHL	33	10	19	2	1	3.72
1966-67	Boston	NHL	34	9	21	2	0	3.70
1967-68	Boston	NHL	28	11	8	5	0	2.87
1968-69	Boston	NHL	24	14	6	4	2	3.08
1969-70	Boston	NHL	37	16	9	11	3	2.98
1970-71	Boston	NHL	38	30	6	2	4	2.53
1971-72	Boston	NHL	38	27	8	3	2	2.71
1972-73	Boston	NHL	45	24	17	1	5	3.27
1973-74	Toronto	NHL	26	12	9	4	1	3.09
1974-75	St. Louis	NHL	30	12	13	5	2	3.10
1975-76	St. Louis	NHL	38	11	17	9	1	3.62
1976-77	St. Louis	NHL	38	13	16	5	1	3.07
1977-78	St. Louis	NHL	12	5	6	7	0	4.15
	Chicago	NHL	4	1	3	0	0	4.25
	total		16	6	9	7	0	4.18

Playoffs

Year	Team	League	GP	W	L	SO	AVG
1968-69	Boston	NHL	1	0	1	0	3.69
1969-70	Boston	NHL	1	0	1	0	4.00
1970-71	Boston	NHL	1	0	1	0	7.00
1971-72	Boston	NHL	7	6	1	1	1.86
1972-73	Boston	NHL	3	1	2	0	3.38
1973-74	Toronto	NHL	1	0	1	0	6.00
1974-75	St. Louis	NHL	1	0	1	0	5.00
1976-77	St. Louis	NHL	3	0	2	0	3.91

NHL Totals:

Regular Season

GP	W	L	T	SO	AVG
591	236	256	87	32	3.25

Playoffs

GP	W	L	SO	AVG
18	7	10	1	3.34

Leo Labine

Regular Season

Year	Team	League	GP	G	A	PTS	PIM
1949-50	St. Michaels	OHA	47	20	22	42	77
1950-51	Barrie	OHA	52	32	46	78	143
1951-52	Boston	NHL	15	2	4	6	9
	Hershey	AHL	53	23	23	46	88
1952-53	Boston	NHL	51	8	15	23	69
	Hershey	AHL	16	7	3	10	33
1953-54	Boston	NHL	68	16	19	35	57
1954-55	Boston	NHL	67	24	18	42	75
1955-56	Boston	NHL	68	16	18	34	104
1956-57	Boston	NHL	67	18	29	47	128
1957-58	Boston	NHL	62	7	14	21	60
1958-59	Boston	NHL	70	9	23	32	74
1959-60	Boston	NHL	63	16	28	44	58
1960-61	Boston	NHL	40	7	12	19	34
	Detroit	NHL	24	2	9	11	32
	Totals		64	9	21	30	66
1961-62	Detroit	NHL	48	3	4	7	30
	Sudbury	EPHL	9	10	10	20	18
1962-63	Los Angeles	WHL	68	30	47	77	90
1963-64	Los Angeles	WHL	70	31	46	77	56
1964-65	Los Angeles	WHL	58	16	37	53	42
1965-66	Los Angeles	WHL	71	33	30	63	33
1966-67	Los Angeles	WHL	70	18	29	47	24

Playoffs

Year	Team	League	GP	G	A	PTS	PIM
1949-50	St. Michaels	OHA	5	1	2	3	13
1950-51	Barrie	OHA	12	13	13	26	36
1951-52	Boston	NHL	5	0	1	1	4
	Hershey	AHL	5	0	1	1	20
1952-53	Boston	NHL	7	2	1	3	19
	Hershey	AHL	3	1	2	3	8
1953-54	Boston	NHL	4	0	1	1	8
1954-55	Boston	NHL	5	2	1	3	11
1956-57	Boston	NHL	10	2	3	5	14
1957-58	Boston	NHL	11	0	2	2	10
1958-59	Boston	NHL	7	2	1	3	12
1960-61	Detroit	NHL	11	3	2	5	4
1961-62	Sudbury	EPHL	5	0	4	4	4
1962-63	Los Angeles	WHL	3	1	0	1	2
1963-64	Los Angeles	WHL	12	10	12	22	10

NHL Totals:

Regular Season

GP	G	A	PTS	PIM
643	128	193	321	730

Playoffs

GP	G	A	PTS	PIM
60	11	12	23	82

Johnny McKenzie

Regular Season

Year	Team	League	GP	G	A	PTS	PIM
1953-54	Calgary	WCJHL	34	6	8	14	12
1954-55	Medicine Hat	WCJHL	39	14	4	18	33
1955-56	Calgary	WHL	1	0	0	0	0
1956-57	St. Catharines	OHA	52	32	38	70	143
1957-58	St. Catharines	OHA	52	48	51	99	227
1958-59	Chicago	NHL	32	3	4	7	22
	Calgary	WHL	13	2	5	7	18
1959-60	Detroit	NHL	59	8	12	20	50
1960-61	Detroit	NHL	16	3	1	4	13
	Hershey	AHL	47	19	23	42	84
1961-62	Hershey	AHL	58	30	29	59	149
1962-63	Buffalo	AHL	71	35	46	81	122
1963-64	Chicago	NHL	45	9	9	18	50
1964-65	Chicago	NHL	51	8	10	18	46
	St. Louis	CHL	5	5	4	9	17
1965-66	Rangers	NHL	35	6	5	11	36
	Boston	NHL	36	13	9	22	36
	Totals		71	19	14	33	72
1966-67	Boston	NHL	69	17	19	36	98
1967-68	Boston	NHL	74	28	38	66	107
1968-69	Boston	NHL	60	29	27	56	99
1969-70	Boston	NHL	72	29	41	70	114
1970-71	Boston	NHL	65	31	46	77	120
1971-72	Boston	NHL	77	22	47	69	126
1972-73	Philadelphia	WHA	60	28	50	78	157
1973-74	Vancouver	WHA	45	14	38	52	71
1974-75	Canada (Summit Series)		7	2	3	5	14
	Vancouver	WHA	74	23	37	60	84
1975-76	Minnesota	WHA	57	21	26	47	48
	Cincinnati	WHA	12	3	10	13	6
1976-77	Minnesota	WHA	40	17	13	30	77
	New England	WHA	34	11	19	30	25
1977-78	New England	WHA	79	27	29	56	61
1978-79	New England	WHA	76	19	28	47	115

Playoffs

Year	Team	League	GP	G	A	PTS	PIM
1953-54	Calgary	WCJHL	5	0	0	0	2
1954-55	Medicine Hat	WCJHL	5	0	0	0	4
1955-56	Calgary	WHL	2	0	1	1	2

Year	Team	League	GP	G	A	PTS	PIM
1956-57	St. Catharines	OHA	14	9	11	20	50
1957-58	St. Catharines	OHA	8	8	4	12	19
1958-59	Chicago	NHL	2	0	0	0	2
1959-60	Detroit	NHL	2	0	0	0	0
1960-61	Hershey	AHL	8	3	6	9	10
1961-62	Hershey	AHL	7	1	2	3	19
1962-63	Buffalo	AHL	13	8	12	20	28
1963-64	Chicago	NHL	4	0	1	1	6
1964-65	Chicago	NHL	11	0	1	1	6
1967-68	Boston	NHL	4	1	1	2	8
1968-69	Boston	NHL	10	2	2	4	17
1969-70	Boston	NHL	14	5	12	17	35
1970-71	Boston	NHL	7	2	3	5	22
1971-72	Boston	NHL	15	5	12	17	37
1972-73	Philadelphia	WHA	4	3	1	4	8
1976-77	New England	WHA	5	2	1	3	8
1977-78	New England	WHA	14	6	6	12	16
1978-79	New England	WHA	10	3	7	10	10

NHL Totals:

Regular Season

GP	G	A	PTS	PIM
691	206	268	474	917

Playoffs

GP	G	A	PTS	PIM
69	15	32	47	133

Peter McNab

Regular Season

Year	Team	League	GP	G	A	PTS	PIM
1973-74	Buffalo	NHL	22	3	6	9	2
1974-75	Buffalo	NHL	53	22	21	43	8
1975-76	Buffalo	NHL	79	24	32	56	16
1976-77	Boston	NHL	80	38	48	86	11
1977-78	Boston	NHL	79	41	39	80	4
1978-79	Boston	NHL	76	35	45	80	10
1979-80	Boston	NHL	74	40	38	78	10
1980-81	Boston	NHL	80	37	46	83	24
1981-82	Boston	NHL	80	36	40	76	19
1982-83	Boston	NHL	74	22	52	74	23
1983-84	Boston	NHL	52	14	16	30	10
	Vancouver	NHL	13	1	6	7	10
1984-85	Vancouver	NHL	75	23	25	48	10
1985-86	New Jersey	NHL	71	19	24	43	14
1986-87	New Jersey	NHL	46	8	12	20	8

Playoffs

Year	Team	League	GP	G	A	PTS	PIM
1974-75	Buffalo	NHL	17	2	6	8	4
1975-76	Buffalo	NHL	8	0	0	0	0
1976-77	Boston	NHL	14	5	3	8	2
1977-78	Boston	NHL	15	8	11	19	2
1978-79	Boston	NHL	11	5	3	8	0
1979-80	Boston	NHL	10	8	6	14	2
1980-81	Boston	NHL	3	3	0	3	0
1981-92	Boston	NHL	11	6	8	14	6
1982-83	Boston	NHL	15	3	5	8	4

NHL Totals:

Regular Season

GP	G	A	PTS	PIM
697	298	367	665	127

Playoffs

GP	G	A	PTS	PIM
104	40	42	82	20

Rick Middleton

Regular Season

Year	Team	League	GP	G	A	PTS	PIM
1971-72	Oshawa	OHA	53	36	34	70	24
1972-73	Oshawa	OHA	62	67	70	137	14
1973-74	Providence	AHL	63	36	48	84	14
1974-75	Rangers	NHL	47	22	18	40	19
1975-76	Rangers	NHL	77	24	26	50	14
1976-77	Boston	NHL	72	20	22	42	2
1977-78	Boston	NHL	79	25	35	60	8
1978-79	Boston	NHL	71	38	48	86	7
1979-80	Boston	NHL	80	40	52	92	24
1980-81	Boston	NHL	80	44	59	103	16
1981-82	Canada (Canada Cup)		7	1	2	3	0
	Boston	NHL	75	51	43	94	12
1982-83	Boston	NHL	80	49	47	96	8
1983-84	Boston	NHL	80	47	58	105	14
1984-85	Canada (Canada Cup)		7	4	4	8	0
	Boston	NHL	80	30	46	76	6
1985-86	Boston	NHL	49	14	30	44	10
1986-87	Boston	NHL	76	31	37	68	6
1987-88	Boston	NHL	59	13	19	32	11

Playoffs

Year	Team	League	GP	G	A	PTS	PIM
1973-74	Providence	AHL	15	9	6	15	2
1974-75	Rangers	NHL	3	0	0	0	2
1976-77	Boston	NHL	13	5	4	9	0
1977-78	Boston	NHL	15	5	2	7	0
1978-79	Boston	NHL	11	4	8	12	0
1979-80	Boston	NHL	10	4	2	6	5
1980-81	Boston	NHL	3	0	1	1	2
1981-82	Boston	NHL	11	6	9	15	0
1982-83	Boston	NHL	17	11	22	33	6
1983-84	Boston	NHL	3	0	0	0	0
1984-85	Boston	NHL	5	3	0	3	0
1986-87	Boston	NHL	4	2	2	4	0
1987-88	Boston	NHL	19	5	5	10	4

NHL Totals:

Regular Season

GP	G	A	PTS	PIM
1005	448	540	988	157

Playoffs

GP	G	A	PTS	PIM
114	45	55	100	19

Mike Milbury

Regular Season

Year	Team	League	GP	G	A	PTS	PIM
1972-73	Colgate	ECAC	23	2	19	21	68
1973-74	Boston	AHL	5	0	0	0	7
1974-75	Rochester	AHL	71	2	15	17	246
1975-76	Boston	NHL	3	0	0	0	9
	Rochester	AHL	73	3	15	18	199
1976-77	United States (Canada Cup)		5	1	3	4	16
	Boston	NHL	77	6	18	24	166
1977-78	Boston	NHL	80	8	30	38	151
1978-79	Boston	NHL	74	1	34	35	149
1979-80	Boston	NHL	72	10	13	23	59
1980-81	Boston	NHL	77	0	18	18	222
1981-82	Boston	NHL	51	2	10	12	71
1982-83	Boston	NHL	78	9	15	24	216
1983-84	Boston	NHL	74	2	17	19	159
1984-85	Boston	NHL	78	3	13	16	152
1985-86	Boston	NHL	22	2	5	7	102
1986-87	Boston	NHL	68	6	16	22	96

Playoffs

Year	Team	League	GP	G	A	PTS	PIM
1974-75	Rochester	AHL	8	0	3	3	24
1975-76	Boston	NHL	11	0	0	0	29
	Rochester	AHL	3	0	1	1	13
1976-77	Boston	NHL	13	2	2	4	47
1977-78	Boston	NHL	15	1	8	9	27
1978-79	Boston	NHL	11	1	7	8	7
1979-80	Boston	NHL	10	0	2	2	50
1980-81	Boston	NHL	2	0	1	1	10
1981-82	Boston	NHL	11	0	4	4	6
1983-84	Boston	NHL	3	0	0	0	12
1984-85	Boston	NHL	5	0	0	0	10
1985-86	Boston	NHL	1	0	0	0	17
1986-87	Boston	NHL	4	0	0	0	4

NHL Totals:

Regular Season

GP	G	A	PTS	PIM
754	49	189	238	1552

Playoffs

GP	G	A	PTS	PIM
86	4	24	28	219

Doug Mohns

Regular Season

Year	Team	League	GP	G	A	PTS	PIM
1953-54	Boston	NHL	70	13	14	27	27
1954-55	Boston	NHL	70	14	18	32	82
1955-56	Boston	NHL	64	10	8	18	48
1956-57	Boston	NHL	68	6	34	40	89
1957-58	Boston	NHL	54	5	16	21	28
1958-59	Boston	NHL	47	6	24	30	40
1959-60	Boston	NHL	65	20	25	45	62
1960-61	Boston	NHL	65	12	21	33	63
1961-62	Boston	NHL	69	16	29	45	74
1962-63	Boston	NHL	68	7	23	30	63
1963-64	Boston	NHL	70	9	17	26	95
1964-65	Chicago	NHL	49	13	20	33	84
1965-66	Chicago	NHL	70	22	27	49	63
1966-67	Chicago	NHL	61	25	35	60	58
1967-68	Chicago	NHL	65	24	29	53	33
1968-69	Chicago	NHL	65	22	19	41	47
1969-70	Chicago	NHL	66	6	27	33	46
1970-71	Chicago	NHL	39	4	6	10	16
	Minnesota	NHL	17	2	5	7	14
1971-72	Minnesota	NHL	78	6	30	36	82
1972-73	Minnesota	NHL	67	4	13	17	52
1973-74	Atlanta	NHL	28	0	3	3	10
1974-75	Washington	NHL	75	2	19	21	54

Playoffs

Year	Team	League	GP	G	A	PTS	PIM
1953-54	Boston	NHL	4	1	0	1	4
1954-55	Boston	NHL	5	0	0	0	4
1956-57	Boston	NHL	10	2	3	5	2
1957-58	Boston	NHL	12	3	10	13	18
1958-59	Boston	NHL	4	0	2	2	12
1964-65	Chicago	NHL	14	3	4	7	21
1965-66	Chicago	NHL	5	1	0	1	4
1966-67	Chicago	NHL	5	0	5	5	8
1967-68	Chicago	NHL	11	1	5	6	12
1969-70	Chicago	NHL	8	0	2	2	15
1970-71	Minnesota	NHL	6	2	2	4	10
1971-71	Minnesota	NHL	4	1	2	3	10
1972-73	Minnesota	NHL	6	0	1	1	2

NHL Totals:

Regular Season

GP	G	A	PTS	PIM
1390	248	462	70	1230

Playoffs

GP	G	A	PTS	PIM
94	14	36	50	122

Andy Moog

Regular Season

Year	Team	League	GP	W	L	T	SO	AVG
1978-79	Billings	WHL	26	13	5	4	4	4.13
1979-80	Billings	WHL	46	23	14	1	1	3.67
1980-81	Edmonton	NHL	7	3	3	0	0	3.83
	Wichita	CHL	29	14	13	1	0	3.33
1981-82	Edmonton	NHL	8	3	5	0	0	4.81
	Wichita	CHL	40	23	13	3	1	2.99
1982-83	Edmonton	NHL	50	33	8	7	1	3.54
1983-84	Edmonton	NHL	35	27	8	1	1	3.77
1984-85	Edmonton	NHL	39	22	9	3	1	3.30
1985-86	Edmonton	NHL	47	27	9	7	1	3.69
1986-87	Edmonton	NHL	46	28	11	3	0	3.51
1987-88	Canada (National Team)		27	10	7	5	0	3.58
	Canada (Olympics)		4	4	0	0	1	2.25
	Boston	NHL	6	4	2	0	1	2.83
1988-89	Boston	NHL	41	18	14	8	1	3.22
1989-90	Boston	NHL	46	24	10	7	3	2.89
1990-91	Boston	NHL	51	25	13	9	4	2.87
1991-92	Boston	NHL	62	28	22	9	1	3.23
1992-93	Boston	NHL	55	37	14	3	3	3.16
1993-94	Dallas	NHL	55	24	20	7	2	3.27
1994-95	Dallas	NHL	31	10	12	7	2	2.44
1995-96	Dallas	NHL	41	13	19	7	1	2.99
1996-97	Dallas	NHL	48	28	13	5	3	2.15
1997-98	Montreal	NHL	42	18	17	5	3	2.49

Playoffs

Year	Team	League	GP	W	L	SO	AVG
1978-79	Billings	WHL	5	1	3	0	5.50
1979-80	Billings	WHL	3	2	1	0	3.16
1980-81	Edmonton	NHL	9	5	4	0	3.65
	Wichita	CHL	5	3	2	0	3.20
1981-82	Wichita	CHL	7	3	4	0	3.18
1982-83	Edmonton	NHL	16	11	5	0	3.03
1983-84	Edmonton	NHL	7	4	0	0	2.74
1984-85	Edmonton	NHL	2	0	0	0	0.00
1985-86	Edmonton	NHL	1	1	0	0	1.00
1986-87	Edmonton	NHL	2	2	0	0	4.00
1987-88	Boston	NHL	7	1	4	0	4.24
1988-89	Boston	NHL	6	4	2	0	2.34
1989-90	Boston	NHL	20	13	7	2	2.21
1990-91	Boston	NHL	19	10	9	0	3.18
1991-92	Boston	NHL	15	8	7	1	3.19
1992-93	Boston	NHL	3	0	3	0	5.22
1993-94	Dallas	NHL	4	1	3	0	2.93
1994-95	Dallas	NHL	5	1	4	0	3.47
1996-97	Dallas	NHL	7	3	4	0	2.81
1997-98	Montreal	NHL	9	4	5	1	3.04

NHL Totals:

Regular Season

GP	W	L	T	SO	AVG
713	372	209	88	28	3.13

Playoffs

GP	W	L	SO	AVG
132	68	57	4	3.04

Cam Neely

Regular Season

Year	Team	League	GP	G	A	PTS	PIM
1982-83	Portland	WHL	72	56	64	120	130
1983-84	Portland	WHL	19	8	18	26	29
	Vancouver	NHL	56	16	15	31	57
1984-85	Vancouver	NHL	72	21	18	39	137
1985-86	Vancouver	NHL	73	14	20	34	126
1986-87	Boston	NHL	75	36	36	72	143
1987-88	Boston	NHL	69	42	27	69	175
1988-89	Boston	NHL	74	37	38	75	190
1989-90	Boston	NHL	76	55	37	92	117
1990-91	Boston	NHL	69	51	40	91	98
1991-92	Boston	NHL	9	9	3	12	16
1992-93	Boston	NHL	13	11	7	18	25
1993-94	Boston	NHL	49	50	24	74	54
1994-95	Boston	NHL	42	27	14	41	72
1995-96	Boston	NHL	49	26	20	46	31

Playoffs

Year	Team	League	GP	G	A	PTS	PIM
1982-83	Portland	WHL	14	9	11	20	17
1983-84	Vancouver	NHL	4	2	0	2	2
1985-86	Vancouver	NHL	3	0	0	0	6
1986-87	Boston	NHL	4	5	1	6	8
1987-88	Boston	NHL	23	9	8	17	51
1988-89	Boston	NHL	10	7	2	9	8
1989-90	Boston	NHL	21	12	16	28	51
1990-91	Boston	NHL	19	16	4	20	36
1992-93	Boston	NHL	4	4	1	5	4
1994-95	Boston	NHL	5	2	0	2	2

NHL Totals:

Regular Season

GP	G	A	PTS	PIM
726	395	299	694	1241

Playoffs

GP	G	A	PTS	PIM
93	57	32	89	168

Adam Oates

Regular Season

Year	Team	League	GP	G	A	PTS	PIM
1982-83	RPI	ECAC	22	9	33	42	8
1983-84	RPI	ECAC	38	26	57	83	15
1984-85	RPI	ECAC	38	31	60	91	29
1985-86	Detroit	NHL	38	9	11	20	10
	Adirondack	AHL	34	18	28	46	4
1986-87	Detroit	NHL	76	15	32	47	21
1987-88	Detroit	NHL	63	14	40	54	20
1988-89	Detroit	NHL	69	16	62	78	14
1989-90	St. Louis	NHL	80	23	79	102	30
1990-91	St. Louis	NHL	61	25	90	115	29
1991-92	St. Louis	NHL	54	10	59	69	12
	Boston	NHL	26	10	20	30	10
	Totals		80	20	79	99	22
1992-93	Boston	NHL	84	45	97	142	32
1993-94	Boston	NHL	77	32	80	112	45
1994-95	Boston	NHL	48	12	41	53	8
1995-96	Boston	NHL	70	25	67	92	18
1996-97	Boston	NHL	63	18	52	70	10
	Washington	NHL	17	4	8	12	4
1997-98	Washington	NHL	82	18	58	76	36

Playoffs

Year	Team	League	GP	G	A	PTS	PIM
1985-86	Adirondack	AHL	17	7	14	21	4
1986-87	Detroit	NHL	16	4	7	11	6
1987-88	Detroit	NHL	16	8	12	20	6
1988-89	Detroit	NHL	6	0	8	8	2
1989-90	St. Louis	NHL	12	2	12	14	4
1990-91	St. Louis	NHL	13	7	13	20	10
1991-92	Boston	NHL	15	5	14	19	4
1992-93	Boston	NHL	4	0	9	9	4
1993-94	Boston	NHL	13	3	9	12	8
1994-95	Boston	NHL	5	1	0	1	2
1995-96	Boston	NHL	5	2	5	7	2
1997-98	Washington	NHL	21	6	11	17	8

NHL Totals:

Regular Season

GP	G	A	PTS	PIM
908	276	796	1072	299

Playoffs

GP	G	A	PTS	PM
126	38	100	138	56

Willie O'Ree

Regular Season

Year	Team	League	GP	G	A	PTS	PIM
1951-52	Fredericton	City Sr.	6	10	4	14	2
	Fredericton	NBJHL	3	2	0	2	0
1952-53	Fredericton	NBJHL	12	15	3	18	6
	Fredericton	NBSHL	2	2	0	2	0
1953-54	Fredericton	NBSHL	23	7	11	18	15
1954-55	Quebec	QJHL	43	27	17	44	41
1955-56	Kitchener	OHA	41	30	28	58	38
1956-57	Quebec	QHL	68	22	12	34	80
1957-58	Boston	NHL	2	0	0	0	0
	Springfield	AHL	6	0	0	0	0
	Quebec	QHL	57	13	19	32	42
1958-59	Quebec	QHL	56	9	21	30	74
1959-60	Kingston	EPHL	50	21	25	46	41
1960-61	Boston	NHL	43	4	10	14	26
	Hull-Ottawa	EPHL	16	10	9	19	21
1961-62	Hull-Ottawa	EPHL	12	1	2	3	18
	Los Angeles	WHL	54	28	26	54	57
1962-63	Los Angeles	WHL	64	25	26	51	41
1963-64	Los Angeles	WHL	60	17	18	35	45
1964-65	Los Angeles	WHL	70	38	21	59	75
1956-66	Los Angeles	WHL	62	33	33	66	30
1966-67	Los Angeles	WHL	68	34	26	60	58
1967-68	San Diego	WHL	66	21	33	54	54
1968-69	San Diego	WHL	70	38	41	79	63
1969-70	San Diego	WHL	66	24	22	46	50
1970-71	San Diego	WHL	66	18	15	33	47
1971-72	San Diego	WHL	48	16	17	33	42
1972-73	New Haven	AHL	50	21	24	45	41
	San Diego	WHL	18	6	5	11	18
1973-74	San Diego	WHL	73	30	28	58	89
1978-79	San Diego	PCL	53	21	25	46	37

Playoffs

Year	Team	League	GP	G	A	PTS	PIM
1951-52	Fredericton	City Sr.	8	10	5	15	18
1952-53	Fredericton	NBJHL	4	5	0	5	2
1953-54	Fredericton	NBSHL	25	15	10	25	10
1954-55	Quebec	QJHL	17	7	6	13	10
1955-56	Kitchener	OHA	8	4	3	7	6
1956-57	Quebec	QHL	10	3	3	6	10
1957-58	Quebec	QHL	9	4	2	6	8
1962-63	Los Angeles	WHL	3	2	3	5	2
1963-64	Los Angeles	WHL	12	4	8	12	10
1967-68	San Diego	WHL	7	2	2	4	6
1968-69	San Diego	WHL	7	3	3	6	12
1969-70	San Diego	WHL	6	6	3	9	4
1970-71	San Diego	WHL	6	4	1	5	14
1971-72	San Diego	WHL	4	0	1	1	2
1972-73	San Diego	WHL	6	1	4	5	2
1973-74	San Diego	WHL	4	3	3	6	0

NHL Totals:

Regular Season

GP	G	A	PTS	PIM
45	4	10	14	26

Playoffs

GP	G	A	PTS	PIM
0	0	0	0	0

Terry O'Reilly

Regular Season

Year	Team	League	GP	G	A	PTS	PIM
1968-69	Oshawa	OHA	46	5	15	20	87
1969-70	Oshawa	OHA	54	13	36	49	60
1970-71	Oshawa	OHA	54	23	42	65	151
1971-72	Boston	NHL	1	1	0	1	0
	Boston	AHL	60	9	8	17	134
1972-73	Boston	NHL	72	5	22	27	109
1973-74	Boston	NHL	76	11	24	35	94
1974-75	Boston	NHL	68	15	20	35	146
1975-76	Boston	NHL	80	23	27	50	150
1976-77	Boston	NHL	79	14	41	55	147
1977-78	Boston	NHL	77	29	61	90	211
1978-79	Boston	NHL	80	26	51	77	205
1979-80	Boston	NHL	71	19	42	61	265
1980-81	Boston	NHL	77	8	35	43	223
1981-82	Boston	NHL	70	22	30	52	213
1982-83	Boston	NHL	19	6	14	20	40
1983-84	Boston	NHL	58	12	18	30	124
1984-85	Boston	NHL	63	13	17	30	168

Playoffs

Year	Team	League	GP	G	A	PTS	PIM
1971-72	Boston	AHL	9	2	2	4	31
1972-73	Boston	NHL	5	0	0	0	2
1973-74	Boston	NHL	16	2	5	7	38
1974-75	Boston	NHL	3	0	0	0	17
1975-76	Boston	NHL	12	3	1	4	25
1976-77	Boston	NHL	14	5	6	11	28
1977-78	Boston	NHL	15	5	10	15	40
1978-79	Boston	NHL	11	0	6	6	25
1979-80	Boston	NHL	10	3	6	9	69
1980-81	Boston	NHL	3	1	2	3	12
1981-82	Boston	NHL	11	5	4	9	56
1983-84	Boston	NHL	3	0	0	0	14
1984-85	Boston	NHL	5	1	2	3	9

NHL Totals:

Regular Season

GP	G	A	PTS	PIM
891	204	402	606	2095

Playoffs

GP	G	A	PTS	PIM
108	25	42	67	335

Bobby Orr

Regular Season

Year	Team	League	GP	G	A	PTS	PIM
1962-63	Oshawa	Tor-Jr.	34	6	15	21	45
1963-64	Oshawa	OHA	56	29	43	72	142
1964-65	Oshawa	OHA	56	34	59	93	112
1965-66	Oshawa	OHA	47	38	56	94	92
1966-67	Boston	NHL	61	13	28	41	102
1967-68	Boston	NHL	46	11	20	31	63
1968-69	Boston	NHL	67	21	43	64	133
1969-70	Boston	NHL	76	33	87	120	125
1970-71	Boston	NHL	78	37	102	139	91
1971-72	Boston	NHL	76	37	80	117	106
1972-73	Boston	NHL	63	29	72	101	99
1973-74	Boston	NHL	74	32	90	122	82
1974-75	Boston	NHL	80	46	89	135	101
1975-76	Boston	NHL	10	5	13	18	22
1976-77	Canada (Canada Cup)		7	2	7	9	8
	Chicago	NHL	20	4	19	23	25
1977-78	DID NOT PLAY						
1978-79	Chicago	NHL	6	2	2	4	4

Playoffs

Year	Team	League	GP	G	A	PTS	PIM
1963-64	Oshawa	OHA	6	0	7	7	21
1964-65	Oshawa	OHA	6	0	6	6	10
1965-66	Oshawa	OHA	17	9	19	28	14
1967-68	Boston	NHL	4	0	2	2	2
1968-69	Boston	NHL	10	1	7	8	10
1969-70	Boston	NHL	14	9	11	20	14
1970-71	Boston	NHL	7	5	7	12	25
1971-72	Boston	NHL	15	5	19	24	19
1972-73	Boston	NHL	5	1	1	2	7
1973-74	Boston	NHL	16	4	14	18	28
1974-75	Boston	NHL	3	1	5	6	2

NHL Totals:

Regular Season

GP	G	A	PTS	PIM
657	270	645	915	953

Playoffs

GP	G	A	PTS	PM
74	26	66	92	107

Brad Park

Regular Season

Year	Team	League	GP	G	A	PTS	PIM
1965-66	Toronto	OHA	33	0	14	14	48
1966-67	Toronto	OHA	28	4	15	19	73
1967-68	Toronto	OHA	50	10	33	43	120
1968-69	Buffalo	AHL	17	2	12	14	49
	Rangers	NHL	54	3	23	26	70
1969-70	Rangers	NHL	60	11	26	37	98
1970-71	Rangers	NHL	68	7	37	44	114
1971-72	Rangers	NHL	75	24	49	73	130
1972-73	Canada	(Summit)	8	1	4	5	2
	Rangers	NHL	52	10	43	53	51
1973-74	Rangers	NHL	78	25	57	82	148
1974-75	Rangers	NHL	65	13	44	57	104
1975-76	Rangers	NHL	13	2	4	6	23
	Boston	NHL	43	16	37	53	95
1976-77	Boston	NHL	77	12	55	67	67
1977-78	Boston	NHL	80	22	57	79	79
1978-79	Boston	NHL	40	7	32	39	10
1979-80	Boston	NHL	32	5	16	21	27
1980-81	Boston	NHL	78	14	52	66	111
1981-82	Boston	NHL	75	14	42	56	82
1982-83	Boston	NHL	76	10	26	36	82
1983-84	Detroit	NHL	80	5	53	58	85
1984-85	Detroit	NHL	67	13	30	43	53

Playoffs

Year	Team	League	GP	G	A	PTS	PIM
1965-66	Toronto	OHA	14	1	0	1	38
1966-67	Toronto	OHA	8	4	3	7	17
1967-68	Toronto	OHA	5	0	6	6	37
1968-69	Rangers	NHL	4	0	2	2	7
1969-70	Rangers	NHL	5	1	2	3	11
1970-71	Rangers	NHL	13	0	4	4	42
1971-72	Rangers	NHL	16	4	7	11	21

Year	Team	League	GP	G	A	PTS	PIM
1972-73	Rangers	NHL	10	2	5	7	8
1973-74	Rangers	NHL	13	4	8	12	38
1974-75	Rangers	NHL	3	1	4	5	2
1975-76	Boston	NHL	11	3	8	11	14
1976-77	Boston	NHL	14	2	10	12	4
1977-78	Boston	NHL	15	9	11	20	14
1978-79	Boston	NHL	11	1	4	5	8
1979-80	Boston	NHL	10	3	6	9	4
1980-81	Boston	NHL	3	1	3	4	11
1981-82	Boston	NHL	11	1	4	5	4
1982-83	Boston	NHL	16	3	9	12	18
1983-84	Detroit	NHL	3	0	3	3	0
1984-85	Detroit	NHL	3	0	0	0	11

NHL Totals:

Regular Season

GP	G	A	PTS	PIM
1113	213	683	896	1429

Playoffs

GP	G	A	PTS	PIM

Johnny Peirson

Regular Season

Year	Team	League	GP	G	A	PTS	PIM
1945-46	McGill Univ.	Mtl-Sr.	6	13	5	18	0
1946-47	Boston	NHL	5	0	0	0	0
	Boston	EHL	10	5	10	15	24
	Hershey	AHL	26	11	11	22	32
1947-48	Boston	NHL	15	4	2	6	0
	Hershey	AHL	36	14	26	40	39
1948-49	Boston	NHL	59	22	21	43	45
1949-50	Boston	NHL	57	27	25	52	49
1950-51	Boston	NHL	70	19	19	38	43
1951-52	Boston	NHL	68	20	30	50	30
1952-53	Boston	NHL	49	14	15	29	32
1953-54	Boston	NHL	68	21	19	40	55
1954-55	DID NOT PLAY						
1955-56	Boston	NHL	33	11	14	25	10
1956-57	Boston	NHL	68	13	26	39	41
1957-58	Boston	NHL	53	2	2	4	10

Playoffs

Year	Team	League	GP	G	A	PTS	PM
1946-47	Hershey	AHL	11	3	2	5	10
1947-48	Boston	NHL	5	2	3	5	0
1948-49	Boston	NHL	5	3	1	4	4
1950-51	Boston	NHL	2	1	1	2	2
1951-52	Boston	NHL	7	0	2	2	4
1952-53	Boston	NHL	11	3	6	9	2
1953-54	Boston	NHL	4	0	0	0	2
1956-57	Boston	NHL	10	0	3	3	12
1957-58	Boston	NHL	5	0	1	1	0

NHL Totals:

Regular Season

GP	G	A	PTS	PIM
545	153	173	326	315

Playoffs

GP	G	A	PTS	PIM
49	9	17	26	26

Bill Quackenbush

Regular Season

Year	Team	League	GP	G	A	PTS	PIM
1940-41	Toronto	OHA	13	4	9	13	0
1941-42	Brantford	OHA	23	5	29	34	16
1942-43	Detroit	NHL	10	1	1	2	4
	Indianapolis	AHL	37	6	13	19	0
1943-44	Detroit	NHL	43	4	14	18	6
	Indianapolis	AHL	1	1	0	1	0
1944-45	Detroit	NHL	50	7	14	21	10
1945-46	Detroit	NHL	48	11	10	21	6
1946-47	Detroit	NHL	44	5	17	22	6
1947-48	Detroit	NHL	58	6	16	22	17
1948-49	Detroit	NHL	50	6	17	23	0
1949-50	Boston	NHL	70	8	17	25	4
1950-51	Boston	NHL	70	5	24	29	12
1951-52	Boston	NHL	69	2	17	19	6
1952-53	Boston	NHL	69	2	16	18	6
1953-54	Boston	NHL	45	0	17	17	6
1954-55	Boston	NHL	68	2	20	22	8
1955-56	Boston	NHL	70	3	22	25	4

Playoffs

Year	Team	League	GP	G	A	PTS	PIM
1941-42	Brantford	OHA	7	2	4	6	8
1942-43	Indianapolis	AHL	7	0	1	1	6
1943-44	Detroit	NHL	2	1	0	1	0
1944-45	Detroit	NHL	14	0	2	2	2
1945-46	Detroit	NHL	5	0	1	1	0
1946-47	Detroit	NHL	5	0	0	0	2
1947-48	Detroit	NHL	10	0	2	2	0
1948-49	Detroit	NHL	11	1	1	2	0
1950-51	Boston	NHL	6	0	1	1	0
1951-52	Boston	NHL	7	0	3	3	0
1952-53	Boston	NHL	11	0	4	4	4
1953-54	Boston	NHL	4	0	0	0	0
1954-55	Boston	NHL	5	0	5	5	0

NHL Totals:

Regular Season

GP	G	A	PTS	PIM
774	62	222	284	396

Playoffs

GP	G	A	PTS	PIM
80	2	19	21	8

Jean Ratelle

Regular Season

Year	Team	League	GP	G	A	PTS	PIM
1958-59	Guelph	OHA	54	20	31	51	11
1959-60	Guelph	OHA	48	39	47	86	15
	Trois-Rivieres	EPHL	3	3	5	8	0
1960-61	Guelph	OHA	47	40	61	101	10
	Rangers	NHL	3	2	1	3	0
1961-62	Rangers	NHL	31	4	8	12	4
	Kitchener	EPHL	32	10	29	39	8
1962-63	Rangers	NHL	48	11	9	20	8
	Baltimore	AHL	20	11	8	19	0
1963-64	Rangers	NHL	15	0	7	7	6
	Baltimore	AHL	57	20	26	46	2
1964-65	Rangers	NHL	54	14	21	35	14
	Baltimore	AHL	8	9	4	13	6
1965-66	Rangers	NHL	67	21	30	51	10
1966-67	Rangers	NHL	41	6	5	11	4
1967-68	Rangers	NHL	74	32	46	78	18
1968-69	Rangers	NHL	75	32	46	78	26

Year	Team	League	GP	G	A	PTS	PIM
1958-59	Guelph	OHA	10	5	4	9	2
1959-60	Guelph	OHA	5	3	5	8	4
	Trois-Rivieres	EPHL	4	0	3	3	0
1960-61	Guelph	OHA	14	6	11	17	6
1961-62	Kitchener	EPHL	7	2	6	8	2
1962-63	Baltimore	AHL	3	0	0	0	0
1966-67	Rangers	NHL	4	0	0	0	2
1967-68	Rangers	NHL	6	0	4	4	2
1968-69	Rangers	NHL	4	1	0	1	0
1969-70	Rangers	NHL	6	1	3	4	0
1970-71	Rangers	NHL	13	2	9	11	8
1971-72	Rangers	NHL	6	0	1	1	0
1972-73	Rangers	NHL	10	2	7	9	0
1973-74	Rangers	NHL	13	2	4	6	0
1974-75	Rangers	NHL	3	1	5	6	2
1975-76	Boston	NHL	12	8	8	16	4
1976-77	Boston	NHL	14	5	12	17	4
1977-78	Boston	NHL	15	3	7	10	0
1978-79	Boston	NHL	11	7	6	13	2
1979-80	Boston	NHL	3	0	0	0	0
1980-81	Boston	NHL	3	0	0	0	0

NHL Totals:

Regular Season

GP	G	A	PTS	PIM
1281	491	776	1267	276

Playoffs

GP	G	A	PTS	PIM
123	32	66	98	24

Sergei Samsonov

Regular Season

Year	Team	League	GP	G	A	PTS	PIM
1994-95	CSKA Moscow	CIS Jr.	50	110	72	182	—
	CSKA Moscow	CIS	13	2	2	4	14
1995-96	CSKA Moscow	CIS	51	21	17	38	12
	Russia (World Juniors, Pool A)		7	4	2	6	0
1996-97	Detroit	IHL	73	29	35	64	18
	Russia (World Juniors, Pool A)		6	6	1	7	0
1997-98	Boston	NHL	81	22	25	47	8

Playoffs

Year	Team	League	GP	G	A	PTS	PIM
1994-95	CSKA Moscow	CIS	2	0	0	0	0
1995-96	CSKA Moscow	CIS	3	1	1	2	4
1996-97	Detroit	IHL	19	8	4	12	12
1997-98	Boston	NHL	6	2	5	7	0

NHL Totals:

Regular Season

GP	G	A	PTS	PIM
81	22	25	47	8

Playoffs

GP	G	A	PTS	PIM
6	2	5	7	0

Derek Sanderson

Regular Season

Year	Team	League	GP	G	A	PTS	PIM
1962-63	Niagara Falls	OHA	2	0	0	0	10
1963-64	Niagara Falls	OHA	42	12	15	27	42
1964-65	Niagara Falls	OHA	55	19	46	65	128
1965-66	Niagara Falls	OHA	48	33	43	76	238
	Boston	NHL	2	0	0	0	0
	Oklahoma City	CHL	2	1	0	1	0
1966-67	Niagara Falls	OHA	47	41	60	101	193
	Boston	NHL	2	0	0	0	0
1967-68	Boston	NHL	71	24	25	49	98
1968-69	Boston	NHL	61	26	22	48	146
1969-70	Boston	NHL	50	18	23	41	118
1970-71	Boston	NHL	71	29	34	63	130
1971-72	Boston	NHL	78	25	33	58	108
1972-73	Philadelphia	WHA	8	3	3	6	69
	Boston	NHL	25	5	10	15	38
1973-74	Boston	NHL	29	8	12	20	48
	Boston	AHL	3	4	3	7	2
1974-75	Rangers	NHL	75	25	25	50	106
1975-76	Rangers	NHL	8	0	0	0	4
	St. Louis	NHL	65	24	43	67	59
	Totals		73	24	43	67	63
1976-77	St. Louis	NHL	32	8	13	21	26
	Vancouver	NHL	16	7	9	16	30
	Kansas City	CHL	8	4	3	7	6
	NHL Totals		48	15	22	37	56
1977-78	Pittsburgh	NHL	13	3	1	4	0
	Tulsa	CHL	4	0	0	0	0
	Kansas City	CHL	4	1	3	4	0

Playoffs

Year	Team	League	GP	G	A	PTS	PIM
1962-63	Niagara Falls	OHA	1	0	0	0	0
1963-64	Niagara Falls	OHA	4	0	1	1	0
1964-65	Niagara Falls	OHA	11	9	8	17	26
1965-66	Niagara Falls	OHA	6	6	0	6	72
	Oklahoma City	CHL	4	0	4	4	5
1966-67	Niagara Falls	OHA	13	8	17	25	70
	Oklahoma City	CHL	2	0	0	0	0
1967-68	Boston	NHL	4	0	2	2	9
1968-69	Boston	NHL	9	8	2	10	36
1969-70	Boston	NHL	14	5	4	9	72
1970-71	Boston	NHL	7	2	1	3	13
1971-72	Boston	NHL	11	1	1	2	44
1972-73	Boston	NHL	5	1	2	3	13
1974-75	Rangers	NHL	3	0	0	0	0
1975-76	St. Louis	NHL	3	1	0	1	0

NHL Totals:

Regular Season

GP	G	A	PTS	PIM
598	202	250	452	911

Playoffs

GP	G	A	PTS	PIM
56	18	12	30	187

Milt Schmidt

Regular Season

Year	Team	League	GP	G	A	PTS	PIM
1933-34	Kitchener	OHA	7	2	4	6	2
1934-35	Kitchener	OHA	17	20	6	26	14
1935-36	Kitchener	OHA	5	4	3	7	2
1936-37	Boston	NHL	26	2	8	10	15
	Providence	AHL	23	8	1	9	12
1937-38	Boston	NHL	44	13	14	27	15
1938-39	Boston	NHL	41	15	17	32	13
1939-40	Boston	NHL	48	22	30	52	37
1940-41	Boston	NHL	45	13	25	38	23
1941-42	Boston	NHL	36	14	21	35	34
1942-43	MILITARY SERVICE						
1943-44	MILITARY SERVICE						
1944-45	MILITARY SERVICE						
1945-46	Boston	NHL	48	13	18	31	21
1946-47	Boston	NHL	59	27	35	62	40
1947-48	Boston	NHL	33	9	17	26	28
1948-49	Boston	NHL	44	10	22	32	25

1949-50	Boston	NHL	68	19	22	41	41
1950-51	Boston	NHL	62	22	39	61	33
1951-52	Boston	NHL	69	21	29	50	57
1952-53	Boston	NHL	68	11	23	34	30
1953-54	Boston	NHL	62	14	18	32	28
1954-55	Boston	NHL	23	4	8	12	26
1955-56	Boston	NHL	DID NOT PLAY - COACHING				

Playoffs

Year	Team	League	GP	G	A	PTS	PIM
1933-34	Kitchener	OHA	4	2	3	5	0
1934-35	Kitchener	OHA	3	2	2	4	0
1935-36	Kitchener	OHA	4	4	1	5	11
1936-37	Boston	NHL	3	0	0	0	0
1937-38	Boston	NHL	3	0	0	0	0
1938-39	Boston	NHL	12	3	3	6	2
1939-40	Boston	NHL	6	0	0	0	0
1940-41	Boston	NHL	11	5	6	11	9
1945-46	Boston	NHL	10	3	5	8	2
1946-47	Boston	NHL	5	3	1	4	4
1947-48	Boston	NHL	5	2	5	7	2
1948-49	Boston	NHL	4	0	2	2	8
1950-51	Boston	NHL	6	0	1	1	7
1951-52	Boston	NHL	7	2	1	3	0
1952-53	Boston	NHL	10	5	1	6	6
1953-54	Boston	NHL	4	1	0	1	20

NHL Totals:

Regular Season

GP	G	A	PTS	PIM
776	229	346	575	466

Playoffs

GP	G	A	PTS	PIM
86	24	25	49	60

Eddie Shore

Regular Season

Year	Team	League	GP	G	A	PTS	PIM
1924-25	Regina	WCHL	24	6	0	6	75
1925-26	Edmonton	WHL	30	12	2	14	86
1926-27	Boston	NHL	40	12	6	18	130
1927-28	Boston	NHL	43	11	6	17	165
1928-29	Boston	NHL	39	12	7	19	96
1929-30	Boston	NHL	42	12	19	31	105
1930-31	Boston	NHL	44	15	16	31	105
1931-32	Boston	NHL	45	9	13	22	80
1932-33	Boston	NHL	48	8	27	35	102
1933-34	Boston	NHL	30	2	10	12	57
1934-35	Boston	NHL	48	7	26	33	32
1935-36	Boston	NHL	45	3	16	19	61
1936-37	Boston	NHL	20	3	1	4	12
1937-38	Boston	NHL	48	3	14	17	42
1938-39	Boston	NHL	44	4	14	18	47
1939-40	Boston	NHL	4	2	1	3	4
	NY Americans	NHL	10	2	3	5	9
	Springfield	AHL	15	1	14	15	18
1940-41	Springfield	AHL	56	4	13	17	66
1941-42	Springfield	AHL	35	5	12	17	61
1943-44	Buffalo	AHL	1	0	0	0	0

Playoffs

Year	Team	League	GP	G	A	PTS	PIM
1923-24	Melville	SSHL	11	10	8	18	0
1925-26	Edmonton	WHL	2	0	0	0	6
1926-27	Boston	NHL	8	1	1	2	40
1927-28	Boston	NHL	2	0	0	0	8
1928-29	Boston	NHL	5	1	1	2	28
1929-30	Boston	NHL	6	1	0	1	26
1930-31	Boston	NHL	5	2	1	3	24
1932-33	Boston	NHL	5	0	1	1	14
1934-35	Boston	NHL	4	0	1	1	2
1935-36	Boston	NHL	2	1	1	2	12
1937-38	Boston	NHL	3	0	1	1	6
1938-39	Boston	NHL	12	0	4	4	19
1939-40	NY Americans	NHL	3	0	2	2	2
	Springfield	AHL	2	0	1	1	0
1940-41	Springfield	AHL	3	0	0	0	2
1941-42	Springfield	AHL	5	0	3	3	6

NHL Totals:

Regular Season

GP	G	A	PTS	PIM
550	105	179	284	1047

Playoffs

GP	G	A	PTS	PIM
55	6	13	19	181

Allan Stanley

Regular Season

Year	Team	League	GP	G	A	PTS	PIM
1943-44	Boston	EHL	40	40	32	42	10
1944-45	Porcupine	NOHA	—	5	4	9	7
1945-46	Boston	EHL	30	8	15	23	35
1946-47	Providence	AHL	54	8	13	21	32
1947-48	Boston	QSHL	1	0	0	0	0
	Providence	AHL	68	9	32	41	81
1948-49	Rangers	NHL	40	2	8	10	22
	Providence	AHL	23	7	16	23	24
1949-50	Rangers	NHL	55	4	4	8	58
1950-51	Rangers	NHL	70	7	14	21	75
1951-52	Rangers	NHL	50	5	14	19	52
1952-53	Rangers	NHL	70	5	12	17	52
1953-54	Rangers	NHL	10	0	2	2	11
	Vancouver	WHL	47	6	30	36	43
1954-55	Rangers	NHL	12	0	1	1	2
	Chicago	NHL	52	10	15	25	22
	Totals		64	10	16	26	24
1955-56	Chicago	NHL	59	4	14	18	70
1956-57	Boston	NHL	60	6	25	31	45
1957-58	Boston	NHL	69	6	25	31	37
1958-59	Toronto	NHL	70	1	22	23	47
1959-60	Toronto	NHL	64	10	23	33	22
1960-61	Toronto	NHL	68	9	25	34	42
1961-62	Toronto	NHL	60	9	26	35	24
1962-63	Toronto	NHL	61	4	15	19	22
1963-64	Toronto	NHL	70	6	21	27	60
1964-65	Toronto	NHL	64	2	15	17	30
1965-66	Toronto	NHL	59	4	14	18	35
1966-67	Toronto	NHL	53	1	12	13	20
1967-68	Toronto	NHL	64	1	13	14	16
1968-69	Philadelphia	NHL	64	4	13	17	28

Playoffs

Year	Team	League	GP	G	A	PTS	PIM
1947-48	Providence	AHL	5	0	0	0	4
1949-50	Rangers	NHL	12	2	5	7	10
1953-54	Vancouver	WHL	13	2	5	7	10
1957-58	Boston	NHL	12	1	3	4	6
1958-59	Toronto	NHL	12	0	3	3	2
1959-60	Toronto	NHL	10	2	3	5	2
1960-61	Toronto	NHL	5	0	3	3	0
1961-62	Toronto	NHL	12	0	3	3	6
1962-63	Toronto	NHL	10	1	6	7	8
1963-64	Toronto	NHL	14	1	6	7	20
1964-65	Toronto	NHL	6	0	1	1	12
1965-66	Toronto	NHL	1	0	0	0	0
1966-67	Toronto	NHL	12	0	2	2	10
1968-69	Philadelphia	NHL	3	0	1	1	4

NHL Totals:

Regular Season

GP	G	A	PTS	PIM
1244	100	333	433	792

Playoffs

GP	G	A	PTS	PIM
109	7	46	43	80

Don Sweeney

Regular Season

Year	Team	League	GP	G	A	PTS	PIM
1983-84	St. Paul	H.S.	22	33	26	59	—
1984-85	Harvard	ECAC	29	3	7	10	30
1985-86	Harvard	ECAC	31	4	5	9	12
1986-87	Harvard	ECAC	34	7	4	11	22
1987-88	Harvard	ECAC	30	6	23	29	37
1988-89	Boston	NHL	36	3	5	8	20
	Maine	AHL	42	8	17	25	24
1989-90	Boston	NHL	58	3	5	8	58
	Maine	AHL	11	0	8	8	8
1990-91	Boston	NHL	77	8	13	21	67
1991-92	Boston	NHL	75	3	11	14	74
1992-93	Boston	NHL	84	7	27	34	68
1993-94	Boston	NHL	75	6	15	21	50
1994-95	Boston	NHL	47	3	19	22	24
1995-96	Boston	NHL	77	4	24	28	42
1996-97	Boston	NHL	82	3	23	26	39
	Canada (Worlds, Pool A)		11	1	3	4	6
1997-98	Boston	NHL	59	1	15	16	24

Playoffs

Year	Team	League	GP	G	A	PTS	PIM
1987-88	Maine	AHL	6	1	3	4	0
1989-90	Boston	NHL	21	1	5	6	18
1990-91	Boston	NHL	19	3	0	3	25
1991-92	Boston	NHL	15	0	0	0	10
1992-93	Boston	NHL	4	0	0	0	4
1993-94	Boston	NHL	12	2	1	3	4
1994-95	Boston	NHL	5	0	0	0	4
1995-96	Boston	NHL	5	0	2	2	6

NHL Totals:

Regular Season

GP	G	A	PTS	PIM
670	41	157	198	466

Playoffs

GP	G	A	PTS	PIM
81	6	8	14	71

Cecil "Tiny" Thompson

Regular Season

Year	Team	League	GP	W	L	T	SO	AVG
1924-25	Duluth	USAHA	40	17	20	3	11	1.38
1925-26	Minneapolis	USAHA	36	—	—	—	10	1.64
1926-27	Minneapolis	AHA	38	17	11	10	9	1.42
1927-28	Minneapolis	AHA	40	28	47	5	12	1.23
1928-29	Boston	NHL	44	26	13	5	12	1.15
1929-30	Boston	NHL	44	38	5	1	3	2.19
1930-31	Boston	NHL	44	28	10	6	3	1.98
1931-32	Boston	NHL	43	13	19	4	9	2.29
1932-33	Boston	NHL	48	25	15	8	11	1.76
1933-34	Boston	NHL	48	18	25	5	5	2.62
1934-35	Boston	NHL	48	26	16	6	8	2.26
1935-36	Boston	NHL	48	22	20	6	10	1.68
1936-37	Boston	NHL	48	23	18	7	6	2.22
1937-38	Boston	NHL	48	30	11	7	7	1.80

1938-39	Boston	NHL	5	3	1	1	0	1.55
	Detroit	NHL	39	16	17	6	4	2.53
	Totals		44	19	18	7	4	2.42
1939-40	Detroit	NHL	46	16	24	6	3	2.54
1940-41	Buffalo	AHL	1	0	0	0	0	1.50

Playoffs

Year	Team	League	GP	W	L	SO	AVG
1925-26	Minneapolis	USAHA	3	3	0	2	0.33
1926-27	Minneapolis	AHA	6	3	3	1	1.33
1927-28	Minneapolis	AHA	8	4	0	5	0.38
1928-29	Boston	NHL	5	5	0	3	0.60
1929-30	Boston	NHL	6	3	3	0	1.67
1930-31	Boston	NHL	5	2	3	0	2.27
1932-33	Boston	NHL	5	2	3	0	1.23
1934-35	Boston	NHL	4	1	3	1	1.54
1935-36	Boston	NHL	2	1	1	1	4.00
1936-37	Boston	NHL	3	1	2	0	2.67
1937-38	Boston	NHL	3	0	3	0	1.70
1938-39	Detroit	NHL	6	3	3	1	2.41
1939-40	Detroit	NHL	5	2	3	0	2.40

NHL Totals:

Regular Season

GP	W	L	T	SO	AVG
552	284	194	75	81	2.08

Playoffs

GP	W	L	SO	AVG

Cooney Weiland

Regular Season

Year	Team	League	GP	G	A	PTS	PIM
1923-24	Owen Sound	City Jr.	9	33	5	38	—
1924-25	Minneapolis	USAHA	35	8	0	8	—
1925-26	Minneapolis	CHL	26	10	4	14	20
1926-27	Minneapolis	AHA	36	21	2	23	30
1927-28	Minneapolis	AHA	40	21	5	26	34
1928-29	Boston	NHL	42	11	7	18	16
1929-30	Boston	NHL	44	43	30	73	27
1930-31	Boston	NHL	44	25	13	38	14
1931-32	Boston	NHL	46	14	12	26	20
1932-33	Ottawa	NHL	48	16	11	27	4
1933-34	Ottawa	NHL	9	2	0	2	4
	Detroit	NHL	39	11	19	30	6
	Totals		48	13	19	32	10
1934-35	Detroit	NHL	48	13	25	38	10
1935-36	Boston	NHL	48	14	13	27	15
1936-37	Boston	NHL	48	6	9	15	6
1937-38	Boston	NHL	48	11	12	23	16
1938-39	Boston	NHL	45	7	9	16	9
1939-40	Boston	NHL	DID NOT PLAY - COACHING				

Playoffs

Year	Team	League	GP	G	A	PTS	PIM
1923-24	Owen Sound	City Jr.	15	37	9	46	—
1925-26	Minneapolis	CHL	3	1	1	2	0
1926-27	Minneapolis	AHA	6	4	1	5	0
1927-28	Minneapolis	AHA	8	2	2	4	0
1928-29	Boston	NHL	5	2	0	2	2
1929-30	Boston	NHL	6	1	5	6	2
1930-31	Boston	NHL	5	6	3	9	2
1933-34	Detroit	NHL	9	2	2	4	4
1935-36	Boston	NHL	2	1	0	1	2
1936-37	Boston	NHL	3	0	0	0	0
1937-38	Boston	NHL	3	0	0	0	0
1938-39	Boston	NHL	12	0	0	0	0

NHL Totals:

Regular Season

GP	G	A	PTS	PIM
509	173	160	333	147

Playoffs

GP	G	A	PTS	PIM
45	12	10	22	12

Ed Westfall

Regular Season

Year	Team	League	GP	G	A	PTS	PIM
1957-58	Barrie	OHA	51	3	10	13	60
1958-59	Barrie	OHA	54	4	10	14	63
1959-60	Barrie	OHA	48	7	28	35	63
	Kingston	EPHL	1	0	0	0	2
1960-61	Niagara Falls	OHA	48	9	45	54	72
	Kingston	EPHL	2	0	0	0	0
1961-62	Boston	NHL	63	2	9	11	53
1962-63	Boston	NHL	48	1	11	12	34
	Kingston	EPHL	21	5	16	21	14
1963-64	Boston	NHL	55	5	1	6	35
	Providence	AHL	13	1	3	4	8
1964-65	Boston	NHL	68	12	15	27	65
1965-66	Boston	NHL	59	9	21	30	42
1966-67	Boston	NHL	70	12	24	36	26
1967-68	Boston	NHL	73	14	22	36	38
1968-69	Boston	NHL	70	18	24	42	22
1969-70	Boston	NHL	72	14	22	36	28
1970-71	Boston	NHL	78	25	34	59	48
1971-72	Boston	NHL	71	18	26	44	19
1972-73	Islanders	NHL	67	15	31	46	25
1973-74	Islanders	NHL	68	19	23	42	28
1974-75	Islanders	NHL	73	22	33	55	28
1975-76	Islanders	NHL	80	25	31	56	27
1976-77	Islanders	NHL	79	14	33	47	8
1977-78	Islanders	NHL	71	5	14	19	14
1978-79	Islanders	NHL	55	5	11	16	4

Playoffs

Year	Team	League	GP	G	A	PTS	PIM
1957-58	Barrie	OHA	4	0	0	0	4
1958-59	Barrie	OHA	6	0	4	4	2
1959-60	Barrie	OHA	6	0	4	4	28
1960-61	Niagara Falls	OHA	7	2	7	9	6
1963-64	Providence	AHL	3	0	0	0	4
1967-68	Boston	NHL	4	2	0	2	2
1968-69	Boston	NHL	10	3	7	10	11
1969-70	Boston	NHL	14	3	5	8	4
1970-71	Boston	NHL	7	1	2	3	2
1971-72	Boston	NHL	15	4	3	7	10
1974-75	Islanders	NHL	17	5	10	15	12
1975-76	Islanders	NHL	8	2	3	5	0
1976-77	Islanders	NHL	12	1	5	6	0
1977-78	Islanders	NHL	2	0	0	0	0
1978-79	Islanders	NHL	6	1	2	3	0

NHL Totals:

Regular Season

GP	G	A	PTS	PIM
1220	231	394	625	544

Playoffs

GP	G	A	PTS	PIM
95	22	37	59	41

Tommy Williams

Regular Season

Year	Team	League	GP	G	A	PTS	PIM
1958-59	United States	(National Team)	50	21	12	33	22
	United States	(Worlds, Pool A)	8	7	0	—	—
1959-60	United States	(Olympics)	7	4	6	10	2
1960-61	Kingston	EPHL	51	16	26	42	18
1961-62	Boston	NHL	26	6	6	12	2
	Kingston	EPHL	36	10	18	28	35
1962-63	Boston	NHL	69	23	20	43	11
1963-64	Boston	NHL	37	8	15	23	8
1964-65	Boston	NHL	65	13	21	34	28
1965-66	Boston	NHL	70	16	22	38	31
1966-67	Boston	NHL	29	8	13	21	2
1967-68	Boston	NHL	68	18	32	50	14
1968-69	Boston	NHL	26	4	7	11	19
1969-70	Minnesota	NHL	75	15	52	67	18
1970-71	Minnesota	NHL	41	10	13	23	16
	California	NHL	18	7	10	17	8
	Totals		59	17	23	40	24
1971-72	California	NHL	32	3	9	12	2
	Boston	AHL	31	8	15	23	8
1972-73	New England	WHA	69	10	21	31	14
1973-74	New England	WHA	70	21	37	58	6
1974-75	Washington	NHL	73	22	36	58	12
1975-76	Washington	NHL	34	8	13	21	6
	New Haven	AHL	20	4	16	20	4

Playoffs

Year	Team	League	GP	G	A	PTS	PIM
1958-59	United States	(National Team)	5	1	1	2	0
1960-61	Kingston	EPHL	5	0	2	2	0
1967-68	Boston	NHL	4	1	0	1	2
1969-70	Minnesota	NHL	6	1	5	6	0
1971-72	Boston	AHL	9	2	6	8	6
1972-73	New England	WHA	15	6	11	17	2
1973-74	New England	WHA	4	0	3	3	10
1975-76	New Haven	AHL	3	0	1	1	0

NHL Totals:

Regular Season

GP	G	A	PTS	PIM
663	161	269	60	177

Playoffs

GP	G	A	PTS	PIM
10	2	5	7	2

ADDITIONAL TITLES FROM SPORTS PUBLISHING INC.
Great Books for Boston!

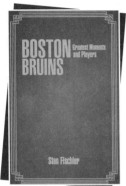

Boston Bruins: Greatest Moments and Players is available in a leatherbound edition that is restricted to 250 copies. Each individually numbered book is autographed by **John Bucyk, Pat Burns, Ed Westfall**. The gold-trimmed leaherbound includes a certificate of authenticity and makes a perfect gift or collector's item.

Order Now!   *Limited edition!* $74.95

Superstar Series!
Great books for younger readers!

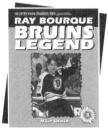

Ray Bourque: Bruins Legend allows readers to follow Bourque's 20-year career with the Bruins. Bourque is tied with Gordie Howe for most first team All-Star berths and holds other records that are described in *Ray Bourque: Bruins Legend*.

5 X 7 softcover   *96 pages* $4.95

Drew Bledsoe: Patriot Rifle details Bledsoe's life and how he has become one of the elite quarterbacks in the NFL. Bledsoe is the youngest player to surpass the 10,000 yard passing mark. Find out more facts and interesting stories about Bledsoe in *Patriot Rifle*.

5 X 7 softcover   *96 pages* $4.95

Pedro Martinez: Throwing Strikes gives readers the complete story behind the 1999 MVP. More than just a look at his baseball accomplishments, it also details the pressures and expectations placed on this Dominican Republic native.

5 X 7 softcover   *96 pages* $4.95

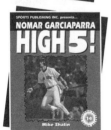

Nomar Garciaparra: High 5! follows Garciaparra's unseasoned yet illustrious career. After his 1997 rookie the year award, Garciaparra has continued to impress Red Sox and baseball fans alike. Discover the secrets behind Garciaparra's success in *High 5*!

5 X 7 softcover   *96 pages* $4.95

Great gifts for children of all ages!

ADDITIONAL TITLES FROM SPORTS PUBLISHING INC.

Great Books for Boston!

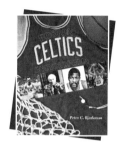

Boston Celtics Encyclopedia is the first and only encyclopedia to date on professional basketball's most-celebrated franchise. Follow their run of 11 world champions in 13 seasons, their tremendous battles with the Lakers in the '80s, and much more. This is a must have for Celtics fans from every generation.

Reserve your copy today!

8 1/2 X 11 hardcover   *350 pages*   *$34.95*

The Red Sox Encyclopedia is the ultimate reference book on the Boston Red Sox. This volume includes season by season details and over 175 great pictures of Fenway Park and Red Sox players. Descriptions of Young, Speaker, Williams, Yastrzemski, Evans, and many more are included in this magnificent volume.

Perfect for the Red Sox fan of any age!

8 1/2 X 11 hardcover   *271 pages*   *$39.95*

The Red Sox Encyclopedia is also available in leatherbound edition limited to 500 copies. Each individually-numbered copy is autographed by **Bobby Doerr**, **Mel Parnel**, **Frank Malzone**, **Rico Petrocelli**, and **Johnny Pesky**. The gold-trimmed leatherbound edition makes a great gift or collector's item.

Certificate of authenticity included!   *$129.95*

Fenway Saved is a lovingly drawn picture, in text and photographs of Boston's fabled Fenway Park. It features interviews, essays, and photographs from the oldest major league park still in use. Fenway was the site of the early exploits of Babe Ruth, the golden age of Ted Williams, and many other legends. Get your piece of history with Fenway saved.

8 1/2 X 11 hardcover   *140 pages*   *$29.95*

Order Today!